9780814206140

Wolf Creek Station

Historical Perspectives on Business Enterprise Series
Mansel G. Blackford and Austin Kerr, Editors

The scope of the series includes scholarly interest in the history of the firm, the history of government-business relations, and the relationships between business and culture, both in the United States and abroad, as well as in comparative perspective.

Regulated Enterprise
Natural Gas Pipelines and Northeastern Markets, 1938–1954
Christopher James Castaneda

Managing Industrial Decline
The British Coal Industry between the Wars
Michael Dintenfass

Henry E. Huntington and the Creation of Southern California
William Friedricks

Making Iron and Steel
Independent Mills in Pittsburgh, 1820–1920
John N. Ingham

Eagle-Picher Industries
Strategies for Survival in the Industrial Marketplace, 1840–1980
Douglas Knerr

A Mental Revolution
Scientific Management Since Taylor
Edited by Daniel Nelson

American Public Finance and Financial Services, 1700–1815
Edwin J. Perkins

The Passenger Train in the Motor Age
California's Rail and Bus Industries, 1910–1941
Gregory L. Thompson

Rebuilding Cleveland
The Cleveland Foundation and Its Evolving Urban Strategy
Diana Tittle

**Daniel Willard and Progressive Management on the
Baltimore & Ohio Railroad**
David M. Vrooman

Wolf Creek Station

Kansas Gas and Electric Company in the Nuclear Era

CRAIG MINER

Ohio State University Press
Columbus

Copyright © 1993 by the Ohio State University Press.
All rights reserved.

Library of Congress Cataloging-in-Publication Data

Miner, H. Craig, 1944–
Wolf Creek Station : Kansas Gas and Electric Company
in the nuclear era / Craig Miner
p. cm. — (Historical perspectives on business enterprise series)
Includes bibliographical references and index.
ISBN 0-8142-0614-X
1. Kansas Gas and Electric Company. 2. Nuclear industry—United States—
History. 3. Wolf Creek Nuclear Generating Station (Kan.)—History
I. Title II. Series.
HD9698.U54K365 1993
33.792'4'09781645—dc20   93-14241
CIP

Text designed by John Delaine.
Type set in ITC New Baskerville.
Printed by Bookcrafters, Inc., Chelsea, MI.

The paper in this book meets the guidelines for permanence and durability
of the Committee on Production Guidelines for Book Longevity
of the Council on Library Resources.

Printed in the U.S.A.

9 8 7 6 5 4 3 2 1

Contents

Preface		vii
Introduction: Chrome-Plated Dreams		1
1. An Exotic Animal		25
2. Atoms and Aquarius		57
3. Days to Remember, Days to Forget		84
4. Fire and Water		110
5. Where the Hell is Beto Junction?		142
6. The Sunflower Alliance		174
7. Wolf Creek Express		202
8. Power Block		227
9. Prudence or Perfection		254
10. "We Are Not a Monster"		278
Conclusion: All Are Punished		301
Notes		333
Bibliography		375
Index		383

Preface

This history originated in 1988 during a conversation with Robert Rives, group vice president for Kansas Gas and Electric Company (KG&E). He explained that KG&E had been occupied since 1968, when its natural gas supply was threatened by the beginnings of the "energy crisis," with the construction of new power plants to change its generating capacity from 100 percent natural gas to some mix of other fuels. While all the elements of this, including the joint construction with other Kansas utilities of several advanced coal-fired plants, were dramatic, the most significant of the company's activities was its decision to become lead utility in building the first and only nuclear power plant in Kansas—the Wolf Creek Generating Station near Burlington. By 1988, that project had been in the public eye for twenty years and had generated an enormous record of fact, opinion, and emotion. Even among those who had experienced the events surrounding the building and operation of Wolf Creek (Rives was company spokesman through most of it) the complexity and multiple perspectives of the story made it resemble the famous nineteenth-century diplomatic conundrum involving the German duchies of Schleswig and Holstein. Three men understood it, said a wag at that time. One is dead, one has gone mad—I am the third, and I have forgotten.

Like many modern corporations, KG&E saw the need to halter the chaos and provide an objective record for future debate by commissioning a fully documented history to be published and evaluated independently of the company or its immediate supporters and detractors. That history would serve as an internal management tool. The recent history of KG&E was so dominated by the Wolf Creek experience that there was no understanding the corporate culture without reference to those times. It brought to mind the Ancient Mariner in Coleridge's poem, who seized the wedding guest and said, "There was a Ship." A second, broader purpose was to begin the process of taking the Wolf Creek story for the general public out of the realm of self-interested acrimony and limited perspective in which it had incubated.

The "Wolf Creek Era" for KG&E, Rives thought, was like no other period in the company history. An arms-length, well-researched and accessibly written history of it, using all the sources, written and human, that were yet at hand, could have significance beyond what one would expect from an account of a single power plant in a plains state. That such a history would be controversial, however it was written and by whomever, Rives never had a doubt. But to wait until emotion had entirely cooled was to miss some of the material and much of the application.

A nuclear power plant anywhere is a modern icon of considerable beam. It is like a big telescope—enormous, heavy, almost brutish and yet delicate—sensitive to the slightest change in the controlling hand or device. It is simple on the outside, a windowless, monochromatic facade of concrete looking for all the world like a huge set of child's building blocks that came only in circles and squares. It is made in two parts, a steam system and a nuclear heat generator. The steam system is basically nineteenth-century technology, albeit with considerable "superpower" twentieth-century twists. The rest of it, the nuclear part, is state-of-the-art science of near science fiction style. Visitors, with sensors hung all over them, passing through one checkpoint after another, feel some fear, but also awe. They see the size, the power, and the beauty. The sight of the storage pool for spent fuel rods at Wolf Creek, its boron water an unearthly deep clear blue against spotless stainless steel walls, is an aesthetic sight exceeded only when, with house lights off, a fuel rod actually comes through from the reactor, lighting the pool and the eyes of the observers with another unique blue glow of radiation, called the "Cherenkov" effect. Like other great feats of engineering it is a symbol as much as a tool and, like them, it is a symbol with more than a single meaning.

The KG&E building in Wichita, where Wolf Creek's owners planned, is also a monument to quality engineering with a touch of experiment about it. It is one of the few places where you can see Westinghouse elevators clad in stainless steel with brass trim. The lights are on all the time because they provide part of the building's heat (there are no light switches) and in the winter the windowsills are hot—they are also part of the radiant heating system.

Like the power plant, the sight of the office building may well affect different people differently. To some it suggests the no-nonsense functionalism of modern America. To others it is a sign of an impersonal, standardized bureaucracy, uniformed and arrogant, complete with automatons working at rooms full of identical metal desks.

For that reason the history of this nuclear plant reminds this author of a contrapuntal baroque fugue—pure polyphony that takes its timbre from the times, but is in a large way independent of the instruments on which it is played. The music is that of America changing, and the stakes involved have to do not only with the future of nuclear power, but with changes in ideas: of risk, profit, community, environment, standard of living, quality of life, and others.

KG&E's Bob Rives was and is a modern corporate public relations man. He understands that even a complex history is a simplification, but that the "story" cannot be credibly reduced to pamphlet size. He knows that corporate history nowadays is not a form of advertising. Academic historians, with their own values and reputation to protect, are not about to work under company strictures designed to ensure that the end result resembles an industrial "Lives of the Saints." No company could have been more respectful of an author's independence than this one was, nor more helpful in finding for me the research help I needed.

No history is written without documents, and no good history is constructed without a balanced collection of sources reflecting the major angles on the case. The company had collected the most complete body of documents on Wolf Creek anywhere, and they were anything but selective to the company's interest. About 40,000 *pages* of newspaper clippings from Kansas and the nation, and nearly 70 *volumes* of hearing transcripts on Wolf Creek only began to tap the company archives. Histories have more "flesh" if the historian can freely talk to the participants on the inside as well as the outside.

Company sponsorship likewise offered this advantage. The "fishbowl" nature of the events ensured that much of this material is available to the general public in segregated sections of libraries. The U.S. Nuclear Regulatory Commission and the Kansas Corporation Commission sponsored and promoted such availability, not only to involve an informed public in the decisions, but to ensure that a raw record was accessible to those wishing to expand or check up on historical accounts that will continue to appear.

The research took more than two years. Doubtless in the material are sources for many specialized studies, sociological and political as well as historical. But it seemed clear that the first cut of the mass should be a comprehensive, comprehensible narrative—academically respectable, but with the prime audience being the nonspecialist reading public. The key challenge was to simplify and to transmit the verve without distortion.

The goal in this writing is as stated by Thomas Macauley in his 1828 essay "History": "The instruction derived from history," he writes, should "be of a vivid and practical character. It would be received by the imagination as well as the reason. It would be not merely traced on the mind, but branded into it." He goes on:

> History, it has been said, is philosophy teaching by examples. Unhappily, what the philosophy gains in soundness and depth the examples generally lose in vividness. A perfect historian must possess an imagination sufficiently powerful to make his narrative affecting and picturesque. Yet he must control it so absolutely as to content himself with the materials which he finds. . . . No picture . . . and no history, can present us with the whole truth: but those are the best pictures and the best histories which exhibit such parts of the truth as most nearly produce the effect of the whole. . . . History has its foreground and its background: and it is principally in the management of its perspective that one artist differs from another. Some events must be represented on a large scale, others diminished; the great majority will be lost in the dimness of the horizon; and a general idea of their joint effect will be given by a few slight touches.

Few any longer pretend it is possible to lay it out as it actually happened, but the semblance must ring true. If history left out nothing, Macauley notes, "the Bodleian library would not contain the occurrences of a week." Instead, an actual history "begins in novel and ends in essay."[1] Its methodological bones should not show. It should not be only a case or illustration of something irresponsibly broader, any more than it should be a public relations tract or a call to action. Whether the history is of medieval religion, eighteenth-century literature, or near contemporary nuclear debates, the rules are the same. Above all, the simple fact must be recognized that most readers are interested in history, but not in historians. The objective is to provide a true, balanced, and recognizable account, not present evidence to win a lawsuit, design a generator, convince a regulatory body, or awe an academic conference. Anthony, Earl of Shaftesbury, who well understood controversy, wrote in the eighteenth century, "Nothing affects the heart like that which is purely from itself and of its own nature, such as the Beauty of Sentiments; the Grace of Actions; the turn of Characters and the proportions and features of the human mind. . . . The horse alone can never make the Horseman, nor limbs the Wrestler or Dancer. . . the skill and grace of writing is founded in knowledge and good sense. . . ."[2] To quote a more recent authority, just as this was being written a "Peanuts" cartoon portrayed Charlie Brown worried about a worldwide cookie shortage. "There's only one cookie left in the whole world," he tells Snoopy. "Look! I had it framed for you." Snoopy, after taking the momento to his dog house, reflects a moment and then eats the cookie. As to the frame—"I can always put my grandmother's picture in it," he reasons.[3] Same point!

Emerson's strictures in his "American Scholar" talk of 1837 are doubtless impossibilities. But it does not make them less inspiring to scholars, and particularly historians of business. "It came to him short-lived actions," Emerson wrote about his hypothetical scholar who was also an experienced man, "it went out from him immortal thoughts. It came to him—business; it went from him—poetry."[4] There is enough charge in the actualities of business—a human challenge perhaps second only to war—to make a kind of poetry. The dreary reputation of much serious business history with general readers can be laid at the doorstep of historians.

As much of what an author can empathize with or illuminate in history comes from experience as from books. My wife Suzi, for example, has kept me in contact for years with "live" examples of those seriously concerned about the impact of nuclear power on the physical environment and the safety of families. Work with Willard Garvey at Garvey Industries over the past several years has added direct action in business, with its sometimes harrowing incontrovertible direct feedback on the consequences of one's own decisions, to my observations of businesspeople over decades of being in their offices rummaging through files. Garvey in turn has appreciated the necessity for stepping back sometimes for a broader look, and therefore supports a professorship in the history of business at Wichita State University, which I presently hold. Interestingly, Garvey, who might seem to some to be the quintessential "big businessman" in Wichita, was a vocal opponent of several aspects of Wolf Creek. It illustrates how unexpected the affinities in this case became.

Since the modern world is not the most friendly place for the relatively uninterrupted concentration preparing and writing history requires, I acknowledge my coconspirators in quasi-monkish isolation. KG&E provided a hideaway where the records could be assembled, as well as the research funding itself. I thank Lyle Koerper, of Western Resources, Inc., in Wichita, for his great help with the text revision, and especially for locating many of the photographs used herein. I acknowledge, too, the help of Michelle McGowan Craig on the final revision. Thanks also go to Donna Dilsaver for her special help throughout. I thank others, as well, too numerous to mention, for their invaluable assistance. Notable among this group are those individuals interviewed for this book, who graciously donated their time and were so forthcoming in helping me complete this history. I also wish to thank Lynne Bonenberger, my editor at the Ohio State University Press, and freelance copyeditor Robert Marcum for their work in bringing this manuscript to publication. Suzi Miner and my boys, Hal and Wilson, forebore many times the attention from me they deserved because Dad felt he was not yet finished repaying the debt he thought he owed to the other writers of books. For tolerance of things not fully understood comes special thanks, and the hope that those who supported the writing of this book may find uses for it that involve its content and not just its bulk.

Introduction
Chrome-Plated Dreams

> Historians have been overconfident about the wisdom to be gained by distance, believing that it confers objectivity, one of those unattainable values in which they have placed so much faith. Perhaps there is something to be said for proximity.
> —Simon Schama, *Citizens: A Chronicle of the French Revolution*

> Like the pyramids, nuclear power stations are historical artifacts of enormous richness, for they vividly embody the basic economic and social relationships of the society that produced them.
> —Mark Hertsgaard, *Nuclear, Inc.*

> All complicated territories need simple maps; and . . . vice versa.
> —Jack Matthews, *Memoirs of a Bookman*

Invisible forces, whose operation, logic, and controls are not directly observable or comprehensible by simple analogy, have always experienced rough going in gaining acceptance in democratic societies. Volumes have been written about the adjustments required by the appearance of the locomotive in the sylvan American landscape of the early nineteenth century.[1] No doubt there were critics of bringing fire into caves. Electricity was a public mystery with dangers less obvious than the open flame. Protestors originally resorted to electrocuting dogs in public to illustrate the hazard.[2] In the middle of the twentieth century came a new means of generating the electric power that was by then universally accepted as a social and economic boon: nuclear fission. While it had many potential environmental and economic advantages, nuclear power generation introduced radiation, another invisible and risky force with which the public and public processes had to deal.

This time the adjustment was made more difficult because the initial awareness of the force by the masses came through its use in a bomb designed not only to kill, but to terrorize an intransigent enemy. Hiroshima and Nagasaki were irretrievably connected in the press with fission in all its manifestations. No amount of public relations craft could totally change "atomic" to "nuclear" in lay vocabularies or accomplish Eisenhower's purpose, stated in his 1953 "Atoms for Peace" speech, of converting radiological swords into plowshares, and putting the Promethean forces unleashed to end a barbaric world cataclysm calmly to work in hospitals and power stations. A nuclear power station with a mushroom cloud behind it was an irresistible image to editorial cartoonists from the 1950s through the 1980s. "It's like," wrote one analyst, "if Edison had invented the electric chair and then tried to market light bulbs."[3]

Early locomotives were named, not numbered, and the engineer decorated the interior like a personal office. They, like their elder cousins the stationary steam engines, tended to be custom built in small numbers and decorated with naturalistic motifs. It followed that they were thought of for a time as "Iron Horses," trainable as animals were, and as much as horses an extension of nature to the hand of humankind. Only later were these "mass machines" perceived as dehumanizing and threatening.[4]

So it was with nuclear power plants. At first they were custom built—no two were just alike—and each had an individual mix of risky and benign operating characteristics. Sometimes they were named for utility executives or scientists, but more often they took their monikers from the local landscape. Certain of the names had a sinister sound. There was Diablo, Black Fox, Comanche Peak. That was because the frontier itself had had its frightening side, and the unfamiliar yet majestic landscape conjured names suggesting both power and menace. The names of most nuclear plants, however, were innocent, localized, and almost friendly—Callaway, Seabrook, Palo Verde, Nine Mile Point, Marble Hill, Waterford, South Texas, Tyrone, Sterling, Grand Gulf, Hope Creek, Catawba, and even (at first) Three Mile Island. There was expectation that they would be as natural a part of the landscape as the topographical features for which they were named.

Wolf Creek Generating Station, Kansas, is of the frontier variety. Yet despite the slight menace in the name, it was early thought that the construction of a power plant, even a nuclear one, sited on a 10,000-acre prairie reserve in one of the least-populated counties of a presumably conservative heartland state could hardly generate substantial social and political fireworks. KG&E, a 47 percent and managing owner of Wolf Creek, was unquestionably favorably known as a Wichita cultural and political, as well as economic, institution. The other major owner, Kansas City Power & Light (KCPL), also 47 percent, had followed so careful a course through its history that Mr. Walter Bridge, Evan Connell's fictional version of the ultimate Kansas City fuddy-duddy, had chosen KCPL securities to pass out to his children under the Christmas tree.[5] Kansas Electric Power Cooperative, Inc. (KEPCO), while ultimately taking only a 6 percent share of the new plant, lobbied long and hard on behalf of its presumably eminently sensible farm constituency for a bigger piece of the plant that it was assumed would take low-cost, reliable power into the twenty-first century.

It is a fair conclusion that Wolf Creek in fact *did not* generate more than its share of controversy. Despite sharing the huge time and cost overruns typical of its 1970s and 1980s kin, Wolf Creek *was* completed. Many in the same era were never finished, due to protest, cost, or both. Others suffered delay and financial escalation that make the Kansas project appear a model of efficiency and restraint. The protests at the plant site near Burlington, Kansas, on the state capitol steps in Topeka, and before company offices in Kansas City and Wichita never made the national headlines accorded to the mass infiltrations of Diablo and Seabrook. However, all the elements and all the players typical of nuclear power plant construction in the United States during the critical "decades of debate" in the history of nuclear power—the ones leading to the entire eclipse of the industry by the late 1980s—were present in Kansas. The history of Wolf Creek, from its inception in 1968 to its commercial operation in 1985 and its changed place in the 1990s, is in microcosm, but hardly in miniature, reflective of an as yet incompletely documented watershed in United States industrial and political history during that era.

Kansas, after all, is not the stagnant backwater that certain readers of popular literature might imagine. From the "bleeding Kansas" days when it was the stage for a moral struggle over abolition, through its pioneering in the "reform" of Prohibition and its national prominence in the Populist and Progressive eras from the 1890s through 1920, the state was perceived as cracked perhaps, but never complacent.[6] It had the distinction of being by turns, and at times seemingly simultaneously, one of the most entrepreneurially capitalistic states in the country and one of the most socialistic. It could breed the most extraordinary economic innovations, and then in periods of economic crisis and political protest turn on them like a frustrated mother devouring her young. It was the home of land leagues, proposing abolition of private property as early as the 1860s; it was the site of Haldeman Julius's socialist paper *The Workingman's Advocate*, and the headquarters of the Little Blue Books; it was one of few states dominated by the People's Party in the 1890s, and one of the few instituting alien land acts and corporate regulation; it was the state that proposed in 1905 putting prisoners to work building a state-operated refinery to regulate Standard Oil; it was early with women's municipal suffrage and the city commission/manager form of government; and it was the pioneer in the Progressive Era of such regulatory innovations as the Board of Public Utilities and the Industrial Court. Even in the 1930s it gave rise to such radical politicians as John "Doc" Brinkley, the goat-gland specialist and demagogue *par excellence*, before setting into a post–Dust Bowl spell of seemingly comfortable Republican conservatism.

Robert Bader, in his recent interpretive study of the image of Kansas, calls it an "eclipsed civilization," and contends that the "dirty thirties" permanently crushed the radical cockade of Kansas, and diminished its interest to the rest of the world.[7] If there is truth to that contention it is also true that the raw material for a struggle over the proper nature of progress remained, and the forces on both sides of the question remained, in potential at least, sufficiently equal that no issue symbolic enough to rouse real passion of this type would be easily carried. Both its entrepreneurship and its protosocialism had the common denominator of "practical idealism." Kansans had a reputation for taking ideas, technological or political, seriously and trying to implement an actual better world based on their dreams. Kansas "fits," wrote a local editor once, "are irregular, but always acute, always sure to come, always exciting and nerve-racking. They are bred in the bone and carried like cottonwood seed in the wind. The ozone is congested with hysteria all the time and in the public mind is as easily touched off as a natural gas well."[8] It was to this volatility William Allen White referred when he asked in a nationally famous editorial, "What's the Matter With Kansas?"[9]

Kansas was a bellwether, all right, but perhaps nothing was especially wrong or right with her that was not at least an embryonic feature of the rest of the country, too. The coming of the nuclear power issue to Kansas, first in the debates over high-level waste disposal at Lyons in the early 1970s, and then in the long-lasting Wolf Creek confrontation, brought a return of the historic Kansas battleground that had traditionally reflected the heart of the nation, ideologically as well as physically. California was California, but events in Kansas, whether they concerned slavery, Indian policy, railroad building, free silver, labor relations, or nuclear power, could not be written off as an aberration. There is no question among the early students of the era that the decades from 1965 to 1985, precisely the period of Wolf Creek construction, were a true watershed for the American electric utility industry generally, and its nuclear branch particularly—a time when the assumed consensus among the industry's stakeholders broke down and there was a struggle for "rerationalization" among managers experiencing "culture shock."[10] And, like the nation, Kansas people try to readjust the mix there of tradition and opportunity. In 1990 there was a sign on the marquee of a motel in western Kansas near Dodge City that read "American-owned." Enough said.

The building of Wolf Creek was a technological feat; it was also a social and political event. But at base, and particularly at first in the minds of its promoters, it was a part of a corporate strategy to provide service and profits into the future as businesspeople saw it. While "local occurrences in the later twentieth century are never entirely local," the truth in the cliché that "all history is local history" should not be lost sight of in an attempt to escalate the story into a case study.[11] This history, as much as any other serious account of the past, seeks truth amid sources admittedly laced with propaganda. Like every other history, however, it fails to cover the real waterfront, and has a point of view that is related to its author, to the mix of sources, and to the focus chosen to reduce a chaos of information to a tale that hangs together.

There can be several fair and legitimate but different histories of a drawn-out multifaceted "event" like the building of Wolf Creek. In this case the "point of view" is both the plant specifically and the company that managed its construction and initial operation—the Kansas Gas and Electric Company, headquartered in Wichita. That the perspective is from "inside" the gates does not preordain lack of sympathy for or information about the rest of the players.

That company officials would be linked as much in history as in actuality with their opponents and regulators was a fate they neither wished nor expected to escape. In fact, even at a short distance in time, there is much grudging respect and sometimes surprising insight and empathy evident in executive offices for the protestors, and with the activists for their corporate counterparts. But, though a regulated utility operates, relatively, in a "fishbowl," and therefore the public record of its doings is more complete than would be usual with a business, it is almost a feature of the process that the corporate "applicant" must be, for the most part, cast as the villain. Intervenors, and often journalists and academic analysts, believe that in nuclear plant hearings there is a tight connection between utilities, regulatory bodies, politicians, and consulting "experts," which acts to intimidate and lock out the public.[12] It is therefore easy to miss the perception by the corporate planners and operators that they are far outnumbered by the "gallery" of citizens and press to whom, if the regulators and politicians were not playing in 1967, they certainly were ten years later.

It may seem ludicrous that a "giant" corporation undertaking a multibillion dollar 1150 megawatt nuclear plant project should itself feel "intimidated." Yet aggressive and numerous Lilliputians can truss up any Gulliver, and have brought many a nuclear project to its corporate knees. Also, while KG&E was often characterized as a giant, a grasping monopoly rolling in millions that could not even be counted by the "little people" it was oppressing, size is a matter of perspective and perception. The utility saw itself as the "little guy," hounded from all quarters, and in some sense the underdog. It was smaller than many of its suppliers and contractors (Westinghouse, General Electric, Bechtel), smaller (in ultimate resources at least) than the regulatory establishment with which it had to deal, smaller than the international energy companies who in some sense set the scene in the field, smaller than its individual critics *en masse,* and smaller than any other utility that ever completed a nuclear plant in the United States. During the history of its Wolf Creek project KG&E saw its bond rating reduced from AA+ to "speculative grade," its sterling reputation in the community become so suspect that Reddy Kilowatt was called Ready Killalot, and its CEO and board members taking angry calls, sometimes death threats, at home and late at night over a period of years. That brand of "intimidation" is part of the account, too.

What to one side was "determination" to the other was "stubbornness," but no one can spend the years it takes to research a history without the undeniable realization that the leaders all around, however they disagreed, were all "true believers." They—vice presidents, farmers, attorneys, state legislators, marchers, commission and board members—fought for a vision of a better world they held in their minds. No crasser motive would have sustained them, no clash of less titanic and honestly held ideological proportions would have justified the time, emotion, and expense Wolf Creek consumed. It was *the* feature of a number of whole careers.

Both sides thought of themselves as "keepers of the plains." The graphic symbol of the Wolf Creek plant was a sharp-eyed wolf's head in a circular field designed for KG&E by Wichita Native American artist Blackbear Bosin. Blackbear also designed, KG&E engineers constructed, and the company erected in 1974 on the grounds of its 1910 electric power plant along the Little Arkansas River in Wichita, a 44-foot-high metal sculpture of an Indian looking skyward, called "Keeper of the Plains." The idea had its genesis in a hospital visit of KG&E's Elmer Hall, *the* company pioneer in promoting nuclear energy, to the artist in 1968, just at the point where serious planning for the Wolf Creek plant was getting under way.[13]

The "Keeper" appeared just before the construction permit hearings on Wolf Creek, and in the midst of considerable controversy among landowners and environmentalists about the site selection. It was a typical KG&E community project, though for a time it became an object of ridicule and parody by the company's detractors. Yet, the statue became in time as close to a universally accepted icon of Wichita as any. In 1990 local developer Jack DeBoer suggested that, as the centerpiece of a $375 million downtown revitalization plan for the city, the "Keeper" be rebuilt 299 feet high, just a foot shorter than the Statue of Liberty. That would ensure that it finally would "outgrow" its original connection with the most controversial utility project ever in Kansas.

The "dreams" of the utility people were based on the amazing history of electricity, not only as a technology but as a business, in providing a more comfortable standard of living at cheaper prices to millions of people. Edison gave us the devices, and, among others, Samuel Insull, once Edison's secretary, developed the centralized, regulated investor-owned utility network that by taking advantage of economies of scale, and by spreading a base load generating capacity, which could not be stored in large quantities or for a long time, over many kinds of customers using it at different times and at different rates, made the commodity much cheaper than each customer could acquire individually. Utilities had a relatively large fixed investment in relation to the annual business done and found division of patronage and the consequent dilution of earnings especially difficult.

The idea emerged that electric utilities were "natural monopolies," and that, as with telephone companies, it was a waste to duplicate facilities, despite the political and economic problems that the absence of market regulation through competition might bring.[14] Some say the companies made a Faustian bargain to gain the monopoly status. If so, in recent times there have been more than a few utility executives who imagine that Mephistopheles is making his final settlement call early and often. The government gave the utility exclusive rights within a territory. It also provided them an opportunity to earn a "reasonable" return on investment for "prudent" capital expenditures. In return the utility became a quasi-public operation, subject to not only scrutiny, but also second-guessing by persons with little expertise in utility technology and less sympathy with utility "needs." The utilities got also in the bargain an "obligation to serve," which included providing an adequate, continuous, and reliable supply of electric power to whoever demanded it whenever they wanted to switch it on.

Thus came to the investor-owned utilities (IOUs) either the best or the worst of both the public and the private worlds, depending upon one's information and interpretation. Financing was private and voluntary, but returns, rather than coming from multiple individual consumer decisions in a competitive voluntary market, depended on costs allowed and prices (rates) approved by public regulatory bodies. In the case of construction of new generating capacity, for example, the company made the decision concerning likely increase in demand and need, raised the money and constructed the plant, and then went before a regulatory body (in Kansas since the 1930s the Kansas Corporation Commission) that determined whether the decision was wise and what return should be allowed on the investment.

While there were "agreed upon" rules governing how regulatory commissions would judge these things, and though for years in times of declining rates public utility commission hearings at the state level were low-key affairs with little public interest or participation, there was no question that utilities' economic decisions were not entirely based on their own boards of directors' estimate of the responses of consumers, nor necessarily "controlled" by regulatory precedent should the public become actively involved. However, the system was so successful for so long in virtually everyone's view— stockholders got steady if unspectacular returns on "safe" utility portfolios and consumers got power for every new device at rates that were decreasing absolutely as well as relatively—that any philosophical objections or serious thinking about "worst case scenarios" were far in the background. Above all the electric industry more than any other satisfied the desire of "materialistic" and "progressive" Americans for a technology that tangibly advanced comfort and cleanliness with no seeming uncontrollable side effects.[15]

Kansas's utility history was typical or better. Electricity began there as a business with numerous, small competitors. Wichita, for example, had two electric power companies using differing technologies when electric power was introduced there in the mid 1880s. However, because small-scale applications were relatively inefficient and because the improving technology could not be adequately applied and managed by small companies run by local businessmen with little technical expertise and marginal access to capital, early electricity in Kansas and elsewhere was characterized by regular outages, constant complaints about service and rates, and calls for direct government ownership and operation of a service that the public thought must be the subject of a business conspiracy against consumers.

In the first decade of the twentieth century, however, there were revolutions in electric technology, in power plant fuel, and in utility corporate organization that changed the picture dramatically and, most thought, permanently for the better. One element in Kansas, the discovery and application to power generation of abundant and inexpensive supplies of natural gas, was an advantage that state had over many others. However, the application of new forms of organization and the gaining of technical expertise through consolidation regionally and through ownership and technical advice nationally, was a phenomenon throughout the country.

KG&E was incorporated under the laws of West Virginia on December 11, 1909, and began operations in Kansas March 1, 1910 after having purchased several companies providing gas and electric service. It shortly expanded throughout southeast Kansas by purchasing 39 utility companies and consolidating many of them. While providing first-time electric service to over 60 new communities, it was able to abandon almost immediately 13 generating plants. For the first time in the territory there was substantial application of electricity to industry. This was an important factor in reducing rates, as not only did the peak needs of factories vary over any 24-hour period from those of residences, but industrial use could help moderate seasonal variations in electric demand so as to use power plant capacity more constantly. Peak demand in the early era came in the winter, due to longer use of lighting. By the time of the planning of Wolf Creek, however, the universal use of air conditioning in Kansas made the summer peak substantially greater than the winter, and therefore made sales in the winter, even at bargain rates, of even more importance in amortizing the cost of generating facilities.

This geographical, functional, and financial integration of the regional electric business by KG&E was possible because the fledgling Kansas company had access to the technical expertise, state-of-the-art equipment, and financial clout of the General Electric Company. GE, which sold equipment to the various local utilities, was having trouble with collections because of these companies' financial instability. It therefore formed a separate corporation, Electric Bond and Share Company, to assist GE's debtors in financing and operating their properties. KG&E was organized by American Power & Light Company (AP&L), a subsidiary of Electric Bond and Share, which owned utilities in Arizona, Florida, Minnesota, Montana, Nebraska, New Mexico, Texas, and other states. That connection remained until 1948 when, due to pressure from the federal 1935 Public Utility Holding Company Act, AP&L's equity in KG&E began to be sold to the public. The transition was complete on July 6, 1949, when "the company's owners moved to Main Street U.S.A."[16]

With early financing available from that consortium, and with a regional "monopoly," KG&E was able to make capital investments in advance of rate collections which created the volume and efficiency to, in common with utilities around the country, actually reduce rates while providing better service to a larger number of people. The company changed all its customers to 60 cycles and was a pioneer in regional interconnection and power sharing within a large transmission grid, thus further ameliorating the cost impact of local demand variations. In 1923 it built a 138,000-volt transmission line through the Flint Hills from a substation not far east of Wichita to its proposed new 15,000 kilowatt (kw) Neosho coal generation station (finished 1924) south of Parsons, and 107 miles southeast of the line's beginning. In 1925 it sold all its gas business (mostly in Wichita) to focus exclusively on electricity. KG&E, like counterparts elsewhere, integrated forward into appliance sales and sending representatives to help consumers install and use electricity, until this function was restricted by state legislation promoted by those fearful of corporate bigness in 1931.

The results were stunning. The calls for public ownership of the electric "service" were stilled. The price of electricity in the KG&E service area was immediately cut from 11 to 10 cents per kilowatt-hour. It had been as high $7.50 per kilowatt-hour in 1886 (a more common average estimate is 25 cents), and it would be 2.5 cents per kilowatt-hour in 1959. It was 1971 before KG&E applied for its *first* rate increase since 1910, and in 1974 KG&E rates were still 43 percent lower than the national average. In Wichita electric generating capacity tripled between 1916 and 1924 as lower rates encouraged tall buildings, and electric elevators and streetcars were the making of the downtown. A southeast Kansas newspaper in 1922 concluded: "Thus all this part of Kansas will soon be under the blanket service of one big electric light and power company serving not only the cities but the smaller villages and in many cases the farm homes themselves. The result of this can be only beneficial because it will modernize not only the small town life in this part of the state but even of the farm homes where no current is used now. It will make this part of Kansas a better place to live and when that is done it will increase the natural development of another one of the great industries which can and will contribute immeasurably to the lasting prosperity of the general public."[17]

The years were kind to that initial vision. KG&E took full advantage of large discoveries of natural gas in Kansas and Oklahoma, and built large power plants in the 1930s and 1940s that provided electricity for Wichita homes and the city's defense-burgeoned aviation industry at rates that were among the cheapest in the country. These increasingly large gas-fired plants were not named for inert features in the landscape, but for KG&E chief executive officers whose pride these metal towers on the prairie were—L. O. Ripley, Murray Gill, Gordon Evans. The last gas unit built, Gordon Evans 2 (1964), was at 380,000 kw capacity the largest gas plant then in use west of the Mississippi and the seventh largest in the United States. It cost $26,000,000, but was one of the cheapest ever based on cost per kilowatt-hour generated. Its monitoring computer was only the fourth of its kind in the nation, and it was thought that its entire output would be needed by 1971 thanks to a demand growth rate that doubled every seven years. The utility was connecting all electric homes and apartments all over the city at discount rates, and air conditioning was the near-universal answer to the sweltering Kansas summers. Wrote KG&E president Evans in 1964: "No end to this kind of growth is in sight."[18]

To the engineers and the managers this history of economic and technological achievement really was a kind of poetry . . . a spirit vision, chrome-plated and updated to the twentieth century. The introduction of nuclear power was the panacea that would sustain the revolution.[19]

That this should be so was neither new nor unusual. Emerson wrote in 1860 that "the motive of science was the extension of man, on all sides, into Nature, till his hands should touch the stars, his eyes see through the earth, his ears understand the language of beast and bird, and the sense of the wind; and, through his sympathy heaven and earth should talk to him."[20] William Dean Howells, looking over the great Corliss steam engine that ran the equipment in the government building at the U.S. Centennial Exposition in 1876, observed that the engine showed a good deal more application of talent than the exhibits in the art building. He commented: "It is [in] things of iron and steel that the national genius most freely speaks."[21] One historian of technology believes that the nineteenth- and early twentieth-century inventors, both of machines and the systems that applied them in the world, thought of themselves as the equivalent of artists in a new Renaissance. Like artists they often encountered in childhood a world that disappointed them and so withdrew "to spaces of their own making, filled with the devices of their imagination" in an attempt to "change or make anew the world."[22] The Brooklyn Bridge, completed in the mid 1880s, was widely admired not only as engineering, but as functional art and powerful symbol.[23] Henry James wrote with trepidation but admiration that the "applied passion" of science and machinery was the key to understanding New York City in 1907.[24] And Hart Crane in the 1920s wrote an American epic poem, *The Bridge*, with the "choiring strings" of the Manhattan to Brooklyn suspension bridge serving as a symbol of America's history and future.[25]

Wolf Creek Station would not be as intimately familiar to daily travelers as the Brooklyn Bridge, but it was every bit as awesome, fully as mysterious and even more vital to the operation of everything from the clock that awakened people to the devices that cooked their dinners and kept them warm at night. It was linked to lives in a way that was bound to be emotional, and that emotion in the minds and souls of its proponents could take the form of fierce optimism and powerful belief that nuclear power was the crown of a progression that had taken humankind out of caves and toward the stars.

In the 1950s it appeared that the progressive mindset of better living through high technology would sweep the field alone. In the 1960s and 1970s it became clear that it would not. Rachel Carson's *Silent Spring* (1962) created fundamental doubt that the DDTs of the new era were boons without cost. The Vietnam War not only introduced deep doubt about the efficacy of technology and its controllability by "systems," but illustrated that what some considered the mechanical juggernaut of science was not unstoppable.

The atomic bomb continued to be an issue. A survey as late as 1984 indicated that the public did not have a clear idea of the distinction between nuclear plants and atomic bombs, and that this was a key restraint. Of those who thought a bomblike explosion at a nuclear plant was possible, 60 percent were against nuclear power. Of those who knew that an explosion was impossible, 88 percent supported the plants.[26]

The complexity of the modern world gave an advantage to "experts," who in the golden era of Edison and Insull—also that of

Walter Lippmann, Thorstein Veblen, and the "technocrats"—appeared to be on the verge of engineering society and its "irrational drift" with the same mastery they applied to dynamos. However, what technological historian Thomas Hughes calls "a gigantic tidal wave of human ingenuity and resource," of which electricity was only one, though a central, part, revealed eventually its dark side. Hughes writes that his 1989 book *American Genesis* is about "an era of technological enthusiasm in the United States, an era now passing into history." In its place, Hughes says came an emphasis on the part of a counterculture on "the organic instead of mechanical; small and beautiful technology, not centralized systems; spontaneity instead of order; and compassion, not efficiency."[27] Richard Hirsh identifies what he calls a "sociotechnical" revolution beginning in the 1960s when consumers and regulators both began to distrust "the actions of elitist technical managers."[28]

Not only did the Icarian pride of those subscribing to the technological vision mask some dangerous flaws, but there were counterdreams of solid provenance, which periodically languished in America but never died. Kansas Populists of the 1890s had not been Luddites, rushing to smash machinery and the advantages it brought, but they had objected strongly to the dangerous and dehumanizing aspects of technological civilization. They never accepted the inevitability of some of the accompaniments of industrialization, but rather blamed the human organizers of the machine and corporate systems for socially inappropriate and narrowly conceived choices. "Our size," wrote Henry Demarest Lloyd in 1894, "has got beyond both our science and our conscience."[29] So it was with nuclear "brotherhood." The complexity of the new technology strongly suggested conspiracy to some: the requirement for advanced education and access to massive capital to be a nuclear "insider" created an automatic corporate and personal elite, which must be nefarious.

Paralleling that type of thinking was a long, recurring American affinity for "the simple life." The interpretation dated at least from Jefferson of the virtue and political value of the straightforward yeoman living in a rural area and working with simple hand tools as contrasted with the artificial and inferior "company man" produced by the fast and complex life of cities and crying for "needs" that reflected only a form of civilized illness. Should production of "luxuries" (of wealth or of convenience) exact too much of an environmental or human price, the answer to these thinkers was to do without, and be in some important ways better off in the process.[30]

Primitivism as an ideal is more common in a highly civilized and urbanized society than in one closer to the actual primitive. Sailing is fun as a recreation, but might not be such a desirable way to haul freight each day. The same is true of living in a tent and cooking on a wood fire. It was easy to take potshots at people who complained about new ways of generating power while they lived amidst the comforts that power brought. Yet the pervasiveness of electricity from central power plants in mid-twentieth-century Kansas could be interpreted as undesirable dependence as well as evidence of free choice. And, it should be emphasized, few of the protesters were suggesting eliminating electricity, and most of them rejected as a gross exaggeration the idea that opposing nuclear power was opposing modern civilization.

Related, but not identical, to "simple life" thinkers were the advocates of a "sustainable" technology. One of the most articulate and sophisticated published advocates of this idea in the nation, Wes Jackson, makes his headquarters on an experimental farm (the Land Institute) in Salina, Kansas, and was directly involved in protests against Wolf Creek on the grounds that the whole nuclear application was a short-term stopgap, which depleted irreplaceable resources and fundamentally upset the proper human relation with the biosphere. Descartes was wrong, Jackson avers, Kant was wrong, Bacon was wrong, and much technological thinking is wrong in perceiving things and solving problems through the senses of an organism solely and from a single perspective in a vast and interdependent continuum. To a politician, maybe to an engineer, a century was an eternity; Jackson points out that in relation to the possible future of the species and its complex evolutionary past, it is an instant, but an instant in which the whole enterprise can be compromised or destroyed. The very complexity of the prairie itself, on which the new power plant was to stand, should give pause to the engineers with their hardheaded certainties.[31]

Jackson is a former professor with a Ph.D. who has given up his academic post to apply what he believes he has learned. Doubtless he represents an extreme in depth of documentation, level of commitment, and breadth of alternative vision. It is clearly true that most opponents, as well as proponents, wanted the plant stopped or continued for far more prosaic and immediate reasons. Yet it is unwise to limit analysis to those issues isolated completely from their broader context. For hardly any of the players, when one talks to them, omit philosophy at some level or a vision of the true and moral "good life" as a motivating factor. Utility executives in charge of Wolf Creek are not necessarily readers either of Adam Smith or Paul Pilzer's recent book *Unlimited Wealth.* Pilzer there argues that the very definition of "economics" as the distribution of scarce resources is a flawed one and that the application of technology means in effect that resources and wealth are unlimited.[32] Likewise, the counter-nuclear movement in Kansas did not consist of people carrying Wes Jackson books in their knapsacks. Still, there was a broad commonality among the Wolf Creek groups, however divergent they were with each other as well as on details internally, that would have provided two broad sympathetic audiences for these teachings at the philosophic extremes. Barry Commoner once explained his stance against nuclear power by saying: "What confronts us is not a series of separate crises, but a single basic defect—a fault that lies deep in the design of modern society."[33]

It is true, of course, that those in the counter-nuclear movement were the ultimate "second-guessers." There was no avoiding observing that they were not the people who were making the decisions and would not be held responsible for the results of the decisions, except, of course, as ratepayers. That, however, is a philosophical difficulty of any opposition. They were criticized for not proposing reasonable alternatives. The best alternative to nuclear was coal, but its disadvantages were several, and it was not a clear winner over nuclear in cost, reliability, or impact on the environment. Other alternatives proposed—wind and solar power, for example—were investigated extensively during the Wolf Creek construction permit hearings and later, but showed little promise of immediate application. Blaming the "establishment" for not pursuing these harder in the past did not change the dilemma for those facing the current decision. Nor was it helpful to suggest simply waiting until something satisfactory (cold fusion, perhaps?) came along. One cartoon showed a bird publishing a newspaper in a treehouse. Due to the concern about nuclear power, he writes, we are not converting to electric typewriters, but are keeping our diesel-powered ones. The point was incontrovertible.

That certain ideas of the intervenors contained features of Marxism should neither obscure the fundamental Americanism of the protest, nor suggest that subscribers to the counter-dream necessarily advocated a socialist state. Among the people opposing the Wolf Creek plant were some who were anticapitalist and many who objected to the form of capitalism that had developed in the late twentieth-century United States. But there were also near libertarians, who felt that the government in league with the utility represented a threat to freedom; farmers protesting the state-imposed right of eminent domain; environmentalists (state socialism has never been known for its fine environmental record); physicians and scientists objecting to health risks and flawed technology; large and small businessmen, concerned about the cost/benefit ratio; and entrepreneurs who valued the efficiency and flexibility of a decentralized economy, which would contrast as sharply with Karl Marx's ideas as with those of Samuel Insull.

All who were enthusiastically involved in the Wolf Creek issue on each side of the question had their fears as well as their hopes. The utility executives' fears were of the country backsliding into relative poverty and of the conveniences that were supposed to free people for a higher life yielding to the historic round of dawn to dusk human drudgery. They feared too that the engine of wealth creation that had operated in the United States so successfully would be damaged so that, as was true in so many places, the humanistic dream of equality might consist of just an equal part of nothing. That these types of concerns overrode even the profit motive that might seem preeminent has been characterized by some students of the industry as one of its vulnerabilities in the 1960s.[34] The opponents' fears were that the irreplaceable gift of nature might be permanently compromised for ignoble ends, that corporate power over basic industries might compromise choice and freedom in a democracy, that the cost of the new power plant would cripple the regional economy, and, most prominently, that nuclear power, though statistically so safe, was theoretically so dangerous that the worst case risk was simply unacceptable.

The great bugaboo was radiation. It was the national phobia, justified or not, about radiation which all parties eventually concluded was the single central reason that nuclear power did not succeed in the 1970s. While the utility people had concerns too about the danger of a "loss of coolant" accident (they did not like terms like *melt-*

down) they emphasized that nuclear was the "prettiest pig at the fair"—that the practical near-range alternatives to nuclear power for electrical generation, such as coal, posed cost and environmental risks that were probably greater.[35] Be that as it may, responded the intervenors, the risk was not to be tolerated—not by the relatively few people living in the vicinity of the plant site, not by the workers there, not by anyone. Margaret Bangs, a Wichita woman who found herself in the early 1970s suddenly in the midst of the battle over Wolf Creek, recalled that, while costs and the reliability of the technology later took their place among her concerns, her initial reason for attending hearings was the unshakable image of Hiroshima and Nagasaki. Her commitment was to act on behalf of her grandchildren to keep anything connected with atomic fission out of the state of Kansas.[36]

Radiation, long before atomic bombs, was connected in the public mind with the menace and possible threat to the privacy of the human body of invisible rays. Despite the fact that human life had evolved in and in fact depended upon a background of low-level radiation, a 1989 *National Geographic* article correctly concluded that "hardly a word in any language generates more anxiety." Invisible and powerful rays have been associated with the gods of myth and with the "incinerating, transforming, enslaving" death rays of the Buck Rogers comics.

In nuclear power plants the radiation was perceived as both "artificial" and "unnecessary." Ironically, by far the greatest radiation health hazard in America in the 1980s was natural radon gas leaking into homes sealed up by energy-conscious Americans trying to save energy to avoid building nuclear power plants.[37] The greatest regular radiation levels to workers in the operating Wolf Creek plant came from the same source.[38] Human-created nuclear power posed a special psychological menace in its emission of rays and its residue of poisons. The fission process itself, transforming as it did a seminatural element into an entirely new one, smacked of medieval alchemy; those who feared nuclear power perceived technological necromancers, perhaps in league with the devil, and railed at them for trying to accomplish the seemingly rational task of turning valueless materials into gold.

Scientists and engineers might think their parallel task was nothing more than finding an efficient use for uranium, just as they had for the once-valueless petroleum in the Middle East, but the imagery their method and materials unloosed was powerful and negative. The new Faust, in the form of the scientist, with his assistants the engineers and the business magnates, was the latest version of the mad villain seeking to rule the world. To harness the engines of the stars to run toasters and air conditioners was a blasphemous challenge to the prerogative of the Deity. Radiation exposure could insidiously plant seeds of destruction inside people, cause constant anxiety, and maybe bloom in death years later. The sparkling, stainless steel reactors with their attending spic and span crews could be something "dirty" in image, both physically and morally. From Dr. Strangelove to Jane Fonda, things nuclear were seldom treated cinematographically in a context other than high emergency and deep scheming. Spencer Weart, in his study *Nuclear Fear: A History of Images,* concludes that "radioactive monsters, utopian atom-powered cities, exploding planets, weird ray devices, and many other images have crept into the way everyone thinks about nuclear energy, whether that energy is used in weapons or in civilian reactors. The images, by connecting up with major social and psychological forces, have exerted a strange and powerful pressure within history."[39]

Common suspicion of radiation, of the pride of the experts, and of the greed of the three-piece suits, held together during the Wolf Creek debates what would otherwise have been a motley crew of strange bedfellows and made what might have been a "routine" construction and rate approval for a power plant a significant human drama. Mrs. Bangs remembers that at her first press conference she appeared with a fellow protestor she had never seen. She arrived primly dressed with the full panoply of middle-aged respectability only to find that her cospokesman was to all appearances a hippie on break from a commune. She had difficulty maintaining her composure then, but later delighted to comment that in the 1990s this fellow was a prominent attorney who wore a tie every day and carried a leather briefcase.[40]

Camaraderie in protest, independent of the cause, cannot be dismissed as a factor. However the experts might decry the "haze of misinformation" in which protestors and intervenors supposedly operated, all grant them persistence and solidarity over a long period of time. More than one observer noted that the end of the Vietnam War left an organized protest movement, flushed with its success and nostalgic for the civil rights and war "events" of the 1960s with little *raison d'être*. "Lives that may have lacked meaning had," wrote Samuel McCracken, "for a space, taken on heroic dimension."[41]

James Haines, a KG&E executive who as attorney cross-examined many intervenors, and who was frustrated to have to sit through public hearings where he listened to attacks by protestors who were allowed to enter testimony without being subject to cross-examination, was a former student activist himself and understood the group-identity motivation well. While he agreed that some mothers felt it was their biological destiny to protest nuclear power, he thought most were driven by "political and social hangover from the 1960s": "All of us hung on to that *esprit de corps* and lifestyle long after it expired and tried to bring it back when we could." Yet as little as he once could imagine being a vice president of a utility, Haines did become one. "One of the tragedies of the century," he reflected in hindsight, "is how leadership [in the 1960s] listened to naive youth."[42]

The temptation is an ancient one, documented, for instance, in the Greek tragedy by Euripedes entitled *The Bakkhai*. There groups (called *thiasos*) are described, heavily populated by women, who band together in ecstatic worship of the god Dionysius. More than one commentator has noted that there are modern parallels from sport to war to religion of people trying to escape the "bland ties of social life." What civil authorities then and later feared was that in its pure form this Dionysian *thiasos* had "an unconcern with anything but its own gratification" and was characterized by "immunity to responsible leadership." Within the "ecstacy" of the group (the sexual connotations of the ancient rite are incidental to the phenomenon) ordinary people could feel themselves to be "superbeings" through their obvious collective power. Euripedes has one of his group say: "When the gods crush our enemies, their heads cowed under the hard fist of our power, that is glory!"[43] It is strong stuff, especially when the crushers are ordinary folks, and the crushees are perceived as the arrogant, high and mighty establishment.

The nuclear issue allowed the groups to maintain that high moral aim and to stay in contact with associates they had learned to respect. The nuclear plant was the perfect modern demon as an attack on it was an attack on the large corporation, the government, and the mixed record of high technology at one blow. "Since almost no one yet understands that his welfare depends on nuclear power," wrote a detractor of the protests, "moral indignation against it comes unusually cheap."[44]

The participants agreed about the camaraderie, but naturally did not interpret it as a psychological drive that "explained" the protest independent of the issue. Diane Tegtmeier of the Mid-America Coalition for Energy Alternatives, while recognizing the "ego involvement people who get involved in political issues can succumb to," thought much of what transformed her from housewife to activist was authentic and impressive. The best of the protestors could, Tegtmeier thought, "maintain objectivity and internal control," and connect the local action with a broader arena. Their theme was "common reverence and respect for natural systems," and many of them read widely on the nuclear issue, respected their opponents, learned only reluctantly about the press and the public eye, and guarded against acting like the "crazies" they were purported to be. "For some it was a growing experience," she remembered, "and for others destructive as they went to their weaker sides."[45] In short, the protest group was no more the monolith that the sound bite and the hearing made them out to be than were the regulators or the corporate people.

The whole panoply of hopes and visions alongside the nightmares and fears of a variety of human types were formally arrayed and opposed in Kansas in the particular vise known as the legal adversarial process. While the process had the virtue of ensuring that all facts were "discovered" and that all views got a respectable airing, it forced the adversaries into their most extreme positions. Though some of the expert witnesses advanced their credibility by occasionally admitting either ignorance or the value of some of the opposition's points, most participants in the process, either at the regulatory or press level, did not risk that. For the record it was a battle—an "us" against "them" confrontation, black and white, empty of nuance, and with clear winners and losers. In reality it was anything but.

In 1973, the year the Wolf Creek plant was announced to the public, a book appeared by economist E. F. Schumacher entitled *Small is Beautiful: Economics as If People Mattered*. It became, along with a small shelf of other works (among them John Hersey's *Hiroshima* [1946]; Rachel Carson's *Silent Spring* [1962]; Barry Commoner's *Sci-*

ence and Survival [1966] and *The Closing Circle* [1971]; Herbert Marcuse's *One-Dimensional Man* [1964]; Lewis Mumford's *The Myth of the Machine* [1970]; and Charles Reich's *The Greening of America* [1970]), somewhat of a cult item.[46]

Not only did Schumacher argue that industry to survive must allow for many noneconomic facets of human nature and that we must see ourselves as a part of nature rather than as a force out to conquer it, but that small-scale, nonviolent, and decentralized technology would, if all real costs were accounted for, be more efficient, not to mention more sustainable in the long run than, for example, current utility practices. Schumacher defended private property ownership in small-scale enterprise as "natural, fruitful and just." However, he criticized it in large-scale enterprises (like KG&E) as "a fiction for the purpose of enabling functionless owners to live parasitically on the labour of others." He suggested, therefore, "some degree of socialization of ownership" in large enterprises.[47]

Schumacher's "Buddhist Economics," which contained several sections on alternative energy technology and organization, was clearly less familiar to KG&E executives, engineers, and attorneys than the precepts of Adam Smith or the reports of the Electrical Reliability Council. However, as of about the date of the publication of his book, the isolation of the utility from the manifestations of a wide range of nontechnical thinking that varied fundamentally from its own axioms had come to an end. What KG&E faced was not only different means, but different values and paradigms about the end. It was something for which the background and experience of most utility managers and employees had not prepared them any more than intervenors were prepared to deal with the technical testimony of the ordinary construction or rate hearing. Consequently the alien behavior of both sides, presented as it was in a constrained legal process encouraging polarization of views and reported by a press where sensation sold, tended to reinforce stereotypes, heighten emotion, and vest each side unalterably to its "positions."[48]

The struggle could not have been avoided. Perhaps it should have been no particular surprise. But it was a frustrating time when no one was satisfied either with the terms or with the outcome. For example, between 1968, when planning for Wolf Creek began and 1985, when it went on line, a tremendous amount of "external" future shock went on—the energy crisis came and went, interest rates soared to all-time highs, conservation increased, electric demand in

Kansas and the nation increased more slowly than ever before, and accidents in nuclear power plants from Three Mile Island, Pennsylvania (1979), to Chernobyl (1986), in the former Soviet Union, changed the rules of the regulatory game substantially. Not only were more strict regulations on fire and safety systems instituted, but often plants in the process of construction were required to be changed even though it meant retrofitting at great expense. Just as the planning horizon for power plants was lengthening, the stability of the economic and social milieu was lessening. KG&E sometimes felt change made it a scapegoat—the deep-pocket victim upon whom responsibility for the negatives of change was loaded. Citizens and ratepayers felt that the dead hand of mistaken decision in the past was being immortalized in the cement of Wolf Creek and paid for by a voiceless public. In 1991 the world scene, with war in the Persian Gulf, increasing oil prices, and concern about the "acid rain" from coal plants, looked again more like 1973 than like 1980: there was talk about building nuclear plants again, but no volunteers among the veterans.

To some extent the hatred of KG&E by some was a result of its history of success. "The nearer a large corporation is to filling the role of a parent," wrote Samuel McCracken in *The War Against the Atom*, "by providing an essential service reliably and at minimal cost, the more its exertions will be expected as a right and the more likely the public will be to see it only in terms of its failings, real or imagined. A large proportion of the public seems to view the electric utilities as philanthropic organizations who ought to supply, at convenient rates, electricity generated through politically fashionable means, but always electricity, and as much as anyone wants."[49]

James Haines, KG&E's lead attorney in the acrimonious Wolf Creek rate hearings in 1985, understood that and a good deal else, but demanded at least that the proceedings include a sense of history, and include empathy with the difficulty of decisionmaking forced in dynamic time. "This proceeding is focused on Wolf Creek," he told the assembly. "The central issue, however, is not Wolf Creek, *per se*, but the much larger issue of the meaning of a public utility's obligation to serve and the proper benchmark and perspective for judging a utility's efforts to meet that obligation. Is the benchmark prudence or perfection? Is the perspective from what is known now or what was known when the decision was made?"[50]

KG&E, which six years earlier nearly passed out of existence because of its nuclear plant's supposed failures, was poised in 1991 to pass out of existence because of its successes. The real prize for which the takeover suitors bid was KG&E's 47 percent interest in an operating nuclear plant whose "dark days" of creation were past. Such are the ironies in the passage of little pieces of time.

Wolf Creek is recent history indeed. The plant is running my word processor as I write this. The documentary materials, oral and written, are a little warmer still than historians usually like to handle. The controversy is not antique; the stakes of interpretation are not theoretical. Something very like the events described, in something approaching parallel circumstances, could happen again, and soon. It may be too early to write a history. But it is also too late not to.

1
An Exotic Animal

> For nuclear energy is part and parcel of the revolution that has helped raise the working classes from being beasts of burden to owners of hundreds of mechanical and morally unobjectionable servants. Unless we mean to reverse that revolution altogether, we would be well advised to take a just measure of nuclear technology, assessing candidly both its drawbacks . . . and its advantages . . . and to guide our policy accordingly.
> —Samuel McCracken, *The War Against the Atom*

> It now appears that the environmental problems of oil and coal-fired plants and the upward cost trend of fossil fuels will not be reversed and thus, with good operating experience on the new large nuclear plants, that orders for nuclear units will continue to increase in what appears to be a stable long term trend.
> —Federal Power Commission, *National Power Survey*, 1970

> In 45 years of business in southeast Kansas, the Company has developed an accurate feel for the pulse of the area.
> —KG&E, *The Core of the Great Plains*, 1955

Dwight Eisenhower spoke to the United Nations General Assembly at the approach of the Christmas season of 1953, under the shadow of a cold war with the Soviet Union that, should it move to violence, could potentially unleash atomic bombs of 25 times the force of that used at Hiroshima, and hydrogen bombs equivalent to millions of tons of TNT. There had been many drafts of the message, since called the "Atoms for Peace" speech, which the U.S. president delivered that December 8. His theme was that swords could be literally beaten into plowshares—that the very atomic forces that had both ended World War II and provided its ultimate terror were not permanently wedded to the "dark side." "Occasional pages of history do record the faces of the 'Great Destroyers,'" he said, "but the whole book of history reveals mankind's neverending quest for peace, and mankind's God-given capacity to build. It is with the book of history, and not with isolated pages, that the United States will ever wish to be identified. . . . So my country's purpose is to help us move out of the dark chamber of horrors into the light, to find a way by which the minds of men, the hopes of men, the souls of men everywhere, can move forward toward peace and happiness and well-being."

The instrument of this latter-day peaceful force was the atomic power plant. Nuclear engines held promise in powering submarines since they needed no oxygen, and the naval application under Admiral Hyman Rickover was well advanced by the mid 1950s. There had been a primitive unshielded "pile" that generated nuclear power under the football stadium at the University of Chicago several years before there was an atomic bomb, and it was to these first experiments Eisenhower now suggested returning. That the early reactors were *breeders*—creating more potential fuel in the form of plutonium than they used—was considered an additional boon that would free the U.S. electric grid from the vagaries of the oil and gas supply and provide energy far into the future at a cost relatively, and perhaps absolutely, lower than at any time in American history. "The United States knows that peaceful power from atomic energy is no dream of the future," Eisenhower intoned. "The capability, already proved, is here—now—today. Who can doubt, if the entire body of the world's scientists and engineers had adequate amounts of fissionable material with which to test and develop their ideas, that this capability would rapidly be transformed into universal, efficient, and economic usage. To hasten the day when fear of the atom will begin to disappear from the minds of people . . . there are certain steps that can be taken now." Eisenhower went on to speak of making fissionable material available to utility researchers both domestically and internationally. He ended with an earnest pledge to pay attention to "human aspirations" and not instruments of war: "The United States pledges . . . before the world its determination to help solve the fearful atomic dilemma—to devote its entire heart and mind to find a way by which the miraculous inventiveness of man shall not be dedicated to his death, but consecrated to his life."[1]

On Labor Day 1954, Eisenhower waved a wand from Denver, Colorado, that signalled an unmanned bulldozer to begin construction at Shippingport, Pennsylvania, of the world's first commercial nuclear power plant. The Atomic Energy Commission, formed by the Atomic Energy Act of 1946, was a partner with Duquesne Light and Power Company in this demonstration project, but the free enterprise philosophy and business orientation of the administration in Washington ensured what might have later been termed the "privatization" of the industrial applications of the atom. Amendments in 1954 to the Atomic Energy Act eliminated the earlier prohibition of private use of nuclear materials and authorized the AEC to license private companies to build and operate nuclear plants. A 1964 amendment allowed the utilities to own the nuclear fuel themselves. It was thought that with some early "pump-priming" financially and technically by the federal government, the nuclear business could be taken over quickly by taxpaying, investor-financed utilities, with the government present only as a watchdog over safety and rates. In 1957 the Price-Anderson amendments to the Atomic Energy Act further encouraged utilities by limiting their liability in case of a nuclear accident to a $560 million fund established by the AEC and private insurers. The AEC predicted that there would be 1,000 nuclear plants in operation by the year 2000.

Activity was regular. In 1955 the first nuclear submarine, the *USS Nautilus*, put to sea, followed by the nuclear-powered ship *NS Savannah* in 1959. In 1957 two construction permits, for the Dresden and Indian Point plants, were issued. Westinghouse and GE (with its new slogan, "Progress Is Our Most Important Product") offered utilities "turnkey" contracts to build nuclear plants for a price specified and limited in advance, and there was every prospect that the impetus to creating a new revolution in the industry would be every bit as strong and successful as when the suppliers had first added capital to and encouraged consolidation of utilities in the early twentieth century. Daniel Ford of the Union of Concerned Scientists later characterized the early nuclear program as "the most ambitious construction program in the U.S. since the building of the railroads in the 19th century."[2]

It was a curious mix, however, of public and private initiative, and it was far from certain whether it would result in the best of two worlds or the worst. Throughout the American history of electric utilities there had been an argument over whether these should be a "service" like water, operated by public bodies or a "commodity," controlled by private profit-making enterprises. While the "private" model won, it was far from pure. One text notes that "the electric power industry is the most money-intensive, pervasive and political business in modern America."[3] As with most government intervention in new businesses (the railroads and earlier canals of the nineteenth century are parallel models) action first took the form of promotion, and then later, when the industry was mature and dependent, of ever more stringent regulation.

Doubtless at least the appearance of a private nuclear power industry was inevitable in the United States where investor-owned electric utilities had been for many years an "entrenched culture" perceived as doing the public good and with good consensus among their stakeholders. In Europe the "sociotechnical" situation was markedly different and nuclear energy was developed more slowly, with a more uniform and debugged technology, and far more standardization and centralized planning. While this approach had failed with historical technologies compared with the more wide-open American entrepreneurial model, a number of students have argued that with nuclear power it became the more successful scenario. It was not a field, perhaps, for cowboys.[4]

It appeared in the 1950s that nuclear power would be some time having any impact on Kansas. Since the exploitation of the Hugoton field in southwest Kansas in the 1920s, the state had a nearly inexhaustible supply of cheap natural gas. There was no reason for KG&E to bear the problems of a nuclear plant, or for that matter to fuss with coal or fuel oil.

The corporate culture typical of American utilities, however, was certainly there. The company was confident of proceeding as "an organization of men and equipment established and maintained to render first-class service to its customers at reasonable rates based on sound financing of the enterprise, a cultural wage to its employees, and a fair return on just capitalization. . . ."[5] If the government would stand back, the company believed it could bring the good life through electricity to more and more people in rural areas of Kansas, who once thought a "wire" was something to repair fences and bind grain. "Through the potent 'juice' that the wire brings to him," Wichita editor Marcellus Murdock wrote in 1938, "man is turning everything under his hand into a marionette which he can make perform to his liking by merely touching a button or throwing a switch."[6]

In 1951 GE's ten-car streamlined train followed two Alco PA locomotives through Kansas with an exhibit of 2,000 of "the latest products, systems and techniques for producing and using electric power." KG&E officials were on hand to greet people visiting the train on its May 21 stop in Wichita and promote Reddy Kilowatt as "Your Servant of the Century."[7] The cost of living, the company emphasized, had gone up 85 percent since 1941, while the cost of electricity for the home had during the same period declined 33 percent. While admitting that there might be rate increases in the future, KG&E promised miracles in return. A 1952 company piece predicted that electricity would air-condition homes, regulate humidity, remove dust, circulate insecticides, kill airborne bacteria with special lamps, and control stuffiness. It would pop your meat, electronically tenderized, into the home electric cooker, and dirty dishes would be sterilized while being automatically washed and dried. People would soon enjoy home dry cleaning machines, "probably supersonic," and their TV sets would have 3-D and color. While all this would require three to four times the power standard in the household of 1952, the power would be a bargain.[8] Symbols of company confidence in the 1950s were not only the new gas generating plants (in 1954, 70% of the company's generating capacity was less than seven years old), but a new office building in downtown Wichita, occupied in 1955.[9] The company slogan was "Live Better Electrically."

In 1957 Gordon Evans, CEO of KG&E, gave a major speech to a national conference on electric heating. KG&E was sold on it, he said, because the recent influx of air conditioning had changed its load factor (the ratio between peak and low electric demand) and made winter sales more important. The company was going beyond heating to the "all electric home," including electric water heating, electric cooking, dishwashing, and garbage disposal. The question was not whether there would be demand for these things, but whether power companies could keep up: "The industry as a whole has not had the vision to see where we were going and to be prepared for the tremendous increase in use of our service. We have consistently underestimated the growth and expansion of our business. Generally, the public has been and is ahead of us in their thinking. . . . In the past the leadership in the electric utility industry have been cautious and safe rather than forward looking and progressive." Evans recalled his own grandfather's 80th birthday dinner. When asked if he had seen many changes in his lifetime, the old man said, "Yes, and I was against all of them."[10]

Evans's determination to get and remain "up to date" affected the whole company. KG&E installed computers for accounting, put graphics in its annual reports, and marketed actively to avoid being seen as a fuddy-duddy during future shock. Its 1952 *Annual Report* looked at the company in the context of a Wichita booming from the B-47 and B-52 contracts occasioned by the Korean War, and took as its theme "From Indian Trails to Vapor Trails." The chart comparing residential kilowatt-hour sales compared with average price showed two lines sharply diverging as sales soared and price plummeted.[11] In 1953 the color cover of the *Annual Report* showed an idealized Wichita with a family observing a high-tech exhibit of electrical appliances over the slogan "a city of new customers."[12] Fred Kimball, in a speech to the Wichita Rotary in the fall of 1958, predicted that Wichita would have more than 400,000 people by 1975, perhaps 500,000, with another 100,000 in the county (1990 actual population was 300,000), and that natural resources like coal and oil "will be in abundant quantity."[13]

Consistent with this "progressive" stance, and with a general utility engineering focus on technological leadership, KG&E did not ignore the phenomenon of nuclear power. Utilities had been so successful that by the 1950s they had begun to be perceived by the business community as static, even unimaginative, with a conservative and dull image that did not attract the brightest new engineers.[14] Related, certainly, was the regulatory environment, which caused utility people to be identified sometimes, to their chagrin, with politicians and bureaucrats. The appeal of nuclear power to these people was evident. Not only was it possibly something that would be good for the ratepayers and provide fuel diversity and profits, but, just as important, it returned the high-tech image to a company dominated by engineers and former engineers. There was an excitement in being on the leading edge, even to some degree probably in the idea of controlling something potentially dangerous, that appealed strongly to the utility people of the 1950s. It was an era focused on a technological future, when nearly every issue of *Popular Science* would have a cover showing monorails or helioports on the top of people's homes in the cities of the future. Nuclear power fit right in, both with the utility executives and with their constituents. James Jasper, in his sociological study of the "Political Life Cycle of Technological Controversies," notes that in the initial "pre-political" stage of new technologies there tends to be confidence in experts and a general excitement about the prospects. Jasper believes that in the case of American nuclear plants, this pre-political stage lasted until 1974, by which time the Wolf Creek project was well underway.[15]

At KG&E the catalyst for nuclear power among the engineers was Elmer Hall. Hall, who became KG&E's chief engineer in 1960, had become interested in advanced physics and its application to power devices while a student at Pittsburg College in southeast Kansas, where his father ran the electric plant. Known to his friends as a great scratch-builder of apparatus, Hall got a fellowship in 1934 at the University of Southern California, where he was to assist in the famous Michelson-Morley experiments on the speed of light. At the last minute that opportunity fell through, and in 1936 Hall applied his active mind to a new job as electric substation operator at Mulberry, Kansas. From there he went to KG&E's Ripley gas plant in 1938. All the while, Hall maintained his intellectual connection with the USC experiments, and subscribed to the *Bulletin*, put out by the college, at seven cents a copy. That publication was filled with information on nuclear physics, and when the announcement was made in 1945 of the dropping of the atomic bomb, Hall was in demand at the Ripley plant to explain to others exactly what had happened. Hall organized the initial nuclear teams at KG&E, and was for years a knowledgeable proponent of nuclear power at a high level within the Kansas company. His combination of practical power plant experience, inventive and experimental capacity, and theoretical knowledge, all dating from his youth, gave him credibility on the subject of atomic energy without parallel among his Kansas peers.[16]

The KG&E *Annual Report* for 1954 emphasized that the corporation was "a good neighbor—locally managed and privately owned ... a part of the American System of Freedoms.... Kansas Gas and Electric Company is a wholly independent, business-managed, taxpaying electric utility owned directly by the public." That said, it was noted that while the company itself had not been active in the field of atomic energy it "is following the progress made in the use of atomic energy for electric power production." Several groups of electric utilities were working on the technology, but "economical production of electricity by atomic energy appears to be several years in the future." Kansas would be far from the first application: "With relatively low fuel cost, this area may be among the last where atomic energy will become economically feasible."[17] In 1955 the nuclear note went in a box of "Items of Special Interest" featuring Reddy Kilowatt springing out of an outlet with a pattern of orbiting electrons behind it. It was reported that "in keeping with the Company's policy of long-range planning" it was participating in the activities of an atomic energy study group headed by Pioneer Service and Engineering Company of Chicago. Still there was the caveat that "there are no present indications that the Company, located in an area in which fossil fuels are relatively plentiful and inexpensive, will find it practical from a cost standpoint to convert to the use of atomic energy as a fuel in the near future."[18]

There was a similar modest appearance of nuclear concerns in the employee magazine *Servicegraph*. In 1954 an article appeared entitled "Edison's Lamp and the Atom." Seventy-five years earlier, went the text, "Thomas Edison stood on the threshold of an entirely new technology, whose possibilities could scarcely be imagined and whose problems were considered by many of the best minds of the day to be insoluble." It was now the same with nuclear power, and that problem would be solved "with the enterprise and the realistic spirit of practical service that Edison exemplified. . . ." The first of Edison's electric generators needed over ten times as much coal to generate a kilowatt of electricity as did the 1954 models. That sort of technological progress would be made with nuclear energy. Breeder reactors produced as much fuel as was consumed, "a phenomenon which would have dumbfounded the scientist of 75 years ago." The piece concluded by predicting that it should not take another 75 years to discover the economic peacetime uses of the atom.[19]

Despite these hints to stockholders and employees, Wichitans at large had no special inkling that nuclear power was a consideration with their local utility until 1957. Under the headline "KG&E to Spend $115,000 a Year in Atomic Study," the *Wichita Eagle* announced in August that the company had joined a group of 13 other utilities in a research and development project to find a nuclear power plant design that would be suitable for Kansas and the Southwestern United States region. KG&E would spend $500,000 in the next four years on the research. There was no hint of a negative local reaction. KG&E's exhibit at the Wichita University open house that spring was an Atomic Electric Power Plant diagram. The newspaper ran a large drawing of a plant that was clearly hypothetical, but which showed the press eagerness to visualize high technology on the prairie.[20]

The company magazine went into a little more detail. The industry group was a nonprofit research corporation called Southwest Atomic Energy Associates (SAEA). Gordon Evans of KG&E was its vice president. A total of $5,000,000 was to be raised from the member companies for a four-year research and development program to design a practical-sized reactor that could be operated at the efficient high temperatures and pressures used in modern "superpower" steam plants. The theory in 1957 was that the nuclear plants would be of smaller capacity than the current gas plants. The size of KG&E's Murray Gill plant, for example (245.7 mw), was thought impractical for nuclear because such a nuclear plant would be "tremendous in size and very expensive to build." It was thought that with research a 200,000 to 400,000 kw plant could be "built and operated at reasonable cost."

Clearly that theory underwent some rapid change. The Wolf Creek plant as constructed had a net design electrical output of 1150 megawatts (1,150,000 kw), over four times the size of KG&E's largest gas plant in the 1950s. Gordon Evans would not have been surprised, however, that the company undertook whatever was found necessary. He surmised in 1957 that "over a period of time, the increased demands for fuels may require the use of atomic power regardless of cost," and that the SAEA objectives included demonstrating that private industry was willing and able to take the lead in atomic research without calling on taxpayer assistance. The project, Evans said, would tell KG&E "how and when to bring atomic power to Kansas." He had no doubt that "when atomic power is practicable and when it becomes economically feasible, we'll have it here."[21]

A little over a year later, when the first large-scale (60,000 kw) U.S. reactor at Shippingport, Pennsylvania, had been operating about a year, a second article appeared in the Wichita press. The reporter this time (December 1958) interviewed S. J. Sickel, KG&E's vice president of operations. Sickel emphasized that the nuclear question was primarily one of fuel availability and cost: "Two theoretical lines on a graph, one representing the slow but steady rise in cost of gas, oil and coal, and the other representing the inevitably declining cost of atomic energy, are the key to the future of the world fuel picture." When those lines crossed—and Sickel estimated that might be in about twenty years—a nuclear plant in Kansas would be a possibility.

Sickel acted as KG&E's technical representative to SAEA, which in turn had hired Atomics International, a division of North American Aviation, Inc., to experiment with atomic-powered generators. At North American's Canoga Park, California, plant, research was underway to design a breeder reactor aimed at solving two of the four major problems of nuclear plants—how to keep radioactivity to a minimum and how to cope with corrosion and high temperature. The two additional big questions, left for the moment in abeyance, were waste disposal and the cost of fuel.[22]

Primary information about the reactor process is required to understand the next steps. The nucleus of an atom contains protons and neutrons. Protons have a positive electric charge, and neutrons no charge. In stable form these remain as they are; in unstable form a certain percentage of the atoms is constantly undergoing disintegration or decay. Chemical particles are expelled along with forms of electromagnetic radiation (mostly gamma rays), making these substances radioactive.

The purposeful "splitting" of the atomic nucleus (fission) with the consequent enormous release of energy and change in the atomic structure of the element bombarded was a discovery of the late 1930s. The bombarding was done by "slow" neutrons acting on an enriched isotope of uranium, which was formed from processed uranium oxide called "yellowcake," and was known as U-235. Nuclei were split, giving off other neutrons, which in turn (when the technology was perfected in the 1940s) split other nuclei, forming a self-sustaining chain reaction. The resulting heat made both the power reactor and the nuclear bomb possible. In the power plant the chain reaction was controlled by neutron-absorbing rods and by moderating materials (usually water) contained in the reactor core. In the process, too, the original U-235 had its atomic structure transformed into various "waste" elements, some highly radioactive. The "hottest" of these elements had the shortest life, while those less immediately dangerous because they leaked radiation slowly presented a storage problem because of their long atomic half-life (the time needed for half their atoms to become stable).

One of the possible products of fission, it was found, was a new element called *plutonium* (Pu-239). A reactor could convert nonfissile uranium-238 (which is 99% of natural uranium, as contrasted with the rare uranium-235) into plutonium, which was itself fissionable and could in turn be used as fuel. This process became the basis of the so-called breeder reactor, whose efficiency was so great and therefore its cost so low that it was early assumed that it would be the sole basis for the commercial electric generating industry. It was the dream of the medieval alchemist of turning lead into gold come true. It made unnecessary the huge expensive processing plants, like those at Oak Ridge and Hanford, which during World War II did nothing but extract precious little U-235 from vast amounts of uranium ore.

Another "fertile" isotope of interest to nuclear scientists was thorium-232 (Th-232). When placed as a "blanket" around a nuclear reactor fueled with something else, thorium, like U-238, absorbed neutrons. However, instead of changing to plutonium, thorium was transmuted into U-233, an isotope much like U-235, and usable also as reactor fuel. Sometimes the type of reactor doing this was called a *convertor* rather than a breeder. The standard model was known as a *burner.*

There were differences in the breeder types other than the atomic process. In both boiling water (BWR) and pressurized water (PWR) U-235 reactors, water is used as a moderator to slow the neutrons in the reactor core. Both types are called *light water reactors* because they use ordinary water. In the breeders the blankets do not have moderators, so neutrons strike the fertile material at high speeds. Thus these are called *fast* reactors, and an advantage is that their high-energy neutrons can induce fission and promote rapid decay in many heavy isotopes, including much nuclear "waste." They are cooled by liquid sodium, which does not moderate speed, but has excellent heat transfer qualities and can circulate at atmospheric pressure. A disadvantage to these liquid metal (LMR) reactors, however, is that the coolant is reactive with air and water and requires expensive safeguards to prevent chemical fires and explosions. Second (and more familiar to the public), their byproduct, plutonium, can be used to make atomic bombs, and therefore is a threat to nonproliferation strategies worldwide, and adds danger to terrorism.[23]

The thinking among the Southwest Energy group in the 1950s was to create a "convertor" reactor—initially using a plutonium/uranium mix as a fuel core surrounded with a blanket of thorium. Through the bombardment and transformation of the thorium to U-233 there would be established a pattern of "perpetual creation." Thorium, like the U-238 used in the more standard breeder, was relatively common and inexpensive. The design, as it worked, would make it possible to largely avoid the bugbear of plutonium.

Another advantage of a breeder over a light water reactor to electric utilities related to corrosion and expansion and contraction. In a standard fission reactor pure water was used in a nuclear steam system, which transferred its heat to a physically separate steam system running the turbines and electric generators (water is a good material in that it does not retain radioactivity long). However, it was hard to keep the water pure, and the high steam pressure typical of a modern electric plant as it pressed against metal cladding presented a difficult problem of finding a material that could meet higher nuclear safety standards. Zirconium was effective, but rare and expensive. Stainless steel was not so good, and copper broke down to strontium, which had a half-life of 500 years. Also, at the 1000° temperatures of supercritical generating plant steam systems, expansion and contraction was too much for nuclear tolerances.

The only answer with standard nonbreeder nuclear designs seemed to be to limit steam temperature to 650°, which cut efficiency but increased all-important safety. To the early planners that was not good enough. "This may be atomic power 1958-style," Sickel commented, "but it's steam power 1922-style." With the convertor or breeder, however, 1000° temperatures again became possible because sodium maintained its liquid state at that temperature. Its high boiling point eliminated the pressure on the cladding and therefore did not require such exotic metals.

Of the problems not being addressed by the California research, Sickel thought waste disposal the most important. "In a world powered by atomic reactors," he said, "someone is going to have to give that problem serious attention." Here also, breeders had an advantage, as they left much less waste.

Somehow the waste question, along with many other less fundamental problems, would have to be solved relatively soon, as natural gas in finite supply was perhaps never a rational long-term candidate for boiler fuel, and its cost was slowly beginning to reflect that. Gas, Sickel said, was "becoming a premium fuel," and that was something that a Kansas utility that was 100 percent dependent upon it had to worry about.[24] In November 1959, only a month before the 50th anniversary of KG&E, one of the top research engineers in the United States told an audience in the company auditorium at Wichita that nuclear energy "will become economical as a source of fuel within the next ten years or so."[25]

In December 1960, the Los Angeles experimental reactor built by SAEA "went critical" (nuclear terminology has a penchant for suggesting stress). Internal reports suggested that this sort of reactor would be competitive with fossil fuel in cost by approximately 1972. It was sodium cooled, using an initial mix of plutonium and uranium, but irradiating a "blanket" of thorium, which, when transformed into U-233, replaced the expensive initial fuels. It was known as an Advanced Epithermal Thorium Reactor (AETR)—which helped the public very little in understanding it. The public relations part was as oversimplified as the terminology was over-obtuse. An interested layperson could obtain a booklet from the group called "Citizen Atom, Your Partner in Progress." Most probably did not think of Mr. Atom exactly that way, but they were at a loss for help in how to think of the breeder project in California.[26]

The next step for KG&E was to become involved in a second nuclear research reactor, again with the SAEA group, now expanded to 17 utilities. The utilities were joined by GE, the Atomic Energy Commission, and a West German research firm to construct a reactor in an Ozark valley twenty miles south of Fayetteville, Arkansas. The project was known as SEFOR (Southwest Experimental Fast Oxide Reactor). It was estimated in 1963 that total cost would reach $25,000,000, with KG&E contributing about $400,000. While the company's annual reports contended that all its generating plants built since World War II could be converted to burn coal, and re-emphasized that "KG&E's service area will be among the last areas in which nuclear fuels will be competitive in price with gas or coal," it also pointed out that since 1954 127 U.S. utility companies had played a part in 28 atomic projects at a cost of $1.2 billion.[27] There was even a nuclear reactor in Kansas. One was constructed at the University of Kansas in a room on the west end of campus in 1961 with a capacity of 250 kw, a cost of $147,000, a staff of one, and virtually no press coverage.[28]

Planning for SEFOR began in 1961. The experiment was announced to the public in 1963, the reactor was installed in 1967, initial fuel loading took place in April 1969, and the final experiments of the first planned set were done early in 1972. Like the earlier Los Angeles experiment the initial fuel was a mix of plutonium and uranium, which irradiated thorium. While the reactor could have run a 20,000 kw generator, there was no such machinery installed.[29]

One major result of SEFOR was to test successfully the so-called "Doppler effect" which, it was claimed, would result in automatic, natural temperature control in case the reactor overheated due to systems failures. This effect was demonstrated for the first time at SEFOR under conditions simulating a power excursion with a delay in operation of the SCRAM system (SCRAM, a curious acronym, is derived from "safety control rod ax man," who in early reactors was the manual controller for shutdown). Full power at SEFOR was 20 megawatts (mw). Power could change from 10 mw to 10,000 mw in milliseconds, but the Doppler effect reversed it to 100 mw until the SCRAM system intervened to shut down the reactor.[30]

Reaction in the scientific community and among regulators to the SEFOR experiments was positive, though not all shared the enthusiasm of GE scientist Dr. Karl Cohen, who called it "the most significant single reactor experiment in the Western World."[31] A sign at the plant on the day of its dedication in October 1965 read: "SEFOR—Nuclear Research on the Horizon of Tomorrow."[32]

While safety was a concern with the scientists, and while a prime purpose of SEFOR was to test safety procedures, it was not an obsession. The researchers, however, did not represent a cross section of the public. Plutonium, named for the Greek god of the underworld, had begun to get a reputation with the general population as the most toxic substance imaginable, capable of killing billions of people. It could potentially be used in weapons by terrorists, its effects could be invisible and strike far into the future, and it was the very substance used in the powerful weapon that destroyed Nagasaki. Over the years of debate on nuclear power and experiments with breeder reactors, its sinister public image only increased.

While the risk was never questioned by scientists, they emphasized that it was not an unusual hazard. Plutonium's famous long half-life was due to slow decay through emission of alpha particles, similar to those produced constantly by potassium-40 in the human body. This very leisureliness made it less fiercely radioactive than many fission products, and its usability as reactor fuel was the best insurance that it would not be lying around long as uncontrolled waste. The slow decay was what later allowed the plutonium-powered Voyager spacecraft to broadcast pictures from Neptune many years after its launch and far out of range of solar power. Plutonium radiation could be stopped by a thin sheet of paper or by water, skin (though it could cause burns), or a few inches of air. When ingested, it was not necessarily carcinogenic unless trapped in the body. Plutonium was found to occur naturally in Africa. It was claimed that it was ounce per ounce only one-fiftieth as toxic as arsenic when eaten, that when injected into the bloodstream tetanus toxin was four million times and botulin four trillion times as toxic. Plutonium was only ten times more toxic than the caffeine found in coffee, tea, and colas. "Plutonium is not unnatural," wrote one defender of breeder technology, "it is not immoral and it is not the most toxic substance known to man."[33]

Mel Johnson, who supervised the making of the core for SEFOR and the loading of plutonium as its initial charge, agreed with this assessment. Jesse Arterburn, who worked with Johnson on SEFOR and later headed the Wolf Creek project for KG&E, told associates that in the early days he and other nuclear engineers handled plutonium with their bare hands. The scientists used to say if plutonium were being passed in the urine you were OK as it was not building up. The dark humor was that it was "almost as toxic as an oleander bush."

The point was that many naturally occurring substances and a larger number of chemicals regularly in use in industrial applications (chlorine was a commonly cited example) were more toxic than plutonium when misapplied and sometimes had no half-life at all—that is, their toxicity *never* diminished. That chlorine gas in a military application was a deadly killer did not imply to these men that it was unacceptable in swimming pools, any more than plutonium's applicability to an atomic weapon implied that it was not an "acceptable risk" when used in a reactor core.[34]

True, most commercial reactors used a more conservative, if less efficient, process than the experiment at SEFOR. Nevertheless, the dream of a reliable power supply that was "too cheap to meter" turned on perfecting the breeder and the convertor designs. Not only were the American utilities in the Southwest Atomic Energy Associates interested, but so were Euopean utilities, who participated in that project through an organization called Euratom.[35]

During the construction permit hearings for the Wolf Creek plant in 1975, Samuel Jensch, head of the Atomic Energy Commission subgroup presiding, asked KG&E's nuclear project manager, Jesse Arterburn, "What is SEFOR?"

"My God, man," Arterburn snapped, "this is the most important experiment in the reactor field in the last ten years."

"You haven't changed Wolf Creek since this thing got started to a fast breeder, have you?"

"I wish I could."

"I know you wish you could, but there have been some restraints, I think."[36]

In the 1960s the promise of the breeder was obvious, while the social and political restraints to which Jensch referred were still mostly in the background. Still, the question remained why KG&E, with its low rates and clean gas fuel, should bother with nuclear power at all. There were several answers, some general to the industry, and some specific to Kansas and to KG&E.

First, the company's 1960s load projections indicated a rapidly expanding demand, which would require that new generating plants enter the planning stage quickly. In 1965 the Federal Power Commission issued two thick books, which represented three years of work by 134 utility executives including KG&E's vice president of operations, Stan Sickel. This National Power Survey suggested that by 1980 the nation would use 2.5 times as much electric power as in 1965 and that the cost of this power would go down 27 percent, not adjusting for inflation. Utilities would need bigger plants, in the 1500 to 2000 kw range (1200 mw and up), and there would need to be 700,000-volt transmission lines, about double the then-current standard. Nuclear power would play an increasingly important role, the study said, amounting to one-fifth of the total electric power in 1980. Also more prominent would be coal plants at the mine mouth, based on the principle that one ought to transport the power rather than the coal, and there would need to be more power trades between utilities. The region in the entire country with the highest rate of growth in power use was estimated to be the southwest region, including Kansas, Arkansas, Oklahoma, Texas, and Louisiana.[37] The November 1965 East Coast blackout was a systems error rather than a fundamental shortage, but national publicity about it, its extent (80,000 square miles, affecting a population of 25,000,000) and similar blackouts in Texas and New Mexico the next month highlighted the inconveniences that could result from even a short interruption of electric power.[38]

Second, environmental concerns and legislation, especially the federal Clean Air Act of 1965, were becoming immediate planning factors for utilities. KCPL planners found that the environmental movement caused substantial non–revenue producing expenditures at its coal plants.[39] From the standpoint of stack emissions to the air nuclear plants were the cleanest alternative available—far more so than coal.

Third, there was hope that nuclear fuel would in the long run be cheaper than finite supplies of fossil fuels. If breeder technology could be developed and broadly applied, it could give the United States independence from its dangerous reliance on interruptible foreign supplies of oil by transferring supplies devoted to generating plant boilers to other uses.

None of these reasons to proceed with nuclear power, however, would have been definitive for KG&E had not the supply and cost of natural gas in its region come into serious question. In 1967, KG&E's gas supplier, Cities Service, notified the company that it would no longer furnish gas to any new power plants, that gas supplies to existing customers would be reduced each year, and that it could make no guarantees about the price or availability of any set supply at all in the long term. To a utility that was 100 percent dependent upon natural gas, and whose in-house studies indicated that its obligation to meet demand would require a new plant soon, this was a watershed event.[40] George Roen, a major consultant for the company, later said he suspected KG&E's chairman, Gordon Evans, had been "scared to death" by the sudden change in the company's fuel future.[41] At this juncture for KG&E not only was capacity an issue, but fuel diversity was an even greater problem. "Running out of gas," Elmer Hall told a Kansas Nuclear Conference in

1971, "particularly in Kansas, is kind of like having a car wreck—It's a terrifying experience that always happens to the other fellow."[42]

The KG&E gas plants could be switched to run on fuel oil—they were designed for that. However, operations with oil were messy (no. 6 oil was essentially asphalt, was difficult to store, was dirty, and had to be heated in order to pump), and with every passing year leading to the price and supply actions of the Organization of Petroleum Exporting Countries (OPEC) in 1973, the supply and price prospect for fuel oil looked more and more tentative.[43]

The upshot, therefore, of the gas curtailment announcement was a series of feasibility studies for alternate fuels. While every possibility was investigated over the next ten years (more was done on wind, solar, and biomass possibilities than many critics would admit), the short-term practical alternatives narrowed to two: coal and nuclear. With 235,000 customers depending on power, and demand growth projections running at about 7 percent per year, the option of "waiting to see" how things might develop was one the corporate managers did not want to pursue.[44] Pollution controls on the new model coal plants were experimental, and lead times on nuclear plants were running at least ten years, with the trend being toward longer construction times and more unexpected events.

The first post–gas curtailment study was by an independent consultant retained by KG&E to confirm whether the gas supply and price situation was as critical as stated, or whether it might be in part a "manufactured" crisis by the gas supply company to boom prices. That consultant confirmed there was a real problem. He concluded that known natural gas supplies were inadequate, that Cities Service would probably be unable to continue to serve KG&E, and that the probability of finding another supplier to commence contractual deliveries in 1975 was remote.[45] There followed in the next two years three studies for KG&E by Ebasco, an industry consultant.

Ebasco had done a study in April 1967 because KG&E was considering covering the higher capital costs of larger power plants by constructing jointly with Kansas City Power & Light (KCPL). The conclusion of that study was that a 1973 joint nuclear or coal plant by KG&E and KCPL was economically inferior to the companies' using separate gas-fired peakers to take care of short-term seasonal demands, and leaving the base load generation as it was. Things changed fast, however. The notice from Cities Service came in April, before the ink on the Ebasco report was dry, and a second Ebasco study, submitted in August 1967 concluded that, given the gas situation, initial plant investment was lower for coal, but that the present value of annual operating costs was lower for nuclear.[46] Generation planning events thereafter moved very quickly, and contacts between KG&E and both KCPL and The Kansas Power and Light Company (KPL) intensified, since coal power technology had changed radically since KG&E built its last coal plant in the 1920s.

The thought was that the company would certainly have to move to coal right away, but should not move from 100 percent dependence on gas to 100 percent dependence on coal. Coal was more subject to interruption than gas. Its delivery, especially the clean-burning hard anthracite coal mined in Wyoming, was a rail logistical problem whose solution was not yet evident. Estimates were that the joint plants of the type Kansas utilities began talking about in the late 1960s would use nearly an entire 100-car unit train of coal every day (and for that time the term *unit train* is an anachronism). Coal could to some extent be stockpiled, but the freezing drizzle the climate regularly spouted could create nightmares of accessibility to these piles in the winter.

The alternate of using mine mouth coal was a serious consideration, but supplies were limited and the Kansas coal had a high sulphur content and other undesirable characteristics. This, given the new air pollution legislation, would require expensive and untried technology both in the loading and burning methodology and in the pollution control equipment. Therefore, it was felt almost from the start that KG&E had better have more than one fuel arrow in its quiver. Nuclear power was the only other one practically available.

True, the 1968 Ebasco studies of coal versus nuclear, of nuclear sites, and of the best coal plant site, as well as the January 1968 Stone & Webster study done for the Missouri Kansas Power Pool (MOKAN) on sites, alternatives, and cost-effectiveness of a jointly owned coal-fired plant could be considered internal and were later criticized as perfunctory in their pragmatic, utilitarian focus. But, as KG&E's Wilson Cadman and KCPL's Arthur Doyle later forcefully stated in rate hearings, the companies did not need a spate of consultants' studies to tell officers what seemed to them obvious. "If you're asking me if I can take a 6-inch volume all wrapped up in pretty blue ribbon with some consultant's name signed off on it and a bill attached to it and say: 'This is it.' No I can't," Doyle testified in recalling these times. "We don't have to hire a consultant to tell us that the sun is going to come up tomorrow morning."[47]

At KG&E every day was a planning day, and the crisis was the fuel crisis. The goals, as Cadman recalled, were three: to seek a new source of boiler fuel, to diversify that source, and to consider those sources that would have the least impact on rates.[48] The U.S. annual kilowatt-hour usage for electricity rose 6.5 percent in 1967—right on trend. Capital was available at reasonable rates to build generating plants, orders for nuclear plants were at an alltime high, and the governor's nuclear energy council in Kansas in 1968 endorsed nuclear power as a desirable direction for the state's future power generation.[49] Gas as a future fuel looked out of the question. Therefore in 1967 and 1968 investigations went forward in earnest to plan for the company to obtain a share both in one or more coal plants and a nuclear plant as soon as possible.

It became clear at about the same time, also, that if primary responsibilities were to be divided between utilities, KPL or KCPL would be the logical party to take prime responsibility for the coal plant or plants, given their more current experience, leaving KG&E with the nuclear project. Like KG&E, KCPL was concerned about fuel diversity—being itself nearly 100 percent coal powered, and with its main Hawthorne generating units rapidly aging physically and technologically. KCPL had been involved in nuclear experiments since 1955, and participated in the 1960s in work at Dresden Power Station 1 in Illinois and Peach Bottom 1, built by Bechtel and operated by Philadelphia Electric, but not as extensively as had KG&E in California and at SEFOR.[50] KG&E, said a KCPL executive later "had more need to be interested. . . . We were spreading local coal. The economics were pretty good. We saw nuclear as down the road, but I think we saw it maybe a little further down the road possibly than KG&E did, and they, I would say, had a head start with respect to Kansas City Power & Light Company regarding the use of nuclear power."[51] Mostly, however, it was confessed by all that none of the Kansas utilities had substantial nuclear operating experience. KG&E was as logically placed to take the lead as any.

1968 was a busy year for KG&E, though from the miniscule press coverage of utility events the public hardly knew it. In January an

Ebasco study was completed of four potential sites for a nuclear plant. Given the water supply needed for cooling such a plant, and the geography of power delivery through the grid, only two general areas presented themselves—one south of Wichita, where Wichita interests had proposed to build the Corbin Reservoir on Chakaskia Creek, and the other somewhere near the John Redmond Reservoir, which dammed the Neosho River near Burlington, Kansas, about 50 miles south of the state capital of Topeka. The same month Stone & Webster's study for MOKAN indicated that a 1000 mw jointly owned coal-fired plant at LaCygne, 60 miles south of Kansas City, would be the most cost-effective initial unit among 24 alternatives studied for a coal plant. In February, KG&E, judging correctly that the Corbin reservoir might never be built and estimating that the load center in a joint arrangement with a Kansas City utility would be much closer to Burlington than to Wichita, applied for water rights from the Redmond Reservoir. In March the fifth of the Ebasco studies recommended Redmond as a nuclear plant site. The same month KG&E announced LaCygne 1, a coal plant to use mine mouth Kansas coal and to be built jointly with Kansas City Power & Light Company.

In April, KG&E announced its intent to proceed with plans for a 1000 mw nuclear plant, estimated to be on line sometime after the mid 1970s. The cost was estimated at $200,000,000. The tourist brochures for Redmond Reservoir published by the U.S. Army Corps of Engineers the next year even mentioned the nuclear possibility. Coincidentally, that same April KG&E undertook its first big plunge into computerized operation beyond its IBM electronic accounting machines with the installation of a new GE 415 computer to calculate loading schedules for generators. Utility people began to speak of COBOL and FORTRAN and line printers, while the press called the device "a pinball machine that can do useful work." In July the Governor's Nuclear Energy Council supported the idea that Kansas should be a site for a nuclear plant. Annual U.S. kwh usage in 1968 was up 8.6 percent.[52]

Of course there could be many slips between the cup and the lip in actually building a nuclear plant, and the details of its design were far from set. Harley Macklin and Elmer Hall, both in operations, formed an atomic group within KG&E to work on the question. At that time they were considering an 800 mw plant, but determined that there were real economies of scale involved in making it larger. For about a 10 percent increase in cost it appeared that one could get twice the megawatts.

To do that, KG&E would need a partner. The two prime candidates were Kansas Power and Light, headquartered in Topeka, and Kansas City Power & Light of Kansas City. KPL, partly because it had decided to focus on coal and partly because of suspicion between company officers of KG&E and KPL (which possibly itself turned on age-old rivalry between Wichita and Topeka), rejected the nuclear overtures. That left KCPL.

However, the heavy negotiations on nuclear could wait, as both KG&E and KCPL in their initial talks agreed that a new coal plant was a much quicker way than nuclear to get them both some new generating capacity. Donna Dilsaver, who came to work for KG&E about that time, remembers being handed, to her surprise, a folder labelled "Atomic Power." But the prospect took a back seat to coal. Construction and operation of a new plant, to be called LaCygne 1, would both test the workings of a KG&E/KCPL partnership and provide feedback on the cost and efficiency of a modern, pollution-controlled coal plant versus the predictions for a nuclear facility.[53]

Ironically, the LaCygne 1 plant, completed in 1973, was in many ways a more advanced and experimental facility than the conservative, safety-driven Wolf Creek Nuclear Station would be. "The thing is huge," wrote a wide-eyed journalist viewing the completed plant. It "squats on whole acres of ground," he commented, and occupies its own peninsula in the middle of its own lake. "It whines and howls and throbs and throws off heat and shows a white banner in the sky that might stretch 100 miles or more in the right conditions."[54] Observers from Japan, Germany, Sweden, Great Britain, the Soviet Union, France, nationalist China, and Israel formed a procession in the mid 1970s to observe its technical wonders.

LaCygne 1 was a "totally custom installation." Harley Macklin noted that since no pollution-controlled plant had tried to burn such coal as the Kansas product, LaCygne 1 was "designed in a vacuum." Clifford McDaniel, who was brought in later to do various fixes on it, commented that many of the LaCygne prototype systems were in the "hammer and sickle stage of development," and led to such operating frustration that some of the old hands gave up on it entirely and were "waiting for the company just to give up and bulldoze the whole thing into the lake."

The technique for burning high-ash, high-sulphur Kansas coal was entirely different from the current standard, and the new plant added some twists of its own. LaCygne was "supercritical"—that is, it operated at a steam temperature of over 1000° and at a pressure of 3500 psi, and therefore required ultrapure water and all sorts of protection against corrosion. The steam drove a single high-speed turbine, was reheated and then piped into an intermediate and two low-speed turbines before going to the condenser tubes for reuse. The turbine blades were subject to damage by this process. But the most unusual thing about LaCygne was its boiler. It used an 18-chamber "cyclonic" boiler, which took in coal in one-quarter-inch chunks rather than the face-powder consistency that was usual in electric plants, burned 90 percent of it in a series of small enclosures roaring at internal temperatures of close to 2500°, and then whirled the heat, in a tornadic motion, into the main structure—just as though it were an 18-cylinder coal-fired engine. The high technology got high publicity, but partly because of the problems with LaCygne, no utility built a cyclonic boiler again.

When burning high-ash coal the waste comes out either in the form of particulate fly ash or bottom ash. In a typical modern coal plant, the coal is pulverized and then burned, sending 75 percent of the fly ash out the stack and the rest out the bottom. This was unacceptable with the new environmental standard, and so the cyclone reversed the percentages. The waste from the bottom, however, involved a kind of molten rock that could easily plug small orifices (called *monkey holes*) and cause operating interruptions. Also, the usual relatively simple electrostatic precipitators used for pollution control in an ordinary coal plant were replaced at LaCygne by the elaborate limestone slurry water chemistry needed to meet the sulphur dioxide and particulate standards of the Environmental Protection Agency.[55]

These "scrubbers" were as prototypical as the cyclone boiler. Though the idea had been around since a test in London in 1929, when the LaCygne scrubbers were installed in 1973 the few in use in the United States were having severe operating problems. Union Electric in St. Louis had put in the first full-scale scrubber (other than limited EPA-sponsored experiments) in 1968 on a 140 mw unit, but abandoned it after three years of unsatisfactory performance. The LaCygne unit, built by Babcock & Wilcox, represented over 20 percent of the investment in the plant, covered an area half the size of a football field, used thousands of plastic balls for the chemical reaction, and depended on 7000 hp fans. During the summer the system leaked and in the winter it froze. The lavalike sludge of fly ash and slurry remaining sometimes got so solid it had to be broken up with sledgehammers. The LaCygne 1 scrubbers, the *Wall Street Journal* commented, "aren't exactly low-cost chimney sweeps."[56]

Theoretically, LaCygne 1 made sense. In 1968, coal at 18.5 cents per million Btu was by far the cheapest boiler fuel, particularly if you could use the local product. Mine mouth coal avoided rail strikes and delivery problems and provided jobs in the local economy. However, the plant turned out to be a great operating headache, and the coal it used proved "much more horrible coal than anyone believed at the time." It was 28–30 percent fly ash and 3–6 percent sulphur, compared with western U.S. coal's 5–6 percent fly ash and 1/2 percent sulphur.[57]

While Wolf Creek ultimately outperformed all predictions, LaCygne 1 had an opposite variance. In 1976 LaCygne 1 was still not operating at its rated capacity, and extensive and expensive modifications had to be made to its pollution control system.[58] In its first 11 years of operation LaCygne 1 was unreliable. Only twice in that time did it reach a capacity factor (a measure of actual output) of 40 percent. Also, since it was the policy in Kansas not to allow utilities to charge ratepayers any interest or dividend cost related to capital committed to facilities under construction (construction work in progress, or CWIP) until such facilities were completed and in service, the sponsoring utilities for LaCygne suffered financially during the lag time, especially since the unit did not work reliably and provide the steady base load power for which it was designed. The fact that KG&E's earnings went down 22 percent in 1973 from 1972 was due in no small part to the capital cost and technical and regulatory delays of LaCygne 1.[59]

The plan had been to build two mine mouth coal plants at the LaCygne site. Partly because the coal supply proved not as large as predicted, but partly also because of the operating problems, LaCygne 2, completed in 1977, used Wyoming coal hauled in by rail, had a rated capacity of 630 rather than number 1's 840 mw, operated at 2400 psi instead of 1's efficient but problematical 3500, and used a standard pulverized coal boiler process.[60] The same more conservative design utilizing Wyoming coal was pursued later in the 1970s, when KG&E participated with KPL in multiple plants at the

Jeffrey Energy Center. No one involved with LaCygne 1 ever wanted to see its like again.

LaCygne 1 had not only made "old-fashioned" coal plants look attractive by comparison, it had, by proving the difficulty of "ultra" coal plants and by making Kansas coal use utterly dependent on reliable rail service, enhanced the attractiveness of nuclear as a choice for the energy future of the state. Added to that experience in moving KG&E and KCPL toward bringing their nuclear option off the back burner were national events creating doubts about the coal supply, while moving the utility industry into a level of strictness on the environmental impact of generating facilities that coal was ill equipped to meet. Midwestern coal, for example, often contained significant amounts of uranium, creating the irony that a mine mouth coal plant in Kansas might be a less *radiologically* clean item than a properly maintained nuclear plant. Environmental issues also included acid rain and global warming, which reached the public consciousness in the 1970s.[61] The size of generating units, limited to 10 to 20 mw in the 1920s, had reached the 600–800 mw range in fossil and 900–1200 mw in nuclear due to enhanced technology and better transmission lines, but could hope for few more economies of scale to offset the increased safety and environmental requirements and keep rates traditionally low.

Regulation became a major factor. The Clean Air Act of 1965 was followed at the federal level by the National Environmental Policy Act of 1969, requiring a detailed environmental impact assessment of any proposed federal action, and amendments to the clean air act in 1970 mandating reduced emissions from coal plants. In 1969 there was also new federal mine safety legislation, which increased the cost of coal. During the period between 1970 and 1984 KCPL's coal cost increased 545 percent.[62] In approximately the same period KG&E's natural gas costs increased 1,128 percent.[63] The Atomic Energy Commission (AEC) meanwhile had commissioned a series of studies of the technology, safety, and economics of nuclear plants, collectively known as the WASH series (beginning in 1957), which were meant "to give utilities greater confidence in the economic viability of nuclear plants."[64]

While it was true that when something went wrong in a nuclear plant it would be more serious than with a coal plant, the plans for a nuclear design that KG&E began to pursue in the early 1970s were much less complex in many ways than an equivalent coal facility.

Wolf Creek, for instance, eventually operated at a maximum temperature of 560° in contrast to over 1000° at LaCygne 1 and a primary pressure of 2200 psi as contrasted with 3500 at LaCygne. The conveying systems necessary for coal did not apply to nuclear, while the corrosive and abrasive effects and stack pollutants of coal were nonexistent.[65] It was a little like electing whether to travel by airline or car. The airplane was demonstrably less dangerous statistically, but that was no comfort for white-knuckled fliers who considered the consequences of becoming a rare statistic. And no one involved accurately predicted the special, nonscientific public concerns about radiation and things nuclear.

The early 1970s seemed the right time to get serious. Between 1966 and 1968 U.S. utilities ordered 66 nuclear generating units totalling 57,000 mw capacity. The average size was 850 mw, but 22 of them were over 1000 mw and the trend was to the larger size. The WASH 1082 study in 1968 was the first of a series of AEC-sponsored design studies of 1000 mw nuclear plants, and it projected a cost for a plant to start in 1967 and go on line in 1972 at $134,000,000, or $134 per kw. Though that was a higher capital cost than for coal, it was expected that the fuel savings over the 40-year life of such a plant would compensate. The next year the government studies had upped the cost to $240,000,000, by 1971 to $345,000,000, and eventually, taking into account costs for greater safety protection, to $500,000,000 for the model 1000 mw plant to be begun in 1975.[66] Still, given the obligation to serve and the problems with the alternatives, nuclear was in the race. A national power survey published by the Federal Power Commission in 1970 projected that nuclear power would be 21 percent of all electric generation in 1980 and 38 percent by 1990.[67] Action seemed to confirm this. Between 1966 and 1972, U.S. utilities ordered 213 nuclear plants, 126 of them in the period 1971 to 1974.[68]

In August 1970, KG&E asked Ebasco for a cost estimate for a 1100 mw nuclear plant. The response was $228,000,000. Again in 1971, Ebasco did a study of the alternatives and concluded that nuclear was the best alternative to follow LaCygne 1. The initial idea was that a one-third interest in the new nuclear plant would go to other members of MOKAN. In March, KG&E and KCPL officials met and decided that the most desirable configuration would be a 900 mw plant with 300 mw each held by KG&E, KCPL, and KPL. That month, KG&E and KCPL signed a tentative agreement to jointly build a joint nuclear plant of 800 to 1000 mw at some site (not yet exactly defined) utilizing the John Redmond Reservoir. At a MOKAN meeting that spring, however, a request for interest from other regional utilities in joining in the plant brought no response, and over the next couple of years estimated start and completion dates for the proposed project were regularly set back. KG&E that summer investigated the advantages of an 800 mw plant by comparison with an 1100 mw one more or less on the model of the WASH studies. Its suppliers—General Electric, Westinghouse, and Babcock & Wilcox—informed company executives that a smaller plant would not provide significant cost savings.[69]

Between that initial 1971 preliminary agreement and formal agreement on and public announcement of the Wolf Creek plant in 1973, a development occurred in the Kansas utilities' preliminary nuclear thinking that was to have a profound positive effect on a most difficult period of construction—namely the decision to participate with out-of-state utilities in the development and licensing of a common plant design.

About the time of the joint agreement, the chairman of the AEC made a fiery speech to a group of utility executives on the need to move away from the extreme individualism of nuclear plants. The uniqueness of plants increased costs, complicated licensing, slowed information exchange and diminished safety.[70] In 1972 the AEC officially encouraged the standardization of nuclear plants in order to speed the licensing process.[71] Through 1971 and 1972 KG&E participated in a cost analysis of other nuclear plants, as cost was a concern that was rapidly growing. These studies indicated more than ever that sharing design cost and experience was highly desirable.[72]

The initiative for implementing the standardization idea came originally from an executive of the Northern States Power Company named Wade Larkin. Harley Macklin and Elmer Hall from KG&E were invited by Larkin to technical sessions in Chicago held while LaCygne 1 was being built. These had the agenda of working out with a number of vendors then involved in doing "dog and pony" shows for several Midwestern utilities considering new power plants a means by which a single design might serve the needs of all, while shared development costs would create a more sophisticated model at less cost to each utility.

The acronym developed for this cooperative design organization was SNUPPS. It originally meant Standardized Nuclear Unit Power

Plan Syndicate. However, with rare sensitivity to how language might sound to the public, the organization changed *Syndicate* to *Systems*. Although initial discussions involved twelve utilities, eventually five vendors and five utilities were involved. General Electric, Westinghouse, Babcock & Wilcox, Combustion Engineering, and Gulf General Atomics were the group to bid on what was called the NSSS (Nuclear Steam Supply System)—composed of reactor vessel, steam generators, pressurizer, reactor coolant pumps, and piping required to produce steam through nuclear fission. These bids were submitted in December 1972. All would have the chance to pitch equipment to the whole group, and the whole group would study each element. The utilities—Northern States Power, Rochester Gas & Electric, KG&E, Union Electric, and KCPL—would then design a prototype that would stand up to the tornadoes in Kansas, the earthquakes in Missouri, and the snow in Minnesota. The plan was that the design would extend to six installed plants. Northern States Power planned two units near Durand, Wisconsin, and Union Electric of St. Louis two units on the Callaway site near Fulton, Missouri. The A/Es (Architect/Engineers) and the contractors on each site would be individual, but SNUPPS experience and expertise would play a big role in their selection. High reliability was a priority. The design was to be a "Model T" of the nuclear age using proven technology, and experience gained by any one utility or its employees in construction or operation could be immediately shared with the others.[73]

There was nothing inevitable or even particularly trendy about SNUPPS, despite the AEC encouragement. "Although hindsight might lead one to conclude," wrote consultant Charles Huston in 1984, "that the decision to join the nuclear power plant standardization group should have been obvious, this was not the case in 1972." There was skepticism in the utility industry about whether a group of utilities could coordinate sufficiently to give real benefits. The majority of utilities planning plants at that time did not join a standardization group. SNUPPS was in fact the only duplicate plant project submitted to AEC for licensing involving more than one utility.

Of course, to KG&E and KCPL part of the appeal was experience. Rochester Gas & Electric and Northern States Power had built nuclear plants before and were operating them. It is ironic in retrospect that the experienced utilities failed to complete any of their SNUPPS plants, while the inexperienced ones, KG&E, KCPL, and

Union Electric, finished the only two plants of the original six that ever provided electric power. The failure of four of the plants, however, was not due to the SNUPPS concept—in fact it can be argued that without it the two probably would not have made it through the maelstrom of protest that arose in the 1970s.[74] SNUPPS in hindsight looks wise indeed, and something like it is in the 1990s being regularly suggested as a universal model for any further American nuclear construction.

KCPL did its own 1971 study titled "Generation Expansion Study after LaCygne #1." It considered gas turbines, coal, nuclear, hydro, and power purchases and, like KG&E's Ebasco study, concluded that nuclear was the best bet for plants coming on line after 1978. The early SNUPPS meetings, attended by KCPL people, were the final impetus KCPL needed to offset its doubts about the experience factor, and it joined with KG&E in the nuclear project. SNUPPS, along with their own incremental cost studies, also determined that the two Kansas companies would accept a plant in the 1100 mw range—the size that would fit the needs of SNUPPS utility partners. Remembered Arthur Doyle of KCPL: "It was not a hard decision to make." At the time it was estimated that for the six units planned by the SNUPPS utilities there would be a cost savings of $90,000,000 due to the cooperation. As it turned out, the cost savings of SNUPPS for the Wolf Creek plant in Kansas alone was in the end an estimated $215,000,000.[75]

In January 1973 came the final agreement between the two Kansas utilities to build a nuclear plant on "site C" of the Redmond candidates—a mix of slightly rolling farm and prairie land 3.5 miles northeast of Burlington, Coffey County, Kansas, 28 miles southeast of Emporia, 53 miles south of Topeka, 75 miles from Kansas City, and 100 miles from Wichita, along a little tributary of the Neosho River called Wolf Creek.[76] In February there was a public announcement of what a KCPL attorney later called a "bold construction project."[77]

KG&E did its announcement at a news conference in the hospitality room of its general office building in Wichita. The size was not announced, but it was suggested that the nuclear plant could be as big as 1,200,000 kw and could cost more than a half billion dollars. KG&E would have primary responsibility for the plant, and as of the first of January had hired Jesse Arterburn, former manager of SEFOR and most recently in the nuclear division of General Electric at San Jose, California, to supervise its new nuclear department. The target date announced for completion of the Wolf Creek plant was 1981, a fact for which Arterburn apologized to his colleagues. "Even though I'll be around for many years," he quipped, "I won't be producing any juice until 1981. I hope the rest of you will have some patience with me." Ralph Fiebach, KG&E's president since 1969 and Gordon Evans, the chairman, both made statements at the conference indicating that even those in the company not working directly with the nuclear project knew its significance to the overall strategy of providing reliable service in the future and ushering in a new era for Kansas power generation. "The nuclear plant," said Evans, "is just another means of helping us to do our job."[78] As though to underline the urgency, in October of that year OPEC decisions in the Middle East created in the United States long lines at the gas pumps and front-page concern with the "Energy Crisis."

There was every reason for guarded optimism about Wolf Creek. It was a joint project, which allowed some expected economies of scale. Both utilities involved needed fuel diversity. Neither was putting all its reliance on nuclear power. Power sharing had been used to a great degree to narrow the power gap for Kansas. MOKAN had been in existence since 1962 and the Southwest Power Pool (SWPP) since 1941. The SNUPPS organization was in place to lend the Kansas firms all the experience there was in matters nuclear, and negotiations were going on with some of the best planners and constructors in the business. "Site C" could expect enough water in its eventual cooling lake to serve two power plants, and its isolation from population centers should minimize difficulties in providing for safety of residents. There was support in the right places. So positive was the response in some quarters in fact that in April 1973, KCPL received a show cause order from the Missouri Public Service Commission requiring it to demonstrate why it should not be required to build its nuclear plant in Missouri rather than Kansas.[79]

The *Kansas City Times* was enthused:

> This huge facility, with a capacity equal to two-thirds of the entire present KCPL system, measures the continuing voracious demand for power both in this area and across the nation. It also reflects a considered judgment by the sponsoring investor-owned utilities that nuclear generation is the mandatory answer to tomorrow's needs for electricity, both in terms of fuel supply and control of air pollution.

The new concern over the environment has obligated the light company here not only to spend millions of dollars for smoke control devices at its various coal-burning stations, but has forced a shift from primary reliance on low-cost nearby strip mine coal in this immediate area to low-sulphur coal which must be shipped from Wyoming. And the considerable reserves there are being mined at a rapid rate by various power companies. The high start-up costs of a nuclear power plant, which have delayed the changeover to the "nukes" well beyond the projections of a few years back, now figure to become more acceptable all the time as the costs of mining and shipping premium fossil fuels soar. . . . Thus 1981, in the present struggle by the electric industry to keep ahead of demand, is none too soon to put a major new source of kilowatts on the line in Kansas—and to push that state into the oncoming era of nuclear generation to meet that demand.[80]

KG&E's annual report for 1973 had a color photograph on the cover showing a solitary great blue heron with the sun in the background rising over the pristine mists of the Redmond Reservoir.[81] The company well recognized that a nuclear plant would be controversial, and that events there would get much more public attention than anything that went on at a coal plant. However, in Robert Rives KG&E had an articulate and personable spokesman, and it could hardly have been predicted that the hit-or-miss newspaper coverage of electric power in the 1960s could escalate in the 1970s so much faster than even the cost estimates of the Wolf Creek plant.

KG&E, after all, had an excellent reputation. It had held a series of conferences with its 200-person supervisory force in 1968 on "social responsibility," and had always been in the lead among local corporations looking broadly at the concerns of its customers and community.[82] "In 45 years of business in southeast Kansas," KG&E's chairman, Murray Gill, wrote in 1955 as the company undertook its first nuclear research, "the Company has developed an accurate feel of the pulse of the area. During the last decade we at Kansas Gas and Electric Company have been guided by and have geared our future plans to the quickening of this pulse. Today, with more people, more jobs and more economic security than ever before, the pulse beats of progress are even stronger and faster in the area we serve. The most significant thing of all about this business pulse is that, while it's faster and stronger, it's still, in the best traditions of Kansas growth, *steady*."[83]

The 1960s had been divisive, and there was that Bob Dylan song about the times changing. But times had always changed, and KG&E had changed with them in a measured and rational fashion. There was no reason to think things would now rage out of control. Wrote Wichita energy planner Grover McKee, looking back on that first announcement, "Since KG&E deservedly owned a spotless record for low rates and effective management, many of those who questioned the wisdom of the Wolf Creek decision were treated as lepers, in the Biblical sense."[84]

Events, however, soon brought the "lepers" into the limelight, and proved that the company's sense of the "pulse" had been more an accident of history than a marvel of insight. Quickly, from the seed of protest that was visible when the SNUPPS planners perfected their organization and chose their vendors, grew a great, enveloping, and unexpected tree.

2
Atoms and Aquarius

I hear America singing—the varied carols I hear.
—Walt Whitman

Are we consumers concerned and brave enough to loosen the stranglehold of this shortsighted monster which threatens our civilization?
—Selma Johnson, in *Wichita Eagle*, April 12, 1975

The question of nuclear power should be decided in the town square.
—Albert Einstein

The very afternoon of the public announcement in Wichita, Burlington, and Kansas City of the nuclear project at Wolf Creek, Wilson Cadman, then KG&E's vice president for customer and community services, held a landowner's meeting at Burlington. For some time there was to be no physical evidence of the utility on the farm and ranch land that was to be the plant site, other than a weather tower and some archaeologists, biologists, and botanists working on the environmental report. However, Cadman learned that from the moment of announcement an issue was joined between local farmers and the corporation that represented feelings both far broader than the technical questions of a single power plant and more difficult of solution than any of the engineering questions connected with the power plant itself.

The residents of Coffey County, then the poorest county in Kansas, were supposed to welcome the huge increase in its tax base that would be provided by the nuclear plant and the regional boom provided by the thousands of construction workers that would live in the area during the peak building years. Many, doubtless most, did. KG&E's earliest surveys showed 58 percent of the county's residents for the plant, a relatively small percentage against it, and a large number undecided. But Cadman, beginning his job of smoothing and coordinating relations between the corporation and the community, found one vocal group that was far from following the local Chamber of Commerce line. Some had lived on their farms for generations, and felt that no amount of money would compensate them for their loss in moving. Others questioned the whole idea of taking 10,000+ acres of farm and grazing land out of production for the purpose of an electric plant and its cooling lake. A number were bitter that KG&E was able to exercise quasi-public powers of eminent domain to force the most reluctant to submit to binding arbitration and sell at a "fair" assessed value. A few objected on the grounds that any nuclear plant was a costly abomination, which would endanger the community and its environment in the long term far more than it would benefit it. These would be joined by others from the immediate area, from the cities to be served (Kansas City and Wichita), and from the national antinuclear movement, as it became clear that the licensing and construction of this nuclear plant, even in a remote area of a "conservative" state, would be anything but automatic.[1]

There had been warnings. In 1956 the KG&E company magazine ran a piece titled "A-Power Confuses Public." The great popular misconceptions, the article said, were that the utilities wanted the profits from nuclear plants while asking the government to subsidize the costs, and that substantial decreases in rates would result from the installation of nuclear power, as had been the case with other technical advances in the utility industry.[2] "There is a great deal of uninformed talk today," wrote W. E. Johnson of the AEC, referring to some criticism of SEFOR, "about the peaceful atom and there are allegations that nuclear power has been subjected to forced feeding by some government-industrial complex. Some people seem more interested in arousing public anxiety than true public interest and understanding."[3] By 1962 the company was ready to recognize that "unfortunately, atomic power has become a political question."[4]

Events of the 1960s on the nuclear and other fronts did nothing to diminish the likelihood of an ideological confrontation over nuclear power. The Vietnam war and the civil rights movement illustrated the power of public protest by "nonexperts," the significance of media attention to statements that could be fit into short sound bites, and the vulnerability of some of the factual claims of the "establishment." While several analysts held that the title of a popular book on the 1966 accident at the Enrico Fermi liquid-sodium cooled reactor in Michigan—*We Almost Lost Detroit*—was exaggerated, it was a signal that the safety claims for nuclear facilities were going to be evaluated strictly and publicly.[5]

Virtually all scholars of utility history noted that the 1960s were a period of unprecedented technical, economic, and regulatory crisis and transition for the electric industry. The same decade is highlighted by historians of social protest. "In the late fifties," writes Kenneth Keniston in *Youth and Dissent*, "on one or two campuses . . . lonely radical graduate students began the effort to define a 'New' Left. But for all these premonitions the overwhelming majority of American students and young people in 1960 were politically apathetic, accepting and inert." That changed profoundly by 1970. The percentage of college students who agreed with the statement "America is a sick society" rose through the 1960s, until by 1970 a majority agreed. In 1970 three-quarters of American college students believed that "basic changes" were necessary to improve the quality of life in American society, while only 19 percent believed that the "system" (the electric utilities were a central part of that establishment) was on the right track. These students did not believe the system would reform itself, but would react only to severe pressure from outside. They, Keniston concludes, were "alienated" and saw the future not as utopia, but as frightening, full of decline and danger. While youth were far from the sole element of the Wolf Creek nuclear protest, their energetic rejection of many of the technological aspects of the contemporary world, of "bigness, impersonality, statification and hierarchy" in favor of "simplicity, naturalness, personhood and even voluntary poverty" was a leaven in a sensitive loaf.[6] The coincidence that electric utilities were reaching "stasis" in the 1960s, where further economies of scale and further miracles of technology were no longer possible, meshed chronologically both with the profound intellectual and psychological watershed originating with youth and with the introduction of a nuclear heat source whose implications reverberated strongly and emotionally among both Babbitts and Bohemians, and created a deep example of "future shock." Together with tremendous disruption of financial markets as well as a major energy crisis involving the possibility of war in the Middle East in the 1970s, these elements made a recipe for high "postmodern" drama indeed in the nuclear power field.

The environmental movement, to which the general philosophy

and direct action techniques of the 1960s counterculture were well suited, achieved in the 1960s the legislative framework through which it could split the alleged "good old boy" network between government and the electric business. The Clean Air Act of 1965 was followed by the National Environmental Policy Act of 1969. In 1970 Congress decided that the nuclear business was sufficiently mature to be subject to antitrust provisions. The U.S. Supreme Court's Calvert Cliffs decision of 1971 required the provisions of the National Environmental Policy Act to be applied to the licensing of nuclear plants, including requiring the AEC to hold public hearings at the licensing stage.

The introduction of public hearings and environmental impact statements to the licensing process was, to quote one who studied the effects in Kansas, "a radical change of the process." The AEC declared a year's moratorium on the licensing of new plants just to prepare itself for this increased public involvement. The number of federally approved regulatory guides on nuclear energy jumped from fewer than 5 in 1970 to 60 in 1973, 240 in 1978, and 330 in 1984. The costs of compliance for the industry and the stresses of change increased proportionately. In 1974 the Energy Reorganization Act dissolved the AEC and divided its duties between two new agencies, the Energy Research and Development Administration (ERDA) and the Nuclear Regulatory Commission (NRC). This not only again disrupted the regulatory process and the licensing schedules right at the time the Kansas utilities had submitted their license application, but also represented a philosophic shift. The research and, to some degree, the promotion arm of the old AEC, which worked most closely with the utilities, was now separated from the purely regulatory branch. Most observers had little doubt that the tone of the NRC, as it took the administrative reins in the field in 1975, was much more oriented toward pure regulation and public opinion than had been the AEC during the pioneering stages of the private industry. The middle name of the former agency had been "Energy"; this one was "Regulatory."[7]

A frustrated Wilson Cadman once called the Kansas branch of the nuclear protest movement "pernicious consumer advocates" who created a situation where 99 percent of the utilities' customers' "tails" were being "wagged" by 1 percent who exercised undue influence on the elected and appointive bodies. These people, he averred, had an interest in polarization, and once the polarization was complete could never forgive KG&E for building and operating the Wolf Creek plant successfully. They wanted it to fail and be a financial disaster for KG&E because they, the opponents, had taken such an extreme public position in predicting that would happen.[8]

There was room on the playing field for maneuver. In vague legislative language, such as "inappropriate management decision," "general public interest," "risk inappropriate to the public interest," and even "prudence," lay considerable room for politicians to act as brokers and to change position as it suited their interest. Interest group dynamics ensured that the nuclear licensing issue in 1970s Kansas would not be played out in relative isolation between the Kansas Corporation Commission staff and the utility attorneys, and that it would not necessarily go according to pre-agreed rules and/or promises. "Skilled political entrepreneurs," from Ralph Nader and Barry Commoner at the national level to equally skilled advocates in Kansas, could put nuclear proponents on the defensive by linking them to scandals or associating them with violations of widely held values such as environmental purity, the sanctity of the small farm, or the safety of women and children.[9]

The result of the introduction of these new players was to force utilities, with their obligation to provide reliable power, to deal with an unreliable political atmosphere. A consulting firm commented on this aspect of the Wolf Creek plant history in a section of its 1984 report headed "Frequent and Significant Oscillations in Public Policy During This Period Created Circumstances in Which Unusual Steadfastness of Purpose was a Prerequisite to the Construction of Any Major New Generation Capacity." KG&E was pressured by government first not to use coal and then to use coal as fuel;

> encouraged to invest in generation capacity and then challenged for doing so; supported by public policy in relying on nuclear energy, and then chastised by some groups for doing so; and confronted by a steadily thickening forest of third parties that have been free to criticize management decision, yet have held no accountability for the delivery of essential public services or for the consequences of the course of action they espouse. Finally, utility managements have faced pronounced shifts in regulatory direction regarding energy matters, often with little or no acknowledgment by contemporary regulators of responsibility for decisions prudently reached and

actions implemented in good faith by their predecessors.... Any management that sought to respond to all of the conflicting public and regulatory pressures ... would have found its actions to be conflicting and self-defeating in ways that would have virtually precluded pursuit of long-term investments and maintenance of the ability to meet all reasonable customer needs at lowest feasible cost.[10]

Concrete evidence that direct action and legislative intervention would be a factor in Kansas and that people there were not such "hayseeds" as to be unaware either of the stakes or their potential personal power came in 1970. The issue was the perennial one of disposal of high-level nuclear wastes: the federal government was promulgating some of the earlier of a long series of unfulfilled promises to the public and the industry to designate a site or sites and a method for disposing of the radioactive waste generated by nuclear plants. A prime candidate in 1970 was the salt mines in west central Kansas, especially 1,000 feet below Lyons, a community of about 4,500 people underlain with salt beds 300 to 400 feet thick. The salt had been laid down 250 million years earlier and was thought to have the geologic stability necessary for long-term waste disposal. Salt can withstand high temperatures, and when heated becomes plastic and flows to seal any holes. Its compressive strength and ability to shield radiation is equal to concrete. Tests at the Carey salt mine near Hutchinson, Kansas, yielded good results with simulated radioactive wastes. Consequently, in 1970 the Lyons salt beds were designated by the AEC as the first national repository for radioactive waste. The government proposed purchasing 7,000 acres near Lyons and moved ahead with a federal waste disposal program.

The first official doubts about that plan came from the Kansas Geological Society. Salt was not immutable, its scientists said, and fissures could open. Ground water could seep through the formations and radiation could penetrate the aquifers. Also, with such a long period of slow radioactive decay, movements over geologic time had to be considered. The Pleistocene ice ages were not over, and eventually glaciers would return. These had never reached as far south as Lyons, but could, and this might lead to a dredging of nuclear waste to the surface. Heat could cause explosions, crack the surface rocks, and produce radioactive geysers. The AEC representative and the Kansas Geological Society people met with Kansas Governor Robert Docking early in 1970 to discuss their differences.

Meanwhile the AEC, according to one account, "was moving into Kansas like Quantrill's raiders." The public and press were invited by the AEC to tour the mine sites, there was a briefing at the Lyons Country Club, and the local Chamber of Commerce got a full presentation. The agency drilled a 1,300-foot core at Lyons in the fall of 1970, and went about other testing.

Locals, however, were amazed at the way a federal project was undertaken, and astounded by some of the inefficiencies in field contracting and operation by the bunch that was proposing to manage waste for thousands of years. The acronyms (such as NWTSR2 for National Waste Terminal Storage Repository for Spent Fuel in Bedded Salt) did not sit well, nor did a bureaucracy that required lumber to be shipped in from Alabama rather than purchased locally. Kansas public officials, wondering whether the designation as a nuclear dump was really an honor, took a go-slow attitude. There were hearings on the proposal to fund the operation in March 1971. Kansas Representative Joe Skubitz opposed it on the grounds that Kansans were not being allowed a sufficient voice in the decision. After considerable debate, involving the rest of the Kansas congressional delegation, the proposal was restricted to a test site in a mine that had been abandoned for about 50 years, but was only 1,800 feet away from an active salt mine.

During the tests there was some evidence of leakage and the AEC itself began to have doubts about the salt dome panacea for nuclear waste. The Nixon administration decided not to push it, and by early 1972 there were new ideas afoot for the aboveground storage of the wastes.[11] Twenty years later the question of a permanent federal waste storage site was still not resolved.

The initial selection of Kansas as a waste site did not result in mass action. A Chamber of Commerce-sponsored meeting at the Lyons High School auditorium in June 1971 drew only sixty people away from the harvest fields.[12] It did, however, sensitize the population and politicians there to the volatility of the issue. One of the state's defenses had been that since Kansas did not produce any high-level nuclear wastes, it could not be asked to store them—an argument the construction of a nuclear plant in Kansas would negate. One reporter in particular—Max McDowell, whose pieces appeared in the *Emporia Gazette* and other publications—revisited the Lyons site controversy regularly throughout the planning and construction phase of Wolf Creek. McDowell argued that the idea of storing waste at Lyons had not been finally abandoned in 1972 and that Kansas in the 1980s could find itself with not only a nuclear plant but with responsibility for the waste from plants elsewhere. "It appears that the people of Kansas have been set up," McDowell wrote in 1980. "We are literally going to be dumped on, and the stuff being dumped will be dangerous for centuries to come."[13]

KG&E's people were not asleep as the waste site controversy roiled. However, the public "fallout" was limited, and the issue was argued mostly by experts on technical grounds. Bob Rives recalled that a commitment was made by the company's top management in the late 1960s to make "this operation [the nuclear plant] an open one with ready access to all the decision-making." One of the company's first actions was to form an information unit, which did a public opinion survey at Burlington and met with as many of those groups as it was suspected would tend to oppose the plant (women's groups concerned with the safety of children, landowners, etc.) as possible before the decisions had to be made. Each meeting included a specially trained member of a 20-person task force formed to discuss why nuclear power was necessary. These people also worked at educating the media where reporter turnover was high and the process had to be continuous. The same material was presented in New York City and other financial centers more regularly than had been the custom previously, when KG&E people had appeared before the financial analyst groups in New York once a year or less.

These early presentations focused on the need for a new fuel and on cost issues, not so much on safety, since it seemed to them that the safety record of the nuclear power industry spoke for itself. This was probably a mistake. "They [the public]," said Rives, "think because it's nuclear, it's different. Accidents at nuclear sites, even though they have nothing to do with the atomic apparatus, get big play while much more dangerous situations at coal or gas-fired plants get nary a word."[14]

The company responded generally to changed public concerns of the early 1970s in several ways. Pollution control at its coal plants was a major example. It also, however, did several things in Wichita to go along with the urban renewal and beautification trends of the 1960s. It instituted a considerable program in the early 1970s to beautify its substations. It worked on a joint venture to use warm cooling water to raise catfish. It continued a policy of burying lines that had begun when the whole downtown had been wired underground in 1935. And it was a primary sponsor of a parklike redo of the grounds of its old 1910 plant, including the striking bronze sculpture "Keeper of the Plains."[15]

Interviews with its own employees, particularly the younger ones, told the company that they had different concerns than before. *Servicegraph*, the company magazine, once filled with pictures of the big fish employees had caught on their days off and stories of volunteer efforts by those retired, now focused on youth and on the public issues of war and peace. "We still listen to our parents," said a young employee in May 1970, "but instead of passing our dreams and hopes for world improvements from generation to generation, our generation calls for such changes now." Questions asked of KG&E's "under 30" employees included "Can a young person be an individual in today's business world?" and "In view of all the problems evident in the United States today and actions by the younger generation to 'change things,' how do you feel about your country's future as a nation and for yourself as an individual?"

Answers were to the point and thoughtful. A lineman from Arkansas City did not take the American future for granted. "The things that concern me most," he said, "are the vast amounts of money, material and manpower that we waste in foreign countries; and the amount of people who are too lazy to do anything but march and destroy property and then say they are trying to improve the country.... The horn of plenty is turning into an empty shell." Clark Ritchey, an assistant chief clerk in El Dorado, summarized the answers: "Young Americans, for a number of reasons, are desperately searching for a philosophy, a reason for living, a purpose for existing and walking the face of this planet. The pursuit of happiness as defined by previous generations appears to no longer be valid to a large part of our young people. It is this dilemma to which the under 30s must address themselves in order to maintain a quality 'way of life' in the coming decades."[16]

KG&E learned nuclear public relations lessons at SEFOR, where there was a school tour program. L. R. Wallis, of General Electric's Nuclear Public Understanding and Information Department, said that the problem was that negatives about nuclear power were by the early 1970s "in" among environmental groups, especially warnings about radiation hazards. Engineers lived in another culture, maybe another era. A SEFOR engineer noted that the political trouble with nuclear plants was partly due to "the vocal minority of environmentalists who do not recognize man as part of the environment." "You might imagine me sitting on a log on a beach in California talking with an environmentalist about nuclear power," Wallis said. "The problem is that too often I end up wanting to sit on the environmentalist and talk to the log."[17]

By the announcement of the Kansas nuclear project in 1973 the debate had escalated. In May of that year Ralph Nader and the Friends of the Earth filed suit in federal court asking that 20 operating nuclear plants in 12 states be shut down. The case was thrown out the next month for lack of evidence, but not before Nader had a press conference publicizing his claim that there was scientific evidence that the lives of millions of people were threatened by these nuclear plants.

At KG&E Ralph Fiebach and Jesse Arterburn responded to the Nader publicity by saying first, that new AEC regulations were addressing his concerns; second, that concern with safety by the utilities should not be taken by the public as evidence of lack of confidence in nuclear energy; and third, that Nader's statement that safety backup systems were "crude and untested" was an untrue and irresponsible generalization.[18]

Some newspapers were more willing than company people to scoff outwardly at the pretensions of the "vocal minority" that proposed to stop nuclear power in Kansas. The *Iola Register* on February 6, 1974, ran an editorial entitled "Futility at Wolf Creek." Those landowners around Burlington making a fuss about nuclear safety, the editor wrote, "are largely talking to themselves—converting the saved, as it were—for their cause is lost." There had been no nuclear accidents and the news was full of the energy shortage: "For good or ill, the men and women of the Wolf Creek society at Burlington have been declared out of order by circumstance."[19] A few months later the same paper opined that the common thread of the protest was that authority was not to be trusted, and that the AEC and the utilities were conspiring to hide safety problems. That approach did not make sense to the editor: "Those who assume the power companies in this country would be willing to invest billions in plants that would be hazardous are assuming that they care nothing about profits or safety. . . . Even if one assumes that those who run corporations are heartless scoundrels who think only of profits—not the case, of course—how could they make profit on a plant that explodes and takes all of Southeast Kansas with it? Or one which must be abandoned because it causes harm to nearby residents? It makes no sense, moral or fiscal, to make such assumptions." The protestors, the editor thought, did not understand the extent to which the United States relied on electric power. "Those romantics who believe we can and should solve the energy crunch by going back to a pre-industrial way of life . . . forget that we are not now providing a decent standard of living for the world population. . . . We can be thrifty. We cannot do miracles. Abandoning the technological exploitation of every feasible source of commercial energy would mean abandoning hope for an end to grinding poverty for the peoples of three-quarters of the world."[20]

The promotional view, however, did not blanket Kansas and was questioned ever more aggressively in the nation. A *Wall Street Journal* reporter wrote in May 1973 of nuclear plants that "their unreliability is becoming one of their most dependable features."[21] A report in the WASH series (1400) authored by Norman C. Rasmussen of MIT and published in 1974 concluded that the risk of serious nuclear accident was as unlikely as deaths caused by a meteor, but was at least statistically visible.[22]

These studies and clippings built a file for the organized Kansas opposition. That opposition focused first on the question of land taking. It originated in 1973 around the town of Burlington with a group called Wolf Creek Nuclear Plant Opposition, Inc., consisting at first of 50 farm families, and spearheaded by a "quiet rural woman" named Mary Ellen Salava. Salava's concern began when she, herself a member of one of the pioneer families of the region, saw the pain of removal for her farm neighbors. She then read an article in *Reader's Digest* about nuclear power, sent for materials on the issue, and started early in 1973 writing letters to the editor of the *Burlington Daily Republican,* Glenn German.

German's lengthy responses and those from others printed in the smallest circulation daily newspaper in the country convinced her that intellectual fencing in Burlington ("the catfish capital of the world," population just over 2,000) was not going to make much difference in stopping KG&E's new billion-dollar project.[23] A woman from St. Louis responded to Mrs. Salava in June 1973 questioning Ralph Nader's technical competence, and suggesting that Salava's *Reader's Digest* material critical of nuclear power was probably written by "a sociologist or a Communist"—clearly to this writer there was little to distinguish the two. "Since there will probably be no intelligent rebuttal based on scientific facts," wrote the St. Louis woman, "and emotions are involved, ignorance and misinformation will run rampant concerning the step toward progress of Coffey County."[24] An activist organization seemed the best alternative to this kind of debate.

Although Salava was later described as a woman "unschooled in leadership" her sincerity and energy made up for a world of technique. We citizens, she said at a public forum in May 1974, do not want to take any chance, not even one in ten million, to have a "China accident"—a meltdown that could destroy eastern Kansas and render it uninhabitable for centuries. "How can you compare such safety calculations to one plane crash or a can of green beans?" How could anyone, even MIT's Dr. Rasmussen, "predict either the frequency or consequences of human error or malice?" she wrote. "Odds of a billion to one can be reduced to near certainty by human error or malice. . . . There has never been such monumental risks proposed for Kansas in any other human enterprise." "I'll continue to keep fighting the plant as long as they keep on building it," she said some years later. "I couldn't live with that thing over there." At her son's wedding in 1977 Mary Ellen Salava's frequent statement that "I only want a world for my children to live in" was recalled.[25] It was a forceful and personal message from a mother, and it had a popular power not easily equalled by the combinations of technological acronyms her opponents often used.

Diane Tegtmeier of Kansas City, who entered the opposition shortly thereafter with a substantial scientific background and unimpeachable environmental credentials, observed that Salava and the others had the simple initial motives of fear of having their land taken away and the thought that radioactivity could pollute the relatively virgin local environment. They had lived on farms for generations and had a strong "personal attachment and high degree of reverence for the land." They viewed themselves, Tegtmeier thought, as farm wives just raising some questions, but in time were able to transcend their personal and family issues to bring their organization to a point of general concern for the environment as more data became available. Information on the threats of nuclear power exploded, and *Reader's Digest* was supplemented by articles by Nobel laureates in physics. A Southeast Kansas issue became a world issue, and these women came, "as all of us did," to understand "their own personal power." This understanding led them to take risks that they did not know they were capable of earlier.[26] What began as small informational meetings, like the one in December 1973 when the Wolf Creek Opposition group voted to buy the film *How Safe Are American Atomic Reactors?* for showing to the public in Kansas, soon involved serious litigation, intervention in hearings, sizeable public meetings, and direct action.[27]

There were also other outspoken associates of Wolf Creek Nuclear Opposition.

Alfred J. Winn, a dairy farmer, refused KG&E's offer for his land and resisted the exercise of eminent domain with a lawsuit. "The utility companies claim the right of eminent domain as public do-gooders," Winn said in February 1974. "If they are, why don't they pay the people who have to make the sacrifice of losing their land and homes a decent price. . . . Who said this is a free country and that citizens have rights, must be out of his cotton picking mind. It is bad enough that the government has the right of eminent domain. If utilities and corporations have this right it is terrible. . . . As far as the citizens of Kansas are concerned, if you don't care enough to help us, you really do deserve a nuclear power plant." Winn called the taking of his 320 acres "nazism." When he finally lost his suit in 1976 he did not exit the field quietly. "My whole family has been through pure hell for three years," he told the press and a state senate committee, "because of the eminent domain law and a monopolist utility that has abused it." The newspaper headline was "A Pawn in the Power Game."[28]

One powerful pair in opposition was the Blaufuss brothers, Francis and Tony. Tony was a priest and stated the moral objections to nuclear power well. "Life is more important and injury is more important and the freedom of people to hold their jobs is more important than profit," he said.[29] But Francis was the more outspoken and activist of the two—so much so that he was to lie down in front of the train bringing the reactor vessel into Kansas. He was retired and committed to the cause full time. "Utilities trumpet the 'growing power needs' because they are over-built," Francis wrote in the fall of 1974, "and want to keep expanding exponentially for the sake of greater profits—regardless of the damage to the environment and public health."

Francis Blaufuss's message was broadly that it was selfishness to ask for unnecessary comforts and conveniences at such great risk. People had gotten along with less electricity before and they could do so again. He quoted Ralph Nader to the effect that "if people had their say between the candle or nuclear power they would take the candle." He suggested that all nuclear plants must be stopped by 1976 even if it meant going back to a more primitive and less power-dependent way of life.[30] He himself had an electric cable in his ceiling for heat "but if it will help on the energy shortage I am willing to put in a fire place or a solar panel to help out."[31]

Blaufuss addressed the technical end of things with colorful emphasis on the dangers. It would take as much lead to line the core and the "poison containers" of the new plant, he said, as all the hunters and skeet shooters of Kansas would use for the next 50 years. "You people are being taken for suckers by the AEC, the power companies, and the millionaires."

Blaufuss thought that direct action was the ultimate key to stopping the steamroller. The biggest environmental battle in history was shaping up in Kansas, he said, "and what happened to the SST will be a spring picnic compared to the struggle that is going to come forward on nuclear fission power."[32] He threatened direct action not only in the newspapers, but sometimes in letters directly to KG&E executives, and without benefit of editing. "With a depression coming on," he wrote Bob Rives, "how can you think of such an expansion. The poor people who half [sic] to give up their farms cry on my sholder [sic] to get me to help them. The power companys [sic] have no mercy on them . . . the crocked [sic?] lawyers are alwsys on the power company's side as they have our money to back them. I am afraid their [sic] will be a civil war in this country over these nuclear plants if they are not shut down soon."[33]

The Blaufuss view of things was blared from the hand-lettered pickup truck in which he travelled in his uniform of seed hat and overalls throughout southeast Kansas.[34] It was expressed also in full-page paid newspaper advertisements sponsored by such groups as

Citizens Concerned for the Future, which attempted to counter the utility access to the media in kind. In one ad Blaufuss compared Burlington officials to patients partly under anesthesia. "You County Commissioners of Coffey County and business men of Burlington are being made a laughing stock by the NRC and KG&E. No other place in Kansas has people so stupid as to want such a plant. Other places run them out. I suggest you people of Burlington get off your butts and help the Wolf Creek Opposition stop the plant." Sometimes his message was reduced to a phrase: "Cows may come and Cows may go, but the Bull in this place goes on forever."[35]

Wanda Christy, a newspaper reporter from Burlington, became openly associated with the antinuclear cause. She articulated, with documentation, the theme of rural virtue opposing the grasping corporation. "How can they sell out their neighbors," she said of the local promoters of the plant, "who helped build Coffey County, in the hopes of putting a little more money into a few pockets." This plant's economic promise, she said, was a rerun of the John Redmond boom that never happened. When the reservoir was built people did not get rich, it just ruined the pleasant life they had had. They started locking their doors and taking keys out of their cars and bringing machinery in from the fields at night. Land would be zoned industrial in the wake of the power plant, making taxes prohibitive. "If our country has come to the point that money is more important than people, then we should lower the American flag and run up a new one designed like a dollar bill."[36] Christy was critical of local papers for getting their information from the power companies and the AEC. "If I robbed a bank and you asked me about it I would deny it."[37]

Another player was Dr. Jacob Frenkel, a professor of pathology at the University of Kansas and vice president of the local branch of the Sierra Club. Frenkel emphasized the medical dangers of nuclear power and the unreliability of human judgment "under sudden stress," and also spoke and participated in forums on the broad questions of nuclear power versus solar and wind alternatives.[38] Like the others in the opposition he was much concerned about the "undemocratic" methods that he felt characterized the nuclear license approval process. He criticized Kansas State University for holding a "loaded" conference with only "pro" experts, and he wondered why there were articles worrying about the demands for more public scrutiny of the Atomic Energy Commission. One symposium on that subject was entitled "Life in a Goldfish Bowl." Frenkel's response was "You have to be a shark to have problems living in a goldfish bowl."[39]

It was somewhat difficult to attack Mary Ellen Salava, Wanda Christy, or Francis Blaufuss, except to call them as a group "medieval buffoons," and to argue that sincerity was no substitute for knowledge.[40] For their appeals were general and primarily emotional. However, Frenkel was an "expert" willing to contend on the customary playing field using practical specifics. As the construction permit hearings grew closer, therefore, there were editorials questioning his credibility. The headline of one published at Chanute in 1975 was "Unscientific Doctor." The editor noted that Frenkel had been rebuked for "gross exaggeration" when testifying before the Public Service Commission in Missouri on Wolf Creek's twin plant there. Attorneys had contended that there were errors in his testimony that expanded dangers by 1,000 times.[41] The Burlington paper called him "An Expert Overnight," and suggested he had allowed his scientific judgment to be distorted by his political agenda. The nuclear issue, the editor thought, was a chance for certain people to "express their dislike of everything in America. We have a vociferous group of self-proclaimed experts who are nonexperts, who travel around the country giving testimony based on half-statements and semi-truths. These have attracted the media instrumental to the detriment of the country."

Frenkel's response to all this was that the public should be allowed to determine who is an expert. There were scientists in the past aplenty who had been persecuted by the establishment for speaking the truth, including the ones that contended first that the earth orbited the sun. He went so far as to say that those approving nuclear plants should get a psychiatric examination.[42]

These headliners were joined by many others. Dale Lyon of the Farmers' Union was early active in the antinuclear cause, as was Wes Jackson, the nationally known environmentalist. The American Civil Liberties Union was an ally that could provide speakers, as were the Sierra Club and the Friends of the Earth.

Many folks could be depended upon to write a letter to the newspaper or to KG&E or to turn out for a rally. KG&E, for instance, got a letter from one Loretta Young of Westphalia, Kansas, who imagined a future Kansas "Nuclear Park" with "beds of wild yellow plutonium along tritium walks. There would be shady American elms in rolling uranium fields. Swimming and boating available in neptunium lakes with fluffy strontium clouds overhead. You could drink from iodine fountains and bask in the radium of sunshine." This Nuclear Park could be easily changed to "Memorial Gardens" when the time came.[43] Kay Nolan quoted David Lilienthal on the bright hope of mankind turning into "one of the ugliest clouds overhanging America."[44] Kay Nelson repeated the claim that a 1000 mw plant produces as much radioactivity as 1,000 Hiroshima bombs.[45] Purl Lance of Burlington contended that "people will not do anything until corpse upon corpse are piled high. Then will the public wake up and stop the building of poison plants?"[46] "Dear Guinea Pigs," went an ad sponsored by Kansas LAND (League Against Nuclear Dangers) early in 1975: "Well Guinea-Pigs, It seems as though / You're the very last to know / There's always been an added factor / A second nuclear reactor. / Another unit equal size / Double Killerwatts comprise / You will get twice the radiation / For other states' electrification. / Scientists seem to agree / Nuclear plants aren't danger free. / Who ever gave your consent / To live in this experiment?"[47] What such messages lacked in meter and sometimes in grammar, they more than made up for in passion.

If Wolf Creek Opposition, Inc., represented the grassroots base of the early counternuclear movement in Kansas, the Mid-America Coalition for Energy Alternatives (MACEA) in Kansas City was its intellectual center. Diane Tegtmeier was thirty years old when the plant was announced. She had degrees in physiology and chemistry and four years' work in biochemistry, but during the period of the licensing application was staying at home to take care of two small children. She was active, however, in Kansas City environmental groups, particularly the Citizens Environmental Council.

Tegtmeier was asked in the spring of 1973 by a faculty friend of her husband's to deliver a speech at Kansas Newman College in Wichita, which was having one of the first environmental conferences to be held in Kansas. Though her main work with the Kansas City environmental group had been on organic control of pests in gardens and with recycling, she thought something broader and at the same time more immediate was needed. She had been reading an article by Sheldon Novik about nuclear power in *Environment* magazine, and recognized that the recent announcement of the nuclear plant in Kansas was, or should be, a timely issue for environmentalists. Actually up to that point Tegtmeier, and many other area environmentalists, had welcomed nuclear power as an alternative to the air emissions problems of coal-fired plants, and "we understood why the utility industry welcomed it too because they were getting weary of the problems coal was causing them." However, her reading convinced her not only that nuclear power had its own problems, but that to build a plant in Kansas with significant economic and environmental impact without more public participation than was anticipated was a mistake.

At the Newman occasion Glenn Koester of KG&E made a presentation about nuclear power, and Bob Rives of the company spoke on the history and future of the company's progressive attitude toward the environment. Tegtmeier, however, found that her speech about hazards, despite the positive assurances from the company, struck a chord with the audience, and that "people were shocked this was going to happen in Kansas."

After the afternoon of speeches in Wichita both Rives and Koester spoke with Tegtmeier. There had been questions from the audience about "how do you answer this woman," and the two asked her what organization she was with. She told them that she was not with any organization devoted specifically to the nuclear power question, and remembered later about Rives: "I can still remember the look on his face of utter surprise that people were opposing it." Actually Tegtmeier at that time had little inkling that she would be much involved personally, but that conversation with the two KG&E people in fact was the beginning of "a 14-year relationship with that organization [KG&E]." Rives and Koester offered to provide her with information about nuclear power and did. She went back to Kansas City, continued her newsletter reading, began attending more lectures, and, when her two toddlers would let her, held meetings in her home to pursue some more specific organization directed at the Wolf Creek plant.

"I thought all I would have to do was call a meeting, clean my house, bake some cookies and someone in that group of illustrious experts would assume the leadership." In fact, Tegtmeier became the leader of the new MACEA organization. Dr. Frenkel helped, and William Ward, then assistant attorney general of the state of Kansas, became involved enough that he acted as the group's attorney during the licensing hearings in 1975 and 1976. Ron Henricks, the local coordinator for Friends of the Earth and an early MACEA member, was a civil engineer who understood the water issue, an early bone of contention about the plant. The group made connections with people opposing Nebraska Public Power nuclear projects and with the opposition in St. Louis and other parts of Missouri, and learned about Salava and the others at Burlington.

Coordination proceeded apace and media coverage followed. A meeting was called at the University of Kansas medical center, Frenkel's turf, in January 1974 to request the help of all groups in a coalition to oppose the Wolf Creek plant. Tegtmeier was most impressed by the testimony of the farmers "and the basic injustice that they saw in the right of eminent domain without it ever having been proved that this was in the public interest." The press was invited to the organizational meeting, but most were surprised that reporters even came, and more surprised at the amount of coverage that was forthcoming. Apparently the regional media wanted a debate, and was more than eager to latch on to any organized group that was willing to provide an alternative view. "We suddenly found ourselves as leaders of the MACEA," and launched on a course that would involve testimony before regulators, lawsuits, an introduction to the lobbying of state legislators, and intensive education in economics, law, and hydrology. Initial financial support and office space came from the Environmental Council and the Friends of the Earth, but the real force was Tegtmeier, who had been terrified of giving speeches in college, but now found that a cause she believed in made all the difference.[48]

KG&E's first direct contact with the emerging opposition came with land acquisition. Jack King headed the group of 16 company representatives who started in February 1973 to contact landowners about selling the 10,500 acres required for the plant and for a cooling lake large enough for two power plants, nuclear or coal.

King had been with the company since 1938, and thought he knew his trade. He had faced irate farmers before in getting rights of way for transmission lines, and even had had to deal with environmentalists' concerns about the threat electric lines presented to heron rookeries. But the nucelar plant acquisitions were different.

The strategy by the company was to acquire land quickly and openly and to avoid using the controversial eminent domain authority if possible. The company people's presence was publicized in the newspaper and they had red service trucks all over Burlington. An early office was established in a Burlington motel, and then in a store building. There was an initial public meeting in an armory announcing that the company would be buying land for one to two years. Right away, 3,000 acres were purchased of territory most agreed was some of the worst agricultural land in the county. King was authorized to make offers 25 percent above appraisal, plus pay the moving expenses and abstracting costs that were normally paid by the seller.

Despite this, the reception from the holdouts was unfriendly. Wanda Christy, for example, sold her land late and at a much higher price than the original offer while, all the time, writing letters to the newspaper complaining about the process and about King personally. The meetings with landowners, public and private, were tense. King remembered that some families "talked to us like we were a bunch of crooks," and said that they were being run off their property and that the Chamber of Commerce had known about the project before the landowners did. With a few the offers were taken to court. There were five of these cases and in all of them KG&E paid a higher price than it had for any other land.

Action occasionally went beyond litigation and suspicious comments. There was a bomb threat on KG&E's Burlington office. The company did not imagine it was serious, but since two private citizens lived on the floor above, it was decided to move the area corporate headquarters to the nearby, even smaller, town of New Stawn.

King felt, however, that in the end most accepted the settlements, which ranged from $200 an acre for unimproved pasture, to up to $1,000 an acre for farmland, as fair. KG&E needed only 10,500 acres, but agreed to buy some parcels outside the boundaries of the plant site if people wished to sell. Thus it purchased eventually around 12,000 acres. A few parcels went for unusually high figures: "When you get down to the last two or three and you've got to have them, you say 'what the hell.'"[49]

The landowner negotiations alerted the company that it needed to step up its public information campaign. Two local meetings were held in January 1974, one with the general public and one with business leaders. These were moderated by Wilson Cadman, and attended by King, Koester, and Rives for the company. Cadman explained the conclusions of the site engineers Sargent & Lundy about the cooling system, which in turn dictated the amount of land needed. The decision had been to use a cooling lake rather than cooling towers, due to that method's greater efficiency and lower cost in a plant of this size. He emphasized that the Redmond reservoir had extra capacity built into it on purpose for industrial use and that there were no buyers of these extra acre-feet on the horizon except KG&E. The company in buying the water would relieve the taxpayers of the expense of that part of the maintenance of the reservoir. The water that came nearest the reactor itself would remain in a closed loop and would not be discharged. Over $2,000,000 would be spent on the seismology, meteorology, ecology, and archaeology necessary to create the Environmental Report (ER) and the Preliminary Safety Analysis Report (PSAR) required before a construction permit would be issued by the federal regulators. Much more documentation and investigation would be done before an operating permit was issued. The company had the option of buying all the land and then announcing. It had decided to announce first. Its offers for land were based on its present state, not its anticipated use value. When speaking to the business leaders, Cadman focused on the number of jobs that would be brought to the community and the massive increase in the county tax base. The questions were polite, but suggested that economic development was not going to be the locus of the debate.[50]

The opposition sponsored its own public meetings. There was a debate in March at the National Guard Armory in Garnett. It was organized by the Holy Angels Social Concern Committee, and featured Dr. Frenkel, Dr. Russell Messler from the chemical and petroleum engineering department at the University of Kansas, and Father Blaufuss. Messler was in charge of the nuclear reactor program at the university and had consulted with the AEC since 1951. However, speaking on behalf of nuclear power, he was severely outnumbered, both on the platform and in the audience.[51] Another debate late in April in Burlington was similarly skewed. Dr. Robert Clack, associate professor of nuclear engineering at Kansas State University, faced Frenkel, Lyon of the Farmers' Union, Father Blaufuss, and MACEA attorney Bill Ward.[52] Some meetings brought in outside experts. For example, in April MACEA sponsored a meeting in Kansas City featuring Larry Bogart, head of the Citizen's Energy Council of Allendale, New Jersey. Bogart said that "anything that industry handles on a large scale is not going to be handled well." The audience seemed to agree.[53] By that winter there were town meetings in all parts of the state on the nuclear issue, sometimes including the governor and state health officials.[54]

The opposition groups said that "their" forums were necessary because other formats were dominated by pronuclear forces. A Kansas State University convocation on nuclear power late in 1974 was criticized as a one-sided forum on behalf of the safety of reactors, which opponents called "unworthy of a University."[55] Bob Rives went on a regular circuit with a speech called "Wolf Creek Generating Station: Its Role in Meeting Kansas' Everyday Needs," while company spokespeople continued to respond to every request to explain the plant to small groups.[56] KG&E had presented talks on nuclear power to 155 groups and 6,500 people before October 1973 and before most of the opposition groups had gotten organized.[57] In these talks there were powerful economic incentives offered against what were described as minimal risks. Cadman told the Burlington Chamber of Commerce in the spring of 1974 that there would be over 1,750 people employed in constructing the new plant by 1978, and that 550 new jobs would come to the county during that time. Housing would be needed for over 300 families, over $10,000,000 in materials would be bought locally in the construction period (not to mention ongoing sales during operation), and that between the announcement and 1978 Coffey County retail sales should increase 34 percent. Wolf Creek would remove only 3 percent of the county's agricultural land, and the tax valuation of the plant alone should conservatively be nine times greater than the current tax valuation of the entire county—with all that meant to schools and public services.[58] It was an attractive brew, well packaged, and delivered with a conviction that was as strong, however differing in style, as that of those who were trying to bring the project to a halt.

When there was even representation, proponents early had an advantage because the opponents were not as loaded with nuclear facts as insiders. Dr. Robert Hagen, KG&E's director of plant services for the Nuclear Development Department, organized a graduate-level introductory course in nuclear power, which was taught in 1975 to KG&E employees in the hospitality room of the company offices in Wichita. He advised that the protestors should take a similar course, but implied they would not. "These people usually don't want answers," he said. "They want headlines, and they get them, because criticism of this sort makes good reading." They were well meaning, Hagen thought, but had knowledge "only on the fringes of nuclear technology," while posing as experts.[59] In a television debate early in 1975 between a man from the farmers' union and a representative from the Kansas attorney general's office on the nay side and a KSU professor and a KG&E representative on the aye side, the press thought the result clear. The farmers' union man especially came off poorly, according to one editor in Lyons: "He was an amateur boxer leaping into the ring with the pro and saying, 'hit me!' The pro did, and apparently out of courtesy did not pummel him nearly as hard as he could have."[60] The opposition recognized that passion and appeals to common sense alone would not successfully counter logic and science. Experience and study slowly built a counterargument that met the contentions of the proponents directly as well as obliquely.

Opposition activity, however, was by no means limited to intellectual exchange. Its forte was in fact elsewhere, especially in organizing demonstrations that helped awaken public opinion to the problem even though they seldom themselves provided much information. What they did do was to provide bumper sticker–type slogans, signs that were memorable and that cut through a lot of complex data in a way that moved ordinary people to believe that action by them was justified and possible. In June 1974 protestors gathered in a parking lot behind the Lewis Standard gas station in Burlington and also at the Arrowhead shopping center to protest the plant for the benefit of AEC inspectors visiting the site. Their signs contained slogans such as "Now We Know How the Indians Felt," "Go Home KG&E," "Don't Poison Kansas," and "This Farm is Not for Sale."[61] A nationally known writer and activist, Mary Hays Weik, came to Burlington at that time to speak to the Wolf Creek Opposition group. She had fought nuclear plants in New York City, and explained her method of having people go to court without attorneys as citizen intervenors. From Burlington she went to Wichita where an organization called Citizens Utility Rights Board (CURB), spearheaded by Wichita State University maintenance engineer John Gaddis, and the local chapter of Common Cause were in their formative stages.[62] In July there was a protest gathering in front of a cafe in Garnett as city officials met with KG&E representatives to hear about the economic benefits of the plant. Again there were striking signs: "Refuse to be a Guinea Pig, Stop Nuclear War," "Ban Nuclear Power," "KG&E is Feeding a Big Line of Bull." There were 15 to 25 people in that group (press estimates varied), one teenager dressed in an Indian costume.[63] In January 1975 a tradition began that was to last throughout the planning and construction of the plant. About 100 people gathered on New Year's Day on the steps of the state capitol in Topeka to listen to speakers, and to renew their dedication to fight the plant harder next year than last.[64]

It was going to be a struggle. And it was not to be between a few radicals and a corporation, but increasingly among Kansas interest groups of all shades of opinion and interest. The Wolf Creek issue created some of the strangest bedfellows in state history.

It is interesting also that the populist tendency in the Kansas nuclear debate was not limited to the opposition. There was a grassroots pronuclear activist contingent that began in 1974 and 1975 to supplement planned events from "official" spokespeople with the kind of guerilla action on a thousand individual fronts that had been previously exclusive to the antinuclear forces. These people tended to write to newspapers rather than demonstrate, and to act as individuals rather than groups, but they did not hesitate to analyze the scene in language more direct than utility officials would dare.

Maybe the debate was not being framed with the right questions, wrote John Aker in April 1974. If the question were, do you want autos that pollute the air, the answer would be no. It would be no, that is, if no one asked if we wanted autos that required 15 percent more gas and produced 30 percent less power and cost more. With Wolf Creek the question seemed to be, do we want to live next to a potential atom bomb. The answer was no. Maybe instead, people should be asked if they wanted to pay higher prices for oil, gas, and electricity. Would a fossil plant occupy no real estate? What about its cooling tower, ugly coal pipes, and smokestacks? All heavy machinery was dangerous. How many coal miners had died over the years? "There are many people ready to answer before they have heard all the questions. Has anyone been asked how much they would be willing to pay in order to not have atomic power plants in Kansas? I think my answer would depend on whether this luxury would cost me two cents a year or $200 a year."[65]

Often "professional" writers to local papers emphasized the miniscule dangers. If all power were nuclear, said one, the risk would be the equivalent of smoking one cigarette every eight years or being one one-hundredth of an ounce overweight or spending a day in Colorado, slightly more exposed to the sun's radiation.[66] Ralph Nader, said one writer, was not always to be believed: "He draws on hundreds of minor steam-pipe accidents to foster the vision that mushroom clouds are just over the horizon."[67]

The grassroots promoters were not short either of criticism of the style and motives of the nuclear opposition. The editor of the *Iola Register* called them "romantics" who subscribed to a conspiracy theory and deeply distrusted all authority.[68] Michael Mann of that same town said he thought that the protest came from a Kansas moralistic tradition gone overboard. He had "never in my 20 years of life seen a more narrow-minded, change-fearful moralistic community. When I first read the *Register* 'Forum,' there were complaints that public nudity might become a way of life. Now everybody and his brother is afraid that the AEC is about to take over Eastern Kansas and turn it into a huge pile of radioactive debris." There was good for the region in the plant, and "with all evil comes an equal amount of good." Fear of death, no matter how remote, was crippling action to improve life. Mann quoted Alan Watts, himself one of the darlings of the counterculture, to new effect: "When survival becomes a compulsion, it becomes a drag."[69]

Some broadened the analysis further, making the Kansas issue a case of something larger than even the nuclear question. Wrote one man: "Maybe they [the opponents] enjoy being involved in the controversy? . . . In trying to protect the consumer from the alleged 'evils' of nuclear power, critics are doing the consumer a great disservice by robbing him of the most economical means of producing power today. Don't let facts stand in the way of an anti-intellectual, anti-consumer campaign."[70] Dr. Peter Beckmann, a professor of electrical engineering at the University of Colorado, was quoted in Kansas to the effect that "the anti-nuclear movement is now at last taking off its environmental mask and turning into a political movement closely allied with the radical left."[71]

Because there were so many forums and so many styles, there were those who called for a single venue to thrash it all out under the public eye. The *El Dorado Times* printed an editorial in January

1975 called "Probe the Atom Plant."[72] The regulatory process in fact was about to provide the setting for a formal confrontation. Public hearings on the construction permit for the Wolf Creek plant were set to begin in October 1975. Although the intervenors were limited in what they could discuss, and though not every group could achieve the standing to intervene, MACEA and the Kansas attorney general's office did intervene, and promised to ensure that the hearings would not be an inside gathering with preaching to the choir.

In preparation for the hearings, groups proliferated and gatherings escalated over the summer of 1975. An alternative July 4 celebration was held at the shelter house at John Redmond Reservoir sponsored by the Kansas LAND, Wolf Creek Nuclear Opposition, Inc., and the People's Energy Project (PEP) of Lawrence, Topeka, and Kansas City. Represented also were the Women's International League for Peace and Freedom, Kansas Farmers' Union, MACEA, Common Cause, the Fund for Peace, and the American Civil Liberties Union. Balloons were released with cards attached saying that they represented the spread of radioactive fallout in case of a nuclear accident.[73] That same summer there was a class at the "Free University," located at Wichita State University, entitled "Stop the Wolf Creek Nuclear Plant." Part of the class material showed "Reddi Kill-A-Wallet eating a wallet." CURB's chair, Art Thompson, was a member of that class, and shortly used his information in an appearance before the Wichita City Commission. "Do you believe in free enterprise?" conservative commissioner John Stevens asked him. Yes, Thompson said, but he did not believe in private monopolies.[74]

Before the hearings began, there was considerable criticism of them and their presumably foreordained result. The People's Energy Project group claimed that the official construction permit hearings would not cover the major issues and that it limited participation to those with considerable financial wherewithal. Paul Johnson of PEP advocated publicly owned utilities, excoriated purchase by investors outside Kansas of KG&E securities, and claimed that "the NRC is no more than a rubber stamp for the utilities."[75] PEP proposed to hold its own "counterhearings" on the steps of the capitol at Topeka—a structure that a number of the more radical environmentalists were suggesting should itself be powered by the wind (internal or external was not specified).[76] "The people of Kansas," said PEP petitions at the Kansas State Fair that fall, "should buy out

KG&E and build a system that suits the needs of the people, not profit."[77]

The stage was set for a hot time. KG&E knew it. "We're not the good guys any more," said Don Elliott, a division manager. "A few years ago it was fun to work for the electric company. Everybody liked us.... Now it's not so much fun. The good guys and electricity are mixed up with nuclear energy and people don't know what to make of it."[78]

3
Days to Remember, Days to Forget

> Kansans are not advocating an environmental utopia at the cost of shackling their ability to provide nuclear and other energy necessary to maintain their employment in industry, commerce, agriculture, and public service institutions.
> —State Senator Vince Moore (Wichita), at construction permit hearings, Nov. 1975

> I am here today because I care. I am here today pleading for reason before a panel of judges which cannot know my great concern. There are no mothers representing me on this regulatory commission of my government.
> —Mary Ellen Salava, at construction permit hearings, Nov. 12, 1975

> Whether Wolf Creek Plant ever heats up from nuclear fission would now seem to be a matter in limbo. Today, however, it's hot enough from emotional fever to generate a lot of steam.
> —*Lebo Enterprise,* Jan. 29, 1976

Between 1974 and 1976, and centering around the formal construction permit hearings, there was an attempt on the part of the "professionals," both corporate and political, to move the Wolf Creek issue off the streets and into a formal atmosphere, where access was limited and rules enforced. It was hardly a conspiracy, but rather familiar standard procedure employing a highly evolved system of prefiled and live testimony and cross-examination that many believed was the best of human systems for getting at the truth and ensuring fairness. But, although the legal profession talked about hosting "adversarial" proceedings, to the larger public, which had suddenly become an active and early stakeholder in the matter of utility generating plants, it looked like a pallid "old boy" network. Not only did the construction permit process not quench the fires building outside their venue, but those outside events in the next ten years penetrated to the inside and changed the hearing process itself substantially. The hints were there in 1975, but had the participants in those hearings been able to read the transcript of the supposedly parallel Kansas hearings in 1985 concerning rates and the operating permit for the completed Wolf Creek plant, they would have been amazed at the depth and the speed of the change.

Permitting interested citizens to participate in construction permit hearings was a legal concept that dated to the 1954 U.S. Atomic Energy Act. However, despite growth in the nuclear industry, opposition during the 1960s at these hearings remained "generally muted." Joseph Camilleri, in *The State and Nuclear Power* (1984), attributes this to the signing of the partial Test Ban Treaty in 1963 and community preoccupation with other politically sensitive issues, particularly civil rights and the Vietnam War. The turning point, according to his analysis, came in the late 1960s, and citizen involvement in the hearings concerning the Lake Cayuga plant of New York State Electric & Gas Company was one of its first manifestations. Evidence of change came later in Europe, but was obvious in Germany by the early 1970s.

Theories have been advanced that the growing dissent was contained in clear stages. Camilleri makes the observation that antinuclear protests tended to start "as a local reaction against a particular siting proposal"—for example Wolf Creek—and then "developed into a far-reaching critique of the entire nuclear programme." He writes, "The local community, which we may for the purposes of analysis designate as the *periphery*, was naturally resentful of the dictates emanating from the *centre*, increasingly identified with remote and anonymous political, bureaucratic and corporate decision-making structures." The peripheral specific objections grew into an attack on the central system core, not only the technological, but the political and economic one.[1] Another scholar looking at the phenomenon from a worldwide and sociological perspective, James Jasper, writes in "The Political Life Cycle of Technological Controversies," that media attention is the catalyst that moves the social context of nuclear power from the muted "pre-political" state to the stages of increased politicalization. Drop in media attention likewise tends again to depoliticize things. Even splits among the sides, Jasper emphasizes, are based on values, but are definitely heightened by the media. Eventually the attention spans of both media and public experience "issue exhaustion," and both accept a *fait accompli*.[2]

It is often said that nuclear oppostion is fundamentally "irrational" and driven by simplistic media coverage. The present history has employed a media database that is probably unprecedented in size for any local nuclear issue. The author's conclusion from studying this database is that a careful reading of newspaper reports gives a fairly complete and accurate picture of the development of Wolf Creek, with plenty of data to lead to a reasoned conclusion. No question some of the coverage—most of it in a few newspapers (the *Wichita Sun*, the *Parsons Sun*, for example)—was annoying to the company people for its "sensationalism" or muckraking anticorporate bias (long a Kansas standard). But overall this element was only part of what the newspaper "sponge" picked up from the surrounding atmosphere along with letters to the editor from supporters of the plant, summaries of official reports and hearings, and detailed statements from KG&E's public relations people. It has been noted by theorists that the media is the primary link between the "establishment" and "challenge" activists (both themselves highly nontypical) and the wider public upon which the decision will ultimately rest. That holds true for the Kansas model.

It has also been claimed that media coverage itself tends to increase opposition to debatable technologies among this wider, nonactivist public, but not because of its bias. First, the coverage, giving prominence, as it does, to disputes among experts about safety, may lead to the "rational" decision by the unquestionably underinformed general public that when in doubt it is better to err on the side of safety.[3] Second, the journalistic "balance norm" favors rivals to the official package, especially early, by giving them instant equal status. Rival spokespeople are quoted in parallel with "officials" and with similar frequency, along with a range of liberal and conservative columnists and cartoons. The "balance norm" may also help opposition by its tendency to reduce controversy to two competing positions, thus assigning to the opposition more unity than it may have.[4]

While the general public may be underinformed (partly its own doing), it is not underexposed. In the week following the Three Mile Island (TMI) accident in 1979, for instance, over 40 percent of the network news was devoted to that issue.[5] And it is clearly true also that the direct action tactics of the nuclear protest not only influenced the frames of the official procedings, but influenced the nature of media coverage as well. TMI and Chernobyl would have been covered differently had they occurred in 1970.[6]

It is a lesson of this study and the nuclear debate in general that "establishments," technical, economic, or political, are no longer able consistently to frame the relevant questions about the technology over the long period of time it takes to build a plant in the midst of rapid change elsewhere. It is not just the inadequacy of their answers that is the problem, it is the inappropriateness of their questions. The issue was framed in the 1960s as one of technical feasibility and economic advantage. Those were debatable and were debated. But a host of "unanticipated issues," combined with events such as a drop in electric demand nationwide, were not only unanticipated, but unprecedented in American history. The debate not only could not be controlled procedurally, it could not be controlled substantively. The shifting frames for analysis show up more in the media than in other forums because the media appears daily, has fewer constraints on change, and reacts more quickly.

It must be emphasized that media coverage, especially local coverage of the debate on a specific plant, is not a sideshow to the "real" event taking place in the traditional forums and revealed in such standard scholarly sources for business history as annual reports, government documents, and court transcripts. Nuclear power, writes one student of the impact of media in the national debate, has a culture, like every other policy issue, and that culture is not only reflected by, but is developed in the media. The metaphors, catch phrases, visual images, moral appeals, and other symbolic devices that characterize an ongoing discourse are encountered as "interpretive packages," and the debate may be seen as a symbolic contest over which of these packages will prevail. Parallel to this on a cultural level there is a cognitive issue of individuals making sense of issues for themselves and deciding on action. Media discourse, argue William Gamson and Andre Madigliani, is part of how individuals construct meaning, and public opinion is a part of the process by which journalists and other "cultural entrepreneurs develop and crystallize meaning in public discourse." The media, these authors conclude, offers "condensing symbols" through its interpretive packages, which make it the central organizing frame for making sense of relevant events. The frames themselves are neither for or against, but profoundly ambivalent. Sometimes they resonate with larger cultural themes, and sometimes they set up a dialectic between cultural themes and counterthemes.

When issues become as complicated as they got with Wolf Creek, and when they are, as a matter of policy, in the public forum, there is no substitute for simplifying, even stereotyping in communication. There must be a kind of "mythology" created in the sophisticated sense of *myth*, not as something untrue, but as something that gets at deeper truths beyond literal truth through powerful condensing symbols. That process got a late start with the proponents, was a powerful weapon with the opponents, and developed primarily in the print media. "Through the agency of symbolic appeals," writes one student of the nuclear power debate, "emotional arousal may reach levels which leave a mass audience susceptible to mobilization beyond institutional bounds."[7] Once the building of an electric power plant would have received almost no newspaper coverage. In this history of a nuclear plant built in the 1970s and 1980s such coverage is a major research element.

True, slogans, drama, and bipolar debate were ready made particularly for the television media and a developing "sound-bite" atmosphere, but newspapers in Kansas did a good job of illuminating the complexity, providing straight information (often at a level that was challengingly sophisticated, technically, legally, and economically, for much of its readership), and of providing a forum for many ideological points of view and conclusions. Other than the built-in bias by which coverage itself influences events toward the opposition, as mentioned above, the medium was not the message, except, certainly, insofar as the modern media was a contributing factor in making public participation in technical decisions something far more threatening to a preplanned program than the progressive reformers of the early twentieth century probably imagined.[8]

These theories all have application to Wolf Creek. The opposition there had its origin at the local periphery and with specific local economic, but nonnuclear issues subject to broader ideological overtones (namely the land taking). This expanded to broader environmental and technical concerns as the movement evolved, and moved into a political stage thanks partly to the largely unexpected level and consistency of media coverage. Diane Tegtmeier was someone whose concerns were both broader and more intellectual than, say, those of Mary Ellen Savala, but she became a catalyst and a group spokesperson in a highly political confrontation the moment a microphone was thrust before her. Given that events had become political the moment MACEA intervened in the construction permit hearings, and given that the local media had found in it a genuine bridge between the official view, the minority opposition, and the "undecided" public on an issue packed with symbolism and emotion, much of the rest followed naturally.

The legal proceedings leading to the 1975 and 1976 construction permit hearings began with KG&E's application in April 1974 to build a 1150 mw nuclear generating plant. A representative of the utility filed the application at federal offices in Bethesda, Maryland, paid a $125,000 application fee and submitted twenty copies of a 1,000-page draft of the environmental report. Shortly thereafter the required preliminary safety analysis report was filed, incorporating the standard data generated by the SNUPPS group for its six identical plants. These two documents, along with input at a series of hearings, would be the basis for the NRC's decision whether to issue first a limited work authorization (LWA) and finally a construction permit (CP) for Wolf Creek.[9] Jesse Arterburn of KG&E commented that the company had spent $2,500,000 for these studies and that "there isn't another system in the world that has so many backups unless it is a spaceship."[10]

In the fall of 1974 the three-member panel from the Atomic Safety and Licensing Board that was to hear the case was selected. Samuel Jensch, the chair, was chief administrative law judge for the AEC (soon formally to be the NRC). The other members were Lester Kornblith, a technical member of the AEC Safety and Licensing Board panel in Washington, and Dr. George Anderson of the Department of Oceanography at the University of Washington at Seattle.[11] Preliminary sparring for the construction permit hearings began on May 19, 1975, with a meeting in Lawrence, Kansas, where there was discussion among utility and intervenors' attorneys and the NRC about what questions would be discussed at the formal hearings in the fall.[12] These discussions took place immediately in the wake of a fire at the Tennessee Valley Authority's Brown's Ferry nuclear plant, which closed down both its reactors, and got considerable publicity in Kansas.[13]

Bill Ward of MACEA was there, as was Jim Lawing of the Wichita branch of the American Civil Liberties Union. That was expected. More surprising and controversial was the participation as intervenor of the attorney general of Kansas. The attorney general himself, Kurt Schneider, though denying bias, was outspoken in his questioning of the plant, and had seriously considered, while attorney general-elect, intervening in a lawsuit brought by landowners at the Wolf Creek site against the utility.[14]

There had always been a question about the relation of the states to atomic plants built within their borders, and some legislation in the 1950s addressed it in a limited way. However, through two decades the states "generally confined their activities to study groups and advisory panels." They recognized that uniformity in regulation was necessary to avoid hindering firms that operated across state lines, and they were basically more eager to promote atomic energy than fearful of its potential effects.[15] That attitude definitely changed in the mid 1970s. States all over the country were intervening actively to create almost the parallel of the "Granger laws" of exactly 100 years earlier when public outrage at the abuses of powerful rail corporations and warehouse companies had galvanized the states into regulatory action of their own, however nonuniform.

Involvement by the attorney general's office had begun in 1974 under Attorney General Verne Miller. A key player in the office was Bill Ward, later attorney for MACEA. Ward made numerous statements to the press justifying a role for the state in the hearings, which had traditionally been a federal/utility show. He said that while assurances had come from the AEC and the power industry that the state's concerns were insignificant, these assurances seemed to him and other staffers "more the products of inventive salesmanship than of an objective assessment of costs and risks as compared with available alternatives." The attorney general's office had questioned the AEC before, when Lyons was picked as a waste disposal site in 1970, and "we were, frankly, appalled by the AEC's apparent failure to take certain common sense steps." The intervention of the attorney general certainly suggested that opposition had proceeded beyond a few radicals. Ward said, "If we had not . . . become convinced that there were alternatives to nuclear power for Kansas, we might not have intervened in the proceeding. We realize that sufficient electric energy is critical to our way of life and to our aspirations as a society."[16]

Ward, who typifies the unusual phenomenon of public official as "responsible" radical, was more expansive in an interview with the *Wichita Sun* in January 1975. He told the paper that it was unlikely the state's points would prevail in the permit hearings. "The outcome is predetermined," he said. "The AEC stooges in Washington will grant the license anyway. Just like in the hearings the AEC has already held, they will say the safety and environmental issues have been satisfactorily answered. What we need is somebody living here in the State of Kansas to take a look at these issues and see whether these fears are legitimate." Ward said that the alternatives to halting the construction through the NRC process were first, a law to be passed by the Kansas legislature forbidding the construction outright or establishing a mechanism for state-controlled construction hearings, such as through the KCC; second, action by the KCC "regardless of whether it receives a mandate from the legislature"; third, a "favorable" decision in the state courts. "What are we getting ourselves into," Ward argued, "when no official of the State of Kansas exercises the authority to make a decision on this kind of power plant which could have all kinds of potential dangerous safety and environmental effects on the people of Kansas for decades?" Wind and solar power could do Wolf Creek's job without any of its dangers. Ward hoped that these questions would be raised at the federal hearings, but was more concerned that the decision itself be "taken out of the hands of the AEC and put under the control of the State of Kansas."[17]

"We have reached the conclusion," the official attorney general's release of 1974 stated, "that a nuclear power plant should be constructed in Kansas only after every reasonable effort has been extended to achieve the legitimate energy goals of such a project in other ways." The concerns of the office were transportation, disposal of radioactive waste, and costs. It said that the utility's environmental report was inadequate, failed adequately to address the effects of a potential accident, and did not contain a good evacuation plan. Attorney General Miller asked for a year's delay in progress on the plant. "We are confident that the problems of providing an adequate energy supply will yield to courage, imagination and cooperation in a spirit of mutual concern for the well-being of the people of Kansas."

Some said then that those statements were the opening salvos of

Miller's campaign for governor.[18] The same charges of exploiting a political issue were directed at his successor, Kurt Schneider. "For environmentalists and displaced landowners to organize and take an adversary position with respect to the Wolf Creek plant is understandable," said one Kansan. "The issue is one on which reasonable people can disagree. For the attorney general of Kansas to take up the cudgel for one group of Kansans to combat the interests of another suggests a kind of bureaucratic arrogance. Mr. Schneider sets an extraordinary precedent in putting the resources of his office on one side of a controversial issue where no Kansas law has been violated."[19]

It turned out, however, that the intervention of the attorney general in the construction permit hearings was only the opening salvo in a series of legislative and administrative state actions regarding Wolf Creek that went well beyond the traditional ratesetting role of the KCC in applying formulae to rates at the time of the completion of a generating plant. Notwithstanding the insistence of the AEC that nuclear plant approval and regulation *per se* was purely a federal matter, Wolf Creek and its contemporaries were too hot as regional political issues to expect states and even municipalities to watch the proceedings from the sidelines.

Utilities were concerned about escalating costs and the delay of rate relief, and so themselves indirectly encouraged a more active and early role for the Kansas state government in nuclear matters, as well as changes in regulatory attitude at the state level that might, in the interest of economic development, contravene the increasingly harsh federal stance. KG&E asked for a rate increase in 1971 and was turned down. In 1973 it requested 19 percent and got 11 percent, and there was a question, on which KG&E prevailed in court, whether the KCC should remove one-third of the LaCygne Station investment from the rate base. Late in 1973 Blyth, Eastman, and Dillon rated nationwide a factor for electric utilities called "regulatory climate." The best rating, as far as utility investor confidence was concerned, was a 1; the worst a 5. Of 36 states studied, only three—Kansas, Missouri, and Kentucky—got a 5! Two of the three were locations for SNUPPS nuclear plants.

According to Murray Weidenbaum, a St. Louis economist and former assistant secretary of the treasury, the decisionmaking procedures of many state regulatory commissions needed to be modernized, but would probably not be. There were political pressures on state commissions, close as they were to the grassroots, that, Weidenbaum said, "often have no basis in economic logic. The average citizen may be bored stiff by discussions of equity financing and debenture indentures. But he or she certainly knows what a 'brownout' or power failure or lack of electric service is all about. The close connection between the two just has to be made."[20] Reality was that utilities proposing nuclear plants in the 1970s could not rely on ever more difficult approval by the NRC as assurance of acquiescence at the state and local level. "Since there is no other place people can get power," said Gordon Evans, who retired as KG&E's chairman in 1975 after 50 years in the business, "people have always been a little suspicious of us." Evans, however, was philosophical about the resulting stress. "I suppose I don't strive for peace of mind," he said. "If you do that you get lackadaisical. If there isn't a little tension in your life you're not worth shooting."[21]

In the months leading up to the construction permit hearings, the opposition provided company officials with plenty of tension. Ralph Nader, one local editor put it, "would like to do to the nuclear power industry what he did to the Corvair."[22] Nader was disappointed in the tepid press response to his convention "Critical Mass '74," but predicted that "once the media sinks its teeth into the nuclear tiger's neck it will never let go."[23]

Mary Ellen Salava and the Wolf Creek Opposition translated on the local level. Salava praised the attorney general for intervention: "When one considers the dimensions a nuclear disaster can take, the most exhaustive research is the minimum precondition Kansas must require before permitting atomic power plants to be built within her borders. The cost of such research leaves the initiative to Topeka."[24]

By 1975 the media, mainline and specialized, had definitely become a factor in the nuclear debate in Kansas. The *Wichita Sun*, a journal that carved out an investigative niche in 1975, editorialized regularly about Wolf Creek and KG&E. It suggested that Kansas should become a pioneer in the application of solar energy rather than having a nuclear plant. What would happen, a *Sun* staff writer asked in January 1975, if when the utility's 20-year uranium contract with Westinghouse ran out in 2002 uranium had passed from the scene as natural gas "has now"? A communications specialist at KG&E, speaking to the *Sun* reporter, could only answer that he guessed in that event the plant would just sit there unless some other use could be found for it.

"What other use—do you mean a breeder reactor?"

"In the back of some persons' heads that's what they're thinking about."

There followed a long account of the dangers of plutonium.[25]

The concerns of the investigative reporters of regional newspapers had long centered on corporate corruption, as that kind of story met a receptive audience among many Kansans. Such revelations about the utility "monster monopolies" added vulnerability from a new angle by expanding further the local and technical concerns to a questioning of the larger economic and political "systems" of which these problems could be seen as inevitable symptoms.

One of the *Sun*'s young star reporters, Barry Paris (later a nationally noted author of literary biography), drew attention early in 1975 with articles questioning KG&E's expenditures on advertising. At issue was the allegation that KG&E spent five times as much on advertising in 1973 as it did on research and development—a ratio, it was implied, inappropriate in these times of conservation. KG&E claimed that the *Sun*'s advertising figures were inflated by a factor of three, and that the high figure came from Federal Power Commission required financial reporting that lumped unrelated matters into the advertising category. Gordon Evans pointed out that the company had not done any sales advertising for appliance use or use of electricity—"it's more for the *wise* use of electricity and conservation." But the article, with its claim that the current rate request would raise the company's rate of return from 7.72 percent to 8.36 percent, and given its circulation among state legislators, was bound to cause ripples in the midst of rate and construction permit hearings.[26]

Fred Kimball, KG&E's senior vice president, who was one of the topics of Paris's attacks in subsequent *Sun* articles, noted that this was about the time of Watergate and that muckraking was the style. Young reporters fighting for bylines looked for the negative. "You could do something great for the community and it would be buried in the classified pages, but if you had someone break a leg on a power pole it was three inch tall headlines across the top of the paper." The *Sun* tried to get Kimball to say that part of his salary was given him on the understanding that he would use it for political purposes, and Kimball was hurt that there were implications he was a crook: "He [Paris] kind of tore me to pieces." While there were those who defended Kimball privately and in letters to the editor, they were few. "It was a time," Kimball noted, "when a lot of people began to withdraw from public exposure."[27]

One man, writing his complaint to the *Sun* about the KG&E articles, thought it went further than reporters looking for reputations and newspapers looking for sales. Robert Peck of Wichita noted that he considered the advertising article "a masterpiece of innuendoes." His major complaint was the implication that profit was a dirty word: "May I remind Mr. Paris, the author, that if he had made a profit at running his own newspaper he would still be in business and not working for you." Peck argued that private enterprise was more efficient than government, and it was more efficient because of the profit motive. The alternative to KG&E passing on its cost to consumers was government ownership of electricity. "In fairness to KG&E, I think your paper should present the private enterprise side of the story. Profit is not a dirty word."[28]

Peck's comments drew their own sharp response. Bill Hawks of Wichita wrote the *Sun* saying he had "become intensively fumed over the inaccuracies and childish brutality displayed in a morally reckless response to a fine article about KG&E in the Feb. 5 issue of the *Sun*." Hawks said he was "appalled" by Peck's "placement of corporate profit so righteously above the American people in order of importance. Such a sly way of putting human greed before human need." Utilities, Hawk said, were not part of the competitive free enterprise economy, which was doomed anyway in the absence of consumer choice.[29] Such was the tenor of the debate as it warmed. A KG&E executive took a picture of a hand-lettered sign on a fence post near Burlington: "You can fool them now. What will you tell them later?"[30]

Another issue highlighted by the *Sun* was insurance. Early in 1975 the paper ran an article headlined "Nuclear: Who'll foot bill in case of accident?" Homeowners' insurance contained exclusion clauses against nuclear accidents and the Price-Anderson Act limited recovery from any one accident to $560 million.[31] Letters to the paper pointed out that private insurance companies were providing $300 million in insurance to nuclear plants and would provide more if the government stepped out. The chance of an individual death due to meltdown was set at 1 in 300,000,000 as contrasted with a 1 in

4,000 chance of dying in a car.[32] Utility executives noted that insurance company experience with nuclear claims made them vigorously compete to cover plants, which were statistically among their safest risks and largest returns. Despite such responses, however, the idea that nuclear plants were so dangerous that insurance companies would not insure them was a simple concept and provided strong ammunition for the opposition.

KG&E increasingly prepared to meet objections in the public forum as well as in hearings and court by making sure that every employee was an informed spokesperson in formal and in casual social situations. As early as July 1974, President Ralph Fiebach followed up 26 informational meetings with employees with a typescript of each of the questions and answers about the Wolf Creek project. Questions included "Why are we building the nuclear plant in the Burlington area? What will we do if for some reason we cannot build the nuclear plant? Is the cooling system from our plant self-contained or do we return water to John Redmond Reservoir? Will there be more than one unit at the nuclear plant? Are we paying excessive prices for . . . land? Are the objectors to the nuclear plant crackpots or are they really disturbed about the location of the plant?" and even "What do we do about cemeteries at the nuclear plant site?"[33]

In addition to employee education, the company involved several high-profile experts to get the pro argument in the press when the grassroots support seemed weak or when the reporting was particularly inaccurate. Prominent among these in 1975 was Dr. N. Dean Eckhoff, director of the Center for Energy Studies at Kansas State University. There is no more danger to radiation from a nuclear reactor, Eckhoff liked to say in speeches, than in sleeping with your wife for eight hours. "I guess there's a spectrum of some people really concerned over safety—really fearful," Eckhoff said. "I tend to think they are naive, I don't think they have looked at the literature. Of course, my thoughts are from a biased viewpoint." One of the problems, the professor thought, was the tendency to "weasel-word." No academic would ever want to say anything was impossible—that there was a zero probability to anything. But when they admitted there was *some* chance of a nuclear accident it was interpreted to mean a significant chance.[34]

Yet no matter what the information provided to the press, Ralph Fiebach remembered, "the kind of story they presented to the public was always one of sensationalism. The way the headline would read it would start spooking people before they ever read the content of the article." People wanted a guarantee, Fiebach said. Some in the utility thought they should give it, but should any prediction made prove false it could ruin tenuous credibility; therefore, often claims against the plant were hard to refute.[35] Also the press and the public tended toward undefined threats rather than specific dangers to which the utility might effectively respond. "It is the diffuse or undefined threat, the boogieman if you will, that spooks the general public," wrote R. W. Clack of the Kansas State nuclear engineering department. "It is the nuclear boogieman that Ralph Nader is most skilled at manipulating."[36]

The statistics and analysis were not really a "story," while the saga of Karen Silkwood, killed in a November 1974 auto accident while on her way to a meeting with a *New York Times* reporter to speak of security violations and plutonium leaks at a Kerr-McGee plant in Oklahoma, was a human drama, and a mystery of the sort that riveted readers.[37] The scientific explanations of the nature of plutonium did not get as much print in a year as the saga of the Oklahoma union organizer would draw in a good week a year after her death. And the specter of the evil, exploitative corporation, meddling in the black arts and cavalier about the safety of those it used, was suggested by the Silkwood stories and affected the image of KG&E in Kansas as well as Kerr-McGee in the neighboring state. A Kansas paper under the headline "The Devil's New Disguise" noted that "'Nuclear' has become the modern word for Devil in some lexicons. It is a transmutation that excludes reason."[38]

The Wolf Creek Safety Report, being technical and not much subject procedurally to formal public comment, caused nothing like the furor focused on the Environmental Report. A subcommittee of the National Advisory Committee on Reactor Safeguards heard three hours of testimony from engineers before 50 spectators in September 1975 and accepted the safety features of the Wolf Creek plant. The only requests for more information concerned the waste and fuel storage building design. The full committee met in Washington on October 9 and also approved.[39] Actually, questions about the safety and waste regulations caused a months-long delay in the issuance of a construction permit for the Wolf Creek plant after the hearings had ended, but not before a court ruling charging the NRC with failing to consider adequately certain atomic power risks in licensing plants in Michigan and Vermont.[40]

The Safety Report emphasized the universality of the SNUPPS design and addressed not only the seismology but the "mean annual tornado frequency" (3.8) of the region. History showed that the plant could regularly receive as much as 80 mph straight winds and a direct tornado hit about every 340 years. It even noted that the heaviest hailstone in the United States, weighing 1.67 pounds, was observed in Coffeyville, Kansas, 80 miles from the site, and that hailstones 3 inches in diameter were not uncommon in Kansas. The plant had been designed accordingly. The report contained an extensive appendix entitled "Chronology of Radiological Review of the Wolf Creek Generating Station," which contained letters from SNUPPS and others on the design, and accounts of SNUPPS meetings.[41] The conclusion was that Wolf Creek was a conservative design, overbuilt and overdesigned in many ways at great expense by the SNUPPS groups, which hoped to amortize the cost over several utilities. Both the design and the safety report were created for experts by experts, and both sides were relatively satisfied.

The Environmental Report was different, not so much in its construction and acceptance by utility and NRC staff and consultants, but in the volume and depth of comment it generated outside the "club."

The U.S. Nuclear Regulatory Commission, Office of Nuclear Reactor Regulation, published the *Final Environmental Statement Related to Construction of Wolf Creek Generating Station Unit 1* in October 1975. It contained sections on regional demography, land use, water use, historic and archaeological sites, geology, seismology, meteorology, terrestrial and aquatic ecology, as well as a complete description of the proposed plant and its systems with an analysis of their environmental impact. The report also addressed the costs and benefits of alternatives to nuclear power as an energy source for the region and the need for additional power generating capacity. The environmental report and accompanying safety report were done twice, once in 1975, prior to the hearings to grant a construction permit for the plant, and again in 1982, in connection with Wolf Creek's application for an operating permit. The National Environmental Policy Act of 1969, which required the environmental report, charged the federal government to fulfill the responsibilities of each generation as trustee for the environment for succeeding generations; assure for all Americans safe, healthful, productive, and aesthetically and culturally pleasing surroundings; attain the widest range of beneficial uses of the environment without degradation, risk to health or safety, or other undesirable and unintended consequences; preserve important historic, cultural, and natural aspects of our national heritage; achieve a balance between population and resource use which will permit high standards of living and a wide sharing of life's amenities; enhance the quality of renewable resources and approach the maximum attainable recycling of depletable resources. All these factors were to be overbalanced by a consideration of "the relationship between local short-term uses of man's environment and the maintenance and enhancement of long-term productivity." The environmental report was sent out for comment to the Advisory Council on Historic Preservation; the Department of Agriculture; the Department of the Army, Corps of Engineers; the Department of Commerce; the Department of Health, Education and Welfare; the Department of Housing and Urban Development; the Department of the Interior; the Department of Transportation; the Energy Research and Development Administration; the Environmental Protection Agency; the Federal Power Commission; the Office of the Governor, State of Kansas; and the Chairman of the Coffey County Commission. Each of these agencies had its own legislative charge, constituency, and tendency.[42]

The conclusion in the environmental report was that Wolf Creek should be granted a construction permit despite some unavoidable adverse environmental effects. Some 10,500 acres of land would be taken out of agricultural use; construction activities would disturb 200 of these acres and the cooling lake flood about 5,000. The staff agreed with the utilities that, while the cooling lake was too big for one plant, there were economic reasons to justify it in case a second plant were needed on the site. Fifty households would be affected and 25 would need to be removed. Construction would reduce aquatic populations in the lower half of Wolf Creek, and when the cooling lake was filled 15 stream miles would be lost as running water aquatic habitat. It was thought that loss of aquatic biota in this section of the creek would be more than compensated for by the establishment of these in the lake through both natural colonization and the introduction of game fish. There would be some mortality of fish in the plant intake structure. The plains harvest mouse and the badger, both rare in the upper and middle Neosho River basin, would lose habitat.

Perhaps most important of the effects, given the subsequent debate on it in Kansas, was that "during post drought periods, withdrawal of makeup water could significantly reduce flows available in the Neosho River," thus extending drought conditions, not only for fish, but for people in the towns that drew their industrial and domestic water supplies from that river.

The environmental report focused on the fish. The Neosho madtom was the snail darter of the Kansas issue. It was on the American Fisheries Society Threatened Species list, and it was possible that the fish would be stressed by the building of the plant "possibly beyond their capacity to recover." Other rare fish—the highfin carpsucker, gravel chub, river redhorse, and bluesucker—might suffer significant reductions. Among the provisos suggested by the NRC staff in granting the construction permit was that "the applicants shall finalize their contractual arrangements with the Kansas Water Resources Board for purchase of the assumed 55.84 percent of total storage from the John Redmond Reservoir prior to issuance of a limited work authorization or construction permit." That was to prove something more than the administrative detail it was imagined then it would be.

What much of the public most feared among environmental effects—namely radiation—was dismissed in the report in three sentences: "The risk associated with accidental radiation exposure is very low. No significant environmental impacts are anticipated from normal operation releases of radioactive materials. The estimated maximum integrated dose to the population of the United States due to operation of the station is 553 man-rems/year, less than the normal fluctuations in the 21,000,000 man-rems/year background dose this population would receive."[43]

The Mid-America Coalition for Energy Alternatives made a list of objections to the environmental report. Dr. J.K. Frenkel and Diane Tegtmeier, speaking for MACEA, contended that the report failed to consider possible release of radioactivity in an area beyond a 50-mile radius: a 100-mile zone including Wichita, Topeka, and Kansas City should be considered; that it failed to account for release of radioactive material in groundwater and the possibility that the

Redmond Reservoir would not meet needs in times of drought; that it failed to detail the environmental effect of the ultimate accident, a core meltdown, and provide for safe storage and disposal of radioactive wastes; that soaring costs cast doubt on the economic feasibility of Wolf Creek; and that projections of its efficiency and availability were too high.[44]

Eckhoff took on these objections one by one in the press. The 100-mile radius point was not valid, he said, as the possibility of radioactive release in the larger area was no greater than in the smaller area: if the company met the 50-mile test it met the 100-mile test. To suggest that not testing specifically for 100 miles was hiding something from the residents of the major population centers was not common sense. The report did account for possible release of radioactivity in groundwater, and it met standards that were 100 times more strict than for operating reactors in Europe. On considering meltdown, Eckhoff responded that the NRC would determine the adequacy of reactor design, but the chances of being killed by such an event were less than being hit by a meteor. The same was true of storage and disposal of waste—the risk was small and the protection adequate. The cost issue was admittedly a real difficulty—one that would become ever more prominent. Inflation was raising the costs, but, Eckhoff noted, another major contributor "is the inordinate delays caused by the well-meaning, and not-so-well-meaning, disaster lobby." There was confusion about the way statistics on efficiency and availability were quoted, but projections for Wolf Creek were no higher than other operating nuclear plants were achieving. The availability statistics on nuclear plants, which averaged in the 70 percent range, were confused in the press with "load factor," and "capacity factor"—measures of averages versus peak and of actual versus theoretical running efficiency, where the numbers would be lower.[45]

It was pretty complicated for a new reporter with a deadline and a word limit. However, for the careful reader who could get beyond the headlines, the Kansas press purveyed over the years an enormous amount of information on Wolf Creek from multiple perspectives. Certainly, it did not print the entire text of hearing transcripts or required reports, but the summaries were generally accurate and much clearer about the essential facts and conclusions than the primary documents with their convoluted style and introverted jargon.

The opposition organizations not only prepared their own testimony for the hearings and lined up their attorneys and expert witnesses, they lobbied to involve other groups. Particularly of interest was the State of Kansas, through its legislature as well as its attorney general's office. There were several bills introduced in the spring session of the 1975 Kansas legislature to give the state a greater oversight of nuclear plants, and Tegtmeier was in Topeka testifying in connection with these. She said she found the legislature relatively apathetic about the issue, and contended that if the apathy continued "Kansas will give up its right to be involved in the decision-making on the Wolf Creek nuclear plant to the federal government."[46] That was a statement well designed to get the state politicians' attention no matter what the issue.

That the Wolf Creek construction permit hearings would not be without incident became obvious in that prehearing conference in Lawrence in May 1975. The hearing room was full, and not just with official participants, but with press and observers. Attorneys offered motions and procedure was discussed, as expected. Jim Lawing of the ACLU argued, for example, that the hearing date was premature, since the notice was issued before the final draft of the environmental impact statement was published. The early date, he said, denied the opponents the chance to prepare and "permits the hearing procedure to become only a forum for advocates of the application . . . , and equal protection also is denied because it deprives poorly financed critics of a meaningful opportunity to be heard." Bill Ward made motions for the applicant to withdraw and for a summary judgment.

The hearing panel was surprised that the hearing did not stay within the usual parameters for such events. Not only did the attorneys make more radical suggestions, but the public and the press were present in greater numbers than usual, and would not remain silent. Photographers maneuvered to get pictures and sometimes tried to speak. Samuel Jensch, head of the panel, attempted to stop both with less than complete success. Once during an address by an attorney a man in the audience began to speak. Jensch called him down, saying that this was not the time for public input, and that the man should tell his concern to one of the attorneys. "Sir," said the voice from the back, "they don't represent me. I don't know these people. Sir, I don't have a lawyer. I just know what I'd like this commission to look over with reference to the power plant and I am not sure that is going to be done if you just listen to these people."[47]

The level of public interest and input became more obvious at the outset of the hearings proper, which opened in the District Courtroom at the Coffey County Courthouse in Burlington in November 1975. The purpose of the Burlington meeting was to permit the public to make statements and express their concerns. Sessions were held in the evening to allow full access and the reports being discussed were made available at two public depositories, as were transcripts of the hearings as they proceeded.

The public hearings began almost exactly a year after Karen Silkwood's accident. While a federal investigation had revealed that Silkwood had probably fallen asleep at the wheel while sedated with Methaqualone, and that urine samples from Silkwood had been tampered with to indicate plutonium contamination, her family continued to pursue lawsuits and to charge that plutonium rod inspection records at Kerr-McGee were what had been faked. Just as the Burlington hearings began, Kerr-McGee announced it was shutting down the Cimarron River, Oklahoma, plant where she had worked.[48]

Jay Silberg, a KG&E attorney, set the scene for his client by going through the history of the plant from initial site studies to the present. He pointed out that the Advisory Committee on Reactor Safeguards, which was independent of both the applicants and the NRC staff, had studied the application, held hearings, and determined that the plant could be built with reasonable assurance to protect public health and safety. KG&E, Silberg said, had not rushed into this. It had created a nuclear staff (Jesse Arterburn was at the table as evidence) and had selected good contractors. The SNUPPS design was conservative. The Westinghouse pressurized water reactor to be used was an update of a type first used in the 1950s. Polls showed that the public did not want to rely on a foreign energy supply and favored development of nuclear power to avoid this. "Now, all this is not to say that there are no risks with this project. There are risks in any project. There are risks when you cross the street. There are risks when those who are from out of town fly here. There are risks when you drive your car. The point that's important to bear in mind is that the risks associated with this plant have been reduced to the lowest possible level, and there have been studies which have shown that the risks associated with operating a nuclear plant are far lower than the risks you and I commonly accept in our daily lives. . . ." The hearings process was designed to ferret out every possible objection. There were 50 contentions by intervenors that the utility would be required to answer during the hearings.[49]

In contrast, the audience heard a statement from Bill Ward, who emphasized that only three groups had been given intervenor status and that the issues that they could address under the rules were severely limited. Ward said that history had caught up with Wolf Creek: "The decision to build a nuclear power plant at Burlington, Kansas, once arguably justified in the mid 1960s, is today seriously ill-advised." Even the study and hearing process so touted by the proponents of the plant for its fairness would not have existed in its current form had it not been for pressure from environmentalists, such as the ones who were intervening here again. The landmark Calvert Cliffs court decision in 1971 required detailed environmental statements for nuclear plants for the first time. Yet, while the current report was thick, Ward said, it was inadequate, particularly in regard to cost-benefit analysis. MACEA and other intervenors were prevented by the NRC from addressing waste disposal, transportation, and problems of terrorism and sabotage. Ward emphasized that the intervening attorneys were operating *pro bono publico*, and that the organizations they represented did not pay the attorneys' expenses, let alone any fees. This he contrasted with the large sums being spent by the utilities for preparation and representation.[50]

The figures on cost of intervention and the limits placed on what intervenors could do got considerable currency in the press. "Actually," said Diane Tegtmeier, "it is impossible for the average citizen to intervene in these proceedings, effectively or ineffectively." MACEA spent about $400 preparing its testimony, while utility spending in preparation for the hearings was estimated at $10.5 million. It was no accident that MACEA's two economic expert witnesses happened to be from Missouri: that was the maximum travel expense the organization could afford.[51] Tegtmeier thought the NRC itself was not "doing a good job of representing the public interest. They are not looking for the best people to represent alternatives to this plant."[52]

The attorneys' opening statements were followed by a wide variety of comments from the public. They stood up one after another, and the panel heard the whole range of Kansas reason, emotion, and interest running sequentially from one end of the spectrum to the other.

Jo Ann Klemmer, of the Topeka branch of the Women's International League for Peace and Freedom, said that the plant would cost too much and that damage it might do was uninsurable. Edith Lange made an appeal based on her mistaken impression that the plant was to be fueled by plutonium. John Decker, city attorney for Wichita, stated that Wichita favored the plant, as its energy department had determined that fossil fuel available for Kansas in the future was minimal. "If we do not have industry in Kansas, we are not going to need homes in Kansas," Decker said. Louis Stroup of Kansas Municipal Utilities, Inc., spoke in favor for the same reasons. Gas was skyrocketing in price and coal supplies were being tied up by environmental concerns. Margaret Bangs of Wichita, who was concerned that her city had taken a position without asking its citizens, expressed her fear as a mother. "I am petrified; I hate to talk but I am so concerned I am going to speak." Harold Wilson, president of the Wichita Labor Federation, AFL-CIO, thought the fears came from distorted imagery: "One of the issues usually raised at a hearing of this nature is that a nuclear power plant is a potential bomb, and probably to the layman whose only frame of reference is viewing a mushroom cloud on television, or reading the editorial comments of the devastation of an atom bomb, I think this is appropriate and sounds conceivable. However, the facts do not support this belief." Wolf Creek would help the construction trades in a down time, while solving the energy problem would be the greatest boon imaginable to employment generally. Bud Grant, director of the economic development branch of the Kansas Association of Commerce and Industry, felt the same way. Every dollar paid out of our economy for foreign oil, he said, would provide capital for industrial development that would purchase goods from American business and support jobs for American workers. Tony Blaufuss argued that the "socio-moral" dimension had been neglected. Was it not cynical to endanger the lives of 2,500 people around Burlington when the site decision had suggested it was not worth endangering 150,000 lives at an alternate site? "We need no 'nukes' on the sacred soil of Kansas." Annete Young, a sophomore at Garnett High School, commented on the fact that the NRC would not allow plants to be constructed near large population centers: "My life is just as valuable and important as the lives of people in large cities." Robert Clack, director of Kansas State University's nuclear reactor facility, said 27 years in the nuclear field had left him optimistic about the power source. "If we make the wrong decision at this time we can commit at least one generation to privation not generally known in this country since the Great Depression." State senator Vincent Moore of Wichita, part of the legislature's energy task force, pushed a similar theme. Opposition to Wolf Creek would cost jobs "unless they want to herd sheep and live on mutton." Most of the opposition, Moore said, needed a course in economics—they wanted to kill the goose that laid the golden eggs as they rolled in American luxuries. The current corporate image of KG&E, Moore said, was a carryover from the campus violence of the 1960s. "The public is given the impression that a corporation is a sinister ogre bent on doing in the people. This becomes an acceptable thesis to some as the economic illiteracy of our people becomes more and more apparent." The utility executives, Moore said, were human and had the same human concerns as the people they served.

Francis Blaufuss gave corporate leaders a lot less credit. "In 1981, when this nuclear fuel is loaded into the reactor, I will personally lead one of the biggest protest marches against nuclear power in the history of the world. Now, somebody might want to scatter my blood down Wolf Creek while I am trying to stop this thing, but that's quite all right. My blood is much more pure than the crap that's going to come out of the nuclear reactor." Mometh White, who marketed sweet clover around Burlington, also had a jaundiced view of big business. "Now I am not going to give up my farming for any crazy and un-needed Rockefeller nuclear plant without a good fight." Wanda Christy thought the whole idea of introducing testimony about economic advantage into an environmental hearing was ridiculous. But she admitted money was having its influence: "The proponents have the money on their side to wine and dine and influence and advertise. We haven't the money, but we have spirited people who are willing to do whatever is in their power to put the real truth before the people and try to stop the building of nuclear plants. . . . I do not apologize for emotion; we are talking about people." Lois Platt of Topeka offered a telling challenge: "Now I am an old lady and I don't know too much. I am not a scientist; I am not a politician. And—but I do read. And I suppose, according to our honorable senator, the man that talked first, you would say that I have been sold a bill of goods, and maybe I have. But you have to prove it."[53]

The panel listened, granted requests for some further limited appearances by the public than there had been time for, and dismissed to reconvene January 26 in Kansas City. Attorneys on both sides meanwhile scurried not only to gather information to satisfy the NRC, to address the concerns of businesspeople who feared economic stagnation for a Kansas with an energy "problem," but maybe most to provide the public "proof" one way or the other Mrs. Platt was looking for.

The Kansas City hearings started with more statements from the public. Margaret Bangs drove from Wichita in winter partly because she was upset that the Wichita City Commission had taken a pro–Wolf Creek position. Also, Bill Ward of MACEA had been in Bangs's Sunday school class when he was in the ninth grade, and had encouraged her to participate further in the hearings. Ward told people that Mrs. Bangs had taught him about ethics and that that is why they were all there.[54] She stated that nuclear power had survived only because of massive government subsidies, and she emphasized the unaccounted for costs and the waste problem.[55] Mrs. Bangs was pleased when, during later testimony, Jensch asked her if that answered her question. That action made it clear that individuals and their concerns were being taken seriously.[56]

Some new issues were raised. Paul Schaefer, an engineer at Kansas State, opposed the plant because of its size and centralization.[57] Donna Salava, who gave her experience as "20 years on a tractor and 25 years under cows, milking cows," emphasized that the taking of water by the plant would hurt agriculture. Nancy Jack of the Sierra Club had the same concern: "We would like to remind once again that the John Redmond Reservoir is *public* property and that KCP&L and KG&E are *private* utility business firms. No private entity should be allowed to destroy public property for private gain." It went on until all had spoken. "This is open season," said Sam Jensch, "open shooting."[58]

A tally showed that the proponents of the plant were much in the majority. Sixty-seven people spoke or submitted letters to the board favoring the plant, while 24 opposed it. Among residents of the area the ratio favoring was 24 to 6.[59] This was not untypical of the country at large. A Harris poll in the summer of 1975 showed 63 percent of Americans favored nuclear power, and only 19 percent were actively opposed.[60]

In the Kansas press, both in the editorial and letters to the editor sections, there was some sharp criticism of the opposition to the plant. An editor in Manhattan called the intervenors "Chicken Littles" who ran around crying that the sky was falling. "There is something more lethally dramatic about raising the nuclear specter than coal smoke. All of which is effective, to be sure, but rather too bad."[61] David Lilienthal was quoted in Kansas to the effect that it was sad to see a country with growth potential "dragging itself down in negativism and fear." There was need for positive thinking. "It is time we stopped making heroes of people who talk about things we can't do and honor those who believe there is no limit to human creative ability—political, economic and technical. Nothing that has happened justifies this negativism we have been passing through. I think you can trace the beginnings of what is still called the recession in the implanting of fear that we have reached the end of the road."[62] A *Wichita Eagle* writer commented that the state motto, *Ad Astra Per Aspera* ("To the Stars through Difficulty"), should be changed to "Don't Cross the Street—A Car Might Come Along."[63]

Among the public actually appearing at the hearings the division of opinion was closer—16 for and 14 against. Mary Ellen Salava, though she was only one witness in opposition, presented an 80-page petition with 3,000 signatures.[64] Edith Lange, one of the speakers against the plant, suggested that there be a public referendum to give a true picture of opinion.[65] A minister, writing to the Burlington paper, pointed out that, even if opponents were in the minority, it was not just a matter of counting. He compared the hearing process to the discussions among the beach promoters in the recent movie *Jaws*. It was a question of economics versus life. "One feels at times that those in the industry who do know the truth are willing to throw us to the nuclear sharks."[66]

A parallel test of the waters, with such even forces that even a savvy politician could not distinguish the way the wind blew, was the public hearing before the Wichita City Commission held on January 22, 1976. Commissioner James Donnell, a dentist with a special interest in energy, stated early in the month that "this is not an effort to frustrate KG&E, yet they have made some wrong predictions." Commissioner Connie Peters thought that attorney Decker had gone too far in Burlington: "My impression was that we authorized him to make a statement that we do need the energy but that we would not take a position for or against the nuclear power plant."[67] Still, the major local paper thought that having to have the hearing was unfortunate: "The idea of holding a high school debate and a town hall type meeting to help city commissioners decide whether or not the City of Wichita will support the proposed Wolf Creek nuclear generating plant project seems a little ridiculous."[68]

The event itself, held on an icy Thursday evening, was a surprise to any who might imagine that the Wolf Creek matter could be contained in respectful debates among attorneys, executives, and regulators. It lasted until past midnight and "pitted professor against professor, businessman against businessman and neighbor against neighbor." Sixty people appeared, twice as many as spoke at the "official" hearings at Burlington and Kansas City. Discussion was to be limited to the economic aspects, but emotion could not be contained.[69] At the end of over five hours of testimony, the commissioners found no acceptable path through the maze except to sidestep the issue. The result was that the commission would not specifically endorse nuclear power, "but if that fuel met our needs best we should use it." The resolution, adopted at 1 A.M., was a masterpiece of doublespeak, illustrating how controversial the issue had become. "RESOLVED: That the citizens of this city recognize the needs of proceeding with plans for additional and alternative course of energy . . . for the future and we support efforts for an early decision to proceed with plans to produce whatever generating facility may be necessary and at the same time encourage all efforts for energy conservation at all levels."[70] The accurate headline after a day of thinking about it was "A-Plant Position of City Unclear."[71]

The same might be said for the rest of the state.

4
Fire and Water

As the terrifying roar of the Hiroshima bomb dies to the whispering burn of the whirling generators, it will not be said the the atomic furnaces arrived on the plains of Kansas by legislative mandate following deliberation and study of all aspects of nuclear power. Rather it will be said that its arrival was born of illegal contract and nurtured by an undue haste to lock the people of Kansas into . . . surrendering a portion of the state sovereignty in violation of the constitution . . . and to subsidizing the two power companies at the expense of all water users of the state who are not guaranteed their water costs for the next 40 to 80 years.
—State representative Arthur Douville (R), March 10, 1976

So really what you get down to is looking at some guesses based on statistics, not just the fellow that you know down the street.
—Bill Ward, Feb. 2, 1976, construction permit hearings

I don't like to see a good man browbeat.
—Jesse Arterburn, Feb. 25, 1976, construction permit hearings

At mid decade in the 1970s, KG&E learned that there was nothing at all that could any longer be considered routine about the construction of a generating plant that happened to use nuclear power as a heat source. To the company, however, the reaction seemed extreme. "Raising the temperature of the water a few degrees," one U.S. nuclear plant executive commented, "is no reason for a civilization to commit suicide."[1] To the intervenors, however, each step in the approval process, perhaps itself relatively trivial, was a vital piece of a total that was anything but insignficant. Critics were not allowed by the procedures to make broad-gauged or philosophical attacks. Their strategy had to be to focus on the local and on the specific as these arose in the approval process. For that reason certain expected "automatics"—things the utility considered "givens" for which approvals must be sought for any power plant—became in the case of Wolf Creek major public battles. Writes one student of the nuclear power fights: "Although ordinary citizens had only limited access to technical information on the dangers associated with atomic technology, they sensed something had gone terribly wrong, not just with nuclear power, but with the industrial and governmental forces that produced it."[2]

At Wolf Creek, as all over the country, nuclear protest was evolving from "pressure group" or "elite quarrel" to "mass movement." Sociologists have speculated that to some degree it was a case of "status disorientation"—that a small pressure group lost power in the formal hearing processes, and engendered a mass movement to get it back.[3] In any case the stages are generally delineated as beginning with legal protest, moving to direct action, and peaking in a social movement that was not exclusively focused on nuclear power, but had as goals decentralization, egalitarianism, and participatory democracy.[4] At each philosophic broadening the numbers that came under the umbrella, and whose individual beliefs had significant overlap with the ideological themes of the movement, increased, as did the pressure they could bring to bear, both at the scene and nationally, on a local project.

Of particular interest in studying a local project is the contention that protest all over the country might have been partly motivated by the feeling the local citizens had of the alien nature of the nuclear plant in their own landscape. This kind of analysis parallels that done by Leo Marx in his seminal sociohistorical work *The Machine in the Garden*, a study of the impact of the introduction of the locomotive in the nineteenth century to American ideas of landscape. Marx uses many nontraditional sources, including paintings showing locomotives and factories in arcadian settings and fiction such as Nathaniel Hawthorne's "Celestial Railway" to analyze the accommodation that was eventually forthcoming. Something similar probably had to happen with nuclear power at every site and at all sites before it had arrived symbolically and visually to the mass psychology.[5] One author notes that there is a "provincial-suburban" fix in peoples' attitudes that "requires a frame around any experience in order to recognize it," or at least "an idea of what a given place is and what one is supposed to do there." For many people nuclear plants were "unreal because [they existed] outside all recognized frames."[6] Wolf Creek ultimately had to seem real to Kansans, an accepted part of the local landscape, or no amount of technical argument could sell it to them.

Fuel and water supply questions were, of course, basic. The planners, however, thought they had arranged these well and favorably and that these matters would hardly cause a ripple in the hearings, much less in the press. Two surprises changed that. First, in the cases of both fuel and water, there were chinks in the armor of the united "establishment" position. Westinghouse and KG&E fell into litigation over fuel that spread through the newspapers the flaws in the early dreams about "turnkey" nuclear plants with abundant, cheap fuel. And on water, there were slips in going through the bureaucratic hoops that allowed for charges of conspiracy and conflict of interest between the utility company and state boards, which in turn opened Pandora's box concerning the specter of drought in a prairie agricultural state.

But errors and omissions would hardly have escalated as they did in these and other preliminary matters had there not been ever-increasing pressure by opponents to drive wedges into the slightest openings in order to split the entire monolith asunder. No opportunity was ignored to do battle, as it was well understood that at some point the economic and political momentum favoring the completion of the plant would be overwhelming.

Cost projections, which began to be questioned seriously at the Wolf Creek construction permit hearings, were central and hugely significant, but difficult to debate to immediate, definitive conclusion. Estimates and assumptions there, as well as on the potential income side, were based on recent history, and a stronger argument could often be made by addressing the known past than to speculating that the unknown future would be fundamentally different. Governments dislike fundamental discontinuities as much as businesspeople considering long-term capital investments do. And there were major philosophic differences about how to calculate cost-benefit ratios. Therefore, the critics of the plant made their stands where they could, whether the problem debated was at the top of their list of dangers or not. There were few precedents nationally for actually stopping nuclear plant projects at any stage, especially after the initial construction permit had been issued. The familiarity of abandoned or interminably delayed projects in process, mired in unprecedented cost escalation and regulatory change, was a phenomenon that developed over the next decade with Wolf Creek's contemporaries because of histories paralleling in many ways the one unfolding in Kansas.

What were called the "limited appearance" statements from members of the public not specifically called as witnesses by the official intervenors—MACEA, Wolf Creek Nuclear Opposition, Inc., and the Kansas Attorney General's office—were taken November 12–13 at Burlington and January 26 in Kansas City. The rest of the construction permit hearings took place between January and June, all in Kansas City, except one session in Bethesda, Maryland. Each of the 50 contested issues, as well as many uncontested ones, were addressed by witnesses, and answered in official findings. The contested issues included prominently that the Environmental Report did not adequately evaluate the impacts of operation of Wolf Creek on the Neosho River and its impoundments; that the report failed to assess the effects on agriculture of the removal of the 10,500 acres of land from production; that the spent fuel pool proposed did not have adequate capacity to allow for unavailability of adequate reprocessing or off-site spent fuel storage; that it had not been adequately demonstrated that there would be uranium available to fuel the plant over its lifetime in the absence of a federal breeder reactor or plutonium recycling program; that the utilities' analysis of the cost of the plant was inadequate and was a severe underestimate, due to numerous claimed errors, from interest costs to lack of margin for safety requirement changes, underestimate of decommissioning cost and overoptimistic availability factor; that the applicants failed to consider sufficiently an alternative site; that they failed to study adequately the alternative of a coal-fired plant; that they overestimated demand growth in their projections; that various energy conservation strategies were not taken seriously enough; that alternative means of generating electricity, from synthetic fuels to combustion of trash to wind power to use of agricultural wastes might singly or together replace the need for Wolf Creek; and that the applicants' emergency evacuation plans were inadequate to protect the public health and safety. After the hearings proper closed the intervenors filed one more claim: that the utility did not have a valid contract for its water supply.[7]

Uranium supply (Contention I-12) was one of the first issues taken up in the technical portion of the hearings, and it was one of those that spilled over most and longest into the press. John Patterson of the U.S. Energy Research and Development Administration noted that supply estimates of any fuel were based on the state of knowledge at a point in time, and were usually underestimates of what turned out actually to be available. Imminent depletion of natural gas, for example, had been predicted since the early years of the twentieth century. Alfred James III, a petroleum geologist appearing for the intervenors, agreed with the history, but disagreed with the interpretation. "It should be apparent," he said, "that estimates of undiscovered potential resources represent a goal for exploration. . . . But to utilize such estimates as a resource base for an expensive facility that will be dependent upon the realization of such goals is scientifically and economically unsound."[8]

The issue was not only the price of uranium ($30 per pound at the time of the hearings and increasing rapidly), the shortage of reprocessing plants, and the possible control of supply by U.S. corporations and/or foreign cartels, but KG&E's specific lawsuit with Westinghouse over Westinghouse's repudiation of its original obligation to supply uranium for Wolf Creek.[9]

Westinghouse in the late 1960s and early 1970s followed industry practice by making contracts with numerous utilities, including KG&E, to deliver uranium at a set price (about $9–10 per pound) to plants that used its equipment. It was a competitive strategy against Babcock & Wilcox, Combustion Engineering, General Electric, and other vendors of nuclear equipment, and it seemed one of modest risk. The AEC in the mid 1950s had offered uranium for $8 per pound to all who would buy, but rescinded this in the mid 1960s because it had a 100 million pound inventory. The expected scenario was a long-term fuel glut at low prices. In the late 1960s uranium was being quoted at $9.50 per pound for delivery in the 1990s.

As with so many other things, however, there was a major change in the fuel context in the 1970s. In 1972 Australia halted production of its huge uranium supply, and shortly thereafter the Arab oil embargo encouraged nuclear plants and put pressure on U.S. supplies. Some countries banned uranium exports and some U.S. utilities began stockpiling it. In 1974 the price doubled to $15 per pound. In the fall of 1975, with the price still rising, Westinghouse defaulted on fuel contracts worth in the neighborhood of $2 billion. Its problem was that it had promised 74,000,000 pounds of uranium, owned only 14,500,000 pounds, and the futures market had turned against it. By 1976 the price was $40 per pound with 1980 futures at $51.25.

Westinghouse defended its action in two ways. First, it highlighted a section of the Uniform Commercial Code that stated that a delay in delivery or even nondelivery is not considered a breach of contract if made impracticable by an unforseen event. Second, it claimed that this unforseen event was an international "cartel" that had been formed by Gulf Oil and others to conspire to raise uranium prices. On the theory that the best defense was a good offense, Westinghouse filed a $5.6 billion damage suit against 29 companies alleged to be in the cartel. Utilities with contracts, including KG&E, claimed that Westinghouse had just guessed wrong and now refused to take responsibility. Twenty-seven utilities eventually sued Westinghouse, several joining in a class-action suit.[10] It was a field day both for attorneys and for antinuclear and anticorporate forces who concluded that the greedy had finally set upon each other.

As with so much else the fuel situation for Wolf Creek was more complicated and less dangerous than it seemed on the surface. Dr. Robert Hagen, who had been hired by Jesse Arterburn in 1974 to add expertise to the KG&E nuclear team, had considerable knowledge and experience with nuclear fuel. A native Kansan, he had a Ph.D. in nuclear engineering, experience with the nuclear navy and Babcock & Wilcox, and a tough-minded attitude that KG&E need not and should not be intimidated by the corporate size of Westinghouse in this matter. But while Hagen was certain the utility could prevail in litigation with Westinghouse and keep a good fuel contract and price, he recognized that Westinghouse's attempt to renege on the contract was a "rude awakening" that suggested a "whole new world" for utilities in relation to nuclear vendors. The assumption with KG&E and many other utilities was that companies like Westinghouse would act as brokers on fuel, just as they had once promised to provide turnkey, complete nuclear plants. All these illusions now came suddenly to an end, making it clear that the local utilities would have to hire their own nuclear teams and deal with these issues directly and expertly. As Hagen remembers it, the Westinghouse people walked out the back door after having informed him of their decision about Wolf Creek fuel and their various defenses, and the media walked in the front door "and asked me

95 questions about fuel supply." It was a tense and defining moment. Utilities around the country, dealing for the first time with primary radium suppliers, made some immense mistakes, spending multimillions for fuel that was never delivered. KG&E in all aspects of the evolving and changing fuel situation did far better than average. "Kansans are pretty tough fighters," Hagen said, "when someone comes down and really gives us a battle." Hagen himself too was knowledgeable and experienced, and it made a difference in this area that would have a positive cost impact for many years into the future.[11]

The intercorporate fight over fuel got considerable publicity locally, and did nothing to calm the fears of those who were arguing that Wolf Creek might cost consumers far more than anyone anticipated, both to build and to operate. KG&E's deal with Westinghouse was for seven years of fuel at a fixed price and an additional 13 years that provided for adjustments based on production cost and market price when delivered. Westinghouse was willing to abide by the "escalator" clause, but not by the first seven-year fixed price.[12]

This was an unwelcome complication just as the public spotlight was on the construction permit hearings. Bob Rives told the local press that even if there was a sharp rise in uranium prices it would have a relatively slight impact on the price of electricity: a doubling of uranium prices had about the same effect on ultimate power prices as a 10 percent rise in the price of coal at a coal plant. Glenn Koester, vice president for operations, said the company had "verbal assurances" from more than one company of an alternative supply. However, editors and intervenors at the hearing noted that the price had risen sharply, KG&E's "sure" supply had come unravelled, experts disagreed as much about the future supply of uranium as they did about that of oil and gas, and there could be more fuel surprises by the time Wolf Creek went on line.[13]

KG&E pursued an independent, unusual, and, it turned out, ultimately very successful strategy in the fuel controversy. It did not join the class-action suit, and did not accept distributions Westinghouse made from its uranium inventory as full settlement, but rather demanded a jury trial in Kansas. It acquired legal counsel who had lost an earlier case against Westinghouse, and who was hungry enough for a victory this time to go beyond the ordinary in effort. And it had by this time enough internal technical expertise to prepare a strong case.[14]

On October 1, 1975, the company brought suit against Westinghouse in the U.S. District Court at Wichita, one of the first utilities nationally to do so. It cited Westinghouse's unilateral repudiation of its June 12, 1974, contract with the Kansas utility to provide uranium for twenty years. The suit requested treble damages, saying that Westinghouse violated antitrust laws by trying to tie the sale of uranium to fabrication services, and asked that Westinghouse be forced to pay the extra costs of any uranium that KG&E had to buy from other sources.[15]

There was an additional wrinkle. An administrative judge in Washington, DC, ruled in January 1976 that KG&E would have to make the Westinghouse fuel contract public. The Atomic Safety and Licensing Board of the NRC confirmed this, saying that KG&E should give the terms to consumer groups and the Kansas Attorney General, who argued that such information was necessary to assess properly the ultimate cost of Wolf Creek. "The trend and tenor of court decisions are confirming the principle of the public's right to know," said the board, "and certainly electric power consumers are needing something more than secret pricing of the components of their electric rates." Kansas Attorney General Schneider agreed that revealing all would lead to "much more public awareness of the tremendous cost of these plants," and a move toward alternative energy.[16]

KG&E objected to making the contract public on the grounds that one of its terms was that it be kept confidential. Should that clause be violated by KG&E now, the contract would be void by its action and the chances of recovery from Westinghouse, at great benefit to Kansas electric customers, would be lost.[17] The struggle over confidentiality continued for a long time. An appeals board of the Nuclear Licensing Board, for example, ruled in April 1977 that the company would have to reveal the price part of the contract, though not the fuels fabrication part.[18] However, KG&E attorneys ultimately prevailed in both the confidentiality hearings and in the Westinghouse lawsuit.

In 1977 KCPL and KG&E formed their own fuel company, Utility Fuels Company, to utilize uranium mined in the Grants, New Mexico, region to guarantee supply, while at the same time pressing to collect the price differential from Westinghouse.[19] In 1978 the first court judgments came down against Westinghouse—the judges accepting the utilities' characterization of Westinghouse as a "corporate gambler."[20] The final 1980 settlement with the Kansas utilities, after a four-year dispute, was worth $94,000,000 in cash, uranium, and fuel fabrication and engineering services at a discount, representing a default on deliveries of 3.7 million pounds of uranium promised them by Westinghouse.[21]

In hindsight, KG&E's handling of the Westinghouse matter was recognized as having been brilliant. Its nuclear fuel costs, as a result, were a bargain for it and its ratepayers. As early as 1977, the Arthur Little firm, which did one of the first outside studies of KG&E management for the Kansas Corporation Commission, concluded that KG&E's fuel strategy was especially impressive.[22] The Cresap, McCormick and Paget study of 1980, after the final settlement was announced, was more fulsome in its praise: "KG&E's handling of the uranium contract dispute was very effective and showed great resourcefulness on the company's part."[23] The evidence of the effect both of the settlement and of later fuel management and wise playing of the market by KG&E for Wolf Creek was clear as the plant later operated. In 1992, for instance, Wolf Creek Station, Kansas, had the lowest fuel costs of any nuclear plant in the United States by a wide margin.[24] The roots of that statistic were in 1976.

In 1976, however, the final result on fuel was not predicted, there was great clamor for publication of all the "corporate secrets" involved, and journalists concluded that the Westinghouse case confirmed "how vacillating government officials, over-eager nuclear reactor salesmen, naive utility officials and profit-hungry uranium producers combined to create one of the most complex and lawsuit-filled debacles in the history of American business."[25] Phillip Knighton, an attorney and geologist in Wichita, filled most of a newspaper page in March 1976 with an argument that fuel supply for Wolf Creek was pure speculation—a "matter of statistical inference rather than geological fact." Even should uranium be available, Knighton said, some had estimated it would cost $100 to $200 per pound.[26] All of this did nothing to aid KG&E officials in trying to focus on one crisis at a time. "Our company," wrote President Ralph Fiebach, "is very aware of social trends which are growing throughout this nation. People increasingly are dissatisfied with business, government and most other institutions."[27]

The discussions at the permit hearings on uranium supply and price, as well as those on plant cost, decommissioning cost, and the accuracy of KG&E's demand projections often addressed the econometric analysis of the expert witnesses brought forward by MACEA. The first hearing witness to introduce the mathematical modeling typical of the econometric technique was M. Jarvin Emerson, who appeared on February 2 and discussed both uranium supply and the forecasting models. While admitting that "the state of the art of applied demand analysis of electricity is unsettled and will probably remain so for some time," and also that "econometric techniques rely upon data reflecting past experience," as did any other, Emerson presented a careful alternative scenario, which predicted that costs would be much higher than the utility said they would be.[28]

The testimony created much discussion about the econometric methodology in general, with the general conclusion that no matter how sophisticated the technique, the projections were only as good as the assumptions that drove them. There was also bias in favor of pragmatic calculations based on experience rather than theory. Chairman Samuel Jensch was blunt. "I don't know," he said, "but we get the impression that the econometric models are going to solve the world's problems. . . . Sometimes I wonder if those persons who are kind of close to the ground on these things, and give some horseback projections . . . are perhaps better than all these sheaves of paper, econometric models. . . . These company people . . . they know their products . . . and they have a feel for the market of the products of the companies they are serving. And they kind of throw out projections of need that I don't find reflected in all these coefficients of P_y and X and so forth. And the fellow knows whether the beans are going to sell in the fall, and how the beets are going to stack up in the refrigerator and that sort of thing." It was a homey analogy, and one that appealed strongly to the applied science side of the engineering model.

Bill Ward was quick on the uptake in that exchange. He hoped, he said, that all the econometric testimony would not be thrown out in favor of a sort of country boy seat-of-the-pants estimate. The plant would be around for a long time. "So really what you get down to is looking at some guesses based on statistics, not just the fellow that you know down the street."[29]

Basic attitude toward econometric analysis was important to MACEA, as two of its major expert witnesses, Dr. Malcolm Burns and Dr. Michael Viren, also made extensive use of it in their subsequent testimony. Both held Ph.D.s in economics. Viren, assistant professor of economics at the University of Missouri at Kansas City, had worked for Bechtel for four years and been control engineer at the San Onofre 1 Nuclear Station in California. Both men presented extensive econometric models addressing the future demand picture, the fuel supply question, the decommissioning costs, the financing costs and the probable efficiency of the completed plant.

Viren's cost-benefit analysis showed that the net benefit of the plant in 1982 would be minus $468 million with a 55 percent capacity factor and plus $242 million with a 75 percent capacity factor. The capacity factor estimated in the Environmental Report, a nominal 80 percent, Viren said was far too high. Experience indicated that early in a plant's life the capacity factor could be 67 percent, but was likely to decline to 40 percent. The intervenors assumed a 55 percent capacity factor for Wolf Creek and therefore a negative cost-benefit ratio. This negative benefit was especially true if the plant were built in 1982 and demand did not require it until 1990. Viren contended that neither a coal nor a nuclear plant was needed in 1982 and that by 1990, when a generating plant of some sort might be needed, coal would have the advantage. One of the utility's mistakes, he contended, was assuming the demand for electricity was price inelastic, and that it would not slow, possibly rapidly, with the price increases connected with the cost of a nuclear plant. The uranium supply question, he argued, was a "complex economic equilibrium problem" that could not be analyzed properly without sophisticated technique. Also, most large construction projects had a larger contingency allowance than KG&E was providing for Wolf Creek. There needed to be more account taken of the costs of retrofitting as nuclear technology and safety standards increased. Viren suggested 15 percent as an appropriate contingency allowance.[30] While Wolf Creek's performance, at least in its first seven years, indicates that the econometric capacity factor estimates were considerably too low, the contingency allowance suggestions as well as estimates of overall cost and potential demand growth turned out to be more accurate than those of the utility.

The cross-examination of Viren, like the early discussion with Emerson, turned as much on his methodology as on his conclusions. The panel studied an article by Lester Taylor of the University of Arizona titled "The Demand for Electricity: A Survey," which employed econometric methods, and it had explained to it Dr. Burn's Ph.D. dissertation "The Economic Effects of Horizontal Dissolution Decrease Under the Sherman Act: A Portfolio Analysis." The latter used a quantitative analysis of stock and bond prices to examine the impact of the 1911 Sherman Act dissolutions of the Standard Oil, American Tobacco, and American Snuff corporate groups. Still, these witnesses were vulnerable given the atmosphere of the hearings in that they did not have extensive practical experience. Burns had not before the current hearing made demand forecasts for any form of energy. Viren was not constantly in utility work, but had been, and said that keeping up with the literature remained a "hobby" of his.

But, while the utility attorneys tried to characterize the econometricians as impractical, the professors indicated that the utility people were backward. The econometric models of demand that Burns and Viren used built in as variables not only time, but the price of electricity, the price of gas, personal income, temperature, and others "in an attempt to disentangle the various components that determined electrical demand." They then applied a log linear model to this relationship, and came up with the possibility that over the next ten years electric demand could grow at a rate as low as 2.3 percent annually rather than the 6 percent range projected by the utility. When questioned about why the model would not have predicted accurately some actual figures that were already known, Viren's answer was that the average applied in the long term and its inaccuracy at spots did not invalidate it. The most telling question, however, was whether had this exercise been done in 1970 it would have taken account of the Arab oil boycott, double digit inflation, and the decline in real income. The point there was the one admitted by all—namely that the ability of models, no matter how sophisticated, to crunch out accurate forecasts depended on the accuracy of inputs about changes that cannot be forecast. "All forecasting models," Viren said, "whether it be a time trend extrapolation, or it be our econometric model, cannot predict the future."[31]

KG&E's witnesses on the way the company forecast demand and promoted use, such as James Lucas and William Woolery, argued that the utility methods of forecasting demand were a good deal more than rude guesses or straight extrapolations of past trends. Woolery, director of marketing services, pointed out that energy consumption forecasts included assumptions on economic conditions, population growth, price of electric power, household formation, price and availability of competitive fuel, and personal income. In the industrial sector each year the company contacted the 44 largest customers, plus other key industries that represented 65 percent of sales, to get their projections. Woolery himself had been involved directly with this since 1955.[32]

Lucas, the manager of system planning, went into even more detail on the mechanics of energy forecasting. He emphasized that "regardless of the particular method used in developing a forecast, i.e., econometric models, regression analysis, etc., the resulting forecast is based on the judgment of the forecaster." KG&E developed its system peak estimates "after first defining the conditions and constraints within which we believe KG&E and its customers can expect to live and to operate." The company did not do its forecasting in a vacuum. Since at least the east coast power blackouts of the 1960s both the National Electric Reliability Council and various regional groups of interconnected utilities were involved in forecasting. Each region might have a different, and partly unpredictable economic future, but if KG&E were badly off in the method and results of its projections, so were a lot of other utilities.[33]

In general, KG&E did a better than average job among utilities building nuclear plants in dealing with the expert witnesses at various phases of the hearings, from economists to health experts. Not only did the company produce good counterarguments, but it cross-examined rigorously and effectively. Dr. Robert Hagen, who did his time as an expert witness on behalf of KG&E and observed and advised on strategy concerning many of the witnesses in opposition, thought that there were a wide variety of motives for these people stepping forward other than true expertise. Sometimes in the case of an attorney it was a person that was going nowhere in his career, or who was slightly bored with it. Becoming involved in a nuclear case, often *pro bono publico*, gave both attention and stress that could be stimulating. In the case of economists, the opposition witnesses, Hagen thought, were often competent academics, but had little knowledge or experience with either utility financing or the technical requirements of nuclear power. Some expert witnesses, when they perceived they were out of their depth, backed off, and agreed to certify that KG&E's position was right in exchange for not being cross-examined. Others soldiered on, and were often ripped unmercifully on the stand. While all the details of these embarrassments were not evident to the public, they had their effect with the panels or commissions who heard all the hours of question and response in detail. And, in some important ways, it confirmed the basic validity of such a lengthy and thoroughgoing process despite its frustrations and costs.[34]

Contention I-18 was that the Environmental Report was inadequate because a coal plant, using either Wyoming or Kansas coal, was a better alternative than a nuclear plant. Donald McPhee of KCPL took on that question for the utilities. Not only did problems with LaCygne 1 throw doubt upon the most optimistic projections about the operating efficiency of coal plants, but there were considerable problems with transportation, mining, and the environmental effects of coal. KCPL had considered the possibility of a second coal plant at its Iatan location as an alternative to participation in Wolf Creek, and had studies done by Black & Veatch. The findings were that at expected load factors the nuclear plant would be more economical. "In my opinion," said McPhee, " coal is harder to come by than uranium, and we've heard lots of conversations about how tough it is to get uranium. But let me assure you that it's real tough to get coal." Like KG&E, KCPL was concerned about its current dependence on a single fuel, in its case coal.[35]

Few had anything nice to say about operating a coal plant, especially one with pollution equipment designed to get the sulphur and ash out. Steam generators wore out faster burning coal than gas or oil, and there was erosion from ash falling into the furnace and wearing the tubes thin. It was substantially different and in many ways more difficult than running a nuclear unit. McPhee summarized:

> The steam generator . . . is a very big complicated animal. You have to put a lot of fuel in. You have got to take a lot of ash out. You have got to have many sub-blowers on it that you keep in service to keep it deslagged. You have got to have the right amount of air mixture and fuel mixture. And it is a complicated mechanism that has to be finely tuned, kept finely tuned all the time. A nuclear unit, while they might be complicated and expensive to engineer and get into service, they are simple in principle. Their volume of reactor is small. It is a fraction of the size of the large steam generator. And it

is much simpler. It is much simpler in principle. It is a matter of water flowing through, picking up the heat, fuel rods inserted to control it. And it is far simpler. So if you think of the capacity factor or the cruise rating of the nuclear unit versus the fossil unit the nuclear unit is much better.

Bill Ward for MACEA did establish in cross-examination that nuclear units, because of radioactivity, were more difficult to repair and that, while coal plants took a lot of time with smaller things, with "nuclear units, if there is a problem, the problems can be very much more protracted."[36] And the panel was not altogether benign on some of the utility efficiency claims. When Jesse Arterburn quoted *Nucleonics Week* showing that some nuclear plants were running with capacity factors above 80 percent and quite a few in the mid 70 percent range, Jensch said there had been some variance between what this trade paper for the industry had reported and what NRC had analyzed. "I think Mr. Arterburn has backed off from being an economist," Jensch said. "He didn't want to get into that mess."[37]

Of course there was much debate about costs (Contention I-14 (g)). Not only were the official estimates of capital costs and operating costs questioned in detail, but there was much discussion of decommissioning costs. The latter, being 30 to 40 years in the future, and with no federal waste disposal site even for spent fuel rods, much less a disassembled plant, in view, was more problematical than any other prediction.

On costs in general the intervenors in retrospect look prescient, and the utilities' predictions badly flawed. The charge was that the contingency costs possibly were being severely underestimated, and that it was likely increased safety requirements would cause changes in design, operation, and associated maintenance that would increase the cost dramatically. The applicants' judgment here was that in the aggregate such changes would not affect plant costs by more than a few percent nor significantly affect the plant schedule. The SNUPPS design had a substantial margin of conservatism and "there is indication that regulatory requirements are becoming stabilized."

While this conclusion was based on such rational observations as the number of NRC guidebooks, it was given in the wake of the Brown's Ferry moratoriums and just three years before the accident at Three Mile Island. It turned out to be badly mistaken. Decommissioning costs were estimated by KG&E consultants at about

$3,000,000 in 1973 dollars, while the opposition surmised that the cost could end up being more than the cost of the plant itself.[38] The truth will not be known until the twenty-first century.

Safety and health questions occasioned some of the sharpest exchanges. Yes, the safety systems were sophisticated and redundant, but Jensch wanted to know what would happen if the operators happened to ignore the readings on the gauges. People were, after all people, not machines. In fact, this was to be a factor in the Three Mile Island accident. With one of the utility witnesses Jensch went through an entire scenario of a loss of coolant accident at 2 A.M. Suppose, he said, a tornado had struck at the time and all the phone lines were down—how would the plant reach the sheriff? How would evacuation be done? The answer was it would be by radio. "I understand that," Jensch snapped, "but you have a tornado and houses have been destroyed and the sheriff is out maintaining law and order. Are you expecting that there would always be a man there so he could pick up the word? And if he does get the word, what does he do?" What did the applicants intend to do for themselves? Sure, there were letters at the hospitals about this, but was that not just a formality? "Have you just got the letter that we are willing to cooperate," Jensch asked KG&E's Gary Boyer, "and you are willing to cooperate and everybody is cooperating, but you don't know what you are doing?"[39] This time Jensch's pragmatic, common sense approach was working against the utility position on safety through systems, just as much as it had against the theoretical certainties of the Ph.D. econometricians.

Jesse Arterburn intervened in the middle of Boyer's testimony on this as, he said, "I don't like to see a good man browbeat." Arterburn was more assertive, but Jensch hardly backed down on the issue. "I just want an answer," Jensch said. "If you don't give it, you may get the same kind of treatment."

Arterburn went through all the evacuation arrangements at SEFOR and detailed what had been done at Wolf Creek. Jensch responded that there was a drill at Northern States Power a few years ago that was a disaster. It was a nice sunny day and the sheriff had gone fishing. Cars broke down, telephone lines were out, and the whole nonemergency exercise looked like something from the Keystone Cops, or, as Jensch phrased it, "a shotgun going off in the orchard." KG&E's attorneys said that Jensch had gotten his account of the Minnesota drill direct from Ralph Nader, and that was not the way it happened at all. Jensch countered that he got it from *Nucleonics Week*, the same journal KG&E had been quoting to him. The chairman eventually did agree that Arterburn had experience and a plan. "I think your experience, perhaps, with training and development will be a very substantial contribution to the programming for Wolf Creek, if Wolf Creek has any fuel to burn and if there is any water."

"There will be, sir," Arterburn shot back. "Just have confidence it will happen."

"Like Christmas," said Jensch, "we keep waiting?"

"We don't have to wait."[40]

Contention I-14 (a) was that the plant would be a threat to the health of people who worked at it or lived near it, and that the costs of adjusting for this were underestimated. George Leroy, the author of a number of articles about the effect of radiation in humans, based partly on studies of Japanese atomic bomb survivors, criticized the intervenors' contention here. They had, he said, used studies incorrectly "and have offered a greatly inflated estimate of the risk associated with occupational exposure to radiation." Leroy estimated that the death rate from cancer among nuclear station employees would be no greater than other electric power generating stations. He was critical of what he called the "linear hypothesis,"—namely that if radiation is dangerous at high levels of exposure this danger can be used as a point on a curve to predict what smaller doses of radiation might produce. "In simple terms, it is like saying that a bottle of aspirin tablets, 100 aspirin tablets, will kill a certain number of the children who consume 100 aspirin tablets. And that therefore, one aspirin tablet has the potentiality of one-one hundredth of the amount of a whole bottle full. We know intuitively that this is not true. . . ."

Bill Ward in his cross-examination asked whether the mechanism by which ionizing radiation caused cancer was really parallel to that by which aspirin caused injury.

"Well, I'm not sure of course. This is the essence of analogy."

"Well, is this analogy you used to aspirin tablets helpful with respect to—in understanding the mechanism; or is it simply an analogy which often allays the fear of say, an uneducated person or member of the public?"[41]

Leonard Sagan, a medical doctor from California, argued that the public health impacts "ought to be included in the cost-benefit analysis even though they will not be direct costs of the plant." Sagan had written an article in a 1972 issue of *Science* magazine entitled "Human Costs of Nuclear Power," leading to the conclusion that one man-rem of radiation cost $30. However, he said that Wolf Creek's proposed radiation levels were so low that "such a plant could operate for more than a thousand years producing less than a single case of cancer." The risk from a coal plant, with its many chemical effluents, would be far greater to health. Several witnesses quoted a paper by F. T. Sowby called "Some Risks of Modern Life." Sowby studied the risks to people in various occupations. It showed that the risk of occupationally related death for trawler fishermen in the United Kingdom was 5 percent. Coal mining in the United States had a 5 percent risk. For all U.S. industries together the risk was 1 percent. Based on statistics of operating nuclear plants in the United States, the risk of death from working at such a plant was 0.3 percent, or less than a third of the general industrial average, and one-fifteenth the risk from the coal plant that was the utility alternative. While no academic will ever say never, Sagan said "we know more about the hazards and magnitudes of risks associated with radiation exposure than we know about any other industrial or nonindustrial exposure, whether it be chemical or physical." No member of the public should get over 10mr (millirems) a year from Wolf Creek. Watching TV or flying to Denver could result in similar doses, whereas one would get 1,000 times that from a GI series at the doctor or spinal x-rays, and people had been treated with 6,000 times that with no link to further cancer. Sagan was critical when attorney Ward introduced research by Robert Poe suggesting that small fractions of a millirem could be carcinogenic. Sagan called the risk in actual practice from a nuclear plant "trivial, insignificant."[42]

The intervenors called Dr. Jacob Frenkel on the health question. Frenkel had been in the struggle a long time and had an A.B. in zoology from the University of California at Berkeley, an M.D. from the University of California at San Francisco School of Medicine and a Ph.D. in comparative pathology from the University of California at Berkeley. He had used radiation as a tool in research for some of his 113 articles. Frenkel cited the BEIR (Biological Effects of Ionizing Radiation) report, done recently by the National Academy of

Sciences, to indicate that the Wolf Creek plant could cause one excess cancer per 5–22 years of operation. "Whether this is a negligible number depends on one's set of values. Certainly prospective plant workers should be aware of these risk levels." Over the life of the plant, excess cancers could be from 1.34 to 6, costing $20,000 each to cure. There might be genetic effects that would not turn up for years. Wastes, such as strontium-90, cesium-137, and plutonium-239 "should be of ethical concern to citizens and to the power companies who generally take pride in their concern with public welfare. Would it not be better to manage the presently unsolved problems of nuclear power and learn from existing reactors before building additional ones and compounding the problem. . . . I feel that we should prudently be on the conservative side; . . . —even though it has been stated that the proper study of mankind is man—I would not like to use, to risk, more human beings to find out these results."[43]

To that Jensch was his usual irascible self. "I think one of the problems I have about all these groups that get together and are scientific all of a sudden, so they get their typewriter and crank out a report, and everybody says, 'Oh, look, we've got a scientific report from the Blue Goose Creek Alley Crowd; let's see what they say.' And we're supposed to be appalled or surprised or something." Jensch took a dim view of volunteer groups setting standards for government agencies. Nevertheless, the exchanges before him on these various issues were on the record and available to history for what they might come to signify.[44]

There was testimony and countertestimony on every comma and dash of the environmental report beyond these major concerns. Most got about the attention expected, small. There was, however, one exception—the question of water. Few doubted that water would be a concern in the hearings, but it would have been difficult to predict in advance how the rhetoric surrounding the water issue would seize the media, or how the politics of it would occupy the state legislature. During the months of the construction hearings a storm of considerable dimension broke over KG&E and Wolf Creek water rights for Redmond Reservoir—how these were obtained and what the effect of keeping the nuclear plant cooling lake filled would be on a state that had known deep droughts.

While the exchanges on water at the formal hearings were extensive, they were technical and not very quotable.[45] Not so with the debates in the legislature and in the daily and weekly newspapers of Kansas. In January 1976, just as the Kansas City hearings got underway, there were headlines about the "Neosho River Water Grab" that an editor called "a threat to the welfare and indeed the very existence of the river valley and southeast Kansas." KG&E's deal with the State Water Resources Board, it was charged, had been irregular and then had been covered up. In the worst case drought scenario the contract provided for use of Neosho River water for the cooling lake in addition to that normally impounded in the Redmond Reservoir. However vigorously KG&E denied that it would ever take or need to take water for the power plant that was needed for drinking or wildlife, there was little trust by some groups in the corporate good will. "Utilities, of course, operate in mysterious ways that are wondrous to behold, " wrote Clyde Reed, the crusading editor of the *Parsons Sun*. "There is small surprise that the utilities in this case pursue a course of utter caution and silence."[46]

The water issue had the strategic advantage of providing leverage that could be applied at the state level concerning the development of a plant that mostly had only to satisfy federal regulators. A time when representatives of the Nuclear Regulatory Commission were in the state seemed a perfect time to join the dual sovereignty issue. Why should the utilities have any of Kansas's precious water, went the refrain, just so they "can keep their hot, hot radioactive Nukes cool."[47] Fred Weaver, a legislator from southeast Kansas, placed before those at the state house a large photo of the Neosho River nearly dried up in a state of drought, and started his campaign from that point.[48] If the Kansas legislature allowed the water contract to stand or be resubmitted, said Dale Lyon of the Kansas Farmer's Union, it would be "perhaps the most shameful hour in modern times for the government of Kansas."[49]

The passion grew by what it fed on. Legislation was introduced at the state house in January 1976 to block the proposed nuclear plant by nullifying without replacement the contract between the Kansas Water Resources Board and KG&E covering the cooling water a nuclear plant absolutely needed.[50] The *El Dorado Times* called KG&E's contract for water "an insufferable demand." It was brazen and outrageous, the editor wrote, to possibly deny small towns depending on the Neosho River their domestic water in times of drought so that the nuclear plants might survive. "Folks don't understand all the nuclear mysteries. But they realize fully and perfectly what happens when water is scarce. . . . Trickery of this sort can well breed the suspicion of solid deceit."[51]

By Feburary there were charges that the chairman of the Kansas Water Resources Board, Keith Martin, had a conflict of interest because his law firm had performed services for a public utility buying water from the state for Wolf Creek. The attorney general moved to investigate, and the governor promised to look into questions surrounding the chairman and at least one other member, Frank Groves of Arkansas City, who had listed substantial interest in KG&E and KCPL in his financial disclosure statement.[52] Groves couldn't believe that the question was even being asked. "We hadn't been lucky enough," he said, "to sell any water, until the Kansas Gas and Electric Company offer was presented and we accepted it."[53] Senator Ross Doyen felt the same way, and threw all his considerable influence into negotiations to be sure that some contract for the Redmond water was approved. Doyen did not want the state to subsidize the utility by in any way giving the water away, but personally believed that the nuclear plant would be seen as a "godsend" one day. Doyen himself had an engineering background, and felt much of the opposition was based on simple fear of the unknown.[54]

Others went further in analyzing motives. Senator Vincent Moore, a Republican from Wichita and one of the most active defenders of the plant in the state legislature, said the water issue was a smoke screen, and that opponents of the nuclear plant were deliberately distorting the facts in their desperation to stop the plant. "They're out to kill the power plant," Moore concluded, and questioning the legality of the water contract was a way to skin that cat.[55] A state senator from western Kansas agreed that nuclear power was "a highly emotional subject; consequently those stirred with emotions about the nuclear power, combined with the emotional reactions to water, will bring highly charged hearings pushed by publicity-seeking radicals."[56]

Debates over proper use of natural resources and appropriate technology had been a theme in Kansas history, and will continue to be in the future. There was the controversy between 1905 and 1910 over piping gas through and out of Kansas. It was widely charged then that leaking gas would ruin the fertility of farms for a quarter of a mile on each side and that the peril of bursting pipes would force abandonment of homes in wide regions. Some thought the gas lines would make a wilderness of the state. Before that came a similar furor over the earlier coming of railroads to the state. It was said then that cultivation of land in sight of the railroad lines would be impossible because horses would stampede at fire-belching locomotives and bursting boilers would endanger homes. One observer concluded that "fifty years from now, the threats of desolation from Nuclear Power will seem as absurd as those of destruction from railroads and pipe lines seem now."[57]

Be that as it may, the *Emporia Gazette*'s letters section, called "The Wailing Place," was filled with fearful invective in the first months of 1976 on the theme of water as related to nuclear power. Rep. David Miller, Democrat from Parsons, called the water contract "a damned outrage. I don't see how they [the water board] would have the authority to do it. After all, the river is for public use."[58]

The counter was that water priorities were set by the Water Appropriations Act, passed by Kansas in 1945, and that water flow would be adjusted during the worst droughts so there would be no change in the downstream flow. No drought in history had been bad enough to change this. Meanwhile, the KG&E contract for the excess impounded at Redmond in normal times would bring the state a profit of between $7 and $20 million as contrasted with a cost to the state at present to maintain the extra capacity (15% of the total) in the reservoir, which had been requested of the federal constructors of the facility specifically to have water to sell to industry.[59] The state was obligated to pay the federal government $7.9 million for the construction of the extra capacity, and this income would help to do it.[60] State representative John Jefferson of Leavenworth added that the Wolf Creek sale was the only sale to industry from a state reservoir to date, yet Kansas had planned for 13 such industrial impoundments and had completed six reservoirs already with such "excess" water capacity. The total available would be 1 million acre feet, or more than 330 billion gallons, at a cost to the state of over $110 million. Even with maximum contracted use, the federal storage at John Redmond would maintain a flow of 21 million gallons a day into the lower Neosho. If that were not enough, upstream were Marion and Council Grove reservoirs, with 62,700 acre feet of unsold public use storage and more than 10 million gallons a day available for stream flow maintenance. These water decisions would allow Kansas industrial growth in the future, said Jefferson, "but not if the Legislature plays games with individual water contracts. Legislative review was intended to guide major policy decisions, not to administer the water plan from the Legislature."[61]

Bob Rives of KG&E stated the press releases saying that the utility had applied for rights to all the water in the Neosho River were incorrect. The contract was for 80,000 acre feet per year to be diverted at a maximum rate not to affect vested rights and prior apropriation rights. The water would be sold unpurified, and KG&E would be responsible for paying for transporting it to the reservoir from the river only at times of high flow. Some communities were worried because they were using more water already than their legal entitlement, but there would never arise a situation where they could not draw to their total need.[62]

That was a good explanation. But where something as basic as water was involved, no amount of assurance from a corporation was sufficient. Some of the greatest verbal and legal battles in the history of the American West, continued right through the twentieth century, have been and are over water rights. These questions cut to the core of development as well as simple survival in the semi-arid regions, which Kansas bordered on the east. So there were headlines, such as "Utilities Use of Water May Bring Water Shortage." Or, even subtler: "KGE Spokesman Denies Power Plant Will Dry Up Water supply."

In February Keith Krause, the executive director of the state water resources board, was called to appear before the full Kansas house chamber—a very unusual procedure. Krause told the house that the Wolf Creek contract would not cause the Neosho River to dry up, and answered charges by opponents. He said that he wished he could make more deals just like the one with KG&E.[63] Both the senate and house energy and natural resources committees, however, proceeded to schedule public hearings on the topic.[64] In mid February Attorney General Schneider drafted a legal opinion declaring the water contract with KG&E, signed in January, invalid and unenforceable due to conflicts of interest by state water board members Martin and Groves. After a series of meetings with KG&E attorney Ralph Foster, the attorney general agreed he would, with Foster, seek an early review of the matter by the Kansas Supreme Court, but stood by his conclusions. The opinion raised a question in the minds of federal officials then holding construction permit hearings whether federal courts might uphold Schneider's ruling in a year or two and throw a wrench into the NRC licensing works. Naturally also it affected proceedings in the state legislature that turned on upholding the water contract.[65]

Foster and Schneider met with Supreme Court justice Harold Fatzer for ten minutes on February 20. Foster could not get Schneider to bring the case before the court. A *quo warranto* proceeding by Schneider would be in effect challenging his own action. The court could not act unless someone brought action.[66] Eventually KG&E filed a petition asking the high court to overturn Schneider's opinion, and the Supreme Court agreed to take original jurisdiction without the usual appeal process through the district court. Both sides were sensitive. Foster commented the attorney general was "an unusual animal." Schneider complained that the hurry-up in the courts might forestall needed legislative action, and he called the utility's case, which contended that there could be no conflict of interest because the price the water board could take for water was set by law, "contrived."[67] "I feel," said Schneider, "as if the train just left and I got hit with the caboose."[68]

The politics of the matter was labyrinthine. Kansas governor Robert Bennett, who in contrast to Attorney General Schneider was generally a supporter of the Wolf Creek project, announced on the heels of the attorney general's opinion that he planned no action to oust members of the Water Resources Board for conflict of interest, though the matter could be brought before the Governmental Ethics Commission. Bennett called the water issue a "technical fly in the ointment," but admitted that ultimately it would be up to the courts: "My compensation doesn't include legal advice to the state."[69] Bennett went further, however, and endorsed nuclear power. In a press conference that soon followed the nationally publicized resignation of three nuclear engineers from General Electric in protest of nuclear power, Bennett argued that Kansas ought to welcome some nuclear power. "I think we are in an energy ethic," he said. "Everybody expects to drive to work, to live in lighted and heated homes, everyone is using energy in everything they do. We have to utilize everything we have available to satisfy the energy demands of the public. . . . In my opinion, a nuclear power plant can be built which would be safe." The water question would have to be satisfactorily resolved.

Probably the statement that had the largest impact on the public imagination regarding the water fight, however, was not the governor's, but one made in February 1976 by the U.S. Fish and Wildlife Service. After a study of the issue an official of that agency wrote a letter to the NRC that was intercepted by the Associated Press. In the letter the Wildlife Service official speculated that in extreme dry weather, with the power plant water contract in effect, the Neosho River could become "disconnected pools," and downstream fauna and flora could be extremely affected.[70] That brought people to town meetings in the Neosho valley, and forced KG&E to send teams to attend these meetings. "I think," said one onlooker, "we've stirred up some interest in water."[71]

The public looked to the legislature, which must reject or modify the water contract within sixty days of its signature, that is by March 11, 1976, or have it go into effect.[72] Should the contract be rejected, the law was such that another contract could not be submitted until the 1977 legislative session, causing a year's delay in the plant.[73] Late in February, SB 986 was introduced into the legislature at the request of State Senate President Ross Doyen. It permitted the state water resources board to renege on the contract and submit a new contract to the legislature in its current session. The bill provided for a 30 rather than a 50-year contract as originally written and recommended adjustments in the charges every ten years.

"I'm just afraid," said Doyen, "we're going to sit here with a barrel of water and nobody to take a dipper full of it."[74] "Here we are," said a state representative, "the first time we try to approve a contract under the procedures we set up under the Water Rights Act and request the additional storage capacity, saying they can't have the water. It reminds me of a man dying of thirst in the desert when he has water because he is afraid to use it because of something that might happen in the future."[75]

KG&E prepared its employees and the media with a "Fact Sheet Concerning Water Supply for the Wolf Creek Generating Station." A Kansas City group, said the document, "is lobbying to attempt to have the Kansas legislature disapprove a contract under which the state has agreed to provide water from John Redmond Reservoir for use in generating electricity." MACEA, the utility said, was urging people to write their legislators on the issue and then to inform MACEA how the legislators responded. A question being asked legislators was whether it was wise to sell Redmond's water reserves to a single user. KG&E's response was that "the question is moot. Whether the water is sold to one user or to several, the effects would be the same on Redmond and the Neosho. What's very important is what would happen if the power suppliers cannot obtain the water." It was easier to ensure that the state not run out of water, the utility said, than that it not run short on energy. Replacing the Wolf Creek facility with several smaller plants could end up using more land and water, the very resources the intervenors were trying to conserve. "Actually," went the internal document, "MACEA makes few bones about the reason it wants legislators to say 'no' to the contract. It opposes nuclear power and even suggests that the water contract might be workable if a coal plant were to be constructed on Wolf Creek instead of a nuclear facility." The group's contention that coal plants used less water than nuclear plants was, KG&E said, "off badly." What was happening was that the opponents were trying to make "a nuclear issue out of a non-nuclear matter." That should not happen. "The power suppliers who have contracted for the water with the state will need the water whether they build a nuclear plant, coal plant, or, for that matter, a solar plant. The contract should stand on its own merits."[76]

An expanded version of this document was released to a number of newspapers.[77] Shortly, in a letter to employees from KG&E President Ralph Fiebach, the company recommended that employees write their state legislators with their views on the water question. The company's first application for water, in 1968, had been its very first act toward building the Wolf Creek plant, and it would be especially ironic if denial of that water were to be the event that ended the quest.[78]

One of those who did write was Jack King, KG&E's land condemnation expert. He got a swift and straight reply from his representative, Ruth Luzzati. She was opposed to the water contract being approved by the legislature at this time, she said, "because I have carefully studied the contract itself. Have you?" It was, she said, not well drawn and the terms were not in the interest of the people of Kansas. "It is grossly unfair for the representatives of the Utilities and the Chamber of Commerce and the *Eagle-Beacon* to imply that those of us who oppose the water contract are obstructing growth, progress, new jobs, etc. We are, to the contrary, trying to do what we were elected to do—protect the interests of the people of Kansas, their water supply and ultimately their pocketbooks."[79]

Luzzati, while not the issue leader in the legislature (that role was played by Fred Weaver in the House and John Simpson in the Senate), was part of a coalition of legislators that shared a growing consensus and concern about aspects of Wolf Creek's progress. It was not necessarily an antinuclear coalition *per se*, she says, but Bill Ward and others from MACEA were definitely a lobbying presence and were doing a good deal of education in the legislature to counter the "tireless" lobbying of the KG&E group. "The halls swarmed with KG&E people," beginning in this period, Luzzati recalls, and there was as well an organized letter-writing campaign by employees, of which King's letter was a part. Her interpretation of this zeal was partly that the company and its people had made Wolf Creek the prime event of their lives, and had staked fame and reputation on its success. There was an early stereotype of the opposition as a radical longhaired fringe group of ecological extremists, and it was during the water fight that it became more clear to the media that those with serious doubts were much more varied than that, and included a good number of legislators.

According to Luzzati, the water issue was a "strategy" to call wide attention to the Wolf Creek issues, and water was concentrated upon because water issues always created broad interest in prairie Kansas. Publicity about the water contract could not only point up some possible conflicts of interest between state officials and big business, but could play on the "giveaway" price in the original contract and the drama of drought disasters and the drying up of small town industry. Water, she thought, had "more sex appeal" than any other state issue, and to connect it with the nuclear power issue at this point was to guarantee that the Wolf Creek question would be front page news.[80]

Luzzati's Wolf Creek file reveals something of what legislators were hearing and doing at the time. She collected clippings of Wolf Creek from all over the state, and regularly replied to newspaper editorials about it. For example, when the *Wichita Eagle* in February 1976 ran an editorial entitled "We May Need It," Luzzati shot a letter to the editor. The editorial had contained a mild threat: "Of course if there are future brownouts or blackouts because alternative concepts of energy production weren't developed in time, the legislators who blocked the Wolf Creek project—if indeed they do—will be safe. Voters will have forgotten who the key opponents were. And, meanwhile, their opposition to the project makes them very popular with the growing number of Kansans who like to fear the worst because fearing the worst is very stylish these days." Luzatti's letter, never published, charged the editor with "gliding over" the facts in the water controversy, namely, "should we approve the contract to give that plant a 50-year supply of water at questionable terms with no legislative review of the effects, not only on the people who depend on the Neosho River's flow, but on the entire state." She was, she pointed out, one of the sponsors of HCR 5043 disapproving the contract, and wished an investigative reporter would ask her for more information. "I must disagree with your editorial's assumption that this is a popular position to take.... In the long run, I can face up to being accused of contributing to a 'brown out' much better than being accused of selling out the rights of Kansas citizens to their water. Brown outs are bad; dust bowls are worse."[81]

There were also in Luzzati's file clippings from around the country on nuclear power and nuclear power contractors, as well as ephemera—pamphlets and broadsides—from local opposition groups like Wolf Creek Nuclear Opposition, Inc. This material was filled with facts, and the pamphlets regularly took the form of "did you know," or "we would like the public to know." Added to that were many letters from constituents, fellow legislators, and lobbyists, as well as notated excerpts from hearing testimony—in short, evidence of considerable unemotional preparation for a completely rational battle on the issues.

A good part of the letters do reflect views opposing the nuclear plant completion in general and not merely concern about the water cost or supply. There is no question either that there was a network forming of people willing to write letters to legislators and to company officials and to appear at hearings. "We are turning up some very interesting data as a result of our resolutions to disapprove the water contract," Luzzati wrote a constituent. "We have to work like pulling elephants' teeth to get it, however, even from our own state employees, let alone the utilities and other interested parties." To another she wrote that "we must have hearings and public debate on these matters or we are not acting as responsible representatives of the people, in my opnion."[82] Later in the spring she wrote that "I think there is a good chance of the water contract having to be re-negotiated on better terms for the state, but the heart of the problem may not be addressed."[83]

The "heart of the problem" was no doubt the broader issue of having nuclear power at all. Hearing testimony on the water question included, for example, considerable argument about the appropriateness of fission power for Kansas.[84] The perception of water being attached to the larger nuclear issue in fact offended some legislators who were otherwise allies in the fight against the original water contract. For example, Jim Lawing, a house member from Wichita who was pushing bills to change the water contract, wrote one of his constituents that, while the initial water contract was a bad one, the debate on it was a catspaw for something different. "While I have strong reservations about the efficacy of a nuclear economy," Lawing wrote, "I do not believe in using the water contract as a collateral attack on the issue. It is not for the legislature to vote for or against nuclear power. That issue is before the Atomic Safety and Licensing Board, and I am happy to leave that responsibility in its capable hands. But I don't believe the people of Kansas ought to write a bad contract."[85] Shades of opinion were many and the issue was hardly the bipolar one the press, in the interest of simplification, might wish for.

KG&E's position got an ally from an unexpected source when Maverick Cole, a high school student from Burlington, wrote his local paper expressing the view that the younger generation, who had to worry about where jobs were coming from, ought to favor the new plant. Maybe some of the opponents locally were prejudiced about other races moving in with the construction workers. Would the plant not lower taxes for locals? And if John Redmond was built for flood prevention and in case of drought, "what about the billions and billions of gallons of unused water flowing down the Neosho River every year. Someone might as well be using that unused water, why just let the water go to waste when it could be used." Cole suggested that everyone needed a more open mind "instead of just thinking of themselves, but for other people and the community."[86]

The other side was equally active. The Sierra Club in 1975 had called for a moratorium on all nuclear plants, and was active in the Wolf Creek issue.[87] On February 12, 1976, it sent an "Action Alert" letter to its Kansas members about the Wolf Creek water contract. The contract, the letter said, was "ruinous" and would "render the John Redmond reservoir nothing but a big cooling pond for the nuclear plant." To stop it "instant and massive help is needed statewide." Sierra members were urged to appear at February 18 hearings before the state house and senate committees on energy and natural resources. The utilities were determined to "go nuclear," and these "stockholder-owned, dividend-paying" corporations had negotiated a 50-year contract to take 9.6 billion gallons a year from the reservoir at a price of only 6 cents per thousand gallons. This amount was the entire John Redmond allocation for industry and 55.85 percent of the total water storage in the reservoir. "None of the water withdrawn from the reservoir would be returned to the river or the reservoir even somewhat warmer; most of it would evaporate while cooling the reactor." Downstream communities, "fisherpersons," and hunters would suffer. "Some legislators may feel that they aren't involved and tend to regard it casually. However, if all the water supply water of John Redmond is sold to the power companies for the WCNGS, no body of water in the state will be 'safe' from future power plants and heavy industry through the precedent set at Redmond." The Sierra Club, Kansas Chapter, said that it did not want Kansas to run out of abundant, clean, and cheap electricity, but that it did not have to be generated by a nuclear plant in Kansas. "'Scare' tactics by the utilities already have begun. Many people don't care where their electricity comes from, as long as it comes. Such apathy is our worst problem. . . ." John Redmond Reservoir, the letter concluded, was built at taxpayer expense for flood control, water supply, water quality control, recreation, and fish and wildlife. "It was *not* intended as a huge public subsidy of a private power business."[88] Commented an editor in El Dorado: "Sic 'em Sierra!"[89]

The step of voiding of the water resources board contract while at the same time amending the state water contract law to allow a new contract to be approved was taken by the state legislature in early March, while the State Supreme Court was hearing arguments.[90] On March 8, in a seeming reverse of at least an informal promise, the Supreme Court dismissed the water proceeding, stating that it did not have jurisdiction and that the matter would have to be heard first in the district court.[91] Not a few editors were happy. The *Parsons Sun* concluded that "I don't think that KG&E . . . should receive any special treatment just because it is one of the largest corporations in the state of Kansas."[92]

Debate in the legislature was emotional, and support or opposition did not line up purely on partisan lines. Representative Arthur Douville of Overland Park, a Republican, made an impassioned statement implying that Wolf Creek was a kind of successor to the atomic bomb. Fred Weaver of Baxter Springs, a Democrat, took the same line. "We got us a pickup load of plastic milk jugs," he said, "and each time [we] drive by John Redmond we're going to get some water. They're not going to get all of it."[93]

Compromises were eventually reached. A new water contract was submitted by the water resources board and was signed by Governor Bennett on March 11. This version amended the 50-year term to 40 years and provided for renegotiation of the price every ten years. It was forwarded by the state water board with Groves and Martin, whose interest had been in question, abstaining. There had been a strong move in the legislature to reduce the amount from 26 million to 22 million gallons a day, but that failed. The legislature theoretically had another 20 days to reject this contract or let it stand. Not surprisingly, MACEA not only filed an additional claim about water with the NRC, but in June entered a suit—ultimately dismissed without a hearing—against the validity of the new water contract in the Shawnee County District Court.[94] Some who accepted the resolution of the question blamed KG&E for not getting the proper information about downstream water supply to the public earlier.[95] However, the *Arkansas City Traveler* expressed a common view of both legislators and public in saying that "enough taxpayer dollars and official time have been spent postponing the inevitable."[96]

The great water fight of 1976 is an interesting case study. It was not the first, and would be far from the last of the holding actions and diversions that characterized the ponderous progress of Wolf Creek toward completion. However, it was the last hurrah and the final theater played out before the Jensch panel when Washington came to Kansas for the hearings that spring, and it indicated strongly that the "proven" procedure on approval of nuclear plants would not go forward in Kansas without internal changes and external pressures.

The closing of the hearings proper, after fourteen weeks of acrimony, was on a dismal, wet, late April day in 1976. The attorneys hauled out their records in briefcases and even shopping carts, and awaited the last of the transcript. One NRC staffer said: "Everybody was dead, simply dead."

Some thought there was more understanding, even unity, than when the hearings started. Others were unsure. It was clear to all, however, that the battle would continue, and that the time, energy, and cost expended by the utility on the public relations and political aspects of the plant would be much greater than initially expected. "Far more happened in the lengthy hearings on Kansas's first nuclear power plant," said an observer, "than the 150,000 sheets of paper on which they're recorded can ever show."[97]

When the hearings started in January, there were those who said that construction work on the plant could begin in May.[98] In fact the final conclusions of the panel did not appear until July, and the final and full construction permit to undertake work at the Burlington site was not issued until May 12, 1977. In May of 1976 Governor Jerry Brown of California was talking about the "politics of lowered expectations" while his father Pat advised never to underestimate the power of the nuclear intervenors anywhere, anytime. "These are well-meaning people," the former governor said. "But they're like the Spanish Inquisition. They want to get you on the rack."[99]

Bob Rives, spokesman for KG&E, knew the feeling. In the long interim between the end of the hearings and the first movement of earth near Wolf Creek, he could only exclaim to the hundreds of interested parties, from contractors to bankers, who asked about the schedule: "We're working towards the beginning of work."[100]

5

Where the Hell is Beto Junction?

Like Frodo the hobbit, I would prefer a less risky life.
—Mildred Clapp in *Kansas City Star*, Feb. 20, 1977

I don't want to seem unfriendly. But the less said about Wolf Creek the better. It doesn't matter whether you're for it or against it—it's just better to keep your mouth shut.
—Sales clerk in Burlington, Jan. 30, 1977

We're not trash or riffraff, but human beings with feelings just like you people that were born and raised here.
—Betty Brown, wife of Wolf Creek worker, in *Coffey County Reporter*, Jan. 12, 1978

Beto Junction is a truck stop on I-35 northeast of Emporia, at the east edge of the Flint Hills. Its name is a combination of Burlington, Emporia, Topeka, and Ottawa—any of which may be conveniently reached by making the proper turn from Beto Junction. The place is known for abundant food, homemade pies, convenient gas, and a gritty Kansas working-class ambiance. Most people who have traveled between Wichita and Kansas City with any frequency have stopped there at some time or other, but many would not admit it. Therefore, one of the best-selling items in a store filled with rubber spiders, sunglasses, and pecan logs is a T-shirt with the legend "Where the Hell is Beto Junction?"

There is one other place you reach by turning off the interstate at Beto Junction—the Wolf Creek plant. When the construction permit hearings concluded with no obvious major embarrassments to the plan outlined in the Environmental Report a lot more people, regionally and nationally, began asking the "Where the Hell" question. The plant construction contractors, who had been standing by for two years as the regulatory processes ran their course, began in 1976 to search for manpower, to think about housing in places like New Strawn, Kansas, and to consult highway maps of the Sunflower State.

Each utility involved in SNUPPS was represented by one member on the SNUPPS Management Committee, which had the overall policy responsibility for plant design. In September 1973 SNUPPS created a company called Nuclear Projects, Inc. (NPI), headed by Nicholas Petrick, to advise the member utilities on management in the field utilizing all the experience resident in SNUPPS. In November 1973 SNUPPS set up a number of specialized committees, the most active being that for technical and quality assurance.

These committees represented a significant, formal, and ongoing national network among utilities devoted to sharing technical and management information and experience of all kinds. Nuclear plants have been criticized for being unique creations constructed in isolation. But to a great degree, despite its midlands location and relative distance from major concentrations of nuclear plants, this was not true of Wolf Creek. SNUPPS and its ongoing mechanisms were a major departure from "business as usual" in nuclear plants and one that would have enormous positive impact on the Kansas project.

As early as January 1973, just as the Wolf Creek plant was announced publicly, committees received proposals from five vendors for the NSSS (Nuclear Steam Supply System) as designed by SNUPPS engineers. Westinghouse was selected. A half dozen A/E (Architect/Engineer) candidates were interviewed. The finalists, Bechtel and Fluor-Pioneer, were asked to make detailed presentations, and Bechtel was selected. Bechtel was the most experienced nuclear A/E in the country, and was responsible for over 60 percent of the world's nuclear projects. That contract with SNUPPS was signed in June 1973, and modeling for the plants went forward.

Since the construction contractor and site engineers were field based, these were selected by the lead utilities for each site, with the advice of NPI and the SNUPPS committees, rather than by SNUPPS itself. KG&E narrowed the field for site A/E to Sargent & Lundy and Fluor-Pioneer. S&L was selected because of its greater experience, particularly in designing cooling water reservoirs. There were bids from four construction companies before KG&E selected Daniel International of Greenville, North Carolina. Again the key was experience. Both KG&E and KCPL had had favorable experience with Daniel in building other plants. KG&E believed that since it was short on nuclear experience its contractors should be particularly long on it.

There was to be great controversy about the performance and local behavior of the contractors, especially Daniel, and about the cost plus contract KG&E signed with Daniel. KG&E's original idea of decentralizing responsibility to the contractors and maintaining only a modest site supervisory staff itself eventually went by the wayside, as did the more modest costs associated with that philosophy. Consultants, who later studied the contractor selection process exhaustively, were mostly complimentary about the choices made by KG&E and SNUPPS, especially when compared, not with the ideal, but with the actual alternatives and with the experience of other contemporary nuclear construction projects. Arthur D. Little Company, in the earliest of these reports (1977), stated that "KG&E has made a series of carefully considered choices in its embarking upon a nuclear power program. It has recruited unusually well-qualified and skillful managers to execute that program. We found a resourcefulness and attention to underlying detail that gives us considerable confidence that the overall program will be successful."[1]

A Touche Ross report was less enthusiastic. Thomas Flaherty of that firm suggested in later hearings that KG&E in the construction planning stages "had neither a thorough understanding of project requirements nor a well-defined sense of the scope of project management responsibilities." Flaherty said the search for facility A/Es was limited, and was heavily influenced by Bechtel's previous work for SNUPPS utilities, and also that the evaluation process was limited. Still, Touche Ross agreed that Bechtel was the most experienced in the industry, and did not fault the job it did. Touche Ross thought the selection process for the other vendors was very comprehensive, though the firm suggested there could have been "more aggressive negotiation" in outlining some of the terms of the contracts to establish a better basis for cost control. KG&E's early contractor relation philosophy of "monitoring rather than active leadership," worked well initially. Appointing NPI as KG&E's agent was a good idea, the Touche consultant thought, but NPI was better prepared on the technical aspects of the design than for contract administration or cost control. Jesse Arterburn, who supervised Wolf Creek for KG&E, while qualified, Flaherty claimed, "was hired in a very informal manner that was predicated by a previous acquaintance with him in his capacity at an experimental facility [SEFOR] in the region."[2]

Still, while maybe not rating an "A" grade, the heaviest *post facto* examination did not reveal grievous flaws in the selection of the contractors KG&E had hired as the permit hearings closed. Daniel had never had a "troubled" nuclear project, that is, one that failed because of faulty construction. Negotiating a fixed scope contract with Daniel in the rapidly changing regulatory and technical atmosphere of nuclear plant construction in the 1970s, would have been, many were to confirm, all but impossible. And, as one consultant put it, should such a contract have been made it "would be out of date shortly after you signed it."[3]

It was later estimated that construction preplanning and procurement done by Daniel and SNUPPS, utilizing the detailed SNUPPS model, saved the project in the range of $15 million over other commonly used methods. The fact that Daniel was, by a decision made jointly with the owners in 1976, able to use nonunion labor also resulted in substantial cost savings. The difference between merit shop and closed shop procedures in overtime pay, foreman selection, manpower requirements, production, fringe benefits, and training costs, was estimated in 1984 at $103,967,000 for the project to that date.

In 1974, immediately on its selection as construction contractor, Daniel established a group of five people in Wichita, Kansas, to perform construction preplanning. In April 1976 this team went to Burlington, and moved into a remodeled building, formerly the Peoples National Bank, at Third and Neosho Streets.[4] By the time of the move to Burlington, Daniel had 38 people in Kansas, 29 of whom worked in the KG&E general office building in Wichita. By the summer of 1976 there were about 80 Daniel people in Burlington, and planning was underway for the construction of an administration building to house them at the Wolf Creek site itself. Everything that could be done to prepare access to the site prior to the issuance of the limited work authorization (LWA) was done.[5]

Some Kansans, however, were not content simply to wait for the NRC decision or for the workmen to translate prospects into concrete. A few days after the hearings at Kansas City ended, Clyde Reed in Parsons called for a statewide referendum on the Wolf Creek issue. The hearings had covered technical matters, he said, but the important issues turned on values and ethics. "That is the case in Kansas where the arrogant attitude of Kansas Gas & Electric Co. has pushed other considerations aside in a successful rush for the Wolf Creek power plant. . . . Must Kansas be satisfied with action of the 1976 legislature on selling water for the Wolf Creek [plant] in answer to half-baked arguments thrust upon it by Kansas Gas & Electric and Gov. Robert F. Bennett?"[6]

Governor Bennett was defeated in the November election by a former dairy farmer and state legislator named John Carlin. The press found that 19 of the officers and directors of KG&E had contributed a total of $6,000, and five KCPL people a total of $375 to Bennett's 1974 campaign. Reporters alleged that this revelation "has suggested to some that Bennett's strong endorsement of the proposed Wolf Creek generating station is easily explained."[7] While other papers called this charge "a cheap shot that needs no replay," or "a bunch of bull," it had its impact on those who were grasping at straws to stop the plant.[8] Carlin's campaign materials heavily emphasized the high cost of Wolf Creek, promised to lower utility bills, and made the gubernatorial contest partly the sort of referendum Reed wanted. Nationally, the election of Jimmy Carter to the U.S. presidency the same month was not to have the positive impact on the nuclear industry that some, observing Carter's background in naval nuclear reactors, expected.

Long before the Kansas fall political campaigns heated up, however, KG&E found itself in a regional political quagmire based on its political activities far afield in California. California had a nuclear initiative on the ballot for June 8. Proposition 15 required two-thirds of the state legislators to be satisfied with the operation and waste handling of nuclear power plants in California. Otherwise operating reactors would be required to reduce their operations by 40 percent within one year and no new plants would be licensed. If after five years the vote on the operating plant was still unfavorable it would have to reduce by 10 percent each year. The proposition also proposed to lift the no fault insurance limit of $560 million on nuclear plants provided by the Price-Anderson Act.

Since Proposition 15 was an unprecedented attempt to put direct public control on nuclear power, it was of interest to utilities building nuclear plants all over the nation.[9] Colorado and Oregon had similar questions on their November ballots, 11 states proposed ballot nuclear issues sometime within the year, and the California result would create momentum one way or another.[10] Therefore, electric utilities nationwide, including KG&E, joined the political fight in California with contributions.[11]

Scholars have seen these votes as a major political crisis for nuclear power, and the victories of the utilities' interests in all these cases as an important establishment of forward momentum in public opinion, which was shattered only by the Three Mile Island accident in 1979.[12] Certainly that conclusion is confirmed in Kansas. State legislator Jim Lawing recalls that he, Ruth Luzzati, and about 18 others voted against the water contract. Of these about four were ardently against nuclear power. The others had vague reservations or were voting the wishes of constituents who were concerned purely and only about water. Lawing himself, as has been seen, did not want to tie water to the nuclear power issues, although he already had serious concerns about the cost of the plant, and whether because of that possible high cost, the ratepayers could ever pay for it.[13]

Attorney General Kurt Schneider did not let this action pass unnoticed. Early in June, Schneider filed criminal charges against KG&E under a Kansas law that forbade corporations doing business in the state from contributing money to influence any question submitted to voters. Since KG&E had contributed $3,000 to a group in California, the Citizens for Jobs and Energy, opposing Proposition 15, Schneider said he had a *prima facie* case. Bob Rives responded that KG&E had made the contribution but the statute did not apply.[14] A few newspapers in Kansas argued that corporations ought to have free speech like everyone else.[15]

On June 8 Proposition 15 was defeated in California by a two to one margin. However, it remained an issue in Kansas.[16] Schneider, the day after the California initiative defeat, asked the Atomic Safety and Licensing Board on behalf of the State of Kansas for a two-year delay in the construction of the Wolf Creek plant.[17] This action, based mostly on the fuel supply question, came just before the NRC staff issued a 43-page report (June 18) agreeing that the plant would be needed by 1982 as planned.[18] Governor Bennett quickly sent a letter to Samuel Jensch, chair of the Atomic Licensing and Safety

Board, asking that Dr. Robert Robel, chair of the Kansas Energy Advisory Council, and State Senator Vince Moore be allowed to testify in any further hearings. The governor said he was hopeful that Schneider's request for a delay "will not be misconstrued as speaking for the entire state of Kansas . . . it should be viewed solely as the opinion of one elected official." Schneider commented that he thought the governor's action "presumptuous," since the governor's office, unlike the attorney general's office, had not participated directly in the hearings.[19]

The complexities of the Wolf Creek issue had divided state agencies, as it had every other potentially unified group pressing a hoped-for consensus. The struggle was characterized by temporary alliances among disparate groups, sometimes shifting as the individual aspect addressed changed. It illustrated that rapid change breaks down traditional interest groups, so that business, government, or even environmentalist interest could no longer be simply defined and advanced by a single spokesperson or organization.

The illegal contributions case went to trial late in August in the Sedgwick County District Court. After deliberating 90 minutes, the jury found KG&E guilty on two counts, and dismissed the company's contention that the California election was outside the jurisdiction of Kansas.[20] KG&E was fined $20,000, the maximum penalty, by judge Nicholas Klein, who then suspended half the fine for two years on condition the company not violate any laws during that period. The company attorneys, arguing that the 65-year-old state statute was unconstitutional because it violated the right of free speech, said it would appeal to the Kansas Supreme Court.[21] A couple of weeks later, however, the company withdrew the appeal, and President Ralph Fiebach personally reimbursed the company for the $3,000 contribution and paid the $10,000 fine. The company stated, however, that it had been told the California contributions would be reported publicly and that they were legal under federal and California law. It had not apparently counted on an old Kansas statute and the zeal of the Kansas attorney general.[22]

Reaction in the state was mixed. Some praised "Kurt the nemesis," agreeing that "the need is not so desperate that we can leap before doing all the looking necessary."[23] The other side said that Schneider and the "zealots" were just another special interest. A poll taken by Representative Garner Shriver of the Fourth District, including Wichita, found that 63 percent favored building nuclear plants and only 21 percent did not. In a Topeka radio station poll, also in the spring of 1976, 48 percent said yes, 34 percent no, and 17 percent were undecided. A statewide survey found 59 percent of all Kansans who responded would favor a nuclear power generating plant in their own counties. Asked their preference for nuclear or coal, 64 percent favored nuclear and only 9 percent picked coal. In Coffey County, where the plant was about to begin, 58 percent had no objection, 18 percent opposed it, and 24 percent had no opinion.[24] "Kansans want to go ahead boldly into the nuclear power age," said a Topeka editor, "rather than cowering on the threshold, dependent on Arab oil sheikhs and inventors of contraptions to use solar power and that of Kansas breezes."[25] If the plant were delayed long enough, noted another in Topeka, construction costs would stop it anyway. "Without it, American industry and technology will be a helpless Gulliver staked to the ground by Lilliputian strings."[26] The blunt conclusion of one editor was "There must be an inordinate number of bull-headed people in Kansas."[27]

Also in 1976 the Kansas Supreme Court decided a case brought by KG&E against the Kansas Corporation Commission questioning the Commission's authority to determine whether a certain generating facility was partially used and includable in KG&E's rate base. The court said that "regulatory agencies cannot grant carte blanche authority to construct huge plants just barely more than experimental in nature, and allow the company to charge the expense entirely to the ratepayer—at least not until it works to a substantial benefit to the ratepayer or is within reasonable limits of anticipation of benefits."[28]

At the time the permit hearings started, legislators were considering a generating facility siting bill, requiring legislative approval of new electric generating plant sites and plans.[29] The Kansas Electrical Generation Facility Siting Act was passed in July 1976. Although it exempted Wolf Creek, it included any future nuclear plant, and required a site permit from the Kansas Corporation Commission. Early in 1977 bills were introduced to require direct legislative approval of nuclear plants, including Wolf Creek. Senator Arnold Berman of Lawrence stated, "Nuclear power may well be the social issue of our generation and the legislative is the most legitimate form for dealing with the social concerns of Kansas."[30]

"It is not too late to prevent development of that plant," said John Simpson, a Republican from Salina, on the floor of the state legislature. Simpson said that the legislature reviewed sites for turnpikes, parks, universities, and prisons, and that some states had even put nuclear plant questions on the ballot for the public to decide directly. "It is not enough," he said, "to let appointees, who aren't directly accountable to the public, make final decisions in an area so unique and potentially dangerous as nuclear power." Robert Miller, who sponsored the bill, bristled at charges that it was antibusiness: "Perhaps what these critics really should be saying is that they are not willing to let public policy for Kansas be set by elected representatives. I might be old fashioned, but I still believe in government based on the idea that the people, not private groups or bureaucrats in Topeka or Washington, are the ones who should decide what kind of state we have."[31] KG&E in opposing the bill noted that the federal hearings had already cost the utility $10.5 million, which would eventually have to be passed on to the public, as would the cost of any further process.[32] Miller's bill was defeated in the Kansas House on February 16, 1977.[33]

As though these struggles concerning state authority were not sufficient, on August 13, 1976, the NRC announced that it would stop issuing plant licenses until its staff could complete new studies of nuclear waste storage, nuclear waste reprocessing, and the environmental impact associated with both. This decision was the response to a July 21 ruling by the U.S. Court of Appeals that the commission's method of considering impact before issuing license was inadequate.

The moratorium could not have come at a more inopportune time for the Wolf Creek project, which was hoping to be granted a work permit that very August. KG&E and KCPL responded by asking for a partial exemption allowing them to build access roads and warehouse facilities, move and construct utility lines, and build a 12-mile railroad spur before a final licensing decision was made. John Wigglesworth, an attorney for MACEA, said that MACEA would take the NRC to court if it granted the Kansas utilities' exemption request.[34] The word from Parsons also favored the delay. "Common sense has been injected into the Wolf Creek project for the first time," wrote the *Parsons Sun*. "Kansas Gas & Electric and Kansas City Power & Light have been roaring hell bent ahead damning the uncertainties as they went."[35]

Early in November the moratorium was lifted. The license applications (construction and operating) pending for seven reactors in six states were able to proceed again—including Wolf Creek in Kansas, the Callaway SNUPPS unit in Missouri, and twin units in Pennsylvania known as Three Mile Island 1 and 2.[36] One Kansas editor noted it was about time for a decision. Burlington was expecting the workers. The town had passed a school bond issue of $5.8 million based on an anticipated jump in attendance because of the new plant. The banks there were investing in a mobile home park.[37] Early in December Daniel International threw a Christmas party in Emporia.[38]

The final conclusions of the ASLB panel headed by Sam Jensch were published in January 1977, and even then stated that "our ultimate decision on issuance of a construction permit . . . must await resolution of the excepted matters [primarily the financial capability issue]. Any activities undertaken by the Applicants in the interim, therefore, are undertaken at their own risk." Jensch dissented from the majority opinion, supposedly the first time there had been a split opinion on such a licensing panel. However, his dissent was based on the undue length of the majority decision and its form, "which is like an advocate's brief for brief writers, rather than an adjudication." It was not based on doubt that the hearings had in fact provided "reasonable assurance that the proposed Wolf Creek facility can be constructed and operated (if adequate funds are available) without undue risk to the health and safety of the public."

Jensch did suggest that the term "at their own risk" be defined as to whether it meant at stockholder or ratepayer expense. Stockholder risk and expense, he said, would provide incentive to business management to see that the uneven construction contractor performance typical of earlier plants was not repeated at Wolf Creek. "The stockholder concern," he wrote, "can be continuously expressed whereas rate payers are not as well organized as stockholders to influence management."[39] In his inimitable style, Jensch told the press that the ruling was a "paste pot" recitation of things that had already been said elsewhere—"a fair analysis of this collection indicates that 75 percent of it is trivia."[40]

Trivia or no, the 178-page decision laid most of the official issues of the construction permit hearing to rest, at least until they were raised again at the operating permit and rate adjustment stages when the plant was finished. The findings of fact included that while there would be an effect on water in times of drought, it was acceptable; that the withdrawal of agricultural land was appropriate and negligible; that the planned Wolf Creek spent fuel pool was adequate; that there was a sufficient supply of uranium for the life of Wolf Creek and that it was not dependent on the breeder reactor or plutonium cycle; that 7.5 percent interest rates were reasonable for estimating the cost of the project (that became obsolete fast); that the range of capacity factors for the plant used was reasonable; that the utilities had adequately provided "for the possibility of future foreseeable cost increases due to increased safety requirements"; that decommissioning costs had not been underestimated; that alternative sites would provide no advantage; that nuclear overall was economically preferable to coal; that, while there was criticism of both sides' econometric models, the Burns/Viren alternative demand projection was not as persuasive as the utilities' demand presentation; that energy alternatives such as solar and conservation could not "singly or cumulatively reduce substantially the need for WCGS"; that the emergency plans were satisfactory; and that the plan complied with the Environmental Policy Act of 1969, the Water Pollution Control Act, and the NRC safety and health regulations.

Only one of the intervenors' contentions remained. Contention II-1 was that "Applicants are not financially qualified to construct and operate the WCGS in light of the fact that Applicants have delayed its construction for one year." The board deferred its decision on this contention until after a further special hearing to be held before the final construction permit was issued. "The board has, however, considered the record," the report noted, "on financial qualifications compiled to date and finds that the Applicants are financially qualified to redress any damage caused to the environment in the course of work undertaken pursuant to any limited work authorization that might be issued."[41] With the publication of the report on January 18 the Atomic Safety and Licensing Board ordered the NRC staff to issue an LWA to Wolf Creek, so that earth moving could begin that week.

William Ward of MACEA said he was "appalled" that the LWA could be issued before financial capability could be determined, but said that the matter was too complex to appeal in the seven days the opposition had to file exceptions.[42] KG&E got the word of a "partial initial decision" on Tuesday, January 18, and saw the actual LWA the next week. At that point the design for Wolf Creek was 50 percent finished and equipment orders were at 90 percent.[43] In midwinter, during the worst natural gas shortage in memory, and in bitter weather that had frozen the coal piles at LaCygne, grading and construction of access and storage facilities began at the Wolf Creek site.[44]

The last-ditch effort of MACEA to stop the final construction permit was based on the water issue, and on raising questions about the ability of the utilities to finance the Wolf Creek plant. The former became moot early in December when MACEA's case on the water contract was dismissed by the courts. Legal strategy was then focused on the finance issue, combined with more active public demonstrations. There was a three-day conference at Kansas City in February 1977 to organize May 1 Kansas and Missouri demonstrations against nuclear power to coincide with a massive protest planned that day at the Seabrook plant in New Hampshire. The conference, held at a church and attended by about 50 people, was called "Melt-Down Mid-America."[45]

On the financing, the opposition group achieved an additional hearing in March 1977. MACEA argued, among other things, that disallowance of construction work in progress (CWIP) financing officially in Missouri and by practice in Kansas would make the plant too costly and would damage utility bond ratings to the point they would be unable to raise enough money.

Rate recognition of CWIP, which was in 1977 allowed in 35 states, was a misunderstood concept. Broad implications in the media and political speeches did not help much in the economic education of the public. It was always communicated that CWIP had something to do with allowing for costs of plants under construction, but not complete and in service, in the utilities' rate base. Often the impression left was that CWIP would transfer the entire capital cost of a nuclear facility under construction from the stockholders to the ratepayers, and with it the financial risk if the plant were never finished and never provided power. Readers of newspapers got such explanations as that CWIP was a policy by which customers had to "finance new power plants years before they begin generating electricity," or to "begin paying for new power plants from the time construction begins." Commissioner Richard C. (Pete) Loux argued strongly that utilities should not be able to earn a return until a plant was "used and useful," and that the issue was "who sets the rates—the regulatory commission or Wall Street?"[46] Put that way, CWIP seemed pretty unfair.

However, while most of the public statements made about CWIP were not inaccurate, they were not specific either, and were subject to misinterpretation. The question was only whether a utility could recover in rates as it constructed a plant the cost of financing (interest on debt and return to stockholders for equity) of the construction. It was true that inflation and high interest rates were making this an increasingly substantial item, but it could become even more substantial if, as MACEA charged might happen, prohibition of this recovery caused antsy lenders to lower utility securities ratings and therefore raise the cost of borrowings for plants, and perhaps make the traditional avenues of first mortgage bond issues and long-term fixed rate borrowing unavailable altogether. There was no claim that these interest and return on equity issues charges were not legitimate expenses, which the ratepayers would eventually be required to pay in any case. The recognized accounting practice (called Allowance for Funds Used During Construction, or AFUDC) was to allow the utility to capitalize its costs of financing construction as part of the total cost of these projects, even though it was not receiving cash income to cover these costs as they were incurred. And there was every prospect that paying it later would make the item far more expensive. "What we are doing," said a KCPL officer, "is paying interest on interest."[47]

The bottom line of the CWIP debate for utilities was that an industry that failed to win the affection of investors was dead. Also, with nuclear plants, large size and long lead time, combined with the fuel diversity and shortage questions that were making the Kansas utilities replace a large part of their total generating capacity all at once, made the amount of construction work in progress, on which the utilities in the non-CWIP states were not permitted to earn a current cash return, a substantial percentage of total assets. The total dollar figure of CWIP and the percentage of assets for utilities nationwide increased rapidly. In 1967 it was $4.6 billion (7.1% of assets), in 1973 $20.6 billion (16.6%), in 1978 $42.7 billion (31%). The cost of debt and equity financing for U.S. utilities increased from $189 million in 1967 to $1.2 billion in 1973 and to $2.7 billion, or 20 percent of reported net income, in 1978. In 1982

CWIP reached 43 percent of industry assets and AFUDC 26 percent of net income. "The effect of borrowing large amounts of money over long periods of time at high interest rates to finance nuclear plant construction," noted a financial analyst, "is evident in the fact that AFUDC, as a percentage of all other project costs increases an average of 2.6 percent per month during a project." A consultant noted that "these data illustrate clearly the strain of financing large construction programs over long and inflationary periods."[48]

The opponents disagreed on what it took to woo those investors, and some didn't think private investment was necessary or desirable at all. The suggestion by these critics was that should the private regulated utilities be unable to finance the plants, they could be nationalized or taken over by state governments. "But that," said one analyst, "would be CWIP on a grand scale. Indeed, the essential hypocrisy of the Naderite position can be understood when one realizes that the same people who object to paying farthings for energy through CWIP would often be delighted to pay pounds for it through nationalization." On the other hand, a completely non-regulated private company would bill its customers for construction work in progress any time it could within its price structure, and would borrow capital only when cash flow was insufficient. It was a device for lowering costs and ultimate prices, and therefore keeping a project competitive.[49]

CWIP was made more expensive in Missouri with Proposition 1, which passed in November 1976, thanks partly to help in drawing up the initiative from the Western Bloc and People's Lobby Press of California.[50] CWIP in Kansas was a less cut-and-dried question. For years it had been the policy of the KCC to prohibit consideration of in-progress construction expenditures and finance costs in requests for higher rates. However on December 29, 1976, a District Court ruling in Linn County in a case brought by KCPL reversed that long-standing policy. The court said that there was no statutory authority to deny CWIP financing recovery in Kansas.

The media made it simpler than it was. The headline in one paper was "Ruling Shifts Burden to Consumer." State representative Ruth Luzzati, a Democrat from Wichita, immediately introduced a bill in the state legislature to make it illegal for the KCC to consider current rate recognition of construction work in progress. Meanwhile the KCC appealed the court ruling.[51]

CWIP was debated for some time. Wilson Cadman of KG&E was vocal in arguing that although the plant would be built without it, and though it was never in the cost calculations, allowing construction finance costs in the rate base would save consumers an enormous amount of money in the long run. The legislation to prevent it, Cadman said, was not sound economics, but antinuclear and ultimately anticonsumer. This drew a sharp response from Luzzati, who said, "sooner or later I'm going to lose my temper with that man."[52] Some state legislators claimed that KG&E was doing excessive lobbying on the CWIP issue (nine of the ten utility lobbyists were working on it) which "confused" the members.[53] The *Parsons Sun* commented in its usual vein that "it is too much to expect . . . Kansas Gas & Electric to subside and let the public interest prevail."[54]

The CWIP legislation died in the spring session. However, in September 1977 a special interim committee on energy ordered, by a 5 to 3 vote, the preparation of a new bill to be considered by the 1978 legislature—a move considered a victory for consumer advocates and a defeat for utility lobbyists. Senator Arnold Berman of Lawrence told the press that with CWIP the ratepayers could expect an immediate 15 percent rate increase. The utility argument that not allowing it would mean "catastrophic rate increases five to seven years downstream," was, said Berman, a claim that had been consistently rejected by the KCC. There would be more customers to help pay the cost when the plant finally came on line, the argument went, and, besides, it would be unfair to ask customers to pay now who may have moved out of the area by the time any benefit came from the plant.[55]

An oft-repeated point of proponents of current rate recognition of CWIP was that finance costs did not generate a single kilowatt of electricity. True, but by the time the Wolf Creek plant was finished, KG&E was estimating the extra costs due to not including CWIP in the rate base at nearly $9 million, nearly the initial total estimate for the plant. Phasing in the construction costs would result in gradual increases in rates rather than a "shock" when the plant went on line. It also would avoid AFUDC, an accounting practice unique to regulated utilities. AFUDC permitted noncash "income" attributable to the carrying charges associated with plant construction to be included in current income under the assumption that the plant's full value would eventually be recognized in rates. This could lead to situations where a utility seemed to borrow to pay dividends that were in excess of its cash income though not of its reported income—a situation which could and did create "common sense" impressions in press and legislature unfavorable to the utility.[56]

Ruth Luzzati, who wrote the original bill, put the argument against CWIP succinctly:

> As time goes by there is increased need to protect the individual consumer from excessive utility costs. The investor-owned utilities, in my opinion, are too prone to let the consumer pay the long-range costs of construction which should more properly be paid by their investors (I take the position that if we consumers are to share the risks, then we should be share-holders. But that is another matter. . .). The investor-owned utilities and their supporters will tell you that they need to have CWIP as part of the rate base because borrowing for large expensive projects in the money market is difficult. The facts do not bear out this contention, as the utility bond market, at least as recently as May 1977, was very good. If, however, the prudent investor *were* avoiding a utility's offering, why should we legislators permit the Kansas consumers—our constituents—to be forced to pay for a project they may never live to see built?[57]

Luzzati's mail was so strong on CWIP and the atmosphere changed so rapidly that the bill, which died when it was first introduced, was shortly one that "people were afraid to vote against."[58] In fact, Ross Doyen recalls that he and perhaps one other legislator were the only ones at that point voting against the bill and arguing that in the long run the ratepayers would save if CWIP were allowed.[59]

Early in 1978, a bill amending state statute 66-128 and disallowing current rate recognition of CWIP was passed by the state legislature. KG&E's Standard & Poor rating on its first mortgage bonds immediately dropped from AA- to A, which resulted in about a half-percent increase in interest charges to the utility.[60]

In the rate hearings in 1985, KCPL's Arthur Doyle reflected that the CWIP decisions in both Kansas and Missouri were unfortunate, not so much for the utilities as for the public. "They're victims of some of the short term economies espoused by the antinuclear activists back in the late 1970s," he said, "when in Missouri they had a proposition adopted for CWIP in the rate base and then they sold it to the Kansas legislature in 1978 and what did that do? That raised really the cost of Wolf Creek 50 percent. . . . It's the me generation, the now generation, I want mine now, keep it the lowest possible cost and saddle the kids with it later. That's why we have a national debt of a trillion dollars and we're in deficit besides. This is part of the same philosophy that's going on."[61]

Wilson Cadman of KG&E had a similar view. He denied that KG&E had a lobbying plan early in 1977 to get CWIP restored. However, the utility definitely did have a lobbying plan when the anti-CWIP bill was introduced into the legislature and was pushed in 1978. "I take great pride in the fact that we were successful in being able to complete Wolf Creek in great shape," Cadman said in 1985. "I despair over the fact that we were terribly unsuccessful in our efforts in the Legislature." He went on:

> We have made some very, very long range decisions with the best kind of information available and, believe me, with the very best intentions and we have dealt with a constant moving target with respect to regulations, changing in requirements, changing in, if you will, the public's attitude toward nuclear power. . . . It's a fact that if it has the word *nuclear* attached to it that creates being penalized. I think I would even carry that a step further that the— the concept of prudency and having everything looked at in a retrospective way is a manifestation of penalization of being a nuclear power, the fact that laws are passed that make it more difficult, the change of CWIP and siting and so on are all anti-nuclear. . . . One can construct a bridge and have some problems with that bridge and the public does not care a hoot about that unless the whole thing falls down. In the case of a nuclear plant, each and every thing in that plant that might have a problem and would require correction gains great public attention.[62]

"Many PUCs [Public Utility Commissions]," wrote Robert Glicksman, looking back on the 1970s, "have been unwilling to confine themselves to a consideration of the facts that existed at the time the utility decided initially to build the plant. . . . A review of the prudence of the utility's decisions is meant to provide an incentive for utility management officials to continuously rethink past decisions as new events unfold."[63] Delays, however, were costly. At the LWA stage, each day of debate over the ground rules, each day of further hearings, added $190,000 to a plant cost that was already estimated at over $1 billion. "Those who would delay construction aren't going to take up a collection to defray the cost caused by delay. Kansans who use electric power are going to bear the burden, both as billpayers and taxpayers. The meter in the cab is running."[64]

The basic question of government control of nuclear power, however, was being played out in Washington as well as Topeka, and in more forms and guises than siting and CWIP bills. In March 1977, a bill was introduced in the state legislature to prohibit utilities from including in their rate base expenses for advertising, lobbying, entertainment, contributions to charities, or salaries above $35,000. The governor of Kansas was paid $35,000, was the logic—why should a business executive get more? "Those who do the regulating don't know what they are doing," commented one editor, "and can't resist playing to the peanut gallery."[65] Joe Skubitz, a congressional representative from the Kansas Fifth District, authored and coauthored some of the many bills in Congress designed to give states more power in determining the location of nuclear plants and disposal sites within their boundaries. One bill would have given a state authority to veto construction of a nuclear plant before the NRC could issue a construction permit, and another gave states a veto within 90 days of the issuance of the permit.

The finance hearings, held before the NRC's Atomic Safety and Licensing Board for two days beginning March 22, 1977, examined the CWIP question, fuel availability, and slippage in the so-called "definitive estimate" of cost and in the planned construction schedule. The utilities were put in the position on the one hand of continuing to argue that allowing CWIP in the rate base would be helpful, while on the other hand denying that it was essential. MACEA, meanwhile, pointed to the cost increases and the schedule slips as evidence that confidence in what would happen to the ability to finance in the future was by no means certain. "Applicant's discussion of KCP&L's current ability to finance the plant," noted MACEA attorney Ward, "is equal in significance to the hiker, about to embark on a 50-mile trek, noting that his feet aren't tired."[66]

There had been delays for the hearings and the moratorium, and therefore resettings of the finish date for the plant to correspond with the start date. Six major construction schedules were issued before 1980. There was a conceptual schedule, a management summary estimating the overall time frame for project completion and identifying key milestone activities, though it did not detail tasks. Revision 0, issued in 1975, was the first detailed construction schedule. Revision 1, April 1976, was the basis for Daniel's estimate of construction costs and for the "definitive estimate" of overall cost. Revision 2 was issued when site work began in February 1977, and Revision 3 was a May 1978 update complete with a critical path schedule for planning and integrating all construction activities. The first construction delay was in 1974 due to high capital costs from tight financial markets. This delayed the planned start of construction until January 1976 and the date for commercial operation from April 1981 to April 1982. Revision 2 pushed the on-line date for the plant from April 1982 to April 1983. The utility explanation was that this was due to NRC delays in convening the public hearings and its summer 1976 moratorium on licensing. The delay, however, led to discussion about whether the reason might also be changing actual demand for electricity versus projections, doubt about financing, or both. When site excavation work began in February 1977 it was 21 months behind the original schedule. The time of construction estimated—about 70 to 75 months—remained fairly constant through these revisions. Would not future delays, as civil work progressed to nuclear work, and crews on site became larger and more specialized, be increasingly expensive? The NRC estimated 96 months for completion of Wolf Creek, and the industry average by 1980 was 106 months.[67]

Related to the schedule question was the reliability of the "definitive estimate" of January 1977, which set estimated plant costs at $1.04 billion. The original KG&E press release announcing the plant in February 1973 had stated the cost of Wolf Creek would be "in excess of $500 million." The plan was then for an 800 mw plant with a fuel load date in 1981. Between that time and 1980 seven major cost estimates were made. Early ones included an order of magnitude estimate in 1973 using input from Bechtel on the power block only, preliminary estimate number 1 late in 1974 from Bechtel and Sargent & Lundy data, and preliminary estimate number 2 a year later assuming an April 1982 commercial operating date. The "definitive estimate" was established when the power block design was about 40 percent complete, and was the first estimate capable of being used as a performance baseline for actual construction.[68] The final cost was 288 percent of the 1977 estimate.

Like a lot of other terms used in the nuclear industry, *definitive*, as applied to the 1977 estimate, was not very satisfactory common English. Leonard Wass of the consulting firm Cresap, McCormick and Paget, said that "to me [definitive estimate] means the most misused term that I have faced in the industry." It was coined by Bechtel to mean the first estimate where a reasonable amount of scope was known so that the project could move forward—the first valid benchmark. To the layman, however, it implied an end estimate—complete, bankable.[69]

The dilemma presented by the "definitive" estimate in light of the many future cost increases was outlined by Charles Huston, who was a consultant for KG&E and later an expert witness at the Wolf Creek rate hearings. Nuclear plants had such long construction times, subject to so much regulatory change, that no initial estimate could be used to control costs, as would be true of budgeting in shorter-term projects. Cost estimates were revised yearly for Wolf Creek throughout a construction period that lasted 8 years. Bechtel, which did the original estimate, had done more of these than any other contractor, and Daniel International had more nuclear construction experience than any other construction company. It was reviewed by all the other companies involved in SNUPPS. But that did not mean the cost estimate was definitive in the popular sense. Huston was constantly to argue that Wolf Creek needed to be compared with other contemporary projects that experienced the same inflation and the same regulatory change, not against any point in time estimate. "It's extremely difficult," Huston said, "to start a reconciliation process with an estimate that is completely out of date in terms of its scope."

As it happened, the 1977 estimate included only 20 percent of the engineering scope as the plant was finally constructed. Bechtel at the time thought it was close to 40 percent defined on the scope, but even that was far from complete. Some of the line items were estimates without firm bids. There was no labor cost experience at the site at all yet. Yet, Huston argued, building in a large contingency allowance for possible changes was bad for project management: "We did not want to allow contractors like Daniel and Bechtel to work up, and we approved specifically what we thought they should spend." The only true *definitive* estimate would be one given at the end of the project, which of course would be useless.[70]

This line of reasoning, from the 1977 finance hearings forward, raised some eyebrows among the opposition. It developed a counterargument, presented largely by Richard Rosen in the later rate hearings, that the cost estimates could have been predicted in 1977 by properly estimating the effects of upward trends in the variables, and that long-term cost trends were not much influenced by extraordinary events such as the Three Mile Island accident of 1979.[71] The press and many who wrote letters to newspapers pretty much ignored the technical considerations involved in estimating, and treated variances from the 1977 estimate largely as evidence of inefficient or even imprudent management. Jim Lawing, a state legislator active in the water issue, talked with Wilson Cadman of KG&E at this time about the possible cost. Lawing had been doing some reading about the cost overrun problems of other nuclear plants, and suggested to Cadman that the cost of Wolf Creek could escalate to $2 or $3 billion dollars. That was more than the entire state budget at that time, and Lawing's question was how could the ratepayers possibly handle it, even should there be no special concern about other aspects of nuclear power. Lawing remembers that Cadman gave a definite response that the plant could not cost more than $900,000,000 in the worst case scenario, even if a lot of things went wrong.[72] From a historical perspective about things that could go wrong, such as inflation rates, he was probably right, but there was about to be a major discontinuity in that tradition. It is a pattern in the evolution of the Wolf Creek opposition that what started with landowners and spread to environmentalists reached its apogee when those concerned with cost joined the intervention. The rising cost went from footnote to headline during the construction years.

In the spring of 1977 cost and finance were more than a footnote—they had been the only issues justifying a continuance of the ASLB hearings. However, the brevity of these hearings, and the quick conclusion that finance was not a problem, indicated that it was not yet considered a major stress point by the regulators. On April 18, the NRC issued a second and expanded LWA to the Wolf Creek plant. It allowed work to begin on some permanent buildings, below grade work on the plant itself, and beginning of dams in the lake area.[73] On April 27, the ASLB denied a request by MACEA to reopen the hearings. On May 8, the same organization's requests to set aside the LWAs, and its charges that a KCPL executive had lied in denying that his utility had used CWIP in its cost calculations, were dismissed.[74] On May 12, 1977, came the final construction permit, with the licensing board's ruling that the two utilities had met all federal requirements for construction. The press reports gave the current cost estimate at $1.06 billion, only slightly up from the "definitive" estimate, with the completion date holding at spring 1983.[76]

While this result was not unexpected by the opposition, who had a sort of underground black humor about the ineluctable progress of the juggernaut, the news was as devastating to the intervenors as hearing of the actual death of a patient long thought terminal. While they had no intention of giving up, the construction permit was a major watershed. The next formal hearings would be at the time of the application for a federal operating permit, and the state rate hearings. By this time the plant physically would be a *fait accompli*, and there would be enormous momentum tending toward the conclusion that it should not then be abandoned.

Analysts have pointed out that there are endemic tactical and organizational problems to sustaining protest movements, making crossroads like this one critical. There are problems of allocation of limited resources, appealing to different constituencies without creating a central hierarchy, balancing the moderate tactics that get press coverage with the more aggressive style that tends to hold supporters together, balancing focus on single issues with the broader appeals that attract supporters, and above all simply keeping the coalition together in "slow" times. Protest organizations have no institutional life of their own, and certainly the individuals in the movement do not have the economic self-interest in the preservation of organization and momentum that their equivalents in corporations or government do. All of these tactical and organizational dilemmas faced the Wolf Creek opposition at this juncture.[77]

Michael Viren, who had developed the econometric models for MACEA, felt confident that the opposition would be able to stop the permit on the cost issue. No nuclear construction permit had been denied before, but Viren had hoped his data would prevail. Diane Tegtmeier, who was also crushed by the announcement, tried to hearten Viren by saying "you can't look at things as this period of time and this particular power plant. We are part of a larger process, and we have contributed knowledge and data to the process." In fact, a construction permit *was* soon denied for the Black Fox plant in Oklahoma on the basis of lack of economic need, using the models Viren had developed.

MACEA felt also that it had made considerable inroads with the Kansas legislature. Tegtmeier recalled that the first time she had talked with Governor John Carlin, when he was a legislator, Carlin told her that he didn't think what she was doing was correct from a policy standpoint. However, Carlin allowed Tegtmeier to use his telephone to make long-distance calls, listened to what she had to say, and eventually did a good deal to facilitate citizen involvement in the nuclear issue. Even Robert Miller, who introduced some of the most radical proposals for Kansas regulation of the plant, was at first doubtful that opposition would fit his conservative values. "Why," he told Tegtmeier, "should I believe some information brought to me by a Johnson County housewife about Wolf Creek?" Miller, who was anything but a "wide-eyed liberal commie," became an effective ally of the opposition.

Tegtmeier and the others in MACEA continued to believe that their opposition was neither radical nor unique, but an element of the Kansas tradition, with its emphasis on individual rights and, to some extent, contrariness to establishment assumptions. Tegtmeier, a relatively recent immigrant to the state from Chicago, felt that her experience in the protest "played a big role in my own identity as a Kansan and feeling good about living in Kansas." Legislators, who had been "polite, but did not have the time" initially, by 1977 were contacting the MACEA people for information. Tegtmeier was able to make an appointment for Amory Lovins, who had written an article in 1976 on soft energy paths much employed by MACEA, to talk with Governor Carlin about his ideas.[78]

There was without doubt also some special psychological momentum in the antinuclear movement in Kansas that could survive reverses. Robert Hagen's insight was that it had begun with the AEC's mishandling of the Lyons waste problem before Wolf Creek was a factor. The federal government, Hagen said, thought that "there were a few Indians and cowboys out here and they could do what they wanted. They got the heck kicked out of them. That opposition group tasted success in kicking them out and really whipping them good." The core of that group made the transition to the Wolf Creek issue, which heated up just as the issue of dumping the nation's nuclear waste out in the salt mines of backward Kansas began to die down.[79]

On May Day 1977, an international radical holiday, there was a massive demonstration at the troubled Seabrook nuclear plant in New Hampshire, where a controversial seawater cooling plan had delayed construction repeatedly. Some 1,200 people, supporters of an activist coalition called the Clamshell Alliance, refused to leave their tent camp at the construction site, and were arrested by a force of 350 state troopers and busloads of state police. The Clams made no secret of their plans and hoped for the overreaction they got, and for the media attention paid to "Woodstock generation" types wearing jeans and headbands and carrying guitars being hauled away by neat uniformed officers.[80]

On the same Sunday as the New Hampshire protests, the *Kansas City Star Magazine* published a long article on the Wolf Creek developments called "Showdown Time in Mid-America." Construction activity in Burlington, which had begun on President Carter's inaugural day, was changing the landscape and the surrounding towns quickly that spring. KG&E Vice President Wilson Cadman said MACEA had been a thorn in the side of the utility. "Their leader, Mrs. Diane Tegtmeier, she's a nice girl," Cadman said. "But she's antinuclear. She's for alternatives—wind, solar. We say nuclear *is* the alternative. We want to use the thing at hand to fulfill our responsibility to meet the power needs of our franchise area. . . . Mrs. Tegtmeier wants solar technology. Solar technology! You'd have to cover all of Coffey County with collectors. Mrs. Tegtmeier and her group—no aspersions to her—they're not responsible. When the lights go out, who are they going to blame? The power company. Well, we're just determined to make sure the lights stay on."

The reporter waffled. Three years ago 18 new nuclear plants were ordered in the United States—in 1977 only four. Yet she found nuclear technology, which she had seen firsthand in visits, "incredible." In short "if you are not afraid of a technology that merely requires 100 percent perfection of the persons who manage it, then nuclear power can be pretty wonderful." Like 95 other utilities around the country, three electric companies in Kansas and Missouri (KG&E, KCPL, and Union Electric building the SNUPPS Callaway plant near Fulton) had "put their names in the nuclear pot." The reporter's concluding question was simply, "Did they put them in too late?"[81]

Post mortems on the construction permit were many. "I felt kind of smashed when I heard the news," said Tegtmeier in a newspaper interview. "But I feel in the last four years the mood of the country is changing. . . . You always think you could have done more. But we carried the whole issue one step further than intervenors who came before us, and we have a lot to pass on to the next intervening group. . . . I think too many people get frightened away because they think it takes an engineer or a lawyer to do something. While we need them, we need the laymen too. It's amazing what you can learn when you want to learn."[82] A few days earlier she had said, "We don't consider this the end. We will continue to do all we can to prevent construction of the plant within legal boundaries."[83]

Arthur D. Little, Inc., was hired by the Kansas Corporation Commission in 1977 to do a management review of KG&E at this juncture. The report was completed in October, and outlined the problems as well as the promise in the situation. The consultants interviewed over 100 people in Kansas, mostly in KG&E management, but also a number of community members familiar with the company. The consultants visited all KG&E's generating stations and six of its seven divisions. They reviewed many company documents.

The conclusion was that KG&E was an efficient producer and distributor of electric power whose management and employees worked hard, were loyal to the company, and had "a long tradition of and commitment to public service." However, KG&E was facing not only the problems of other U.S. utilities, including changes in the business and regulatory environment and rapidly increasing costs, but special problems of its own, including prominently a 100 percent change in its fuel base, requiring heavy capital costs to replace generating plants that would otherwise be usable. KG&E should be commended, said the report, "for proceeding in an orderly fashion to shift from dependence on precious fuels. . . . It is clear that KG&E's construction schedule is justified, up to and including the addition of Wolf Creek in 1983, even if the load forecast is too high." The company was in transition from a period when its management was heavily dominated by one man (Gordon Evans) to a more broadly based style involving more delegation of authority. The Little report stated that strategic planning was weak. There was no clearly articulated mission statement, and many parts of the company lacked an "analytical approach to problem-solving and decision-making." KG&E's relationship with the Kansas Corporation Commission was "not as good as those of other Kansas-based utilities." Long-term financeability was a problem. The Little people recommended current recognition of CWIP for Kansas, that the test period for rates be the latest possible with most current plant investment included as well as a "realistic" return on equity. Rate relief from the KCC would need to be "prompt and adequate."

Public relations presented another class of challenges. The company was said by Little to have great sensitivity to low costs and relatively high sensitivity to public and consumer relations. It ranked high with Wichita city officials to whom consumer complaints were often directed. Nonetheless, "reasons for high electric bills are still not well understood by the general public," and the dynamics of building a nuclear plant were more mysterious yet. For example, the consultants' interviews with the public showed them that the word "Kansas" in the utility title led a good number of citizens to believe that it was state owned. KG&E was building the only nuclear plant in the state, the Arthur Little writers pointed out, and "it has become the focal point for criticism from individuals and groups who are opposed to nuclear power. . . . All in all, we think the Company is doing about as much in dealing with . . . these problems as it can. . . . [L]eadership of some of these groups is sophisticated and knowledgeable and it should be expected that their impact will become greater as power costs continue to rise."[84]

Some of the people who commissioned the Little study criticized it. Pete Loux of the KCC said there was "too much puffery" in it, and that Little had acted as an "advocate and advisor" not an evaluator. Wilson Cadman responded that it was an in-depth study, and had been commissioned by the KCC, not the company. The KCC had selected the firm and had authorized the bill of $178,000 to be paid by KG&E customers. It had better be good![85]

KG&E's attitude as it passed the hurdle of the Wolf Creek construction permit was that, with a few exceptions, it was on schedule on its fuel diversity mission. The company activity in coal got much less publicity than its nuclear plant, but new coal construction was adding immensely to Kansas electric utility capacity in this era. Immediately when the troublesome LaCygne 1 went on line in 1973, KG&E and KCPL started work on adjacent LaCygne 2, which was to use cleaner-burning coal hauled from mines in Wyoming by train. LaCygne 2 (630,000 kw capacity, cost $234,000,000) entered commercial operation on May 15, 1977, right on schedule, and just a few days after the granting of the Wolf Creek construction permit.[86] A second major coal involvement by KG&E was the Jeffrey coal units, named for Kansas Power and Light chairman Balfour Jeffrey, and located near St. Mary's, Kansas. KG&E's partner here was KPL. Jeffrey was planned for four units, to become operational in 1978, 1980, 1982, and 1984. Early on a nuclear unit was even contemplated to be part of the complex. It used Wyoming coal, and if fully completed would have a capacity of 2800 mw and serve 1,000,000 customers.[87] KG&E's interest in the first three Jeffrey units was 20 percent (4 was 15%, later withdrawn), and work began on Jeffrey 1 in 1975. Unit 1 was completed in July 1978, on schedule.[88] At its dedication on a 90-degree July day, Vice President Walter Mondale told the 6,000 people gathered that "this is a classic example of how America can solve the energy crisis," and an example as well of "Kansas leading the world." The United States, he said, was the Saudi Arabia of coal producers and this effort of the Kansas utilities was right in line with Carter administration policy.[89]

These were significant projects. One newspaper called them "power plants as big as cities." Jeffrey was to be the largest power plant complex in Kansas and the largest construction project ever undertaken there. There were planned more miles of paved streets, conduits, and underground transmission lines than in most of the surrounding towns. As many as 1,000 workers, requiring their own sewage and water purification plant, worked at Jeffrey, and there would be a permanent work force of 250. In Wyoming there was a $2,000,000 shovel to dig coal at the Amax mines, and the mine supply town of Gillette went from a population of 7,000 in 1970 to 11,000 in 1976. It cost $40,000,000 a year to operate the coal mines there, $1,000,000 of which was spent on environmental programs.[90] Jeffrey 1 went on line in the spring of 1978. Its smokestacks were 600 feet high, and towered over a boiler complex that covered more than a city block. The coal piles covered 200 acres and looked "strangely like a vast black lake." The unit was visible from Topeka, 30 miles away.[91] KG&E spent record high amounts on construction through the 1970s. In 1974 the construction investment was $51.8 million, up from a previous high of $43.2 million in 1971. In 1974 it was $48 million; in 1976 $115 million; in 1978 $134 million.[92] And *then* Wolf Creek construction got started!

Information on the national and regional power situation in

1977 indicated to KG&E executives, as much as did the construction schedules, that the company was on the right track. Elmer Hall and several other executives attended a conference of the Edison Electrical Institute in San Diego, California, in 1975, and heard a navy admiral say that the U.S. military could not protect oil pipelines and harbors in the Middle East, and that an embargo in that region, such as the one in 1973, could not only precipitate another major energy crisis in the United States, but could interfere with the operation of the fleet. The officer said that the navy therefore was planning on all-nuclear ships, and that the utility industry should be thinking the same way about U.S. power plants.[93] In March 1978, the National Electric Reliability Council, which had been formed after the Northeast blackouts of 1965 to survey electric utility capacity, produced its *1977 Annual Report*. Parts of it were never released to the public, and its conclusions were shocking. The report concluded that "the adequacy of electric power supply for the future is in jeopardy," and that by the early 1980s there could well be substantial blackouts in the United States unless construction of generating capacity were greatly expanded. Such blackouts would cause disruption of the industrial sector, adverse changes in lifestyle, and threats to the health and welfare of all citizens. The last gas-fired unit in the country was installed in 1977, and government regulation along with conflicts between environmental goals and energy requirements were slowing the replacement of gas by coal and nuclear tremendously. The association told its members that "it is essential to alert governmental leaders of the trends which are threatening to create an electric power supply system which is neither adequate nor reliable."[94] The council predicted that neighborhood- or government-imposed restrictions on the use of electricity were almost certain as early as 1979.[95]

Washington seemed to agree. James Schlesinger, Carter's secretary of energy, spoke in 1977 of an energy crisis beginning in the 1980s that could be worse than the 1930s Depression and could lead to disaffection with our political and economic situation.[96] President Carter, loath to pursue some of the power generating options in the face of environmentalists, emphasized conservation and got rid of the limos at the White house in favor of leases on small cars.[97] A report released by Senator Edward Kennedy in the fall of 1977 suggested we could have a robust economy while cutting energy growth to zero by 1985. This would, of course, involve changing our economy to one of increased services and fewer solid goods and reducing fuel consumption 40 percent through technology.[98] The press sensed that something was up. "The great organs of popular misinformation and belated intelligence," wrote Ted Brooks, a Wichita energy reporter, "are gradually beginning to recognize a world-wide energy problem that refuses to go away. It is not the flimsy 'crisis' glorified since 1972. It is a dreadful, long-term confrontation between dwindling energy fuels and raw materials on the one hand and a combination of needs and dizzy expectations on the other. . . . As a matter of necessity, not ideology, the apostles of infinite growth, economic development, industrial progress and pollution for profit are in for a hard time."[99]

Locally these warnings rang true. The Kansas winter of 1977–1978 was the coldest in 36 years, there were several coal strikes, a severe natural gas shortage affected the region, and there was a heat wave that summer, driving KG&E's peak load to record highs.[100] However, it appeared that the conservation predictions might not be accurate. There had been a real slowdown in national electric demand growth from the traditional 7 percent a year during the first energy crisis. In 1974 growth actually declined. In 1975 it was up by only 2 percent. However, in 1976 demand increased 5.2 percent and was close to 7 percent in the first half of 1977, ending the year at 6.5 percent.[101] KG&E's average demand growth for 1974 through 1978 was only 2.4 percent, but as the Arab oil boycott receded, the demand trend seemed to be upward.[102]

There were some cracks in the SNUPPS alliance. Northern States Power, the originator of the organization, cancelled its Tyrone 2 plant in January 1974, citing an insufficient need for power. It was rumored by 1977 that Union Electric would cancel the planned second Callaway plant in Missouri. However, these were in the "frosting on the cake" category. There were four SNUPPS plants under construction and expectation of a great deal of information exchange and cost savings through the NPI management company.[103]

Rate adjustments for the generating capacity expansion in Kansas, as it manifested itself in coal plants, were leaner than the utilities hoped, but were regularly granted. In the spring of 1978 KG&E got KCC approval for a $16.3 million rate hike, less than half what it requested, and allowing only a 13.5 percent return on equity (which translated to 9% applied to the whole rate base) compared to the 15.5 percent return on equity the utility thought necessary. Since 1974 the utility had requested rate hikes totalling $52.9 million and had been granted $28.1 million.[104] In the rate case concerning LaCygne 2, the KCC seemed amenable to the idea of using as recent a test period as possible, and even estimating rates on projected rather than historical expenses, subject to refund, to reduce rate lag time.[105] Rate relief was enough to keep things running and KG&E's rates remained among the lowest in the country. A 1977 survey showed KG&E's rates were 185th lowest among 231 utilities (virtually all those in the nation) even though rates had increased 21 percent in the preceeding year. Investor rating services no longer ranked Kansas at the bottom in regulatory environment, and it appeared that there was some room, comparatively with other parts of the country, for further rate increases to replace generating capacity.[106]

At Burlington and on the construction site, activity indicated to one reporter that the "Atomic Spirit is Loose." Derricks and cranes were in evidence, as was Pinkerton security. The largest concrete mix plant in the state, capable of producing 200 tons an hour (a truckload every three minutes), was underway to create the 110,000 cubic feet of concrete required. Twelve-foot diameter pipe was ordered that would draw in cooling water at a rate of 500,000 gallons a minute, and rebar for the 208-foot-high containment building arrived to fit a reinforcement design worthy of a racing car space frame.[107]

Even opponents admitted that the work already done by May was impressive, Daniel had "gouged, chipped and blasted a fantastic hole in Coffey County, just east of New Strawn." There were 570 Daniel people on the job late in May, with 800 expected by summer, and 1,800 to 2,500 by 1980. The construction firm selected workers from over 7,500 applicants, and trained carpenters and electricians in a school building at New Strawn. From the top of a hill of backfill a tourist could see all around the graded area and look over the "lay down yard" where there were five cranes "of the type which customarily light up small boys' eyes," as well as rows of reinforcing steel, stacks of bright yellow girders, and extensions for the cranes to allow them to reach the top of the 20-story containment building. Every rod and part was tagged, and the NRC had on file the exact temperature and time it was made. There was a first-aid building, construction offices, a warehouse, a pipe fabrication shop, an electrical shop, a carpenter shop, and a maintenance shop. The access highway was almost finished and the 12-mile railway spur that would bring in major parts had been started. The dominant feature of the site was the hole, which would be filled with the seven-building "power block." There workers had cut into solid rock to reach elevations measured by electronic transit to the 50,000th part of an inch. Once the exact depth was reached engineers mapped every crack and crevice in the shale base as workers swept away even rock dust to clear the surface for the concrete pads on which the foundation would be set. The deepest part of the excavation was the "key"—140 feet in diameter and 10 feet thick—where 7,000 cubic yards of concrete, chilled to just the right temperature for best curing, would be laid. Bids were being entertained to start dams for an eight-square-mile lake, which would begin filling in 1979 and leave the plant itself on a peninsula on the former prairie.[108] "Dust flies and the earth trembles," wrote a reporter on the press tour, "as man and nature collide in America's quest for energy."[109]

There were strangers in Burlington—construction crews doubled the town's population—and some hard feelings as a result. However, the economic impact on a county that a June 1977 survey ranked the absolute poorest in the state in per capita income was obviously large.[110] By spring a new $6,200,000 school complex was underway in Burlington, as was a $1,000,000 hospital addition. There was extensive work underway on the Burlington water and sewage systems and a new shopping center was being discussed. Sales tax revenues in the city had increased 20 percent over a year earlier, and rents had as much as quadrupled. A house built in 1900 and needing repair sold at auction in April for $28,000. Tourists went in and out of the county courthouse to see the 3/8 inch to the foot model of the Wolf Creek plant, which filled most of the lobby area there. They learned that a 1000 mw electric plant could light 10,000,000 100-watt bulbs, not to mention what it could do for a local economy. "I don't even go into town anymore if I can help it," said a local farmer who had lost his land to the plant. "As soon as you look at those people you can see the dollar signs light up in their eyes."[111]

Not all was rosy, however, in the towns. Workers moving into mobile homes in many of the communities reported that they did not feel accepted. Merchants in stores followed them around, afraid that they would steal something. Women were told when they took their children to enroll in local schools not to reveal that their husbands worked at the nuclear plant. There was lots of gossip about the workers' lifestyle, much of it steamy and uncomplimentary. "We're not trash or riffraff," one wife said, "but human beings with feelings just like you people that were born and raised here. Don't you people realize that this plant was the best thing that has happened to this town in years? . . . Why don't you just give everyone a chance and judge them for what they are—not for what you think they could be. Give us a chance, you might even get to like us."[112]

Mrs. Edith Lange of Burlington didn't think so. It was not so much the people as the activity over in the "wasteland" nearby that annoyed her. "Where could you find a prettier place to live?" she said. "There's a beautiful sky, the climate's wonderful and our garden gives us everything we could want. . . . [pointing to cranes at the construction site] That plant just spoils everything."[113]

During the press tours of the Wolf Creek construction site that followed the issuing of the construction permit, Glenn Koester of KG&E said that "he expected opposition to the project from environmental groups to die down, now that the work permit has been issued."[114] Clyde Reed at the *Parsons Sun* doubted it. "The first battle of Wolf Creek is over," he editorialized, but if the events in New Hampshire were any indication there would be more battles. At least two important questions remained unresolved: could the economics of a latter-day nuclear plant be made to serve the public, and what about fuel and waste storage? "We shall see," the editor concluded, "what we shall see."[115]

6
The Sunflower Alliance

> Let's stop playing games and get on with the work at hand.
> —*Wichita Eagle*, Dec. 9, 1977

> The days of the kangaroo court are over, and we must go to direct action.
> —Francis Blaufuss, Nov. 10, 1977

> Once a person has persuaded himself that he or she has enlisted in a noble crusade to rescue the world from atomic holocaust, any reasoned arguments on the other side become unheard and unavailing. . . . It displays a depth of conviction not matched by good judgment.
> —*Kansas City Times*, Oct. 13, 1978

Recently, there have emerged a group of academics who identify themselves as being involved with the "sociological and historical study of technology." They make some fundamental interpretive points that apply to events at Wolf Creek as they developed in 1978 and 1979.

One central insight is that there is such a thing as the "sociology of technology," and that it is simplistic to isolate the history of a technological "artifact," like Wolf Creek station, from its social, economic, and political context. Instead, the technology must be studied as a part of a "seamless web" involving the society in which it appears and the time of the culture it represents. The technology itself it often part of a "system" and its audience can be characterized, not as a single interest group, but as a complicated "network" of potential consumers or affected parties.

A second germane insight of these scholars is that in all sorts of modern technology from the introduction of the safety bicycle to the application of Bakelite plastic, facts and problems are not simple scientific givens within a well-fixed paradigm community, but rather are subject to "social construction." "In deciding which problems are relevant," write Trevor Pinch and Wiebe Bijker, "the social groups concerned with the artifact and the meanings that those groups give to the artifact play a crucial role: a problem is defined as such only when there is a social group for which it constitutes a 'problem.'" In the Wolf Creek case, the engineer/manager proponents were not able after the mid 1970s any longer exclusively to either define the problems or the questions to be answered, or to exclusively interpret the significance of the facts and statistics they offered. The engineering mentality failed to comprehend fully that to solve *its* problems with *its* solutions was not adequate. True pluralism had come to the utility industry. Problems now had to be perceived as relevant and perceived to be solved by a wide public before what these scholars call the "stabilization of the artifact" as a social phenomenon could occur.

A third important point is that new technologies such as nuclear power do not necessarily inherit the "momentum" of their related systems (in this case, electricity in general). Also the degree to which they gain acceptance and the speed of this may vary considerably over nations and within regions inside nations. What Thomas Hughes calls "reverse salients" could and did develop as organized protest grew. As in guerilla warfare, the opposition was likely to flame up "spontaneously and unexpectedly in several places." And, like guerilla resistance, it was effective out of proportion to numbers when directed at central planners whose "guns" might be the wrong size and aimed in the wrong direction, or who could find themselves the equivalent of the eighteenth-century British troops, proud of their successes in Europe, wearing bright coats and marching through the American forests in lines while ragged frontiersmen and Indians picked them off one at a time.[1]

According to this analysis, while the beginnings of construction at Wolf Creek represented at least "trajectory," and perhaps the beginnings of "momentum" (these historians argue that in the twentieth century there is no such thing as true "autonomy" for a technological system), there was a parallel strengthening of a significant "reverse salient." The inner dynamics of this salient, being more spontaneous and less centralized than the technological establishment itself, are best traced chronologically, and the pattern constructed from specific events that had no preordained relationship, and that were motivated by passion as much as planning. Writes William Least Heat Moon of the problem of writing the "deep history" of a single Kansas county: "It was connections that deviled me. I was hunting a fact or image and not a thesis to hold my details together."[2] In his case it was map quadrants; here it is activist "happenings."

It should not be assumed these "happenings" consisted wholly of longhaired young people carrying signs at a rally or chaining themselves to fences. The Wichita City Commission and its consultants, debating separating Wichita from its long-time connection with the KG&E power grid through the building of a coal gasification plant using an experimental alternative technology, was equally "revolutionary" if not more so. Each of these discrete events was "countercultural" to the technological, economic, and social hegemony of the regional power industry, and was driven by many broad and national trends, but occasioned immediately by the building of the Wolf Creek plant. It is like the causes of the Civil War. There were many, but eliminate the slavery debate and the history as it happened and when it happened becomes incomprehensible. The plant was the symbol, was the focus of all these disparate alternative yearnings. At base, as Margalee Wright, a Kansas Corporation Commission member during the later rate hearings, put it, there was operating in Kansas an innate "distrust of a system that tends to solve problems on the backs of common people."[3]

Perhaps unfortunately, just as the opposition strengthened, the polarization symbolically and physically increased with the isolation of the public from the plant itself. With the series of press tours corresponding with the granting of the construction permit in May 1977, public tours of the Wolf Creek site ended. Kansans could drive as far as the new Wolf Creek visitor center, opened in July on a high spot 2.5 miles east of U.S. Highway 75, and from there could see construction vehicles at the building site as well as mockups of the nuclear systems. But the real thing was off limits.

The site tours ended in response to new federal security rules, not at the behest of the utilities, which thought them good public relations. Educational tours blunted popular suspicion about the secrecy of nuclear plants. As a Commonwealth Edison spokesman put it: "When people can see for themselves what we are doing, they can decide for themselves if it's right. But if they can't see, if they are locked out, what then?"[4]

The problem was the increasing aggressiveness of the nuclear intervenors, and the shift from legal maneuvers in the hearings to civil disobedience on the ground. Partly this was because the legal processes between hearings were neither visible nor available. Partly, it was because Kansas, having no state initiative and referendum, did not lend itself to the political organization of opposition as much as did, say, the state of Washington, where shortly a public power system's nuclear program would be stopped by highly political organizations with a focused economic appeal, using weapons such as the petition drive and political campaigns to oust members of the public power board.[5] Confrontation was the only recourse available to those wishing to stop the Kansas plant during its construction stage. "Wake up and slumber no more," wrote Francis Blaufuss, "—your lives are at stake. We must protest as other countries do. Spain had 150,000, Germany 80,000, France 35,000 and the U.S. at Seabrook 5,000. These were directed at individual plants. I see no reason why we could not muster 100,000 at Wolf Creek."[6]

Most demonstrations were peaceful. But there was some violent rhetoric. Ralph Nader, in the *Village Voice* in June 1977, asked, "Shouldn't you destroy property before it destroys you?" Editors wondered whether the polite trespass typical of plant site demonstrations would become ugly, as with the cycle that had replaced flower children with Weathermen in the 1960s.[7] On the morning of May 24, 1977, the KG&E office building in downtown Wichita was evacuated due to a telephoned bomb threat.[8] Such threats became nearly routine at Wolf Creek.

Stereotyping increased as threats became serious. A columnist compared nuclear protestors with the nineteenth-century English workmen known as Luddites, who went about smashing machinery. Antinuclear partisans were described as presenting "a generally hairy and unkempt appearance." They sat at speeches weaving and knitting things "and their questions tended to be incoherently passionate. They probably went home and ate dandelion hamburgers."[9]

Scott Garten, a particularly outspoken defender of Wolf Creek, wrote caustic letters to the *Emporia Gazette* in the summer of 1977 about the local protestors. He called them "scare mongering varmits," and said that watching a "bunch of these clowns" demonstrate at Wolf Creek on Hiroshima Watch day August 6 would "be as much fun as living next door to a holy roller church." Garten's annoyance was partly based on his own passions, but also on the expansion of the protest beyond the realm of attorneys and intellectuals. "I'd be less inclined to poke fun at these characters if they could demonstrate to me their credentials in the subject at hand. If they could prove that they can cope with university physics and differential equations, I would not turn a tin ear or a glass eye toward their views. As it is, I honestly wonder if any of them can count to ten on a cold day, what with their hands being in their pockets."[10]

Garten, of course, got a response. Peggy Price wrote a letter to the editor saying that she could decipher equations and count and she opposed Wolf Creek. "I was taught as a child that when a person resorts to name-calling, demeaning words and belittling something, you only succeed in reducing yourself in the eyes of those around you." She invited Garten to the next meeting of the Emporia Citizens for Energy Conservation, held at the United Methodist Church. There he was invited to demonstrate his own ability with equations. As to his charge that the protestors were "coming out from under a rock," Price said being under a rock was not so bad as rocks tended to absorb solar energy and were great insulation, "definitely 100 percent better than any building in Emporia."

Why was it so important to demonstrate ability in higher math? wrote another Garten detractor. Do you need ballistics and fluid mechanics to "resolve the effects of a machine gun on a victim?" Were only experts to be in on the debate? Did some group have a monopoly on defining the problems? "It bothers me that discussions on topics important to the public's well-being or detriment, whatever the case may be, are scrutinized so technically by the extremist that they no longer are able to communicate with ease and simplicity the crux of major evidence for or against a decision." Kansans, this man said, were losing the quality of "humble communication": everything written or said about Wolf Creek was so emotional that the state was at risk of becoming a Babel of loud talk.[11] Reddy Communications, which owned the rights to the cute lightning man with the lightbulb head, Reddy Kilowatt, long used by utilities as a symbol, went to court in the summer of 1977 seeking an injunction against groups who portrayed the little character as a purse snatcher, a gambler, and a panhandler.[12]

The antinuclear movement in Kansas inevitably changed as it

grew. The people who would join a march, who would camp in the snow to meet the train carrying in a reactor vessel, who would shout slogans in the street, and who would flirt with arrest, fines, and jail were not necessarily the same type as those who had sustained the countermovement through the licensing process. Things became less polite, and more assertive, even aggressive.

Hiroshima Day—August 6—1977 was the occasion for the largest demonstration yet at Wolf Creek. It was a combination of spectacle, theater, and speeches that came to typify opposition technique when denied "official" access and forced to appeal directly to the public through the media. A crowd estimated between 100 and 200 marched through Burlington that Sunday, saw skits, heard speeches, and released balloons symbolizing radiation. Most were from Missourians for Safe Energy, Wolf Creek Nuclear Opposition, Inc., and the Kansas City People's Energy Project. Some staged a mock "die in" in front of the People's National Bank and Trust Company. It was complete with a simulated Civil Defense announcement, hard hats, and cardboard tombstones with the symbol for radiation danger and a skull and crossbones on them. State Senator John Simpson of Salina, William Ward of MACEA, Wes Jackson of the Land Institute, and Edith Lange of Wolf Creek Nuclear Opposition made speeches. Simpson said the plant "stands as a symbol of the power of the large business over the individual trying to make a living." He claimed it was a waste of land and water, a sign of inflation and was the dinosaur and passenger pigeon of the twentieth century—doomed to extinction. Ward noted that the hearings were over "and now it's time for us to cast the rest of our vote. I think that's why we're all here today." Jackson likened reliance on electricity generated by nuclear plants to drug addiction, and said that withdrawal was easier when you were 8 percent addicted than when 30 percent dependent.

Francis Blaufuss directed the balloon release. Cards on the balloons read, "This card was attached to a balloon released near the construction site of the Wolf Creek nuclear plant. If an actual accident had occurred you would now be contaminated with radiation. Such a major catastrophe almost occurred during the $500 million fire at the Brown's Ferry reactor near Athens, Alabama, on March 23, 1975." There was a place for the recipient of the card to send back name and address, and the card contained the slogan "better active today than radioactive tomorrow." A large banner at the demonstration site read, "If the utility bill doesn't kill You: the radiation Will." Marchers chanted "No nukes, sun power!" as they moved through town on the sidewalks. Around 5 P.M., as the marchers were about to disperse, a truck with Alabama tags drove by, and a man leaned out to shout, "Are you bastards going to pay my salary next week?"[13] It was nothing like the antinuclear protest at Faverges, France, the Sunday before where one was killed and 100 injured in a battle between 30,000 protestors and police during a march on a nuclear plant under construction.[14] But to the clusters of Burlington residents watching from their homes and businesses, it was a sure sign that the construction phase of Wolf Creek would not proceed unopposed.

Another kind of group appeared at the site in October—1,000 people representing families of KG&E and KCPL employees. They too were preparing themselves psychologically for a long battle. "A Day at Wolf Creek" was a four-hour open house and tour held on a cold gray day and fueled partly by the largest cookie order (3,500) ever received by the supermarket in Emporia. After quite a bit of asking for directions, the visitors were directed by Boy Scouts from Burlington into the heart of the complex.

Jesse Arterburn manned the public address system to explain what would go where. One area shaped like a key slot was where the reactor would be placed. A set of huge legs, looking like the temple at Karnak along the Nile, was the turbine-generator pedestal. Everywhere were large cranes, looking like a giant's erector set. Bob Rives and Glenn Koester of KG&E, Don McPhee and Stan Jameson of KCPL, and Wade Pointer and Chuck Kinney of Daniel International were in the warehouse parking lot personally greeting visitors before they attended the slide show inside on the need for nuclear power and the reasons the Wolf Creek decision had been made. Pamphlets were distributed with the theme "From Arrows To Atoms." There were no incidents. People showed the permits they had received from Wilson Cadman, newly promoted to executive vice president, and stood where they were told to stand. "In all my years of security work and dealing with large groups of people," said the Wolf Creek security chief, "I have never seen a more well-mannered friendly crowd than the KCPL and KG&E folks. Even their children are that way."[15]

The field day was followed by 29 customer meetings between company representatives and about 1,000 selected customers of

KG&E. Personal letters of invitation signed by President Ralph Fiebach were mailed to customers, and cookies and coffee were served at the evening gatherings, where a company officer and the local manager presided.[16]

Public relations, however, could not mask that every day of construction provided some new occasion for controversy and disagreement over the quality and safety of the work that was being done and the competence of the workers doing it. As was once said about the cowboys coming into Wichita in the 1870s with the trail herds, the construction workers moved into the area by Daniel were hardly ministers of the gospel. They were, however, a definite part of the imagery connected with the plant during the construction period, and one that could not be entirely controlled by public relations statements from the company.

John Delehanty, a student at Emporia State University, who was hired to do cleanup work, had a not untypical reaction of shock that the people actually constructing such a high-tech facility were not white-coated Ph.D. physicists, but rather the same mix of people that were found on any heavy construction project. They partied all night in nearby towns and then took speed during the day to stay awake. Drug use was widely rumored, mostly marijuana, and Delehanty with the rest of his crew spent their time cleaning cigarette butts and construction debris off surfaces to which critical pieces must mate. Shifts were going around the clock, people were away from their families and living in temporary housing, and the scale and complexity meant that even a small percentage of error could have substantial effects.[17]

Though the "civil" stage of the work did not involve nuclear equipment and was massively heavy (each 40-foot section of water pipe to bring cooling water to the plant from the lake weighed 25 tons and had a diameter of 12 feet), it was delicate in the sense of being critical pieces in a system that had to mesh perfectly and that could not be taken apart to the foundations for repairs.[18] Early on there was a gap between the "culture" of the workers and that of the supervisors, and another gap between the supervisors, who had to get along with and motivate workers to spend long hours in the cold, and the designers, who would have preferred zero-defect procedures and the kind of documentation that would have taken much of workers' time at jobs they were less suited for than primary construction work.

Construction workers became a focus of attention at plants all over the country during the time between public hearings. There were complaints there about defective welds, bad concrete pours, reinforcing bars of the wrong length, switches of identification tags on structural steel components, use of structural components so poorly fitted that they had to be forced into place with heavy machines and held by wire until they could be welded, and poor anchors used to attach pipes.[19] At the San Onofre plant near San Clemente, California, a 420-ton reactor vessel was installed backward in 1977. [20]

On December 12, 1977, a construction event occurred at Wolf Creek that got very little publicity outside the company magazine at the time, but that was to generate in time more print than most would have imagined possible regarding a slab of concrete deep in the bowels of a generating plant. The "base mat" pour was the largest single concrete pour yet in Kansas, and formed the base for the reactor containment building. The mat was specified to be 10 feet thick and 154 feet in diameter, made over cross-hatched layers of thick reinforcing bar (rebar). The concern was that in large pours of this type air pockets or honeycombing and cracks might appear—they did at Callaway. Though these were not dangerous and were easily corrected, the public regarded cracks in a sidewalk or patio as signs of sloppy workmanship and therefore would be shocked to have them show up in this expensive and elaborate job. Therefore vibration was applied during the pour and temperature and curing time monitored carefully.[21]

The pour took 39 hours, and NRC people were on the site the entire time observing the process. So were KG&E agents and substation people to make sure there was no power interruption. A fleet of 12 trucks carried the concrete, which was pumped on the pour with elephantlike nozzles over seven layers of rebar. In all, 6,700 cubic yards were poured—enough to cover 50 acres 1 inch thick. The weather was good, damp and not too cold, almost perfect, the experts said, for such a pour. Wilson Cadman wrote the Daniel people that the pour was "an outstanding accomplishment of quality, efficiency and productivity."[22] Indeed, until the tests in March 1978, of the strength at 90 days, showed the test cylinders to be out of spec, the pour appeared to be as perfect as could be expected. In any event, the March 1978 KG&E *Annual Report* concluded that the pour was another benchmark. "There can be no turning back," it stated.

The utility "is totally committed to the era of change in which we now find ourselves."

Yet while the mega-yards of concrete went in at Wolf Creek, there were those who advocated a return to square one on the fuel diversity question. They suggested, given the price escalation and continued doubts about the safety of nuclear plants, reconsidering a larger role for coal in Kansas. One manifestation of this in 1978 was a call for the conversion of KG&E's Gordon Evans gas plant to coal. Another was a remarkable civic move by the city of Wichita to investigate seriously the construction there of a state-of-the-art coal gasification plant.

The Evans coal conversion idea was instigated by the ever-active MACEA. That organization asked late in 1977 that the Department of Energy and the KCC investigate the feasibility of converting KG&E's newest gas plant, located near Wichita, to coal and if it were feasible to order the utility to make the conversion. Such a coal plant would have a 370 mw capacity, which would just about cover KG&E's 470 mw share of Wolf Creek, and make completion of that plant unnecessary for the southeast Kansas trade territory, MACEA claimed.[24]

The *Wichita Eagle* editorialized that these continued interventions by "the relatively small group of self-styled environmentalists who call themselves the Mid-America Coalition for Energy Alternatives" were silly when the walls were rising at Wolf Creek, and the reactor, being built in Tennessee, was ready for its initial tests. Energy alternatives needed to be investigated, the paper said, but on the suggestion to convert the Evans plant to coal "the figures just don't add up." "Let's stop playing games and get on with the work at hand."[25] A Wichita geologist responded that MACEA was "a public interest group of professionals," not kooks, and that its statistics on demand growth were much lower than those assumed by KG&E.[26] MACEA estimated that customers would save $150 million by converting the gas plant and stopping Wolf Creek.[27]

Late in January 1978 the U.S. Department of Energy decided that Gordon Evans Plant 2 could be converted from natural gas to oil or coal. MACEA said the conversion would cost $95 million and KG&E estimated $190 million. In March the DOE told Representative Dan Glickman, who had presented MACEA's case, that the Evans plant could not be economically converted to coal. The DOE estimated the cost at $133 million and said that was excessive for the benefits gained. Congress was considering legislation to outlaw burning of gas in electric generating boilers, which would mean that if KG&E's gas plants could not be economically converted to coal, there would be all the more need for replacement of their base load capacity by new coal and nuclear plants.[28]

Wichita's coal gasification experiment was a far more extreme proposal, which illustrated dramatically the perception that some new and different energy sources were required in the near future to keep Kansas competitive industrially. Wichita, in common with many American cities, had a plant to convert coal to the city gas supply for several decades beginning in the 1880s and before the arrival of natural gas.[29] The modern proposal, however, was for an entirely different technology. Tentative discussions between engineering firms, prominently Williams Brothers Engineering Company of Tulsa, and the Wichita City Commission and economic development committees began in the spring of 1976 as the result of studies showing that the natural gas shortage would be worse with every passing winter, and that by 1990 there might be no natural gas available for any purpose in Wichita.[30]

KG&E engineers were critical of the Williams Brothers report, which appeared early in 1977, especially because the suggestion that coal gasification was feasible ignored a mass of evidence indicating that Wolf Creek would provide the power more cheaply. Several critics felt the whole idea was a pipe dream of Wichita's economic development department director Grover McKee, admittedly a financial genius with a penchant for grandiose deals, but a mixed track record on implementation. Don Elliot of KG&E estimated that synthetic gas would cost $5 to $7 per million Btus in the early 1980s or a 500 percent increase in the natural gas prices consumers had been paying.[31] The Williams Brothers report concluded that the effect of the coal gas plant on Wolf Creek should be ignored: "We just don't think nuclear has any place in this part of the world. It's different in the East where you have transportation problems and where you have to haul the clean western coal farther."[32]

Although Panhandle Eastern Pipeline Company thought enough of the coal gasification idea to agree to be partners with the city in building it, there was considerable controversy. Coal gasification was not a new process. However, earlier technologies produced what was known as "city gas," and not the higher energy pipeline quality gas that the Wichita plant was advertised to make. No plant in the world could produce that in 1977, and the designs to do it called for about five million gallons of water a day, either a huge railway delivery system or a coal slurry pipeline from Wyoming, and a change in the state law to allow special bond financing and to put the city of Wichita rather than the KCC in charge of rates—fundamental challenges all.[33]

Reverses came. In March 1977, the state legislature turned down the bond bill Wichita was depending on to fund the gasification plant. Mayor James Donnell was angry, but Grover McKee went too far in a public interview by mentioning "those idiots" in Topeka, and was removed as head of the coal gas project.[34] In May there was discussion of the city's buying KG&E's Murray Gill gas plant, just in case the coal gas plant did not produce the high-Btu gas proposed, but could produce gas sufficient to run the electric plant.[35]

In the fall, Ted Brooks, former energy reporter for the *Wichita Eagle*, then writing for the independent *Wichita Journal*, wrote a 15-part series on the coal gas proposal, introducing significant doubts. Brooks said that questions should have been asked long before, but that the town's major newspaper was carried away, like its public officials, with the puff and the unexamined claims of the promoters. Brooks suggested that the city take a hard look at Mark Twain's statement about the three kinds of lies—lies, damn lies, and statistics—and get realistic about the coal gas plant's chances of doing anything but ruining the city financially.[36] The plant would produce 9 tons of sulphur dioxide, 16 tons of nitrogen oxide, 2 tons of particulates, and 1.4 tons of monomethane hydrocarbons daily to add to Wichita's air.[37] Wichita's population was not only not growing, but had actually declined since 1970: "At the present rates, the city will be gone in 100 years or so." That complicated the marketing and would increase the rates.[38]

In mid November a city advisory panel of three business leaders advised cutting the size of the plant in half and doing a feasibility study of whether even that would work. Brooks praised the panel and said that "this column has wrongfully inferred that they had been asphyxiated by the hot air generated in City Hall."[39] Shortly thereafter Grover McKee, at age 44, was suspended altogether from his city duties amid charges that he had misled bond buyers about the coal gas project.[40] When representatives of Energy Transportation Systems appeared in town in December beating the drums for a Wyoming–Arkansas slurry pipeline, there was a jaundiced public reaction. "Implausible as it was," said an observer, "the idea put visions of sugar plums in the heads of the hard-pressed municipals. Officials of KG&E The Electric Co. nearly died of apoplexy."[41] "It's not very good government," one wag commented, "but it's first class comedy."[42]

Wichita decided to have a special "advisory referendum" election on whether to continue moving forward on the plans for the plant. It was considered unwise to put the issue on the regular ballot with the fluoridation and gay rights proposals that had kept the city hopping in those same months.[43] But questions abounded and hurdles continued to appear. The City Commission in January 1978 applied for a $24 million grant from the DOE to study the gas plant proposal.[44] Kansas Governor Bennett stated that the plant must get the approval of the KCC before it was built. City Manager Gene Denton denied this.[45] In the weeks before the election scandals surfaced concerning the operation of the city-owned Wichita Gas Utility, a stopgap measure created by Grover McKee and at first run by the same Williams Brothers Engineering that proposed to build the coal gas plant. Several major industries were cut off from gas supply that winter, and since they had contributed the major funding for the city utility and made many prepayments for gas they now could not get, they were understandably angry and loath to try such devices again on a larger scale.[46] In February, a coal slurry pipeline bill to grant the right of eminent domain to the companies proposing such a pipeline to feed the Wichita plant was defeated in the state legislature.[47]

Meanwhile energy bills went higher. "Your friendly and esteemed gas and electric companies," wrote Ted Brooks, "are not solely responsible for mounting fuel bills. Mother Nature, not to be outdone by their passion for pecuniary gain, has been an important contributor.... Meanwhile the dependable postman has been leaving fuel bills which make strong men weep. Weak women phone the executives of the power and fuel companies to honor them with shameful language. The unfortunate inhabitants of once-envied all-electric homes are becoming permanently ill.... Those who live in the home of the brave will not despair. One can always buy a wood stove and move into the basement or a single room. The furniture and unnecessary parts of the house provide enough fuel to last until grass and trees start growing in the streets. . . . The Wichita commission is always interesting, sometimes astonishing and usually half gassed."[48]

There was of course a massive publicity campaign to promote a positive vote on coal gasification. "A negative vote," Brooks commented, "is equated with backwardness, privation, infertility and people moving to Arkansas." The estimate of $910 million to construct the plant would be more than $2 billion by the time the finance charges were factored in—or more than it was estimated at the time that Wolf Creek would cost—even if things went perfectly. The promoters said there would never be any obligation to the taxpayers, but since the City of Wichita was one of the purchasers, had liability, and had no money but taxes, that seemed a questionable claim. "Directly or indirectly," Brooks contended, "the public will pay. . . . The amount of official misinformation and nonsense that passes for truth is startling."[49]

On March 28, 1978, in the special election, the voters "advised" the City Commission to kill the project. Some analysts said that the public was just disgusted with a liberal City Commission; others that conservative Wichitans would vote against anything that involved potential spending. However, there were those who figured that just maybe there was a common-sense conclusion that coal gasification was a very expensive pipe dream, born of hysteria and visions of leadership. Despite endorsement by all five City Commissioners, the City Manager, and the Chamber of Commerce, the vote effectively ended talk of coal gas in Wichita. Panhandle Eastern Pipe Line Co. and Lehman Brothers Kuhn Loeb, Inc., withdrew as partners, and one of the most spectacular proposals ever advanced by a city for energy independence died quietly.[50]

The design was eventually constructed in North Dakota and, due to technical problems and the deregulation of natural gas prices leading to a suddenly increased supply at a price far below coal gas, was a financial disaster. Hindsight makes the 1978 Wichita voters into geniuses and the city leaders into clowns. However, as cannot be emphasized too strongly, hindsight was not available to decisionmakers at the time. The Wichita coal-gas incident, while seemingly peripheral to the development of Wolf Creek, was a direct threat of an independent alternative by a major KG&E customer, and illustrated not only serious questions about the nuclear route, but also the seriousness with which the energy crisis, about ready to manifest itself strongly for a second time with the revolution in Iran, was taken. Those who in hindsight might suggest that KG&E's gas plants represented "excess capacity" should recall how seriously the coal gasification plant was regarded in Wichita circles.

The fuel mix situation was that same year further complicated by federal action. The Natural Gas Policy Act of 1978—a bill one commentator called a "legislative Loch Ness Monster"—began the process of gas price deregulation.[51] The second shoe was the Fuel Use Act of 1978, which outlawed use of natural gas as a boiler fuel by utilities, setting a ten-year deadline for complete conversion away from it. The act was partially repealed in 1981, when gas supplies increased (thanks partly to the price deregulation), and there was the possibility at that time of applying for exemption from the act, which KG&E did and was denied. In 1978 the Fuel Use Act added importantly to a picture that suggested strongly that KG&E had not only to get fuel diversity, but also to end its dependence on gas entirely, even for local peaking.[52]

Wilson Cadman, who became president of KG&E in 1979, could never imagine how the critics later waved aside the impact the Fuel Use Act had on KG&E in 1978. "Our goal was energy and fuel type," he later testified, "rather than capacity. We could have had a complete cessation of growth in 1978 and because of the law that was the law of the land that was enacted that year, we were absolutely required beyond a shadow of a doubt to plan and develop another kind of generating system." The later repeal of the Fuel Use Act demonstrated to Cadman only the unreliability of government projections and the instability of regulations: "One sweep of the pen takes it away; another sweep restores it in some partiality." The utility, however, could not speculate on future changes, as the 1978 law had a deadline not far beyond the Wolf Creek completion date, and was therefore a "ticking time bomb."[53] The penalty for using natural gas in the late 1980s would be fines and jail sentences, which, Cadman reflected, "was incompatible with my plans."[54]

No matter how inevitable the nuclear option might have seemed from a utility policy perspective, however, nothing about it was a given in Kansas politics. In March 1978, just as the debate about the

Miller bill to require legislative approval of nuclear sites was abating, the news broke that KCPL was negotiating for sale of part of Wolf Creek, as well as the Iatan coal station, to the Nebraska Public Power District. The NPPD needed the power because its partner in building the Ft. Calhoun nuclear plant in Nebraska, the Omaha Public Power District, backed out, leading to the cancellation of that project. Seventeen percent of Wolf Creek would go to Nebraska under the plan, taken from KCPL's share. In addition there was a proposal by Kansas Electric Cooperatives, Inc. (later Kansas Electric Power Cooperative, Inc., or KEPCo) to own another 17 percent of the plant. The Nebraska sale would leave KCPL with 24.5 percent of Wolf Creek and KG&E with 41.5 percent.

The Wolf Creek opponents were quick on the scene. Bill Ward of MAECA said that the sale proposal vindicated the position of the opposition to the plant, as it clearly showed that the growth of electric demand must be slower or rate increases smaller than the company had predicted when it went into the deal.[55] It was true that percentage load growth, especially for KCPL, was at a recent low in 1978, just preceding the unpredicted Iranian revolution and second energy crisis. Load growth for the utility in 1978 and 1979 was -6.3 percent, the low since 1973, though the very next year load growth was 11.9 percent, a ten-year high.[56] State Senator John Simpson spoke out immediately in the legislature: "Should we be developing a nuclear power plant in Kansas for people all over the country?"[57] Four legislators—Simpson, Berman, Miller, and Donald Mainey of Topeka—called for creation of a special legislative committee with subpoena powers to investigate the proposed sale. They charged there was excess capacity, and suggested the solution of abandoning the Wolf Creek construction. "It's good to know right now that we were right," said Diane Tegtmeier of MACEA, "but that alone won't please us. We won't be pleased until the NRC . . . reverses itself and withdraws the construction license for the plant."[58]

A seven-member legislative special committee held meetings, partly secret ones, on the sale issue beginning late in March.[59] The two-day official hearing began on April 13 and covered such questions as "Why was the sale necessary?" "How could KCPL and KG&E overestimate their electrical demand by as much as 4 percent annually as they showed a need for the plant?" "Do the utilities have the financial clout to complete and operate the plant?" "Is there a chance to kill the plant, though it is nearly 8 percent complete?" "Were any Kansas utilities offered the 17 percent share?" "What will be the future needs of Kansans for electricity?"[60] At the same time four state senators in Nebraska introduced a resolution calling for an investigation of the Nebraska power district's role in the sale. A major issue there was the relationship of a public with a private entity. "I don't think public power entities should be lending their credit to a private project," said one Nebraska legislator. "We shouldn't be bailing out a private company."[61] A second legislative objection was legal impediments to NPPD ownership of property outside Nebraska.[62]

The conclusion of the Kansas panel was that the Kansas legislature had not been "deliberately misled" about the sale, but there was a suggestion that laws be passed to eliminate the possibility of the "lack of candor" displayed by KCPL in this case.[63] The Kansas attorney general issued an opinion on May Day that the KCC had no authority to block a sale of power such as the one proposed, either under the 1977 siting act or any other bill.[64] Therefore, despite a bill of $5,700 for the special probe, the committee had to conclude that there was nothing wrong in the sale.[65]

The hearings, however, did provide the opportunity to publicize widely the fact that actual demand growth since 1974 had averaged 1.25 percent a year for KCPL and 2.4 percent for KG&E, while the utilities and KCC staff had projected about 6 percent and MACEA had estimated around 2.5 percent.[66] They also effectively scotched the deal. KCPL had been negotiating with Nebraska for "wheeling" power there since the inception of Wolf Creek in 1973, and the current negotiations had included a provision that KCPL could in return buy up to 25 percent of the Mandan project by which Nebraska, and by extension Kansas Citians, would get cheap Canadian hydroelectric power after 1985. It also allowed KCPL some rights in a Nebraska coal-fired plant.[67] Delicate business negotiations, however, do not thrive in a fishbowl, and the publicity effectively ended them. The Nebraska Public Power District withdrew from the deal in October.[68]

Clearly, the Nebraska sale was an initiative that promised to aid with increasingly dicey financing for Wolf Creek and to relieve Kansas and Missouri ratepayers of the costs of any short-term "excess" capacity at Wolf Creek. Econometrician Michael Viren, called to testify before the special committee, said that while he still thought the plant should be abandoned there was "no doubt in my mind, that the action to sell excess nuclear power now for rights to buy power in the future was in the best interest of KCP&L rate payers."[69] Both KG&E and KCPL started looking for other partners almost immediately. Negotiations with the Kansas Municipal Energy Agency in 1979 for 9 percent of Wolf Creek and 4 percent of LaCygne broke down, but sale of a percentage of KG&E's ownership of Jeffrey Unit 3 to Missouri Public Service Co. went through in 1982, although the KCC subjected it to such rigorous restraints that it never was completed.[70] In playing for double or nothing on the Nebraska sale of 1978, and in speaking of the negotiations as a "plot," the politicians, protestors, and newspapers cut off all prospect of that obvious accommodation. "The probe," said one paper, "has been an ill-disguised last-ditch attempt by opponents of nuclear-fueled electric generating plants to block construction of the Wolf Creek plant."[71]

Dr. Margaret Maxey of the University of Detroit spoke at a KG&E luncheon meeting in April 1978, giving a broad view of current nuclear public opinion. The NAACP had issued a statement favoring nuclear on the grounds that it would help unemployment, there had been thousands of pages of studies of its risks and their solutions, yet it seemed that a vocal group had concluded that more studies meant more danger. "A fear strategy," she said, "has been very carefully orchestrated in this country since the early 1970s," and it was nearly invulnerable to the logic of risk comparison. The ecology movement, Maxey argued, thrived in affluent nations because "they have the leisure time and the sensitivity to look out for rather esoteric problems. Why? Because their basic needs have been abundantly taken care of by their parents, by welfare assistance, by the network of non-profit organizations. They represent a narrow set of interests of a very very small minority."[72]

Narrow or no, the antinuclear protest movement in Kansas continued in 1978 to grow quickly in size, variety, and intensity. At the annual gathering on the Capitol steps in Topeka in January the opposition sang protest songs to the tunes of "I Heard the Bells on Christmas Day" and "Michael Row the Boat Ashore" ("Everyone come take a stand / Hallelujah / Run the nukes right off our land / Hallelujah!"). Paul Schaefer of the People's Energy Project said there that he had asked a legislator if it were possible to sue KG&E

because the utility threatened his children and grandchildren. The legislator replied that it was possible "but KG&E will soon have robbed me of even the money to hire a lawyer and draw up my will."[73] KG&E had been arrogant, came the word from the *Parsons Sun*, and now even newspapers like the *Iola Register*, which had been a utility cheerleader, were changing their tune. "High-handed tactics were employed by the utility, its lackeys and retainers. Everyone else was wrong. Kansas Gas & Electric rode high, wide and not so handsome over all opposition.... But the worm is turning now."[74]

Individual groups began to join into networks and present a united front, while at the same time they became functionally specialized. In April 1978, the groups attacking the Wolf Creek plant from various angles formed a coalition called the Sunflower Alliance, modeled after the Clamshell Alliance, which was so effectively delaying the Seabrook plant. By October a specialized resistance group, the Kansas Natural Guard, was formed within the alliance to take direct action. This included a plan for the first major act of civil disobedience in Kansas. Nonviolent protestors were trained for a planned action involving lying across the railroad tracks when the reactor vessel was delivered to Wolf Creek that winter and thus they faced mass arrest. Relatively few alliance members were willing to take that drastic a step. Guard member Joan Conger said it "shows our frustration. If we thought there were any hope of preventing the plant legally, if there were any substantial hope, we wouldn't do it." But there were suggested actions short of that for all. The alliance, for instance, advised its members to turn off their electricity every Sunday evening from 9 to 9:05 P.M. It would not hurt either them or the utility much, but it was the kind of symbolic protest that galvanized the group and fascinated the media.[75]

The direct action events increased in frequency and size as the weather warmed. Late in June the Sunflower Alliance was able to turn out a "quiet but enthusiastic" crowd of 600 in 100-degree heat at John Redmond Reservoir. Protest folk singer Danny Cox was there to sing "Brown's Ferry Lullaby," and there were trips to the water's edge to take samples symbolizing the drawing of water by the Wolf Creek plant. A large switch near the speaker's platform read "Flip the Switch on Nuclear Power." It was, said one paper, "like a church reunion."[76] The group requested that participants participate in the "switch off" campaign and that they not bring alcohol, drugs, or dogs to the rally.[77]

There were many new faces, and many young ones. But youth was far from the whole. "I just wanted to tell you," said 57-year-old Helen Woodcock of Gridley, "that you shouldn't be fooled by all of these young people walking around with their shirts off. I noticed all of the other reporters talking to all of the young people and taking film of them and I want you to know that my generation is concerned too." Said a Mennonite involved in the social concerns group at her church: "I feel funny among all of these young people." Others liked the age mix. Louis Bodine, 73, said, "People ask me why I don't go to the senior citizens' meetings. I say I want to be with young people, where people are doing things. All they do at senior citizens' meetings is talk about their aches and pains."[78]

A month later, also in stifling heat, a crowd estimated as high as 1,000 rallied at the reservoir and heard Senator John Simpson speak on the threat of the nuclear plant.[79] That event coincided with a four-day demonstration at Seabrook involving 10,000, and drew 20 reporters and photographers and four TV stations into the Kansas sunshine. "Before the snow flies," Francis Blaufuss told the reporters present, "Wolf Creek will be a thing of the past. Today marks the turning point against nuclear power. We will demonstrate and demonstrate—we will not stop."[80]

Protest events began almost to follow a calendar. There was the New Year's rally on the Capitol steps in Topeka, the Hiroshima day rallies on August 6, and the Karen Silkwood day rallies on November 11. The Karen Silkwood protest in 1978 gathered on the Topeka capitol steps, and consisted mostly of young people, including such mainline, but previously not actively antinuclear, organizations as NOW (National Organization for Women). "Our unity and strength," said Karl Shepard of the Sunflower Alliance at that rally, "is stopping the cancerous tyranny imposed by nuclear power." A "human blockade" of the reactor delivery was discussed at Silkwood day.[81]

The press was filled with the debate, and partly in response the rhetoric escalated and the action became more extreme. In October the University of Kansas's journalism lab FM radio station, KJHK, broadcast a "War of the Worlds"–type hoax purporting to be a news story about 15,000 people killed in a nuclear disaster at a plant near Waterloo, Iowa. The news flash reported that the plant had exploded and destroyed the city. As a result of this program, the Federal Communications Commission investigated withdrawing the station's license—the claims made were believable enough to Kansas to represent dangerous distortion.[82] The Kansas Natural Guard performed anti–Wolf Creek skits on the campus. Student members marched past K.U. classrooms wearing gas masks and chanting "Radiation, radiation here it comes," while carrying signs calling attention to the imminent arrival of the reactor vessel.[83]

Around the country the same polarization pattern prevailed, as the most radical and determined elements were attracted to the nuclear issue. At Seabrook opponents of the plant clashed with the Ku Klux Klan, there to support nuclear power. The chant in that bizarre confrontation was "Blacks and Whites, everyone unite! Smash the Klan!"[84] Rhetoric in the Kansas press more and more reflected a radical and even revolutionary, not just a protest, tone. As Shakespeare put it, the movement "grew by what it fed on," and its shape was influenced also by the market in media outlets. Nuclear power, said a letter to the editor, was an "unscrupulous" effort by "money-hungry predators. . . . The nuclear fuel cycle is an evil genie which must be caught, not to be put back in its bottle, but rather to be burned at the stake. This can be accomplished by the women of the nation. . . ."[85] Daniel Ellsberg, of Pentagon Papers fame, visiting Wichita, encouraged the Wolf Creek protests, adding, "I hope the train doesn't run over you."[86]

Even official political rhetoric turned up the wick a notch. The successful gubernatorial candidate that fall, John Carlin, grasped a constituency forming. "It's time we said 'enough' to the big utility companies who are bleeding us," Carlin said in a campaign address. "The people of this state expect and demand that their governor represent the people and not the utilities. The governor's status quo attitude is not only insulting but irresponsible, especially when this attitude costs us millions of dollars in inefficient government and millions of dollars in increased utility rates."[87] It was as though speakers on all sides were testing the limits of invective, waiting for a call to reason, which was slow indeed to come.

The time had long passed when proponents of nuclear power thought that ignoring the opposition was a realistic possibility. The strategy of KG&E as a company was to have officers appear personally in the thick of the debate, and respond orally and in writing and at length. While the "teach-ins" of the opposition went forward, KG&E continued its press conferences and employee tours of the plant construction site.[88] It also sponsored public forums, such as one in November led by nuclear proponent Jan Gerstenhaber, a young woman who addressed the weaknesses in Amory Lovins's "soft path" theory of the future of central utilities. "Sure, I'd like to stay home and not travel around all the time," said Gerstenhaber. "I'd rather sleep in my own bed and not have to take all the abuse we get in the debates, but I think I should do something."[89]

Wilson Cadman in the early spring of 1978 attended a lecture given at Kansas State University by Dr. Barry Commoner of Common Cause, entitled "The Political Implications of Energy Conservation." He followed up with a letter to Commoner. "It was a cold day," Cadman noted with no little irony, "and I found the very attractive and well illuminated auditorium to be a warm comfortable place to listen and finally consider some of your comments. Your charming manner and humorous approach to a very serious problem was well received by a near capacity student and faculty audience."

Commoner had criticized the Carter Administration, the Federal Energy Regulatory Commission, and Secretary of Energy Schlesinger unmercifully and then praised an FERC report that advised solar power. "It is peculiar to me," Cadman wrote, "that you gave the FERC no credit for competency until it came forward with a favorable report on the future of solar energy. It is our studied opinion that solar energy has its place along with all forms of energy to solve this nation's critical energy problem. I do, however, think that you performed a disservice by offering up 'pie in the sky.'" Commoner's suggestion of moving from a central station electric supply concept to a "backyard do-it-yourself" approach Cadman thought unrealistic, especially in the time frame Commoner proposed. "Kansas farmers remember the wind chargers and the Delco plants, yet couldn't wait for central station service from the private companies and the REA. Have we forgotten Red China's 'great leap forward' with a steel blast furnace in every backyard? Did that make a lot of steel for China or was it a great leap backward?" Cadman corrected a number of statistics used in the speech. He then closed by objecting to Commoner's statement that "public ownership of solar power is necessary because the capitalistic system does not work." Capitalism did work, Cadman claimed, in the power industry and in others. "I seriously doubt if your anti-capitalistic statement made a favorable impression on the informed students at Kansas State University." Copies of the letter were sent to the university newspaper, its president, numerous professors, and representatives of utilities around the state.[90]

There is no question that not only KG&E's past positive reputation as a civic-minded corporation, but its continued attitude of patience and direct involvement by officers and employees at all levels gave it a better chance of dealing successfully with objections, influencing the social context, and completing its project than was true of a number of other utility companies. There was a kind of general "knee jerk" hatred for both the corporation and the people who were sometimes called its "lackeys," but when it came down to individuals there was a grudging respect even among the most intransigent opponents of the Wolf Creek plant for Bob Rives, with his calm, respectful, and fact-filled responses; Donna Dilsaver, a pioneer among women executives and a person who could speak to the concern of mothers directly; and even for Wilson Cadman, who, while possessed of a modicum of Irish volubility, certainly did not isolate himself either in fear or out of rancor from the center of the fray. This constant presence not only kept matters in a dialogue rather than a monologue form, but prevented the unchecked escalation of radicalism that occurs when the enemy is unknown and invisible—the kind of fierce hatred that can be engendered in war for a foreign and alien enemy. To say that KG&E people were your neighbors was a slogan to be sure, but it was also true. The critics were neighbors too, whom KG&E officials met at social gatherings and on the street. Generally, the company people stopped and talked when accosted, and did not sneer and turn away. It did not prevent increasing protest, but it was a moderating influence.

The company was not alone in defending itself. There continued to be a grassroots and spontaneous support group as well as opposition. While it is an axiom that people tend to come together more strongly to stop something they fear than to support something they wish for, these pronuclear citizens spent lots of time and print questioning the motives of the opponents and doing some amateur social psychology.

The combination of "church reunion" and "county fair" atmosphere at the rallies was not viewed by all as a sign of seriousness. Maybe, some said, it was a "fad" to join antinuclear groups. "There is a strange element of Americans," wrote the editor of the *McPherson*

Sentinel, "who will rally to most any kind of a protest meeting, march or sit-in." What about real sacrifices? "Let these protestors turn off their electricity and burn kerosene lamps. Turn off their air conditioners. Throw away their electric refrigerators. . . . Turn off and throw away their TV sets. . . . Try this plan and you can bet the present protestors couldn't forget their principles fast enough to buy nuclear electricity."[91] The *Kansas City Times* argued similarly: "Sometimes one has to wonder to what degree antinuclear power protestors are motivated by pure reason and conviction or whether many of them are not merely caught up in the faddish vogue of a currently popular cause and the zestful camaraderie of the picket march. Once a person has persuaded himself that he or she has enlisted in a noble crusade to rescue the world from atomic holocaust, any reasoned arguments on the other side become unheard and unavailing."[92]

A second line of argument was that the protestors were being fed misinformation, and that they were themselves irrational—"kooks." "The timing of the doomcrying varmits who oppose nuclear energy is amazing," wrote one critic in February 1978. "Just two days after Groundhog Day, one of them pops from her hole to monger fear. I hope she will scurry back to her burrow to hide from all that 'horrible' radiation." He said the protests were the product of "disordered, uninformed minds."[93]

More calm, but making the same point, was a Peter Stoler article reprinted in Kansas in the fall of 1978, entitled "The Irrational Fight Against Nuclear Power." The facts dictated nuclear, Stoler said, so why the protest? "Some of it stems from an uneasiness about anything new or different and resembles the passionate, unthinking hostility that greeted powered looms, steam engines, railroads, automobiles and other technological advances. Much of the antipathy is emotional, the product of a 'Hiroshima mentality' that equates nuclear power with bombs and seeks to ban both. Since the U.S. withdrew from Vietnam, resistance to nuclear power has become the new crusade for many members of a society that otherwise lacks compelling causes. Nuclear power is an inviting target for those who revolt against bigness—big science and technology, big industry that must build and manage reactors, big government that must safeguard and regulate them. Part of the opposition stems from a desire to return to the supposedly simpler good old days, in which people would do more for themselves and, as one bumper sticker suggests, SPLIT WOOD NOT ATOMS."[94] Peter Brennan, secretary of labor under Nixon, said that when Carter said that energy independence should be the moral equivalent of war, "he declared war on the wrong people"—namely the utilities. "You can't build anything from conservation," Brennan said. "You can't even build a wheelchair out of the pie-in-the-sky energy schemes being huckstered as substitutes. . . . We are allowing our available energy options to be crippled and broken by government regulations, by a fierce band of no-growth muggers who are assaulting virtually every energy option we can realistically use, and by an American public that doesn't know what's going on and what's at stake. . . . When you're hungry and out of work, it's difficult to enjoy a spotless environment."[95]

Then there were those who said that the protestors were rational all right, and had a point, but were just too fearful—they had seen too many nuclear "creature feature" movies. Everything involved a risk. Went a typical example: "The more meek would undoubtedly insist that every conceivable problem be forecast and safeguarded against before the first electrical plant could start generating. . . . Not too many years ago one would have said it would be impossible for a man to walk on the moon and live to return. Yet we solved that problem just as we have handled many other seemingly impossible tasks. If we are going to keep this country running, maybe it is time we began putting a little more faith in our capabilities."[96] "If the doomsayers had prevailed," said another, "we would still be living in conditions of the stone age."[97] "I'm convinced," wrote a third, "if we'd had nuclear power for thousands of years and some guy tried to introduce fire, he'd have a terrible time."[98] The 100th anniversary in 1979 of Thomas Edison's invention of the electric light bulb encouraged arguments of this type. And the debate over environmental protection versus economic growth in general has continued along much the same lines since.

No alternative to nuclear was simple. Coal continued to be a problem. The winter of 1978–1979 was another cold one, and the operation of coal generating plants was complicated by a long strike by the United Mine Workers.[99] Financing was tightening. In December 1978, First Boston, an investment firm, put securities of all three major Kansas utilities on its "unwanted" list. It cited the election of John Carlin as governor, with his campaign of utility bashing, a "cloudy" regulatory outlook in the state, and climbing interest rates.[100] Utility rates were increasing too slowly for Wall Street, yet too fast for customers. Vulcan Chemical in Wichita, KG&E's biggest customer, announced in 1978 that it was studying creating its own electric plant. It and other industrial customers argued they were being discriminated against to hold residential rates artificially low. Residential customers blamed the industries, whom they said got an unreasonable subsidy.[101]

The construction milestones at Wolf Creek provided multiple opportunities to dig the dagger in and try to turn it. In October 1978 the Kansas public learned that at the 90-day test in March of the base mat pour, a number of the test cylinders cracked at pressure levels that did not meet NRC standards. KG&E explained that the test equipment and procedures were probably faulty, not the base mat, and that even if the tests were correct, the mat was plenty strong and had lost only some of its redundant specifications. But the base mat problem created a substantial regulatory delay and placed a weapon in the hands of those questioning the infallibility of experts in the office or on the site.[102] So focused was the press on the base mat, and on some cracks or "voids," common to all big concrete work, that had been found in walls going up in the containment building, that the news of Westinghouse losing its fuel supply suit—good news for KG&E and Wolf Creek—which came at the same time was almost ignored.[103] Instead, it was suggested by the regional press that the base mat argument and the cracks could make the plant, now 25 percent complete, into a "$1 billion white elephant."[104] "Corrosion, cracks and dents," wrote the Wichita newspaper, "are slowly crippling a growing number of the country's nuclear power plants."[105] It might be noted also that cracks in concrete were much more easily understood by newspaper readers than were uranium contracts.

As the year of the Sunflower Alliance ended, the plant was growing about as fast as its opposition. The framework of the turbine room could be seen and six tiers or "lifts" of concrete had been poured around the reactor room itself to a height of 66 feet above ground. While the strength of the concrete in the reactor room had been questioned, a reporter noted that "a first-hand examination makes it hard to imagine anything ever damaging it." The primary wall was four feet of reinforced concrete, then came a "secondary shield wall" of 3.5 feet of reinforced concrete, and finally a "primary shield wall" with an average thickness of seven feet, four inches. The "short crane" working outside went to 310 feet, the big one reached to 375 feet—the largest of their kind in the world.[106] One newspaper described the plant in the fall of 1978 as the "Monolith of the Prairie." The main impression was "awesome and redundant"—"mind-boggling." Two thousand construction workers were on site making it more so daily.[107]

While the tensioning rings were tightened around the containment building and the concrete went in by the truckload, the direct action groups trained. Their first target was the reactor vessel, which was expected to be delivered at a specially constructed dock at the Port of Catoosa on the Arkansas River at Tulsa and then hauled in a custom rail car to the Wolf Creek site sometime early in 1979. Plans were made to intercept it on the river, and to do so again along the Missouri Pacific rail line at the site itself.

The *Kansas City Times*, commenting, referred to "A Sorry Protest Fleet" and claimed that "such extreme behavior can only damage the credibility of the protestors in the eyes of the public and the governmental regulatory agencies. It amounts to an admission that the objectors' arguments are bankrupt or have not proved persuasive. And in effect it violates the protestors' pledge of peaceful, nonviolent action. . . . The proposed outing is on a par with the gambit of the Save the Whales fans who put out to sea in small ships to interpose themselves between the power harpoons and their intended targets."[108]

But the Natural Guard continued with the disciplined training, including relaxation exercises and discussions of nonviolence and role playing. Participants acted out the part that would be played by power plant workers and police as well as themselves when the day of confrontation came.[109] "We naturally recognize that everyone might not approve of our actions," said Paul Schaefer of the KNG, "but then not everyone approved of the Boston Tea Party."[110] All the trainees in Lawrence were told they should not participate in the reactor action unless they were willing to go to jail. All accepted that. "I don't believe what I'm doing is wrong," said University of Kansas senior and Natural Guard trainee Bill Beems. "If any crime is being perpetrated, it's the construction of that plant."[111]

At the end of 1978 the "reverse salient" in the case of the introduction of the new technological system at Wolf Creek had established a clear enough direction, gathered adequate tools, and reached sufficient strength that a critical confrontation awaited only the proper opportunity, weighted as it must be with the right symbolism and visuals. That opportunity came in the dead of a severe Kansas winter with the arrival of the reactor containment vessel in Coffey County.

7
Wolf Creek Express

This is the key to make the plant work; this is where the nuclear reaction takes place. Once it is there, it will be even harder to stop.
—Andy Allen of Kansas Natural Guard, on plan to stop reactor vessel train, Oct. 11, 1978

No one in state government is equipped to make valid criticism of this plant.
—Kansas Attorney General Robert Stephen, April 12, 1979

It was a long, hearty feast that's now over.
—*Wichita Eagle*, commenting on the history of KG&E, Jan. 22, 1979

There was no break for the holidays.

On December 22, 1978, the NRC ordered that all concrete work at Wolf Creek be discontinued until the base mat question was fully and finally resolved and the Quality Assurance program approved.[1] "There is no question," said one regulator. "The procedure for qualifying the concrete mix was not followed by the contractor. They didn't play by the rules of the game."[2] KG&E officials spent their holiday in Washington talking concrete with regulatory committees.[3]

Two days after the concrete work suspension the 380-ton, $50 million Westinghouse nuclear reactor containment vessel for Wolf Creek left Chattanooga, Tennessee, on an oceangoing "super barge." It was 40 feet long, 20 feet in diameter, made of carbon steel with a covering of stainless steel, and with the planned addition of 193 bundles of uranium fuel rods (55,777 rods total) would become the reactor engine itself. The vessel attracted a lot of attention on the Ohio River. Its route was from there to the Mississippi, then along the Arkansas to Tulsa, where it would be transferred to a 22-

axle rail car for the overland journey to Kansas.[4] On December 29 Bian Hunt of the Sunbelt Alliance of Oklahoma told the press that previous reports of a nonviolent protest of the reactor landing were inaccurate. The protest fleet intended to confront the reactor barge at Catoosa port and stop it by putting small boats in its path at the port's turning basin.[5] On December 31 Nader's Critical Mass organization asked the NRC to suspend Wolf Creek's license, pointing to the base mat problem and saying construction work at the plant was "woefully deficient." KG&E's Rives responded that the Critical Mass letter was "their usual silliness." Robert Pollard of the Union of Concerned Scientists announced he would join MACEA's William Ward at meetings in Bethesda, Maryland, concerning the base mat.[6] That month too, the prime rate on loans went to 11¾ percent, the federal government announced that while Yucca Flats, Nevada, seemed promising there was still no approved federal nuclear waste disposal site, and KG&E quietly paid Coffey County $833,585 for six months of property taxes on the Wolf Creek site.[7]

The new year opened with record low temperatures in Kansas— 20 below zero in several areas on January 2 and 3.[8] The weather delayed the reactor barge, but on January 5 protestors gathered at Catoosa with their canoes and rowboats and their entourage of media. They sang songs with frosty breath wafting from parka hoods ("Hey, oh, hold on; Wolf Creek Nuke is dead and gone") and carried homemade signs ("React or Die," "Radiation Without Representation"). Seventeen people were arrested when they crossed the fence built by Port of Catoosa officials and slid down a snow-covered slope toward the water. They were hauled to jail in a bus, and all but three were released on their own recognizance. Several construction workers jeered. The water temperature of 16 degrees stopped the protest fleet, and the reactor, which had been making progress for eight days behind the tug *J. E. Gegenheimer*, landed without serious incident.[9] After several days of delay due to snow and ice, it was hoisted onto its rail car on January 10, and began a journey in a train that local folk legend dubbed "the Wolf Creek Express."[10]

That same day, a meeting at the plant site between KG&E officials and 100 area politicians concerning the base mat question was cancelled after a telephone call to the Wichita office warned of a plan to disrupt it with a bomb. "Even though I think my electric bills are too high," said an anonymous caller, "I don't want to see anyone hurt." Fifteen to twenty members of the Kansas Natural Guard (KNG) were at the plant gate nearly every day distributing leaflets.[11]

On Thursday evening, January 11, the "Express" entered Kansas. People in towns along the route turned out during the frigid night hours to see the 200-foot railcar and its cargo. An 11-year-old boy commented, "I thought it was going to be a bomb."[12] It did indeed look like a bomb, with a large banner on the side, reading "Wolf Creek Plant: Saves Oil . . . Makes Jobs . . . Saves Money."[13]

Awaiting the train at Burlington was a dedicated contingent from the KNG camped in tents and tepees scattered along a Coffey County back road in the bitterly cold, snow-covered landscape. One tent flew an early U.S. flag adorned with 13 stars in a circle—a symbol that became a regular prop of the protest. The contingent was visited through the night of the eleventh by Coffey County police and firemen in four wheel drive vehicles, who were concerned for their safety in the extreme conditions. Paul Schaefer, 32, one of the leaders, said the goal of the group was simply to regain some control of their lives: "At least I feel good knowing that I tried."[14]

The protest plan had been in the making for over three months. Some would go on to the tracks to "symbolically" and temporarily stop the train with their bodies. Others would stand by in support. Those blocking the track expected to be arrested, and would "go limp" so they would have to be carried off to jail. The Guard allowed no one except its trained members, the police, and the media to attend. Location of the campsite and the confrontation was kept secret and some members acted as informal sentinels to keep out intruders.[15] An observer noted that the "campsite is pervaded with youthful optimism and idealistic determination," and that visiting there was as it must have been visiting General Washington's troops at Valley Forge.[16] "I don't expect any problems," said Coffey County sheriff Earl Freeman. "We'll arrest them and charge them with criminal trespassing, that's all. Then if there are no altercations there will be no further charges."[17]

Tony Blaufuss, the priest, wrote an article about the moral justification for the action. "We decided to participate," he said, "only after a lengthy study of the problems and prayerful consideration of the effects of our action. It seemed to us that we needed to exercise our responsibility to alert people to the dangers. . . . Our intention is not to downgrade the law. . . . However, there are situations when we disregard laws for a more important reason. . . . We believe our action is in the Christian tradition. Jesus taught the primacy of love over law. . . . When there was conflict between breaking a law and helping people (or even animals), he taught his disciples to break the law."[18]

On January 12 at about 2 P.M. the meeting took place between the MoPac train on the Wolf Creek spur northwest of Aliceville, Kansas' and the KNG protestors. The group joined hands and marched to the railroad tracks as the train approached. Several carried signs. "If You Can't Pour Concrete Can You Store Nuclear Waste?" said one. Francis Blaufuss lay down on the tracks after shouting "Take that damn thing back to Chattanooga, Tennessee!" and became the first of 36 people arrested. Seven went to jail.[19] The rest were fined $40 and released.

The train was delayed for 30 minutes, while people circled it chanting "Block that Nuke," and then it went on its way to a welcoming photo session at the plant.[20] KG&E senior engineer John Bailey said the blunt shell was "backed by volumes of test data . . . a thing of technical beauty. . . . Few parts of any space project have had more attention to every detail of construction than this container. It took five years, three months to build the vessel. We know where, when and who poured the steel. We can also track the molding and welding, every inch, day-by-day." When the cranes had "walked" the vessel to its holding pad and most of the workers had left, Arterburn walked over and patted the huge mass. "Welcome home, baby," he said.[21]

"Our message is not violence," said one of the protestors, "our message is peace." The law enforcement officials did their duty respectfully and the media disrupted the ceremony in the most minimal way. Sheriff Freeman, in a freshly pressed uniform and chewing on a cigar, commented: "I've talked to them a little bit. I think they are attacking the wrong end of the horse. I tell them I'm not for or against the plant, but if they put their time in by trying to get Congress to stop this, they'd have a better chance. I guess they like doing this."[22]

Edith Lange objected strongly to editorials that called those arrested "criminals" or media groupies. "The protestors," she wrote, "choose dramatic ways to dramatize those dangers because they want to get the issues before the public, not because they want to have a big lark for themselves. They know that few people read books but that everybody watches television, so naturally they try to attract the cameras. . . . These protestors . . . are not criminals; rather they are the salt of the earth and may well become the American heroes of tomorrow."[23] Onlookers were impressed by the spirit of unity that the event seemed to bring among the participants on all sides. It showed, said one, "that the bond of human dignity can exist even though persons come from different perspectives."[24] This interpretation fits with Kenneth Keniston's analysis of the "Vietnam Summer" youth protest of the late 1960s. "Formal statements of rationalized philosophy," he wrote, "articulated interpretations of history and political life, and concrete visions of political objectives were almost completely absent . . . (and in this respect, as in many others, this is a typically American group). But what did emerge was a strong, if often largely implicit, belief in a set of basic moral principles: justice, decency, equality, responsibility, nonviolence and fairness."[25]

Of course there were some detractors. Wrote one: "May God above bless KG&E and KCP&L and all other large corporations who stand for the American Free Enterprise System. May those who are in the Kansas Natural Guard drown in a river of Russian Communist Vodka!"[26] A newspaper in Ft. Scott attributed the protest to news hunger: "No clown hired to tease children in a supermarket has been less worthy of a banner head line and front page pictures than these exhibitionists. . . . They are the groupies of the news industry. We feed them, groom them, give them their reason for being."[27] Columnist Jim Bishop asserted that "there is fascism in ecology." The nuclear protestors were zealots, he said, "who in the name of clean air and sturdy forests, will strangle us with their antiseptic hands."[28] Concluded a Kansas observer: "As for the 'Sunflower Alliance' and 'Natural Guard,' they are full of hot wind and organic waste."[29]

Relatively, things looked good for the Wolf Creek project early in 1979. The Kansas protest had been defeated before the NRC boards, in the courts, and in the field. The critical equipment had reached the Burlington site, and construction policies had been improved for the move from civil to nuclear construction.

Then came the Ides of March.

Early that month the Seabrook reactor was delivered to its site in New Hampshire. People hurled themselves in front of trucks and blocked the state highway. One hundred fifty-five members of the Clamshell Alliance were arrested. In California activists threatened to cut transmission lines.[30] In March, too, the Karen Silkwood trial opened (with her heirs suing Kerr-McGee for $60 million in damages), the five Wolf Creek KNG activists who went to trial were sentenced, and the movie *The China Syndrome* was released nationwide. KG&E employees were invited to a special showing of the film at Wichita's Cinema West, equipped with an analysis of the inaccuracies of the film published by the Edison Institute.[31] Typically for the company, they did not ignore the problems, but tried to prepare for them.

Then there was Three Mile Island. On March 28 about 4 A.M., the feedwater supply pumps at Three Mile Island Nuclear Plant Unit 2, Harrisburg, Pennsylvania, shut down. The emergency feedwater supply system failed because its valves had been mistakenly closed, and 69 control rods slid into the reactor in an automatic SCRAM. A series of mechanical and human errors left 80,000 gallons of radioactive water on the floor and caused the uranium rods in the reactor to overheat, expand, and break through their protective sheaths, spreading radioactivity. It took far too long for a site emergency to be declared and radioactive steam to be vented. On day 4, March 31, a hydrogen bubble that formed inside the reactor falsely created a fear of explosion and the rumor that the core would be cut off from emergency coolant and subject to further temperature rises and possibly a meltdown. Not until the sixth day did the bubble danger dissipate, allowing the core temperature to fall toward a cold shutdown.[32] The series of related events and errors, happening simultaneously, and all to negative effect, was, in the NRC's definition, "incredible."[33]

Three Mile Island (TMI) was the single most important external event affecting the construction progress, cost of, and regulatory stance toward Wolf Creek in Kansas. Although most students of TMI have suggested that the effects of it and other nuclear accidents on public opinion were temporary, they have also concluded that these effects were strongly negative, increased the size of the antinuclear movement generally, and had an impact at sites quite remote from the accident itself.[34] It certainly undercut the force of the statistics about lack of accidents at nuclear plants, and it galvanized antinuclear opinion among many who had been undecided.[35]

At first many emphasized that overreaction was as dangerous as underreaction. The *Kansas City Star* in April ran a list of historical disasters and possible but overextreme reactions: "1903 Iroquois theatre fire, Chicago, 575 die. As a result all theatres in United States closed permanently—1912 Titanic sinks, 1,517 die—All marine transport banned forever—1918 Brooklyn rail wreck kills 100—Nation's railroads liquidated—1937 Natural gas explosion kills 400, New London Tex. school—Petroleum industry shut down—1942 Fire guts Coconut Grove Boston, 483 perish—All night clubs close . . . —1956 Two planes collide over Grand Canyon, 128 die—World's air traffic grounded forever . . . —1979 Nuclear plant leaks radiation, Harrisburg, Pa.—None die—Government halts nation's nuclear energy program."[36] Conservative James Kilpatrick tried to stop the furor he knew was coming from "calamity howlers and purveyors of panic." He thought TMI was mostly a media event and not a real crisis. "By the ordinary yardsticks," he wrote, "the accident at Harrisburg ranked below a run-of-the-mill train wreck or a 10-car pileup on the freeway," but the novelty made it more.[37] In fact, more people had died at Wolf Creek than at TMI. On May 7, a 35-year-old Daniel employee, David Bailey, died when a falling cable cutter hit him. On February 6, James Hegwald was killed by a falling tree while clearing land for the plant. The newspapers contained the usual obituary, nothing more.[38]

But any thought that TMI could be waved off as "just one of those things," or turned to the utilities' advantage by emphasizing that no one was injured, was dispelled as the reaction to the emergency nationwide appeared over the next months. Mike Royko in Chicago admitted he had trusted the "helpful local nuclear power plant. . . . And I admit that I wanted to trust it, especially with the Arabs goosing the price of our oil-produced energy every time their mad minds twitched." TMI changed that: "Because now the terrifying words aren't coming from the dust-jackets of worst-selling scare books about what might happen. This time the thrilling plot hasn't been something that came out of the mind of a science fiction writer."[39] A letter from some children in Australia asked, "Are Mickey and Donald OK?"[40] Indeed, the TMI accident led to a substantial escalation in questioning the American way of life, modern style.

It was uncertain what would be needed to respond adequately to the public fear. "The public's outrage has to be gauged," wrote the editor in Parsons, Kansas. "Congress could outlaw the whole thing. When you're dealing in the psychological realm, it's awfully hard to predict."[41] Jane Fonda and Tom Hayden began to appear at rallies all over the United States. A nationally syndicated cartoon showed a nuclear plant with steam coming out the cooling tower and slowly taking the shape of Ralph Nader. "Good Grief!" went the balloon caption from the control room, "It's worse than we thought!"[42]

Local reaction was swift and more than verbal. While Kansas Senator Nancy Kassebaum's comment on TMI was simply that "we can't turn back the hands of time because of one incident," other Kansas officials were more disturbed.[43] With the heightened awareness of nuclear dangers in the wake of TMI following so closely on the news of the brief stopping of the "Wolf Creek Express" in Kansas, Francis Blaufuss gained national fame and got mail from all over the United States in response to photos that ran showing him lying down on the railroad tracks.[44] "The purpose of a nuclear reactor is just to boil water," wrote Fred James of Wichita, using an image that was often repeated by opponents. "That's like hitching an elephant to a lawn mower. There are better ways of boiling water."[45] KG&E's Wichita offices were picketed on April 6 by robed figures carrying signs. They wore white face makeup, black shrouds, and orange plastic booties like those worn by plant workers to avoid radiation contamination. There was a rally at the Century II auditorium that day to recognize the dangers of TMI and apply them to Kansas.[46] The next day there were 125 protestors. At the KG&E annual meeting late in May, marchers outside dragged three captive customers around in a ball and chain and stopped passersby for debates on nuclear power.[47] The theme of a Sunflower Alliance rally at Redmond Reservoir on June 5 was "No Need for Wolf Creek: We All Live In Pennsylvania."[48] On June 10 more than 1,000 people, the most ever gathered in an antinuclear meeting in Kansas, braved a hard rain to wave 13-star flags at Redmond Reservoir and hear speakers against Wolf Creek from such new followers of the Alliance as the Kansas Organic Producers, the Socialist Workers Party of Kansas City, and the United Mine Workers.[49] Bob Rives of KG&E said that people were "unduly frightened," but that "we're in a position of having to meet the needs of people. That's the purpose of Wolf Creek." TMI, Rives said, would make Wolf Creek better.[50]

Kansas Fourth District Representative Dan Glickman did not appear to be willing to leave that up to the company. In the days following TMI, Glickman proposed having permanent on-site federal inspectors at every nuclear plant as long as they were running.[51] The *Wichita Eagle* recommended a moratorium on the licensing and building of nuclear plants nationwide.[52] Diane Tegtmeier of MACEA said, "The accident bears out what we've been trying to say . . . unfortunately it does."[53] Governor Carlin supported new siting bills introduced in the legislature for nuclear plants and even for power lines.[54] "They are monopolies with captive customers," said Kansas Senate majority leader Norman Gaar. "We cannot permit them to go on unbridled, without public input."[55] "Those of us who have stood up steadfastly for nuclear power," said a reporter at the *Emporia Gazette*, "are beginning to waver in our tracks. The nightmare at Three Mile Island . . . is enough to shake anyone's faith."[56] TMI, opined Scott Garten, caustic critic of the local protest, "really threw some Chicken Littles into a tizzy."[57]

It struck far more than the fringes, and was hardly a sermon just for people in the choir. People of all shades of opinion interviewed for this book invariably mentioned the importance and the shock of TMI in regard to Wolf Creek. Dr. Robert Hagen, the KG&E nuclear engineer, and Jim Lawing, the ACLU attorney and state legislator, both went to see *The China Syndrome* when it came out and were both overwhelmed that TMI followed so close on the fictional "meltdown" scenario. Lawing, when asked about the outside connections of the local protest—was there any national "conspiracy"?—said if there was it was Hollywood and that movie.[58] Hagen agreed. TMI, he said, had a particularly devastating effect on the "old school" nuclear engineers who genuinely believed that they had built the "perfect machines" in their nuclear plants and that they were really risk free. Engineers of Hagen's generation accepted that there was some risk, but that it was controllable. But people like Jesse Arterburn, who had hired Hagen for the KG&E nuclear unit, were psychologically devastated by TMI and completely surprised by it. According to Hagen, Arterburn was never the same after Three Mile Island. Suddenly he feared lawsuits, and begin to imagine accidents that he had never thought possible before. His separation from KG&E, and from Wolf Creek, was, after that event, only a matter of time.[59] Lawing, Arterburn, and Hagen were hardly "Chicken Littles," and neither were the thousands of others locally and regionally who put down their newspapers with the front page headlines about an accident in Pennsylvania and began thinking hard about the domed structure in Burlington, Kansas.

After TMI, Kansans could say "it could happen here," concerning the operation of a nuclear plant, while the events surrounding that accident gave more currency to the seriousness of dealing with the immediate issue of the questioned concrete work at Wolf Creek. On May 5 a syndicated article by Daniel Schorr appeared around the country that focused on the Wolf Creek concrete question specifically. Schorr got his information from Max McDowell, who had in January ended his career as a Kansas investigative reporter to return to piano tuning at his home in Elmdale, Kansas. Schorr's implication was that McDowell, who had been an antinuclear activist since the Lyons protests in 1970s, and who often appeared as a speaker at the Redmond reservoir rallies, had been forced out of his position as a reporter at WIBW-TV in Topeka because of charges of "overkill" concerning "a crusade a little before its time" on the concrete void at Wolf Creek. The station itself said that McDowell resigned when he was told he could not report exclusively on Wolf Creek; he still wrote articles regularly for the *Emporia Gazette* and other Kansas newspapers.[60]

The "scandal" that McDowell uncovered and Schorr emphasized was the "woefully belated notice" by the NRC of potential deficiencies in the base mat at Wolf Creek, and the "void" in a concrete wall, which Schorr said KG&E did not report to the NRC until McDowell filmed it for the evening news in Topeka. McDowell sent a report to Governor Carlin, and tried unsuccessfully to get the story of the void more fully covered in Kansas newspapers. Then came TMI, and the revelations there of "cover up," and of statements by officials critical of freedom of the press. Suddenly McDowell's "void" story began getting play in Kansas and elsewhere, including Schorr's syndicated piece. "No longer is this Max McDowell's quixotic crusade," Schorr wrote. The Kansas building union's council was instigating its own investigation of the quality of construction at a special office at the nonunion Wolf Creek site, and, said Schorr, "even the complacent, publicity-hating Nuclear Regulatory Commission," was asking for data on the base mat before proceeding. NRC called a public hearing in Kansas on the base mat for May. WIBW received an Associated Press award for McDowell's reporting, which it accepted in the reporter's absence.[61]

Bob Rives responded to Schorr at length in a letter to the press. There was no "scoop" by McDowell on the base mat, Rives said. Several papers had covered it earlier, including the *Wichita Eagle*, which had printed Schorr's article prominently. KG&E made no attempt to hide it. The company, it was true, had not reported the "void" until the day McDowell's story ran, but that was because he was at the plant filming another story when the workmen removed the forms that revealed the void. The company expressly allowed the TV crew to film it. It was unfortunate that the first reporters described it as a "fissure" rather than a void, and that implied crack. One journal claimed that "the concrete is crumbling at Wolf Creek." A *void* was simply a place in the wall that did not fill, and the simple solution was to fill it with concrete. The base mat concrete was strong enough, no matter what reports you believed.[62]

On May 15 the base mat hearings, which KG&E's Glenn Koester called the "Days of the Dungeon," began in the basement of the Coffey County courthouse in Burlington. It was, it was said, "an odd mixture—part detailed technical discussion, part town meeting, part revival tent, and part media event." Four sheriff's officers were assigned to the rear door to stop overcrowding, but even so there were 100 people sitting in the stairwell, while lights from a half dozen TV crews kept the room plenty hot.[63] The base mat problems gave opportunity for many claims against KG&E that were inaccurate or exaggerated. The biggest hole in the pour was four inches square, yet there was a charge that Daniel had buried an air-compressor in the base mat. The charges got so extreme that Don Elliott at KG&E used to joke that apparently people thought the company got rid of its old office furniture by pouring it into the concrete at Wolf Creek.[64] "I apologize for the extreme moods here tonight," said one speaker. "There are some people here with dollar signs in their eyes and chrome-plated dreams. But some of us call this place home, and we want to keep it that way."[65]

There was understandable complaint that the builders should be allowed to judge their own work on the base mat, but there were also data to support the company contention that the SNUPPS design included a good deal of extra strength beyond what was strictly needed.[66] The company concluded that the test concrete cylinders were not set straight, and that there was something wrong with the test machine. The most severe earth movement expected on the site was .12Gs, while the plant specifications, because the single design covered areas more prone to earthquake than Kansas, were for withstanding .2Gs. The 90-day test of the concrete, showing its strength at 4,460 psi, was not the 5,000 psi specified, but more than met all design stresses. Four thousand psi was in fact the standard used in many nuclear plants, and 5,000 psi was a Bechtel requirement, not an NRC one.[67] Perhaps the sample cylinders were stored under the wrong conditions, and almost certainly the tests, conducted on a Sunday, were done with malfunctioning test equipment which positioned the cylinders, but unfortunately the workman did not see a supervisor when the concrete cylinders started breaking and so entire cylinders were not preserved for further tests.[68] The Portland Cement Association tested fragments from the crushed cylinders and concluded the strength of the concrete averaged 6,690 psi.[69] McDowell asked repeatedly if Bechtel had a contract with KG&E relieving Bechtel of responsibility for any design flaw. The answer was only that that information was proprietary.[70]

The base mat question was finally resolved in July after further tests of the suspect concrete by the U.S. Army Corps of Engineers Waterways Experimental Station at Vicksburg, Mississippi.[71] KG&E had presented evidence that the failure of some cylinders at the 90-day tests was an anomaly, and that all cylinders at the 7-day and 28-day tests had tested 5,000 psi or above. New concrete, in the absence of chemical deterioration, which was extremely rare and had been ruled out in this case, invariably grew stronger, not weaker, with time. Charges by Ralph Nader that KG&E had waited six months to notify the NRC of the concrete tests were incorrect. While the NRC did not put a moratorium on Wolf Creek until six months had elapsed, the tests were reported to it by the company the day after they were done. Karl Seyfrit, director of NRC's Region IV in Arlington, Texas, had said when asked by newspapers during the base mat crisis about the quality of work at Wolf Creek: "I wouldn't say that it's outstanding, nor would I say it's at the bottom of the heap. I wouldn't characterize it as greatly different from the norm on such projects."[72]

The NRC conclusion was that the base mat concrete had not

weakened since it was poured in 1977 and that there had been no chemical deterioration. NRC did not go on record about whether the compressive strength was actually the 5,000 psi design specification, but did concede that it did not have to be that strong to meet all stresses to which it might be subjected. While it did not go so far as to approve the base mat, NRC allowed KG&E to suspend its own work stoppage order on concrete.[73]

Glenn Koester remembered later that for the company the base mat delay, coinciding as it did with the TMI events and suggesting, as it did, that the minimal on-site KG&E construction supervision team would have to be greatly expanded, was the low point of the entire Wolf Creek project. Meetings between KG&E and Daniel officials and the NRC often were held at Arlington, Texas, on Saturdays, and then the whole thing had to be explained again in Washington, DC. "We spent so much time with the NRC we should have lived there." The only good point about the base mat delay was that the winter was so bitterly cold that less concrete construction time was lost than might have been the case under milder conditions.[74]

These issues created further polarization over the nuclear issue, which increasingly came to dominate the public mind concerning the Kansas Gas and Electric Company generally. It was noticeable not only in the hearings specifically relating to Wolf Creek, but in all other public hearings involving KG&E. Of 27 people testifying at public hearings on a $36.4 million rate increase request to cover costs of KG&E's share of Jeffrey Energy Center, held at several Kansas towns in August 1979, at least 16 represented antinuclear groups. Wilson Cadman complained that "the [rate] hearing was dominated by special interest groups using the occasion as an antinuclear forum," and said that the whole thing was "a highly orchestrated antinuclear media event dominated by the above-mentioned groups." The response of an editor whose reporter had covered the rate hearing under the headline "Kansans charged Saturday that KG&E is wasting money by building the Wolf Creek Nuclear Power Plant" was that "the reporter's job was to reflect what happened at the meeting, not to attempt to strike a balance of debate where none occurred."[75]

Jack Glaves, special counsel for the KCC at this rate hearing, purposefully pursued a line of questioning on Wolf Creek. "To say this project [Wolf Creek]," he said, "important as it is to the ratepayers of KG&E, is not relevant to a case in which the customers' future rates are set, is ludicrous. . . . Wolf Creek is a monumental part of KG&E's system and a monumental part of its construction budget. It all goes to the financial integrity of KG&E."[76] KG&E attorney Ralph Foster responded that the KCC had granted Wolf Creek a certificate of convenience and necessity, and the company had kept the Commission informed on its progress. "You cannot assume to manage the affairs of a utility under the guise of rate-making."[77] But the Kansas public wanted micromanagement, and by a government agency as close to them as possible. By April 1980 a major study of Wolf Creek, commissioned by the KCC and undertaken by consultants Cresap, McCormick and Paget, was under way.[78] That was not enough for some consumers. "I see that KG&E has done it to us again with the help of the Kansas Corporation Commission," wrote one. "When is the customer going to stop being the patsy of the utilities?"[79]

There was no question that with TMI the national antinuclear movement reached a peak. Few denied that the antinuclear tour conducted in the summer of 1979 by Jane Fonda, Ralph Nader, Tom Hayden, Bella Abzug, and others was "a helleva show."[80] Conservative commentator John Chamberlain, observing the attendance of 20,000 people at one of Fonda's rallies in New York City, could only muse that he was feeling a little forlorn. It had become partly a matter of personality and media. "Jane is a good-looking girl with sensible enough ideas about physical fitness, and she certainly can act. How else could she persuade her myriad followers that she knows more about Southeast Asian politics than the combined faculty of Stanford University's Hoover Institute for the Study of War, Peace, and Revolution? How else could she have established her reputation as a profound Marxist scholar? And how else could she challenge Dr. Edward Teller and former Department of Energy Secretary James R. Schlesinger on problems of nuclear safety?" Chamberlain thought it was a little like Henry Ford, in earlier times, giving opinions on Zionism because he knew how to build cheap cars. "The reason for my depression," Chamberlain concluded, "is that people who can explain what goes on in a nuclear reactor cannot compete with Jane Fonda in show business. The likes of Dr. Edward Teller don't turn out the mobs."[81]

In Kansas the increased intensity was indicated by more and more groups joining the antinuclear crusade, and by a turned up, while at the same time more generalized, rhetoric attacking nuclear power as a whole, and even capitalism, as frequently as it addressed specific problems with Wolf Creek, such as the base mat or the financing. Even local nuclear protest now had the "heft," the national and even global significance and the ideological expansiveness uninterrupted by factual detail, that made for the compact drama on which the media thrived. And it was through the media that the news reached the hearts and minds of the former "free riders," hoping to gain the benefits of protection by the protest without cost, but now galvanized into action. New Kansas groups appeared almost weekly in 1979: SCARE (Salt City Alliance for Responsible Energy); SANE (Salinans for Alternatives to Nuclear Energy); WISE (Women Insisting on Sensible Energy); MANA (McPherson Anti-Nuclear Alliances); CANE (Campaign Against Nuclear Energy); KASE (Kansans for Sensible Energy); RFK (Radioactive Free Kansas); ACE (Advocates for Clean Energy); CREST (Coalition for Renewable Energy Sources).[82]

Among the new voices were those of Chuck and Mary Abbott Mills, who bought KG&E stock so they could advance their antinuclear views from the inside at company annual meetings. The couple wrote a long article for a Wichita newspaper in November 1979, entitled "Nuclear Power: A Consumer Rip-Off." Nuclear power, the article said, was born through "the union of monopolistic corporations and monolithic government. It will only die when enough people stand up and refuse to take it any more." Construction costs on Wolf Creek had already reached the first estimates for the whole plant. There might be a question of uranium supply, as oil companies owned 65 percent of the U.S. uranium reserves and the government the rest. Conservation, they thought, would eliminate the need for the plant entirely.[83]

Bob Rives responded with a long piece entitled "Nuclear Power: Getting the Facts Straight." The Mills' article, Rives said, was filled with errors and was misleading. It was not true that nuclear plants could not get private insurance. It was not true that the United States was running out of uranium. It was not true that the taxpayer would pay for decommissioning. On the question of overbuilding, Rives restated the company position: "It is not generating capacity that is dictating the need for new plants nor is it growth in the use of electricity. It's the need to use different fuels. Just as the number of cars you own doesn't matter if you can't buy gasoline, having power plants is not helpful if they have no fuel to burn."[84]

Communications problems were endemic. The same month the Mills' article was published, the nuclear industry was given the "gobbledygook" award by the National Council of Teachers of English for its media "explanations" of the TMI emergency. There an explosion was called "energetic disassembly," and fire referred to as "rapid oxidation," which was being technically accurate to the entire exclusion of the sense of common discourse.[85]

KG&E's Rives was a better link than most, as he had a journalistic background, humanistic interests, and a firm command of the English language. He had been with the company since 1959, and his loyalty to it was sincere. Most people had no background at all in either heavy construction or things nuclear, so the company public relations staff looked for an "element that made it understandable." Still, Rives had to insist on technical distinctions—in engineering, in management, in finance—from CWIP to "capacity factor"—that seemed arcane and even conspiratorial to many readers. Rives was the first to perceive too that the base mat and void issues, coming as they did at the height of the protest, combined with coincidences like *The China Syndrome* appearing exactly at the time of Three Mile Island, "were grist for the mill" that was grinding out the anti–Wolf Creek material. Nuclear power might be the best of several risky alternatives, but, said Rives, it "forced people to think about things they don't think about. . . . No young mother likes to think about any element of risk."

Nor did company directors and officers much like thinking about getting obscene anonymous phone calls at home late at night, sometimes containing death threats. That, however, became part of corporate life by the late 1970s. No director resigned, and, while there were discussions and scenarios on the possibility of abandonment at the meetings, none, hearing the facts, favored it.[86]

"They [the opposition] feel they invented the word environment," said Marge Setter, a KG&E director and independent businesswoman, "but a lot of us knew how to spell it a long time ago." Setter was, she said, a "flag waver and pure capitalist," and saw no reason to apologize for what the American system had and would do. Along with other directors, Setter was sued by some stockholders over Wolf Creek. Her reaction was calm and ironic. She said she should get her name in the book of world records as the "only white woman ever sued for one billion dollars." Nothing was totally trouble free, Setter opined, Maytag commercials notwithstanding. The hoops nuclear plants had to go through to be commissioned "border on being ludicrous." But there had to be a basic decision to go forward or stop. KG&E was a go-forward enterprise, and Kansas was a state that had to take some risks to grow. "We had swum halfway across the lake," Setter said, "and had to get to the other side."[87] That attitude was shared by top management to a remarkable degree, considering the pressure.

At the plant late in the year that had begun with the Wolf Creek Express, work proceeded, but became more costly as the purely civil part gave way to the nuclear part. Part of the plant was "familiar, commonplace hardware," and part was "alien and hostile," at least at first. The series of events at TMI seemed routine. People had been controlling mechanical processes connected with a relieving of pressure in a steam generation system from the time of the first locomotives. Yet that familiarity, and the relatively slow pace connected with it, could be deceptive, and neither construction nor operation of a nuclear plant could any longer "be dependent upon habits and procedures that have remained virtually unchanged for more than a century."[88] Wolf Creek had reached the "alien" stage, and "reform," if needed, was critical before proceeding further.

It was already too late for some SNUPPS plants. Northern States Power Company's Tyrone Unit 1 in Wisconsin was cancelled in October of 1979.[89] In January 1980, Rochester Gas & Electric, another SNUPPS partner, was forced by the State of New York to cancel its Sterling 1 plant.[90] Each cancellation of a SNUPPS unit added to the cost for the remaining utilities of the SNUPPS design, as well as the pressure on their managements.

Unquestionably, 1979 and 1980 were years of substantial internal change for KG&E with regard to its supervision of Wolf Creek. Although these changes received very little publicity, and may in fact have seemed not only arcane but very nearly incomprehensible in their effect to most newspaper readers, they were credited by later consultants with a critical impact on "saving" the plant in the face of what seemed overwhelming reverse momentum in the sociotechnical atmosphere in the state of Kansas. Einstein once said, "God is in the details." The company seemed to recognize this as it addressed one set of details after another from the perspective of what its executives had learned while listening and not simply resisting during the confrontations with critics. Things had not gone according to the original plan. KG&E was wise to recognize this and to modify that plan rather than stubbornly to stick to its 1968 vision as a second new decade dawned.

There were technical changes. For instance, the design for the nuclear core of SNUPPS plants was changed during the summer of 1979 by Westinghouse. The new one called for 193 fuel assemblies each containing 289 fuel rods with cylindrical uranium dioxide pellets sealed in zirconium alloy tubes aligned in squares called *arrays* with 17 rods on each side. The total mass of uranium dioxide would be 111.4 tons. While operating experience with this new configuration was limited, there had been some problems with the older 15 by 15 rod design, and the lower power density of the new configuration was thought to be an advantage.[91]

Other technical and managerial changes loomed. The NRC had by fall ordered over 60 design changes at Wolf Creek to meet new fire safety regulations alone.[92] The KCC was investigating having state employees train as nuclear operators so they could be assigned to oversee the plant should the state order it.[93] The union battle at Wolf Creek grew stronger, and there was a petition drive headed by Steve Ingram of the Kansas Building and Construction Trades Council to unionize workers at the site. Only one small group of 16 boilermakers, employed by subcontractor Chicago Bridge and Iron, represented unionized labor.[94] The U.S. House debated putting a six-month freeze on all nuclear plant building in the country.[95]

Added to that was an unexpected financial crunch, made no lighter a burden for KG&E by being largely due to external factors. The prime rate at Chemical Bank went up in September 1979 to a record 13.25 percent—which as it turned out was only the beginning of an unprecedented rise. It was 14.5 percent by early October.[96] In the summer of 1979 Standard & Poor downgraded KG&E's preferred stocks and bonds for the second time in a year, and the company postponed the planned August 2 sale of 1 million shares of common stock. S&P said that KG&E's cash flow and earnings projections were "substandard," and that "regulatory treatment which has lagged in the past will be important to whether the company can maintain a reasonable financial balance." The preferred stock rating went from A- to BBB, leaving it below the average for the utility industry though still investment quality. One more step down to BB and it would have entered the "speculative" class.

Staffing at KG&E headquarters at the end of 1979 underwent some changes and received various sorts of analysis. The legal staff became an issue. KCC staff people thought that Ralph Foster as KG&E attorney had a "sweetheart deal." His legal firm was reimbursed for many salaries and was provided with offices and a law library at the utility, with social dues and entertainment expenses paid. Of course Foster was the one who was so often in said staff's hair, and of course they were comparing his so-called luxurious deal with government, not other corporate work. Most utilities had an entirely in-house legal staff, and therefore KG&E could argue effectively that its deal with Foster was a cost saving. Richard C. "Pete" Loux on the KCC, however, was fond of saying that KG&E was thinking of itself as a kind of "glamour" company in the returns it wanted on its stock and the salaries and perks it gave to its executives. This kind of rhetoric had played well in Kansas since the Populist 1890s.

Foster and the KG&E directors believed that this sort of charge was "a partisan effort to keep rates down." They averred that KG&E's Wichita location did not help it in Topeka, and that the KCC staff itself was inexperienced and subject to too rapid promotion.[97] The national mood did not help. "Since March 28 [the date of the TMI accident]," said Foster, "inquiry into things nuclear has been quite the thing. It's quite popular to shoot at electric utilities."[98] KG&E needed well-paid executives, one independent director said, particularly because of Wolf Creek: "It's impossible to predict all of the changes that might be necessary in a project of this size. It's not a piddling deal. . . ."[99] Just as some of the criticism of Foster was surfacing in the fall of 1979, that attorney began working at KG&E full time.

Simultaneously with these events, and as though to cement the utility's determination to push ahead with Wolf Creek whatever the undertow, Wilson Cadman took over as president and chief operating officer. Cadman was a compact, balding, bull-like man, whose ruddy face wore a constant determined expression. He was scrappy, blunt, and had an acerbic wit. Previous president Fiebach by contrast—tall, distinguished, with wavy white hair—looked like one thought a U.S. senator should, and had the smoother, less frenetic style that had served the company well traditionally. The transition at the top was symbolic. The company now had a kind of Theodore Roosevelt at the helm, who, by God, was going to persevere!

Another management change at KG&E late in 1979 was equally significant for Wolf Creek. In September 1979, Jesse Arterburn, KG&E's superintendent of nuclear development since 1973, resigned and returned to California to be with his family. But there were other reasons for his departure. Arterburn, with a small staff, but mostly personally, was trying to supervise the construction by Daniel in a much closer way than had originally been envisioned as a role for KG&E, and he was not happy with what he saw. His father had been in the construction business and had lost all he had— Arterburn was not going to let that happen at Wolf Creek. Originally it had not been imagined that Arterburn would even be resident on the site, but he had insisted on it, saying that he could not find any one that he could trust. The Daniel construction manager, on the other hand, complained that he could not get enough authority to move the project forward, and that Arterburn had $3 million in back invoices on his desk which he would not clear for payment because of some complaint or other with some part of the work.

The showdown really came when Arterburn demanded that Daniel be fired as prime contractor. Fiebach and Koester had a stormy meeting with him, disagreeing with this course. Daniel was as good as any contractor, they said, and plants that had tried changing contractors in the middle of the project had had even greater cost overruns than those that had tried to work out the problems and stick with their original horse. It came down to losing either Arterburn or Daniel, and it was Arterburn who went. Glenn Koester, who was sympathetic with the average workman, for whom Wolf Creek was just a hard, cold job, decided to take more of a role. And the Arterburn resignation, combined with increasing new regulations from NRC and more and more quality assurance requirements, resulted, as well, in a recognition that the original strategy of working through NPI and the contractor with a very small on-site presence for KG&E would no longer work. Arterburn's successor, Gary Fouts, was an experienced construction supervisor who began to build a substantial on-site KG&E construction and quality oversight staff. Later a second specialist, Frank Duddy, was brought in by KG&E specifically to "kick ass and take names" in ramrodding the final fueling and completion stage.[100]

In 1985 Arterburn himself, in a deposition before the Missouri Public Service Commission concerning KCPL Wolf Creek rates, reflected back over the events of 1979 and before. By that time his experience in the nuclear industry totalled 31 years, and he had witnessed all the changes, escalating as they did from the time he moved from the management of SEFOR to KG&E's superintendent of nuclear development.

Arterburn's understanding of his job when he was hired was that he was "project manager with responsibility for the entire [Wolf Creek] effort involved in the design, construction and eventual operation of that facility." Though he admitted there were "certain qualifications" to that responsibility, he certainly perceived it as a thoroughgoing one. He testified that from about 1976 on he had spent the majority of his time supervising Daniel, the construction contractor. In 1979 he had set up a crisis by recommending that Daniel be removed or he would leave the project. "Everywhere you look," he had written, "Daniel has problems, problems primarily created by the lack of management. . . . Daniel shows essentially no leadership in providing resolutions for problems but primarily offers excuses." Arterburn analyzed the problems under "lack of conformance to schedule, lack of conformance to budget and poor productivity."

Arterburn was not satisfied with KG&E management's response to his charges. At first he thought it was their lack of experience with construction projects—"later I came to the conclusion that by that time, they surely understood what was being said but still [had] very little or in some cases no reaction." The quarterly management meetings with KG&E and KCPL, in Arterburn's view, did not change things much. There was, he said, "an atmosphere of silence." In fact Arterburn thought that in pushing for changes he made a mistake because, as he put it, "it began the erosion of my authority to deal with Daniel to the point that now I have essentially none. Furthermore few hard decisions or actions have resulted from the meetings although the clock kept ticking away. The meetings provided a forum in which Daniel could generate their usual 'smoke screen' and lead the management to believe everything was in good order even in spite of my broad side attacks." Arterburn strongly felt that KG&E

and KCPL management had to have some sort of "truth session" with Daniel to make the contractor see the problems *had* to be corrected. Instead, he claimed, there was no clear locus of authority and the Daniel people went around him, Arterburn, to lobby the executives. In brief, Arterburn felt he had the responsibility but not the authority on the project, and Daniel was not taking him seriously, leading to a classic stress point for a manager.

Of course the commissioners and attorneys in Missouri clamped onto this kind of testimony as possible evidence that there was "imprudence" in KG&E's and KCPL's management that would justify cutting the requested rate increases. Over and over Arterburn was questioned about the education and nuclear experience of these other executives who apparently had such a role in making decisions with Daniel, and, of course, in general, their specific experience was less impressive than Arterburn's. The implication was that "they [Daniel] considered me a rather hard taskmaster and they were seeking relief" by doing an "end run." Arterburn confessed that at some of the quarterly meetings he had attacked Daniel "in a very dramatic way" trying to force attention to the problems, and then later realized that "such an antagonistic encounter" could not bode well for the future of the project. However, Arterburn clearly stated his opinion that management of a large construction project should be "highly centralized," in preferably just one individual, and he thought he ought to have been that one. The attitude of Donald McPhee of KCPL, he said, was basically that "you don't fight with a constructor," and Arterburn probably thought Glen Koester was appeasing Daniel, too.

Several consultants (notably Charles Huston) were later to disagree with Arterburn's analysis of proper management style, and Koester's feelings, based on the cost experience of utilities that had fired contractors, have been noted. But in 1979, it was a key issue whether KG&E should take a more active role in management at the site, and how that role should be organized. Arterburn's was one road ultimately not taken. The argument went back also to the whole broader issue of the original construction contract, and the control leverage that could or could not be exercised by a utility on a custom project built in the midst of rapid changes on all fronts.

Personally, Arterburn was bitter not only about the circumstances of his "resignation," but that the announcement in the newspapers gave as a reason only that he wanted to be with his children in California, not mentioning any dispute over how the project was being managed. Still, KG&E executives continued to visit and consult with him in California, and the relation was one Arterburn himself agreed was "amicable."[101]

Dr. Robert Hagen, who was close to Arterburn, does not dismiss also the psychological impact of Three Mile Island on Arterburn's confidence, and confirms his discomfort with the delegation that would have to be done with the new management scenario. To Hagen, whatever the reasons for Arterburn's departure, the change it symbolized had been bound to come ever since the Westinghouse fuel case in 1976. KG&E had to adjust to hiring technical people of its own who had background in nuclear power, not just in buying poles and insulators, and it had to micromanage every aspect of the construction. After TMI in 1979, Hagen said, safety became a predominant factor in discussions of things nuclear, and with the public there was a strong element of resentment of "the technology they can't understand." Kansans, Hagen noted, are independent and stubborn, and perhaps, given TMI, the only reason Wolf Creek was ever finished was that there were independent and stubborn Kansans building it as well as opposing it. Certainly as of that date the previous idea that the plant would surely be finished despite difficulties, that it was somehow inevitable and had been since the early construction permit stages, was no longer an obvious or even a plausible fact. Whether the KG&E officials allowed themselves to think it or not, from 1979 on the survival and completion of the plant was touch and go. Other states were abandoning nearly completed plants, and there was no reason that could not happen in Kansas. Jim Lawing notes that in 1976, at the time of the water fight, the antinuclear movement in Kansas was tiny, seeking temporary allies on desperate issues. By 1980 it was powerful, so powerful that it came close to bringing the plant down. Events of 1979 account for much of the difference.

The change at KG&E in its stance toward construction and the strategic direction that went with it got little publicity, but was massively important. In fact, the departure of Arterburn was a symbolic divide. Ironically, in a way Arterburn's departure represented a kind of victory for the enlarged role for KG&E in micromanaging the site directly that he had always tried, without much support at first, to advance. However, there were substantial differences in the strategy and the style.

Kent Brown, later a group vice president at KG&E, was at that time a consultant for Management Analysis Company (MAC) in San Diego and was retained to assist Koester by analyzing the KG&E Wolf Creek organization and suggesting the best way to expand and restructure it. Brown spent six months analyzing how utilities in the rest of the industry related to their nuclear construction projects, and constructed policies, procedures, and structure.

It was clear that the old idea that utilities in constructing generating plants could "turn over their destiny to an outside consultant who was there on a cost plus basis" ended with the complex requirements of nuclear plants in the 1980s. MAC itself was founded specifically to help utilities make the transition and was a champion of the philosophy of the utility getting in there and exerting control. MAC also worked with Daniel—in fact Daniel was the consultant's first employer at the site. The first assignment there was reviewing how KG&E organized the work in general, and then Brown moved to organizing specific tasks such as piping and welding.[102] Construction work schedules were speeded, and some men were on the job 84 hours a week to try to make up the schedule slippages caused by such events as the base mat controversy.[103]

Brown and others came to agree that amid these details and changes in 1979 or 1980 KG&E as a company buckled down irreversibly to the task of completing Wolf Creek; everything else was secondary. Wilson Cadman said that at the time he took the presidency Wolf Creek "became consuming as far as the company was concerned."[104] Partly it was the 1978 fuel use act, partly it was the confrontations of 1979, partly it was determination not to waste the effort and progress made so far, partly it was the insight that quick completion was the best way to hold down costs, but it was also, for better or worse, corporate pride and unity in the face of adversity. As a planner, Kent Brown had to admire that. It was the ultimate mission statement or strategic intent, "as crystal clear an objective as you will ever find." That vision of a beleaguered "small" utility countering a social reverse, a regulatory morass, and financial uncertainty to finish the task it started stimulated all connected with the Wolf Creek project.[105]

In the fall of 1979 interest rates hit 15.25 percent; they were to be 21 percent before the plant was completed. The Dow Jones average went to an 11-year low.[106] KEPCo and KG&E were in a major argument about the co-op's share of the nuclear plant. Consultants from Cresap were soon to arrive on site to make an investigation that some at the KCC expected would reveal major management problems. But all the while the trajectory was forward for KG&E. On December 5, the cap was placed on the reactor containment building. The trademark dome of a nuclear plant, severe and almost mosque-like, stood at last entire on the Kansas prairie.

The Wolf Creek logo, designed by Wichita Native American artist Blackbear Bosin. (Unless indicated otherwise, all photos and illustrations provided courtesy of KG&E.)

Wilson Cadman, president of KG&E during the Wolf Creek construction period.

A face, and hat, in the crowd, January 1979.

Protestors slide down the icy slope to the Arkansas River as the Wolf Creek reactor barge arrives in Tulsa, Oklahoma, January 4, 1979.

The reactor vessel ready for the final leg of its trip to Burlington, January 1979. Courtesy of the *Wichita Eagle*.

Protestors meet the reactor vessel train, January 1979.

Francis Blaufuss protests the arrival of the reactor vessel train, January 1979.

The containment building under construction, showing the controversial base mat and the elaborate reinforcement and concrete work on the dome.

The reactor vessel is set into place, February 28, 1980.

Kansas Governor John Carlin (second from left) and Attorney General Robert Stephan (center) visit the Wolf Creek site during construction.

A member of the Kansas Natural Guard outside the KG&E stockholders meeting, November 1982.

Part of KG&E's management team in 1984. Left to right: Kent Brown, group vice president, technical services; Glenn Koester, vice president, nuclear; Howard Hansen, group vice president, finance; Wilson Cadman, chairman of the board and president; Robert Rives, group vice president, corporate relations; Ralph Foster, vice president, general counsel; Glen Montague, group vice president, administration.

A small demonstration in Burlington late in the construction period.

Local reaction to the approaching rate hearings, June 17, 1984. Courtesy of Lee Judge and the *Kansas City Star*.

KG&E lead attorney James Haines at the opening of the Wolf Creek rate hearings, 1985.

"Captive customer" confronts "Reddy Kilowatt" outside KG&E's Wichita offices during the 1985 rate hearings.

The interior of the turbine building at Wolf Creek.

Wolf Creek Station, showing the power block, turbine building, support structures, and cooling lake in their prairie setting.

Wolf Creek Station sending out power.

8
Power Block

It's a debate between two alien cultures that speak totally different languages.
—Susan Gale, in *Emporia Gazette*, Feb. 8, 1980

Workmen, leather belts clanking with strange-jawed tools and shoulder-length puggrees trailing beneath the hardhats or tied flaps-up, look like misplaced Turks or Martian cowboys. Color leers against the overall gray—purple pipes, yellow welding screens, glowing red warning lights. Walt Disney's Wonderful World of Atomic Energy.
—*Kansas City Star,* April 6, 1980

We know little more about this $3 billion boondoggle than we did five years ago when it was a $500 million boondoggle—except that it is losing partners every day, that construction continues with costs soaring to the skies, that it may produce electricity we don't need, that it will produce radioactive waste we cannot hide and that all of us will pay for this mistake in dollars and dismay for years to come.
—*Olathe Daily News,* May 6, 1982

Wolf Creek is one of the sounder nuclear projects under way in the country.
—Cresap, McCormick and Paget, consulting report to the Kansas Corporation Commission, 1980

The TMI accident ensured that nuclear power was one of the top issues dividing American society. Gloria and the "Meathead" debated it with Archie Bunker. Jerry Brown hoped to reach the White House with it. Books on nuclear power lined bookstore shelves in 1980, most poorly researched and awkwardly written. The release of the Iranian hostages and the elevation of Ronald Reagan to the White House that year may have encouraged some that "deregulation" would be the rule in nuclear power as well as other energy fields.

However, the "conservative revolution" meant less in the nuclear field than in many others, and the forces arrayed against one another remained firm in their places. "Nuclear power is a religion to its supporters," a Kansas writer mentioned, "and a fanatical obsession to its opponents."[1]

Opposition for Wolf Creek was by now a given, and during the early 1980s, as the eventual cost became better defined and rapidly grew, that opposition got larger and more diverse. All plans, all arrangements were in flux, and came apart regularly. There was bitterness and confusion as facts changed too rapidly for public adjustment or even adequate explanation. The only defense was momentum. Finishing the plant rapidly would minimize the cost escalation, and it would allow the utility to present a working plant, which it would seem unreasonable to demolish or abandon.

Work proceeded as rapidly as possible in bringing to life a series of buildings known as the "Power Block." In January 1980, two pairs of 355-ton steam generators arrived at the site after the arrest of some members of the Sunbelt Alliance at the Tulsa port. The generators, standing nearly 70 feet high and measuring 14 feet in diameter, produce steam to drive the turbine that operates a relatively small, though efficient, single electric generator.[2] In February, the reactor was put in position with only a slight delay due to breakage of a guide pin, and absolutely no fanfare.[3] By June 1980 the plant was 60 percent complete, and the utility began pumping 1,380,000 gallons a day from John Redmond Reservoir into a small lake at the plant used to test the ultimate heat sink dam and some of the systems.

The Power Block section included seven buildings, one housing the reactor, another for auxiliary equipment, and still another for the turbine and generator. Others were for the control of backup diesel generators, fuel, and waste storage. The Engineering Intermediate Schedule detailed 5,000 separate activities, while the Construction Intermediate Schedule listed 2,000 items.[4] The main lake fill began in the fall and by summer 1981 the lake was 58 percent full. Heavy rains kept it well ahead of schedule, requiring little water pumping from Redmond or the Neosho River.[5]

Wages were high, as was overtime, with lots of "boomers" working at the plant. The tasks were specialized and the scale was huge. There were 26,454 pipe hangers to be installed, for instance, many with unusual welds. There were 5.6 million feet of electrical cable. The main buildings had 160,000 cubic yards of concrete. There were 160,000 feet of pipe larger than 4 inches and 133,000 feet of smaller pipe, all of which could leak.[6] The containment building was tested with an air pressure of 650 psi, which it had to withstand with no leaks. The 4-foot-thick walls were actually drawn in half an inch in circumference when steel tendons were tightened to the specified stress by hydraulic rams, in a modern version of a medieval cathedral's flying buttresses.[7] A federal inspection of Wolf Creek in April 1982 concluded that work there was of better quality, with fewer violations, than the national average, and that on the whole the Wolf Creek builders had been "cooperative and responsible."[8]

Progress was tracked on 260 separate systems in the Power Block. To identify them there was an elaborate code documented on cards carried by many employees. There were Bechtel systems and Sargent & Lundy systems, as well as codes for each of the structures in the block. The pipe to go in a certain system was coded by tags with the letters of the system as well as by colors, which were documented on the cards. The BL system, for example, was the makeup water system, and the pipe for it was green. The HB system was liquid radwaste, which shared purple pipe along with some other waste-related systems. The turbine building was Z4.[9]

The whole thing was tended by 1982 by 3,000 workers with a weekly payroll of $1.5 million.[10] It was not always easy to get people with specialized skills to come to Kansas in competition with other nuclear sites where they were in demand, and the nuclear industry by the mid 1980s was not the glamor job it had once been. However, Wolf Creek recruited with ads showing the pleasant lifestyle in rural Burlington.[11] "We do not expect to jeopardize public safety to generate electricity," Glenn Koester said at that time. "We don't think it's that difficult to operate successfully if the plant is working safely. We know what we're doing."[12]

Journalists fell all over themselves trying to crank out cuter or odder descriptive prose on the physical and social impact of high-tech industry on the prairie. "It is sensed before seen," wrote James Kindall in a *Kansas City Star* supplement called "Life in Nuketown": "a still vacuum of distant power, a neck-tensing awareness of alien magnitude. Close. Approaching. Then, quick and surprising, like trees shooting forth sudden spring leaves, it rises from the Kansas sod and sagebrush, a massive, colorless dome attended by praying mantis cranes, and cradled among mounds of skeletal metal bones, the nesting ground of—what?" A local farmer told Kindall they don't have to sterilize bulls any more, they just run them by the plant. Francis Blaufuss told him they were going to have to shut the plant down or "We'll see demonstrations that will make the fall of the Roman Empire look like a spring picnic." But most people in Burlington were not overwrought. "What does a stolid, cud-chewing farm community propped contentedly on the Kansas plains do when the finger-snapping atomic age swaggers into town? The answer is to arch an eyebrow, spit a chaw of tobacco in the street and lean back once again." Kindall could not resist saying that the catfish capital of the world had "gone fission."[13]

Workers at the plant accepted, and even praised it. Said a female security guard (15% of the workers were female) on the night shift: "Every so often God, in his mercy, has given man the knowledge to take one more step up the ladder to a better way of life. . . . As you can tell, I am not a writer, and maybe I am not saying this very well, what I am trying to say is, Thank you, for the chance to be part of tomorrow."[14] Don Burgner, a construction worker, said, "All I can say is it's a good project, it's gonna make wine and nobody's cows are gonna die."[15]

Workers did not take criticism of themselves passively. "Oh, they'll go out and raise hell and kick heads," said a plant training department manager, "but they're a close group of people. You'll see a lot of them on the front pew on Sunday."[16] When, in the summer of 1982, Tom Taylor of the KCC referred to the work at Wolf Creek as "sloppy and lazy," signs appeared along U.S. 75 to wit: "How can you say we are sloppy and lazy? We're the best damned workers in Kansas." "When you work for the K.C.C. how can you call anyone else lazy and sloppy Tom Taylor." "Hey Pete Loux. We trained for our jobs. How did you get yours?"[17] "If the news media, politicians and K.C.C. think they could do a better job," wrote a worker, "I would like very much to see them get out from behind their desks, out of their suits and white shirts and put in 10 to 12 hours in all kinds of weather conditions . . . like the craft people do here at Wolf Creek."[18]

The construction force reacted strongly to charges about alcohol and drug use at the plant, calling some of it "calculated innuendo" that was "absolutely uncalled for."[19] But the construction force was hardly a monolith. There was enmity at the site between workers from the North and from the South, and workers ranged from those who specialized in working at nuclear plants because "they're so critical. So technical. You get down to the finest line of work," to those who drifted around the country working wherever and on whatever the wages were high. Doubtless, as the company claimed, the charges of drug use were exaggerated in the rumor hotbed of a construction site.[20] Also the unions, which wanted the site organized and were annoyed by Kansas's Right to Work law, emphasized that "if it were union labor there would be more control."[21] But there is no question drug use existed. "It's darn sure serious," said one worker who quit the project. "You can't be building a nuclear powerhouse with a bunch of dopeheads and drunks." The wages were $8 to $13 an hour and they brought all kinds. "It's really strange being a construction worker," said one man who would not give his name, "'cause there's a lot of freedom. You can walk around, cuss, raise hell, spit on the floor. Don't need to be decked out and speaking proper. That's why there's a lot of people in it. There's a lot of people who can't cope with society. Can't cope with an office. There's a lot of strange people in construction."[22]

However "strange," the lot of them added much to the Kansas economy. "Those who are calling the costs criminal should view the spectacle of 4,100 workers leaving the construction site north of Burlington at 5 P.M. each day. Imagine, if you can, 4,100 workers in that many cars and more lined bumper to bumper all the way from Burlington to Beto Junction."[23] Late in 1981 there was a wedding between two workers in the turbine building. The female electrician and the male welder wore hard hats and western outfits with the company logo on the back.[24] In May 1980 a proposition to stop the Wolf Creek plant was offered at the KG&E stockholders meeting by Thomas and Anne Moore of Lawrence. The vote against it was 10.1 million shares to 694,177 shares.[25] "Despite the bad-mouthing that the union pushers are doing," said the construction superintendent, "the project continues to progress on schedule."[26]

In June 1980 the plant adopted its logo—a likeness of a sharp and rather slant-eyed grey wolf's head on a large gold star and surrounded by a blue circular field lettered "Wolf Creek Generating Station." The design was by Wichitan Blackbear Bosin, a Kiowa-

Comanche and one of the nation's best-known Native American artists. The Wolf, said Bosin, is venerated in Native American culture: "He was a great hunter and a great provider, but he also possessed an extraordinary knowledge of nature and he lived in harmony with it. He was accepted as a teacher by the Indians and they respected his lessons and they learned them well." The stylized star in the logo was Sirius, the bright star of summer, and around the wolf's head was a blue path representing nature's neverending gift of running water, for plants of all kinds.[27]

The summer of 1980 seemed to reinforce the need for Wolf Creek. That year came one of the "heat storms" that Kansas can experience. On June 25 the official temperature was 103°, but it was 120+ on the asphalt at the Sedgwick County Zoo and 109° at 21st and Grove in Wichita. Electric consumption broke a two-year-old record. There was standing room only at the city pools and hospitals were full of heat prostration cases. People without air conditioners were seen sleeping on their porches to stay away from the hot walls of their houses, and, it was reported, "Even the birds are panting."[28] On July 2 the official temperature in the shade at the airport in Wichita was 109°, and it had been 100+ for eight straight days, setting all-time electric use records every day.[29] The string of 100+ days ran to 14, the mercury reached 110° all too often, and there were 130 deaths in Kansas from three solid weeks of searing heat beyond the usual flames of a Kansas summer.[30]

The heat, however, was not enough to allow ignoring the rapidly escalating costs of the Wolf Creek plant amid rising interest rates and deteriorating securities ratings for the utility.[31] One way to soften the blow to KG&E and KCPL ratepayers was to bring in more partners. However, the Nebraska sale failed, and, in the early 1980s, part of what was considered the "original partnership deal" unraveled.

It was assumed from the beginning—in fact court ordered—that a 17 percent share of Wolf Creek would be owned by Kansas Electric Power Cooperative, Inc. (KEPCo), for distribution of power to its member rural co-ops, of which there were 26. The investment would be funded by KEPCo's federal backer, the Rural Electrification Corporation (REC). However in spring 1979, immediately after TMI, Dale Lyon of the Kansas Farmers' Union, long an outspoken critic of Wolf Creek, questioned in speeches and letters whether that ownership commitment was wise. "I am no expert in such matters," Lyon said, "but recent events relating to nuclear power plant failures give strong indication that this reported 200 million dollar investment of REC monies are being spent on what could be a real bummer." The REC was owned by farmers, Lyon claimed. Were the farmers buying a source of electricity not available elsewhere or were they bailing out some investor-owned utilities who had made a bad decision? Was KEPCo buying responsibility for an accident? And why should the REC help the investor-owned utilities, when its formation in 1936 was due partly to refusal of these same utilities to supply cheap electricity to farmers?[32] Wasn't KEPCo's 17 percent of Wolf Creek like buying a "pig in a poke?"[33] "Farmers' Union is the mother of cooperatives in the United States," Lyon said in the spring of 1980. "We cannot stand idly by while this juggernaut of huge investor-owned utilities combined with the Federally subsidized, non-competitive nuclear industry smashes the very idea of farmer cooperatives and subsequent farmer-control of his source of electricity." Even if nuclear electricity were cheaper than alternates, Lyon said, the co-ops were more important to the farmer than mere price.[34]

KEPCo officials responded that Lyon did not even represent his own union, and that many of its members were apologetic about his stand. KEPCo had been negotiating with KG&E (and suing it) for almost five years to achieve a Wolf Creek share and was not going to lose the momentum now.[35] KG&E was also negotiating by spring 1980 with the Northwest Kansas Municipal Energy Agency for a 5.5 percent share, to cost $70 million, and with other groups of Kansas municipalities who might feel nuclear was the wave of the future.[36] Still, the KFU joined MACEA, the Kansas Organic Producers, and several other groups as intervenors in the 1980 hearings regarding the KEPCo Wolf Creek purchase.[37]

The KEPCo hearings before the KCC lasted four weeks during June and July 1980, and produced 19 volumes (3,834 pages) of testimony. The technical issue was whether KEPCo would receive a certificate to generate and transmit electricity in Kansas. That is, it wanted to become what was known as a G&T, or generation and transmission utility. The reason for that certificate was the proposed purchase not only of a Wolf Creek share, but of hydroelectric power.[38]

Dr. Bob Hagen, who was on the stand for three days on behalf of

KG&E, remembers it as a long, hot summer indeed, and not just because of the weather. Each attorney took a shot at him while the others listened and learned, and Hagen remembers that the objections of his attorney were pretty regularly overruled. In his mind, not only was the KEPCo matter being adjudicated, but the whole post–TMI future of Wolf Creek was, with this opportunity, being put under the white light of state investigation. It was, he said, "as close to a kangaroo court" as he had ever experienced.[39]

Charles Ross, the executive director of KEPCo and a former Topeka newscaster, was so colorful a character that one newspaper said his appearance at the hearings transformed the witness stand "into a stage." Phil Kassebaum, KEPCo's attorney, defended its interest lucidly.[40] The issue was significant. While the two major owners of Wolf Creek were not certain early that they wanted KEPCo involved in Wolf Creek, by the 1980s it appeared essential, especially for KG&E, whose trade area was growing in electric demand more slowly than predicted, to unload at least part of the financial burden of the nuclear plant. KEPCo had already paid KG&E and KCPL $55 million apiece, an amount that would have to be refunded with interest should the application be rejected. More importantly, the total amount expected for the 17 percent share was $245 million.[41]

To quote chapter and verse of the niggling: Some members of Kansas Electric Cooperatives, Inc. (KEC), refused to join KEPCo when it was formed in 1975 as the power supply entity of KEC, and these independent co-ops now felt they were being squeezed out. Some wanted to introduce the KG&E uranium contract into the hearings; others did not.[42] KG&E and KCPL were not the greatest friends of KEPCo. Though the two had approached KEPCo with the idea of a sale, and, although KEPCo saw Wolf Creek as one means of being independent of the investor-owned utilities, its demands quickly became unpleasant to KG&E. KEPCo filed an antitrust suit against KG&E and KCPL in 1973, shortly after Wolf Creek was announced, because the two utilities would not transport power, other than that from Wolf Creek, for KEPCo over KG&E and KCPL lines. KEPCo argued that without that wheeling privilege, Wolf Creek power alone would be less valuable to them. They needed a power mix from several sources, including hydro peaking power from the Southwest Power Administration, and they needed an alternative power source when Wolf Creek was shut down for maintenance and refueling. The two major utilities agreed finally, but only after a lengthy and bitter fight, and after the so-called "territoriality bill," passed in Kansas in 1976, provided protection for the co-op's service areas.

In addition, there was tension arising from the fact that KG&E and KCPL were "private" companies, albeit with heavy regulation, while KEPCo was seen as a model of the dreaded public power alternative, which the problems at Wolf Creek always threatened. Richard Loux of the KCC thought the state as a whole should be considered as one entity in regard to electric transmission that was planned by the state rather than competitively. KEPCo's becoming a G&T might be the opening wedge. "We are a tax-paying group," said a KCPL executive, "whereas they get low-interest loans and are tax-supported."

Thus, the scene at the hearings: "On the one hand was the IOU family—the investor-owned utilities, which belong to the stockholders. On the other hand was the Cooperative family—which has nothing to do with cooperation with each other, but refers to the fact they are not corporate. . . . If disharmony between the two families and, importantly, between the family members themselves weren't enough, the Consumer clan was on hand as intervenors to assure that neither the IOUs nor cooperatives inherit too much of Wolf Creek. Acting as referee was the KCC."[43]

An issue also in the KEPCo hearings was cost—whether the utilities could accurately project the cost of Wolf Creek, and whether KEPCo could afford to chance the cost overruns. It was an early opportunity to address the issue that had become as important, if not more important, than those specifically nuclear fears that had started the protest in the first place.

James Haines, whose first work with the KG&E legal department was on the KEPCo hearings, was concerned that the cost figure that was then being presented by KG&E for Wolf Creek—initially in the hearings $1.3 billion—was "a bad number." Although the utility reviewed that number annually, the timing of the KEPCo hearing was such that it was over before the annual review. Haines thought that it would be poor strategy to focus on the number and then to change it immediately when the hearing was over. It would be better to make the change during the hearing, or at least qualify the number, even though the new number would be 50 percent more than the "definitive estimate," and three times the first vague claims in the late 1960s. Senior management, however, disagreed. While a member of the KCC staff predicted during the KEPCo hearing that the cost of Wolf Creek could reach $1.7 billion, KG&E denied it. However, their own annual review late in the year came up with a number of $1.9 billion. No better number existed at the time of the hearings than the one the company used, but the short time elapsing between seeming certainty and cost change damaged corporate credibility.

Haines remembered later that from his perspective the KEPCo hearings were "the moment of truth" on the economic part of the plant—that time "when people said to themselves this could get out of control." It was also strong reinforcement for KG&E's decision to focus all company attention on the plant. The project seemed too far along to back out, but the rest of the course was going to be tough. "We have to give this project 100 percent of our attention," company officials told each other, "or it is going to strangle us."

Of course, there were no guesses then that the final cost would be $3 billion. "If at any one of the decision points," Haines said, "a clairvoyant had come along and said it would cost $3 billion, it would have been different." There were people who were estimating higher numbers than the utility was for the cost, but they were not perceived at the time to have much documentation or credibility, but were seen rather as ideological, antinuclear troublemakers, who in retrospect turned out to be right, but for the wrong reasons. Haines said later: "It would have been irresponsible to believe them." Had he himself said $3 billion in 1980, Haines thought, he should have been fired. Instead, the company regularly looked at what had been invested in the plant and what it estimated as needed to finish it, and came to the logical conclusion, given those facts, that it should continue. Not that there were not some suggestions, other than the general media hue and cry, that it was time to abandon the project. In later hearings the period 1980–1982 was most often mentioned as a time when, in hindsight at least, that possibility ought to have been given the deepest consideration. Every directors' meeting at KG&E during that period considered it, and the numbers on it were presented.[44] There were rumors much later that sometime during Governor John Carlin's first term he caused a message to be sent to KG&E officials through a state senator that if they would abandon the nuclear project, state legislation would be passed to protect the company from losing what it had invested to date. The company rejected the overture. Other states had tried such deals, and history showed the promises were not to be depended upon. But possibly in Carlin's mind a truce had been offered, and KG&E had in effect said "nuts," and kept on fighting. It may not have helped politically.[45]

Another player entering the lists with the KEPCo hearings who had cost concerns was Brian Moline, counsel for the KCC. Moline felt strongly that the utilities were underestimating the cost impact of TMI, and that the co-ops were not allowing for the probable cost escalation in arranging the financing for their purchase of a share of the plant. During the hearings themselves the cost estimates were changed twice—a signal. Farm communities had a declining population and would have to stick with the deal and its costs for a good long time.

The KCC had put some people at the construction site in 1979 to monitor things—younger accountant types. While KG&E cooperated, Moline remembered, the construction people did not like it much, and there was considerable tension. The KCC staff needed, however, to "get a feel" of the field, as the rate hearings, when they came, were "going to be the biggest thing ever to come down the regulatory pike." The construction was exacting—ducts had to be absolutely perfect, and then when they were the feds changed the specs. Each change increased costs and the prospect that rates would triple suddenly—a prospect that gave politicians and regulators nightmares.

At the KEPCo hearings, Moline got the feeling that the cost projections were just guesses, changing monthly, and thought that the utilities' allowance for contingencies was too small, only about 10 percent. The trend looked like "building in economic disaster for the ratepayers."[46] Moline agreed with Commissioner Loux, who said that after the KEPCo hearings, a new Wolf Creek glossary was needed. The term *negative float* should be defined as the number of days a project is behind schedule; *negative savings* was a loss, slippage, or delay; *post applied fix* was how much it would cost to do the job right the second time; *accounting entry* was an unreal expense; and *cost reimbursement contract* was cost plus profit.[47]

Still, Moline was impressed with the KG&E executives, with

Cadman and Haines particularly—Haines for his brilliance in the hearings, and Cadman for his courage. No one in Cadman's position should have had to put up with the personal abuse he took, Moline said, yet the KG&E president was always sitting in the first row looking right at witnesses who were ready to upbraid him personally. He identified himself with the plant, for better or for worse, and its darkest days were also his personally. By contrast, however, Moline noticed that many of the company people were engineers who "never had to deal with complex interpersonal things," and tended to respond to legislative inquiries with a blank stare and a statement that this was none of its business.[48] That was not satisfactory. 1980 and 1981, particularly during the extended KEPCo debate, was a period when the anti–Wolf Creek coalition began to grow more on the basis of cost than on issues relating to nuclear power *per se*. That coalition began to include business owners from Wichita appearing before their city commission or agitating with the Chamber of Commerce, and not just environmentalists camped along the railroad spur or picketing the gates.

The KCC KEPCo decision, which came in October 1980, allowed the 17 percent share purchase by KEPCo, but the Commission attached a long string of conditions in its 42-page order. These included that KEPCo could not bind its members to sign 40-year full power contracts, a crucial factor in KEPCo's financing the plant. The Commission said that binding the members to a single power source for that long was contrary to the public interest.[49] Another major restriction was that KEPCo could not pay more than 17 percent of the $1.5 billion maximum cost estimate for the Wolf Creek plant at the time of the hearings for its 17 percent share, whatever the escalations before completion might be. A third bombshell was that KG&E and KCPL would be penalized should the Wolf Creek plant not be completed by April 1, 1984 by forcing them to pay KEPCo a return on its investment until completion.[50] Brian Moline explained on behalf of the KCC staff that the Commission limited KEPCo's participation not because Wolf Creek was a nuclear plant, but because KEPCo could offer no assurances of when the plant would be completed or what it would cost: "We would be derelict if we had not examined carefully their efforts to mortgage their ratepayers." Moline denied charges that the commissioners had been influenced by antinuclear groups and that the order was an attempt to sabotage Wolf Creek.[51]

The utilities demanded a rehearing, saying the order exceeded the KCC's authority, was "capricious, unlawful, unreasonable and unjust," and would kill the sale deal.[52] It was denied.[53] Awkwardly, that same week the KCC issued its order, the utilities put out a new cost estimate for Wolf Creek of $1.7 billion—already above the KCC allowance.[54] The completion date estimate was set back a year, to April 1984, and each month of delay added $15 million to the cost.[55] KG&E, KCPL, and KEPCo unsuccessfully sued in Shawnee County District Court to try to modify the KCC KEPCo order.[56]

While the Kansas Farmers' Union hailed the KCC KEPCo decision, KG&E and KEPCo officials deplored it.[57] KG&E saw it as another wrench thrown into its financing plans, and interpreted that the KCC must be getting frustrated with the plant delays and wished to take desperate measures.[58] Wilson Cadman wrote an open letter to "Kansas leaders" emphasizing that several independent consultants, beginning with Arthur D. Little, Inc., in 1977, had given Wolf Creek good marks as a reasonable investment. Cresap, McCormick and Paget of Chicago, hired by the KCC, called it "one of the sounder nuclear projects underway in the country," while R. W. Beck and Company of Denver, retained by the Kansas Municipal Energy Agency, said Wolf Creek was "a low-cost power supply source," for the municipalities. Four studies, none commissioned by KG&E, had four positive findings. "Critics and criticism often make the news," Cadman noted, "while findings of recognized authorities sometimes are overlooked."[59] KEPCo attorney Kassebaum estimated that the Wolf Creek ownership could save KEPCo members $180 million in the first 16 years of operation, that KEPCo's studies demonstrated the feasibility, and that KEPCo had already negotiated a $322 million federal loan for the purchase.[60] KEPCo officials stated that their studies showed that KEPCo participation in Wolf Creek would be feasible even if the cost of the plant went as high as $3.8 billion.[61] "While there may be a great deal of double talk and as much restriction in any final order as the commission believes it can get by with," said a KEPCo spokesman, "I see no way they can get out of this jam."[62]

In the spring 1981 legislative session in Kansas, a bill (SB 80) was introduced to exempt co-ops from the regulation of the KCC and therefore to set aside the restrictions the KCC had imposed in the KEPCo case.[63] Some naturally objected that the KCC was the protector of the consumer and its role should not be diminished. Senate

Bill 80, these interests said, was "a political maneuver," pushed by the utilities because "Wolf Creek is becoming an embarrassing financial lemon, and KG&E and KCPL want to spread the sour taste around."[64] The attack on the KCC, said one staff member there, was part of the Reagan emphasis on deregulation, but it was also due to specific pressure from local utilities. "We have seen it coming," said Tom Taylor of the KCC. "The KCC has been very tough on utility companies and they don't like that. They want to operate without commission or public scrutiny."[65]

The bill was called "special interest legislation" by the critics, and perhaps it was. KEPCo had borrowed money short term at the peak 20.5 percent interest, and approval of its federal loan was delayed because of the KCC order. The interest difference between the market rate and the federal rate would amount to $12 million a year on KEPCo's Wolf Creek investment, or about $1,400 per hour. According to KEPCo officials, the delays would probably serve only to increase the eventual cost of Wolf Creek and diminish its feasibility for KEPCo or anyone else.[66] Meanwhile the main partners had offered a further 9 percent interest to a group of municipal utilities for $171 million.[67] The cost at the Jeffrey plant was escalating almost as fast as that of Wolf Creek, and coal had environmental problems, too. Charles Ellis of KEPCo stated its position dramatically: "KEPCo is like a huge airliner which has passed the point-of-no-return on takeoff. It's either going to fly or there will be one hell of a crash. I have not, now or anytime, any intentions of being the victim of such a crash! We've got the throttle open and the stick back and we're going to take off. I'd advise anybody against the mistake of bailing out now. You're going to get badly skinned up if you do."[68]

Senate Bill 80 passed the Senate in mid-February by a 24 to 9 vote.[69] Governor Carlin threatened to veto it if it reached his desk.[70] Compromises were made in the House in March, and the full House adopted the revised bill without dissent. Under the amended bill the KCC continued to have authority over co-ops in general, and the terms of the bill expired within a year, but the bill did set aside many of the restrictions of the KCC KEPCo order.[71] Carlin signed the bill in April.[72] "It was a meeting of minds," wrote an observer, "legislative and business, that fertilized the egg and brought life to the whole endeavor. . . . Wolf Creek is going to come into existence, everybody ought to just as well stop tormenting it and let it go ahead and happen."[73]

The passage of the bill, however, was far from the end of the snags connected with the KEPCo deal. On July 15 the Rural Electrification Administration denied, for the fiscal year at least, a request by KEPCo for a $432 million loan guarantee to help it buy a share of Wolf Creek. The delay during the KEPCo hearings, the REA said, led to its loan fund being already committed. Permanent denial would force the co-op to go to conventional rather than low-interest government financing.[74]

As a result of this denial, the utilities and KCC staffers in August had a number of meetings with federal officials in Washington to try to expedite the federal loan guarantee. Brian Moline, general counsel for the KCC, wrote a memo on the events there, intended for the KCC, which got leaked to the press. Moline indicated that Wilson Cadman and Arthur Doyle were "visibly shaken" at one point in the discussion and that there were angry, sarcastic exchanges between utility and federal officials. Moline paraphrased Cadman as saying that if the loan were not approved by the end of the year, at which time the provisions of SB 80 expired, "the entire Wolf Creek project would be thrown into chaos." Charles Ross of KEPCo called the leak to the press unethical and an embarrassment to the state of Kansas. Moline only commented that had he known it would become public he would have written it in a different style, but as straightforward information for his employer he would not change a word.[75]

While KG&E officials denied turning pale at the meetings with the REA, the utilities clearly hoped that the REA would approve the proposed KEPCo loan shortly after the end of REA's current fiscal year on September 30.[76] It did not happen.[77] REA in October approved a $200 million loan guarantee for KEPCo to buy only a 6 percent share of Wolf Creek. While utility officials were glad the issue had been resolved, they looked on it, interviewers said, "a bit ruefully."[78] The sale went through January 1, 1981, at that 6 percent level.[79] Jim Haines, at a rate hearing before the KCC, confirmed that this KEPCo share reduction would have a "devastating" financial effect on KG&E. "KG&E," he said, "made it through the '70s by drawing on the residual strength of its financial health. That residual strength is now largely gone. KG&E cannot financially survive another decade of bare bones rate increases."[80]

Nor was news rosy on other fronts. After some time of negotiation a deal for the sale of a 9 percent Wolf Creek share to the Kansas Municipal Energy Agency fell through in the spring of 1982.[81] In the fall of 1981, Callaway 2, another SNUPPS plant, was cancelled completely, and KG&E had its share of Jeffrey 3 on the block to raise cash for Wolf Creek and avoid borrowing. KG&E's periodic cost review now set the price of Wolf Creek at $1.9 billion, and the estimated fuel load date was set back 6 months to December 1983, with commercial operation to begin in May 1984.[82] Price escalation was rapid: in January 1980 it had been $1.3 billion; in July $1.5 billion; in October 1980 $1.7 billion; and now, a year later, $1.9 billion. Arthur Doyle of KCPL stated that he felt the cost could go to $2 billion, and the completion date could slip again.[83] Still, construction proceeded, the design was good enough to be adopted by the British, and momentum seemed irreversible even to many who had opposed the plant. "There is no use trying to pretend we can rewrite history," said Governor Carlin, "or do it all over again. The plant is being built, it's going to have to be paid for at some point and we'll proceed from there."[84]

The Cresap, McCormick and Paget consulting report, entitled "Report on the Financial and Operational Study of the Wolf Creek Nuclear Generating Facility," submitted in November 1980 was a benchmark in that process of resignation, if not enthusiasm. As it was commissioned by the KCC (though the price was assessed against the utilities and eventually their ratepayers) and was at first envisioned as a "probe" that would reveal substantial problems, its relatively favorable conclusions gave the plant credibility.[85] The report used 25 interviews, as well as masses of documents provided by the utilities, to do an analysis extending from the decision to build the plant to the progress of the Power Block currently. In addition to the much-quoted (by the utilities) line about the relative soundness of the project compared with its contemporaries around the country, the Cresap report went into unprecedented detail in analyzing the project from a neutral perspective, and was clearly written to boot.

The consultants concluded that while "the early stages of the Wolf Creek Project were beset by certain significant problems," the decisions of KG&E in 1979 about changing its role, staff, and presence on the construction site had led to major improvements. Principal among these was the direct and extensive personal involvement of KG&E's vice president–nuclear, Glenn Koester, and of Gary Fouts, the construction manager. There had been delays, but these were not simply attributable to incompetence. True, there were work scope changes, which added nearly $20 million, and underestimates of $113 million. Productivity was not as good as had been projected, and there was $13 million in unforeseen construction problems. But external events, or "uncontrollable" factors, were mostly blamed. The work delay over the base mat concrete delayed setting the reactor vessel by 18 months, for example. Additional regulation due to TMI had added over $5 million to the cost in the first year, and more increases were expected. Added state and federal regulation generally had added $81 million to Wolf Creek's total cost. Increased site security due to new NRC regulation added $4 million. Even with the slippage, the Wolf Creek schedule was better than the average of other plants being built across the country at the same time. In fact, of 14 plants that were projecting fuel load in 1982, only one had a projected construction duration shorter than Wolf Creek. Costs were escalating no faster than elsewhere.[86]

The financial challenge of the plant was admittedly great. KG&E, said the Chicago consultants, would need large rate increases before 1984 and over $500 million in external financing—about $100 million a year. Its profit margin and return on equity would drop, even under the best circumstances. Insufficient or untimely rate relief, inability to place stock offerings at reasonable prices, inability to achieve the company's authorized rate of return, failure of the commission to approve the sale of 17 percent of the plant to KEPCo, and a whole list of other contingencies, could put KG&E into a financial emergency.[87]

Most of the Cresap report's recommendations were directed at making KG&E's supervision of the construction field work more effective. Prior to 1980, the report stated, "the owner-utilities' project management concept was inappropriate for a large complex nuclear plant construction project," and its quality assurance (Q/A) staff on site was insufficient. As of July 1980, however, the on-site staff had grown from 3 to 15, and new cost monitoring and schedule computer systems had been developed. This systematized what the Cresap people called a "highly personalized, unstructured and, on occasion, quixotic," prior method of such monitoring. "Without complete and easily understood project status and performance information, the owner-utilities' management can not effectively monitor progress, or ensure that the architect/engineers close out their work in a timely manner." Though the plant's remote location made it difficult to retain experienced general foremen and foremen, this had improved. There was criticism and praise in the report, but the audit was anything but a disaster for the utility. The criticism was specific, and solutions were outlined plainly.[88]

All this made encouraging reading at the corporate offices. However, the public issue of Kansas nuclear power was not to be decided by consultants. Cresap, McCormick and Paget wrote, "Although this report has been prepared so that it is understandable to persons who do not have a technical understanding of nuclear plant construction, the basic subject matter is very complicated, and simplification was possible only to a limited degree."[89] KG&E suggested in its flyer, "The Outlet," which went out with the electric bills, that people order a free copy of the entire report for their public library or university, but probably there were few takers.[90] It was easy for engineers to laugh at some of the critics, and to point out that nuclear technology was not kindergarten, but the fact was that in a representative democracy, the people with the best simplification—or at least the most compelling one—would often prevail. The suggestions for converting Wolf Creek to a coal plant were said by one engineer to be akin to making a sewing machine out of a television set, and by another as like converting a '67 Ford into a pocket watch.[91] Yet it continued to be suggested, and the suggestions were listened to.

Public indignation in the early 1980s was not calmed by reports; instead it was inflamed by news. KG&E and its ratepayers were asked to contribute to the cleanup of TMI, and a bill in the Kansas legislature to prohibit that, introduced in 1982, failed to pass.[92] In November 1981, the NRC estimated that Wolf Creek would not begin commercial operation until early in 1985.[93] In the irony of ironies, Congress in the fall of 1981 repealed large sections of the Fuel Use Act of 1978. This, combined with deregulation of price, made natural gas, whose shortage had started the whole move of KG&E toward nuclear, again a reasonably priced competitor as boiler fuel.[94] In August 1982, the utility confirmed a year's delay in completion, from May 1984 to the spring of 1985. This was blamed on new quality control and safety regulations, and the cost of it was pegged at $1 million per day. There were press rumors that KG&E bills might jump 88 percent when the blessed day of completion at Burlington finally arrived.[95] Flyers circulated in 1982 estimating a possible 200 percent rate hike.[96] The phrase "rate shock" began to appear in headlines, and a new organization called the "Electric Shock Coalition" gained members who had never been in the opposition movement before.[97]

The rhetoric from the opposition, however, showed frustration along with mounting anger. A critic in 1981 said that the "Sunflower Alliance" groups "might as well be punching a pillow," as loose-knit left-wing coalitions kept protests peaceful, but failed in getting their point across.[98] The New Year's Capitol steps rallies grew less boisterous and more poorly attended, as did the Redmond summer happenings. At a nuclear energy protest meeting in Lawrence in the summer of 1981 the comment was that "the flies outnumbered the participants."[99] One hundred people at a TMI commemoration march in 1982 was not like the old days.[100] True, the remaining group was determined. Several chained themselves to the fence at Wolf Creek in the summer of 1983.[101] But the numbers in the field were not impressive. "Our lot in life," mused one opponent "has now been relegated to the position of bailing out fiscal irresponsibility and poor management decisions made by KG&E."[102]

But a certain resignation did not mean that the protest had reached the "post-political stage," or that the technology had garnered acceptance. Bitterness toward the utility companies increased as it appeared more and more inevitable that the plant would be completed, licensed, and would affect rates. In the fall of 1982, a local newspaper concluded "this must surely be one of the worst-planned and controlled construction projects ever done in the United States, perhaps the world. . . . Is American Technology so poor that this is the best we can do? Or are government regulations so complex and self-defeating that this is the only way a plant can be constructed?"[103] One man that fall said the plant "promises to be the biggest white elephant in Kansas' business and industrial history."[104] "Pity poor Wolf Creek," wrote a Kansas editor a few months later, "the nuclear plant that nobody loves. Like an unwanted child with expensive habits, Wolf Creek is straining the affections—to say nothing of the financial support of its parents."[105] By early 1983, the cost estimate for Wolf Creek was $2.5 billion. "This hungry Wolf has been on the loose for a decade. . . . [T]he Kansas Corporation Commission estimates it will cost at least another billion to finish whitewashing this elephant. . . . There seems no end to the waste, the billions upon billions we will be forced to cough over for a project that should have been shut down in the name of common sense years ago. . . . Reading through the flack and between the lines, the utilities have lost their collective shirt, pants and shoes on this boondoggle and they want us to pay for their folly."[106] One newspaper in 1983 called the project "a crock of stink."[107]

The *Parsons Sun* and its editor, Clyde Reed, had been a special KG&E nemesis for some time, and became so much so in 1982 that Bob Rives of KG&E responded at length to one of its patented editorials. Rives quoted a March 23, 1973, *Sun* editorial, to wit: "Kansas Gas and Electric always had had a reputation as a progressive utility staying ahead of the needs and preparing for the future with rare foresight. Its leadership in the nuclear project is in line with its past policies as Parsons and southeast Kansas have known them." What happened to that, Rives asked? Phrases such as "less than candid," "arrogant," "foolhardy," "flacks," "most monstrous error," had crept into the Parsons news reporting on Wolf Creek, but, said Rives, there had not been careful research on the alternatives. Rives offered to send Reed a copy of a *New York Times* article supporting nuclear power—"the kind that gives me a warm glow about the First Amendment."[108] Others commented too on Reed's special gall on Wolf Creek. A writer for the *Emporia Gazette* thought it might be his diet. It was reported that Reed ate shredded wheat, and implied that maybe his brain cells were not getting enough nourishment: "If Mr. Reed is able to write brilliant editorials 90 percent of the time after a meager bowl of straw and bananas in the morning, imagine what he could do with an adequate meal."[109]

Really, though, it was not shredded wheat and it was not just Clyde Reed. It was the tension of a great and expensive unknown toward which a determined utility was pushing hard amid a bevy of second-guessers and some true believers of other persuasions. Lance Burr in 1982 made a run for attorney general of Kansas nearly exclusively on the Wolf Creek issue, criticizing incumbent Robert Stephan for refusing to take an active role on Wolf Creek. Burr described the plant as a "white elephant" and "consumer ripoff," and argued that the attorney general as protector of the environment should oppose it.[110] Burr promised if elected to throw the weight of his office behind seeing that the completed plant never generated electricity.[111]

Cost was the bugbear, and the increasing realization that ultimately the consumers would pay all or most of it. "Remember the good old days," went a fall 1982 letter to the editor. "That was in the days when [if] a company made an error it paid the penalty—not its customers. . . . I hope the same guy who sold them on the Wolf Creek project didn't sell them the Brooklyn Bridge while he had them hypnotized."[112] The Black Fox nuclear plant in Oklahoma was cancelled in 1982.[113] A poll taken by KCPL in March 1983 showed its customers about evenly divided on whether Wolf Creek should be abandoned also. Most emphasized the cost as the big factor ("If it is finished, so are we").[114] Letters suggested Kansans should "kill the Wolf Creek monster . . . before it eats us all up alive in electric bills."[115] The word *monster* was repeated often, often tied to the image of a mutated wolf feasting on inordinate quantities of money. "Won't the Legislature skin this Wolf before it grows more teeth?"[116] At a Redmond Reservoir rally that spring a sign was put up pointing to Wolf Creek and reading, "For Sale. For information call Kansas consumers."[117]

There were calmer voices, of course. Two people writing to the *Wichita Eagle* late in 1983 noted that it was difficult to know all the costs and predict all the changes in technology, law, etc., for a 12-year project. If inflation held at a constant 10 percent, the original $783 million estimated cost of Wolf Creek would be $2.5 billion by now. It was silly to have more KCC studies funded by KG&E and its ratepayers. "They are arguing a fact, like trying to explain why a baloney sandwich tastes like cold cuts on bread." Cheap was not all that mattered. If Wolf Creek worked it would be a bargain in the long run.[118]

Wasn't the media full of scare talk? asked a college professor. Wasn't it amazing that polls of college students and the League of Women Voters showed that both groups considered nuclear power their number one present risk of death, easily outranking motor vehicle accidents, which killed 50,000 Americans a year; smoking, which killed 150,000; and handguns, which killed 17,000? Eighty percent thought nuclear power was more harmful than coal burning, though at least 20 studies concluded otherwise. Many programs in cancer screening, medical care, and highway safety could save thousands of lives each year for less than $50,000 per life saved. Yet the public was spending $50 million per life saved to protect itself against nuclear radiation. They did so, the professor said, because of the journalistic sins of overcoverage and language inflation. *Lethal radioactivity* was an accepted term, though none talked of *lethal water* because of drownings. Interviews in the press were usually not with university professors who published regularly, but with renegades with axes to grind.[119]

While the exaggeration in the safety area was clear, it would have been difficult to exaggerate the difficulty the escalating cost caused KG&E in the early 1980s. When the company announced a cost estimate of $2.67 billion in November 1983, it was the seventh cost revision since the project started, most of them in the 1980s.[120] CWIP was introduced again, again without success, as an aid to financing. In 1980 only 14 states entirely prohibited CWIP from the rate base, as did Kansas, but that did not change the politics there.[121] "Most Kansans wouldn't know a CWIP from a WPA or RBI," said one journalist. "But it's costing them money to be ignorant. Legislative do-gooders have fought CWIP and returned home to woo voters with a 'look what I did for you' story. 'I slapped it to those Big Utility Boys, they can't make us pay for costs of construction until the unit goes on line.' Bull—with a capital boldface B, followed by the U and double L."[122] Such invective, and many hours of lobbying by Cadman and others at KG&E, made nary a dent in the opposition to CWIP.[123]

In May 1982 KG&E suffered what the newspapers called a "1-2 punch" to its finances. It was announced then that KPL and KG&E had ended their negotiations for KG&E's selling its 20 percent share of Jeffrey 3 for $84 million, and the KMEA group of cities said that it would be impossible for it to take a share of Wolf Creek and LaCygne, planned to cost $179 million. Only about a third of the KMEA members would agree to the step, and the stability of the entire organization was threatened by the Wolf Creek controversy. Wilson Cadman commented that if the company could not find another buyer for its Jeffrey share it would have to increase its 1982 money raising goal from $138 million to $207 million and its 1983 financing from $109 million to $124 million. The strategy was to issue common and preferred stock and to sell bonds through KG&E's new European subsidiary, as Europeans were not nearly so spooked about nuclear projects as Americans seemed to be. To keep stock sales an option the dividend was kept up. S&P lowered KG&E's corporate bond rating in the spring of 1982 from BBB to BBB-.[124] This was the lowest notch on the investment grade scale. "It's a money-cruncher," said Loux of the KCC. "But when they complete their construction program, they'll probably turn around and become a blue-chip utility. Until then it's tough sledding."[125]

That summer Gordon Evans, KG&E's "Renaissance Man" died.[126] Electricity use in the entire country dropped by nearly 2 percent, the first significant annual decline since World War II.[127] The national press was full of news of the WPSS bond problems for the abortive state of Washington nuclear plant projects, where customers were paying on $7.5 billion in bonds floated over the last decade on two nuclear plants that had been cancelled.[128] In July 1983 came a default on the WPSS bonds of $2.25 billion, the largest in municipal bond history.[129] Early in 1983 this was followed by the news of the dioxin pollution at Times Beach, Missouri.[130] KG&E, then the smallest utility in the country building a nuclear plant, was getting a reputation as the "little utility that could," but there were those in the company that at times thought maybe it couldn't.[131] Bob Rives commented that it was just another critical time. "I guess in a sense things seem like they're always at a critical point."[132]

The short-term financial crisis brought on by the KEPCo share reduction, the KMEA cancellation, and the inability to sell Jeffrey 3, like the others, was weathered, but the difficulties did not cease. Late in 1982, KG&E sold its Jeffrey 3 share to Missouri Public Service Company, though not without some skepticism from the KCC about the wisdom of selling such low-cost power in order to fund Wolf Creek.[133] However, after KCC approval, that deal too fell apart. The KCC had ruled that rate relief to KG&E for purchased power beyond the first year would remain subject to future rate cases. KG&E thought this was too much risk and cancelled the sale.[134] Instead it asked for a rate increase to cover its Jeffrey 3 expenses, and gave up income as well as the chance to avoid part of the charge of "overcapacity."[135] In April 1983, KG&E first mortgage bonds were dropped by Standard & Poor from BBB- to BB+, and its preferred stock rating from BB+ to BB, both "speculative grade." The concern was about cash flow, and S&P analysts said that "significant reduction of financial stress cannot be realistically expected until at least 1985, when Wolf Creek [85% complete in the spring of 1983] is expected to become operational."[136]

Cadman and financial officer Howard Hansen innovated daily in borrowing. They also continued raising money through stock sales, though the WPSS jitters and the cancellation of the $7 billion Marble Hill nuclear plant of Public Service Company of Indiana caused them to cancel at least one proposed issue. Interest rates in 1983 had declined from their 21 percent high, making the KG&E annual dividend look more attractive to investors. Some, however, unaccustomed to seeing utilities as a "growth" versus an "income" stock, even began to wonder whether the low price of the KG&E stock might one day prove to be a bargain.[137]

Cadman and Hansen went before the security analysts in New York with a 12-minute color film with the theme that it was wrong to paint all nuclear projects with the same broad brush—the one in Kansas was different.[138] Consultants more or less agreed. A Drexel-Burnham-Lambert study in 1984 examined 33 nuclear plants owned by 43 investor-owned utilities and concluded that Wolf Creek was financially sound. It was 11 percent cheaper to build than the average, had a better than average safety record, and was probably not in danger of cancellation. Less encouraging was a First Boston Corporation study of the same year, which evaluated the cost of plants to consumers. Due to KG&E's relatively large share of Wolf Creek, its relatively small customer base, and less than anticipated increase in demand, First Boston estimated that Wolf Creek would be the third most costly plant ever built, in cost to consumers.[139]

The real proof of confidence was in the financial offerings. In March 1984, KG&E sold $100 million in bonds, and some stock, though the latter went at a distressed price of $16.75 a share. The bonds went to institutional investors in what was known as a "private placement," instead of to the public as was traditional. Cadman and Hansen's strategy was to make detailed presentations to specific large investors about the "true picture of Wolf Creek," rather than depending on small investors overwhelmed with negative media publicity. Kansas senator Bob Dole introduced a bill to allow KG&E to use $1.5 billion in tax-exempt industrial development bonds to pay off construction, but this bill was withdrawn shortly when its costs in lost tax revenue were determined.[140] Both KCPL and KG&E set up financial subsidiaries in the Netherlands Antilles, a tax haven in the Caribbean, to attract Eurodollars (KG&E's was called Kansas Gas and Electric International Finance NV). Cadman spent much time in London, where he could deal with all the banks in the world.

KG&E became the first American customer of the Long Term Credit Bank of Japan. In 1980 it raised $124 million, in 1981 $186 million, in 1982 $200 million, and in 1983 $357.6 million. During that last year Cadman was gone from home over 200 nights.[141] The company used credit agreements; revolving bank loans based on a letter of credit from Credit Suisse, New York Branch; short-term borrowing and loans pledging fuel inventories as collateral. Amory Lovins quipped that "they're into about everything except bake sales."[142]

The message to investors was that "Wolf Creek is not a lurid example of corporate mismanagement. It is a victim of unforeseen circumstances."[143] After all, as one executive put it, in utilities in the 1950s "you could have put a gorilla in the chief executive's chair" and the business would have grown.[144] These current trying circumstances would change, and the strong management they built, as well as the efficient nuclear plant the opposition partly molded, would still be there. KG&E's innovation in finance and its salesmanship to the sophisticated investor in the early 1980s was a factor as important as its determined and respectful continued engagement with the opposition in ensuring that the Wolf Creek plant, unlike so many of its fellows, would be finished and would produce power into the future.

Still, there was no question there was an emergency. One wag quipped that he noticed KG&E was worried about unfriendly takeovers, and asked its stockholders for authority to impose "shark repellent." "The best shark repellent they have is Wolf Creek." In the spring of 1984 the cost estimate of the 96 percent complete plant was $2.7 billion, one-third of that representing interest on debt. It was almost like the federal deficit. KCPL's investment in the plant was nearing $1.8 billion, $240 million more than the current value of all their other plants combined. Further delays could cost $50 million per month. The financial structure of the utilities was a little like the plant, some said—strong on the surface, but vulnerable beneath. And then there was the rate battle coming up, when the KCC held hearings specifically on Wolf Creek. "Both sides," Cadman predicted of those hearings, "will end up pretty bloody." If anything should happen to scrap Wolf Creek, said the fixed income manager for Commerce Bank in Kansas City, "we're talking about a virtual wipeout of shareholder equity."[145] As a group of consultants later put it, "KG&E . . . demonstrated its ability to finance its ownership interest in the WCGS under very difficult conditions," but at the same time it increased its financial and business risks "and became very dependent on receiving adequate and fair rate relief in connection with its investment in the WCGS."[146]

Company officials had a worst case scenario on computer, but would not speculate publicly about it. "The moon could fall and hit the plant tomorrow," said KCPL's Doyle. "If you speculate like that you're off in never-never land."[147] Yet operating people inside KG&E began not to like what their calculators showed. "I don't give a damn if the fuel is free," said Bill Woolery. "When your capital costs get away from you you have shot the cost per kilowatt-hour."[148] Lyle Koerper, who by 1984 had replaced Bob Rives as KG&E's spokesman on Wolf Creek, said, "We can't guarantee for anyone this company will be in business three years from now."[149] The word *bankruptcy* began to be mentioned.

In the late months of 1983, KG&E prepared for the beginning in January of the first major set of federal hearings since the construction permit hearings of 1976—those that would result in an operating permit for the Wolf Creek plant.[150] Frank Duddy was in charge at the site for the end game on construction.[151] KG&E was getting kudos from the local press for its "Project Deserve" community charity through which stockholders, employees, and customers of KG&E donated money to a fund that helped the poor with utility bills and equipment repairs.[152] And even the national antinuclear activists gave the Kansas nuclear plant a relatively good rating. Nader's Critical Mass Energy Project rated nuclear projects from 1.00, which meant management attention and involvement were aggressive and warrant less NRC attention, to 2.00, which was adequate, to 3.00, which meant utility attention was acceptable but weaknesses were evident. Wolf Creek got a rating of 1.67 from the group.[153] The public, meanwhile viewed a television special entitled *The Day After*, which, in harrowing detail, documented the potential grisly effects of a nuclear attack on the city of Lawrence, Kansas. Newspaper reviewers did not resist commenting that even a small release of radiation from a nuclear plant could have a similar effect and that "the life of every American would be tainted by such illnesses as cancer and birth defects—or lost to radiation poisoning."[154]

While KG&E remained determined, it was difficult to maintain morale in the ranks. People working in nonnuclear parts of the company felt neglected. This was particularly disturbing in a company that had been known for the personal attention given to line employees by the top people. There was the agony, too, of contrasting stories from the company and in the newspapers, and the necessity for trying to explain to neighbors items the employee did not fully understand. It was a wearing phenomenon to be always and forever, even if you were a secretary at KG&E or a lineman, at a party or out on the lake, the spokesman for and the representative of the nuclear plant that was on everybody's mind. Wolf Creek was difficult for everyone with any connection to KG&E, as much so as ever as the Power Block and its connections neared completion. It was, commented Bill Woolery, "one hellish project. . . . You can't believe how it consumes everything."[155]

9
Prudence or Perfection

> I think by the year 1990, Kansas will be shouting for glee because we have it [Wolf Creek], I really do.
> —State Senator Ross Doyen, March 1, 1984

> I say now is the time to stop Wolf Creek from ever operating. We don't need the power. We don't need the danger. We don't need the bills.
> —Robert Cartwright, in *Wichita Eagle,* March 4, 1984

> There is no need to put our ear to the ground. . . . I think we can feel the thunder at our feet.
> —*Pittsburg Sun,* March 14, 1984

1984 was a famous year—one of those unusual years between decades or turns of centuries that gets any attention in advance at all. This time the notice was due to George Orwell's distopian novel *1984* (1949), about a bizarre and totalitarian futuristic society where information came in "newspeak," and history was rewritten to suit current ideology. Paradoxes—"War is Peace," "Slavery is Freedom"—were accepted by a brainwashed or frightened populace, and deviations from the current "correct" path were punished by aggressive organizations of political militants. Understandably, there was, among the strongly literate at least, no little rumination when the actual 1984 arrived, about the similarities or dissimilarities of American conditions to Orwell's unsettling vision. If such speculation reached Kansas, it applied more directly to the Wolf Creek controversy, now again directly in the public eye, than to most areas of life in "Midway U.S.A." For in the nuclear struggle, ideology met engineering every day. The Wolf Creek controversy was as much about what values Kansans wished to incorporate in their culture, and to what degree any group could impose a set of values on another, as it was about how electricity was to be made. And, while there may not have been wholesale rewriting of history, there were specialized "uses of the past," especially the recent past. The slogans were there, as was, if not "newspeak," at least considerable doubletalk. Naturally both sides saw the other as the totalitarian threat, clouding the future.

The debate over nuclear power generally has been called a pivotal and typical event in the history of "late capitalist development." "However strong the commitment to market principles," writes Joseph Camilleri, "the nuclear fuel cycle presupposes, by the very fact of its organizational and technical complexity, a degree of centralized coordination which only the state is able to offer." Government has, he says, an "endogenous structural role in economic management." State intervention at Wolf Creek, through the formal hearing processes, from licensing to rate hearings, was indeed a constant. However, as already suggested, state centralization was no more readily accepted by the public in the flux of change in the 1970s than was corporate power. Government, while posing as the "friend of the people" in controlling utilities and protecting against nuclear hazards, revealed in the shine of publicity its own weaknesses as well as its arrogance. There was a "preoccupation with legitimacy" in the 1970s, and the formal and intimidating state processes, which were supposed to seal that legitimacy for the new technology while seemingly rapping its promoters on the knuckles, failed fully to do so this time. Camilleri argues that worldwide "the nuclear controversy generated both new and old forms of conflict, each superimposed on, and interacting with the other." One of the new forms was that nuclear power became a focal point of a larger movement committed to resisting the "colonization of the life-world," and represented a threat to the legitimacy of regulator as well as regulatee.[1]

In the case of Wolf Creek this was most evident in the rate hearings before the KCC and in the legislative events surrounding them. While the "prudence" and "hindsight" issues were debated rather technically against the backdrop of unprecedented legislative direction for the hearing process, adjudicators, witnesses, and attorneys were deeply aware that the storms boiling around this single plant in Kansas were of a type that might be far less containable in the vessel of established procedures and powers than was the atomic fire in the dome near Burlington.

The operating license hearings on Wolf Creek began on January 17, 1984, in Coffey County, and moved to Emporia in February. This type of hearing generally was calm, as approval was almost automatic, but that very month an operating license had been denied a completed nuclear plant—the Byron Nuclear Power Station near Rockford, Illinois, built by Commonwealth Edison Company of Chicago. The cost on that plant had risen from an original estimate of $1.4 billion to more than $7 billion.[2] Also, as seemed almost usual, the real benchmark event of the licensing hearings had its film parallel and accompaniment. The movie *Silkwood*, produced by Mike Nichols and starring Meryl Streep, was, as much as *The China Syndrome* had been, a panegyric against nuclear power—this time, however, slightly less well-crafted. "Rarely," wrote a reviewer, "has better talent been squandered on a sappier story." It reflected, that analyst said, what historian Richard Hofstadter had called "the paranoid style in American politics"—i.e., the idea that everything was the result of a plot. The message of the film was that we don't see ourselves, as engineers do, "inhabiting a world of unavoidable choices and risks, but as slaves to brooding circumstances and vague menace which we might escape if management weren't so greedy and secretive."[3] The movie, said a Kansas editor, was appropriate to 1984, as it was "merely the latest in a recent and corrupt tradition that consciously falsifies history and delivers checkable lies to its gullible audience." The quantity of Quaaludes in Silkwood's system at the time of her car accident, the editor noted, was high, and that of plutonium low or nonexistent.[4]

Silkwood was based, however loosely, on fact, and current news reinforced that. In January of 1984 the U.S. Supreme Court ruled 5 to 4 that state juries may impose heavy damages to punish nuclear plants that recklessly cause radiation injuries, and it restored a $10 million punitive award against Kerr-McGee that had been thrown out in the court of appeals.[5] Kansas Attorney General Robert Stephan emphasized that the Silkwood court decision meant that the federal government was not going "to lock the state out from ensuring that its people have recourse for injuries under state law," and that could have application to several aspects of Wolf Creek.[6]

There was a strong voice for moderation of the attacks at this late stage. A large ad in the *Wichita Eagle* in February 1984, signed by numerous prominent citizens, called KG&E a good citizen of the community, which had suffered from the longest and most negative and intemperate media attention ever directed at a generating plant project. It was time, the ad said, for more fairness toward the utility.[7] A business group complained that "we are deeply concerned that the heavily biased and negative media attention on Wolf Creek Generating Station is creating a dangerously unstable business climate in Wichita and the entire state of Kansas."[8] A letter to the editor in Wichita compared the cost of one killowatt-hour of electricity with the cost of the newspaper. In 1945, both were 3¢. Now (1984) the daily paper cost 25¢ and Sunday 75¢, and a killowatt-hour cost 6.9¢. People had been thrilled when the nuclear plant was announced and then "along came the 'nervous ninnies' and the 'kook groups' with all their loud-mouth protesting to cause delays. They always delay the work because various commissions apparently are more concerned with the whines of those squeaking wheels than getting on with the worthwhile business at hand."[9] Grover McKee, Wichita's former advisor on the coal gas plant, admitted he had opposed Wolf Creek, yet suggested that now that it was here it was time for a change of tune. The city should focus on "how we get ourselves out of the mess we're in rather than engaging in spear-rattling, chest-beating and public floggings of KG&E, which was, I remind you, a kind friend of long standing until a few short months ago."[10] Many were shocked when a small lead statue of an English hare put alongside a pool in Wichita's Heritage Park in memory of a sister of Wilson Cadman was singled out from the other sculptures and smashed by vandals on the anniversary of her death.[11] Yet few expected that a change of atmosphere would be suddenly forthcoming, after so many years of polarization and bold statements. "The Chicken Littles, Turkey Lurkeys and Ducky Luckys," said one wit, "are now roosting in Kansas. Their normal call of 'nu-clee-r ca-tas-tro-fee' is now a raucous 'too-hi, too-hi.' The purpose is the same: to frighten away the perceived interloper from Wolf Creek. As a robin fights its own reflection at a mirror or windowglass, this non-endangered species battles a non-existent enemy. Its understanding and comprehension of reality is imperfect."[12]

The operating permit hearings were real enough. Amory Lovins was brought to Kansas for a fee of $4,000 to appear, and said that KG&E was financially sick, commenting (mixing his paleontological metaphor a bit) that Wolf Creek was like a dinosaur trapped in a financial tar pit.[13] The Citizens Utility Rate Board (CURB), founded by Sue Horn Estes in Wichita late in 1982, proposed that the official state agencies were not enough to protect the consumer. While CURB originally was to have been supported financially by membership contributions, which the utilities would help it solicit, it eventually came to be supported by the ratepayers of the utilities that it attacked.[14] It was joined in opposition by the Electric Shock Coalition, formed in the spring of 1983, which was to be to the rate hearings what the Sunflower Alliance was to the construction years.[15] The Kansas Natural Resource Council, successor to MACEA, came out against completing Wolf Creek, charging that the company was not being honest about projected rate increases. It was time to stop unquestioned growth, the organization stated.[16]

People in suits and ties joined those in tie-dyed jeans and work shirts this time. The support of the Wichita Chamber of Commerce could not be depended on by KG&E. The Chamber had been "besieged by questions" from businesses about electric rates and had appointed a task force to reexamine the Chamber's 1976 position supporting Wolf Creek on the grounds that it was a step in ensuring a healthy economy.[17] Bill Easton, a Wichitan who ran a foundry with an electric furnace, considered moving it out of town. He was for nuclear power, but not Wolf Creek. "You had the best data, plans and brains of the utility," he said, "—and circumstances just caught up with them. The whole plan for the plant was a mistake."[18] A group of small Wichita businesses formed an organization called the Alliance for Liveable Electric Rates (ALERT) headed by Linda Weir-Enegren, an owner of LS Industries. Enegren, with her business background, unquestioned credentials as a caring volunteer, and a style that mixed research with strong emotional appeal, was to be a formidable force in the Wolf Creek consumer movement over the next few years. "An investment is an investment," Weir-Enegren said. "They pay their money and they take their chances. It is extremely unpalatable to us for KG&E to ask to be immune from the whole free-enterprise system."[19] Willard Garvey, a Wichita real estate developer and entrepreneur, was disturbed at the "business-government" partnership represented by a regulated monopoly. "There is plenty of blame to go around on Wolf Creek," he wrote. "But isn't the root cause that politicians and political monopolies have little incentive to control or reduce costs to the citizens?" Garvey recommended complete deregulation of utilities: "The competitive pricing system is the consumers' and taxpayers' sole salvation."[20] The Libertarian view was related. Bill Earnest, the chair of the Kansas Libertarian Party, and not frequently associated with the left-wing progovernment types who were in the anti–Wolf Creek ranks, opposed not nuclear power, but the system of which Wolf Creek was a part. "If an unfriendly foreign power," he wrote, "had attempted to impose its methods of producing and selling electricity on us, we certainly would have viewed it as a hostile act." But there seemed to be willingness to accept the "nightmarish trauma" imposed by Kansas's own legislature to administer "fair" prices in utilities. The free market, Earnest said, would determine what was overcapacity and who should pay. "Abolish the Kansas Corporation Commission, and then adjourn the legislature."[21] Strange bedfellows perhaps, but all tending in the same direction, and with the potential to form a formidable front. "What next," came the cry. "Will KG&E ask that we give our first born, our blood, or the gold from our teeth?"[22]

An example of the state of the media amid all this pressure came in March 1984 when a controversy erupted about a front page Sunday story in February featuring an interview with KG&E's Wilson Cadman, Bob Rives, Kent Brown, and a reporter for the *Wichita Eagle*. The reporter, Steve Tompkins, had on that occasion quoted a 1973 order of magnitude cost estimate, dated February 18, 1973, and giving the projected price of the plant at $783 million. He then went on to say that in August of 1973, KG&E had set up a model of a nuclear plant at Wichita State University and Elmer Hall had appeared at a press conference claiming the price was $500 million. The implication was that the company knew then that the figure was wrong, and had purposefully withheld the document from the public.[23] Tompkins's rhetoric was bold. The headline was "KG&E Bet Company on Wolf Creek," and the claim was that "an examination of company and government documents shows the trail of the Wolf Creek project is littered with mistakes in planning and management, costly delays and warning signs about a declining nuclear industry that KG&E failed to heed."[24]

Something about the document did not make sense to KG&E officials, especially since they knew they had not knowingly been involved in any such coverup. They contacted Elmer Hall, who remembered the document, went back to the archives and found it, and proved that the newspaper date had been altered to reflect earlier knowledge by the company of the higher estimate than had actually been the case. Even with the right date, the document had been a mistakenly high estimate for the time, and was corrected at the time by Bechtel.[25] The reporter, and the editor and publisher of the Wichita newspaper, were called to a meeting at the KG&E offices, where the evidence was presented to them of the obvious forgery. The document's original date could not have been before January 1974, months after the project was approved. "I never saw the blood drain out of two men's faces so fast in my life," Cadman remembered. Tompkins denied wrongdoing, but was suspended and eventually resigned. The *Eagle* management advised their ambitious reporters that seeking the Pulitzer Prize for muckraking reporting could and should only go so far.[26] The paper admitted in print that it had made a "serious error."[27]

Given the media controversy, there was relatively little fireworks before the new three-person Atomic Safety and Licensing Board group at the hearings themselves, much less so than in 1976. The opposition seemed almost to grant the NRC momentum, and saved much of its force for the KCC rate hearings, where cost and the question of who paid could be placed at the center of things. Wanda Christy and Mary Ellen Salava were there as intervenors, as they had been since the first land taking and the formation of the Wolf Creek Opposition in the early 1970s. Also officially intervening was Kansans for Sensible Energy (KASE). Contentions were divided into many subsections, but addressed overall just two remaining issues—the adequacy of the evacuation plan in case of emergency and the financial qualifications of the utilities building the Wolf Creek plant. The board addressed the evacuation contentions at length, concluding in both cases that the plans were acceptable and the license should be issued.

The financial contention, introduced by KASE, was dismissed before the hearing. A federal court had ruled in response to KASE in 1982 that the financial health of utilities does not affect operational safety and did not therefore merit consideration at licensing hearings. A federal appeals court panel in February 1984 reversed that by ruling that the NRC must consider a utility's financial health before awarding it a construction permit or operating license. However, the NRC left its prior rule in effect for the time being until it could draft a response to the court. KG&E, of course, worried that KASE could still threaten the operating license on financial grounds later, thus causing delay and additional cost. Other issues than evacuation and financial were not considered at all at this stage, partly accounting for the quiet at the hearings.[28]

The NRC operating license hearings were just an event in a long federal final approval process. KG&E applied for an operating license on August 5, 1980.[29] It submitted its final environmental and safety reports on Wolf Creek to the NRC in the spring of 1982. The final operating license was not issued until March of 1985, though an "initial" decision came in July 1984. A full power permit waited until June 1985 when all the "hot tests" of Wolf Creek at partial power and the fuel load had been completed.[30]

At the KCC and in the Kansas legislature, things were not so orderly. Ordinarily and historically, utility rate cases were as uncontroversial as NRC final operating license hearings. Decisions had been made with the best information available at the time, the plant had been built, and the ratepayers needed to pay for it. Kansans, however, were in no mood to play out that scenario. Wolf Creek had been a top newspaper issue in Kansas for several years. It was the second biggest story in state newspapers for 1984.[31] The opinion that had been generated was bound to have its day again in some powerful forum or another before electricity from Wolf Creek went out over the lines.

The legislature was first. The publicity and the political pressure resulting from reports of possible "havoc" in KG&E rates when Wolf Creek came on line created a strong movement in the legislature to increase the powers of the KCC to disallow certain expenses for completed generating plants, including adjustments for "overcapacity," and "imprudent" investment or management by the constructing utility, as that was evaluated by the Commission after hearing witnesses.[32] A rancher, Don McGinnis, became a local folk hero in 1983 when he won a battle with KCPL and stopped the utility from stringing a high-voltage power line across his ranch in Anderson County. McGinnis, in his hat and boots, had his picture in papers around the state, along with the description of his lifestyle, including keeping a pair of lions and a B-26 bomber.[33] A protesting individual had triumphed over big business in that case, and some saw no reason why the model could not be applied to stopping Wolf Creek also, or at least to burdening the utility stockholders and investors for a long time, if not permanently, with much of the bill.

There was no shyness about expressing opinions. "If a small business made such mistakes," wrote an editor in Pratt, "the proprietor would bear the loss and his customers would buy elsewhere."[34] Wrote another: "Why must Kansas continue to play the sucker? By all indications, we're the biggest bunch of cauliflower-eared rubes west of Moses Malone. We'd plunk down our last quarter for another look under the walnut shell. . . . After all we bought Wolf Creek. Or, the Legislature did."[35] A rate shock bill, one editor thought, would send a much-needed message to the Wolf Creek builders, who "should have realized the folly of Wolf Creek years ago." Conservation, he said, was "a nightmare that must haunt many a bigwig at KG&E and KCP&L."[36] Economic opinion could be blunt. "Let the owners (stockholders)," wrote one man, "who have been getting fat at public expense over the last 50 years absorb some of the loss."[37] Another suggested that a few alterations be made to the Wolf Creek dome and a telescope be installed in it. Lacking that, local ranchers could store alfalfa there. "Stories about waste and mismanagement are enough to cause a C.P.A.'s eyes to roll back in his head."[38]

A bill was introduced in the Kansas legislature in January 1984 to ban any nuclear plant in Kansas until the waste disposal problem was solved. This was modeled on bills in other states, but did not have much of a chance of passage. More promising was "rate shock" legislation, which began in that month to be pushed in the state legislature by the KCC and its chairman, Michael Lennen. "It's something we want to nail down," said Lennen. "The commission's authority to address the issue of excess capacity is unclear." The KCC wanted flexibility in how it determined excess capacity, but did not want to be faced with the choices of "all or nothing," "needed or not," and "used and useful" on the generating plant, as would normally have been the case. In addition to the capacity legislation, there were bills discussed that would allow the KCC to address the question of decommissioning and of management prudence.[40]

Not only had the protest movement changed and strengthened after TMI in 1979, but the legislature had changed too, and the new legislators were much more willing to be activist on the Wolf Creek issues.[41] The membership of the KCC was also undergoing change exactly at this time, and Governor John Carlin was not appointing "business as usual" conservatives.[42]

The members of the KCC did not think of themselves as media stars, and did not especially relish the public attention the traditionally obscure regulatory body was about to get. However, Lennen thought that the role of the KCC as "a kind of surrogate for the marketplace," required it to develop a model of a reasonably priced base load plant as a standard for economic prudence or valuation, and to analyze deeply the entire history of the Wolf Creek construction with an eye to evaluating management and, if necessary, "punishing" it (no one liked to use that term) as the marketplace supposedly would have. In the process Lennen personally gained more respect for the actual market as a regulator than ever—the administrative process was a very imperfect substitute. The KCC frankly did not have the staff to investigate by itself such issues even if it had the power, so at the same time it requested legislative approval to hire outside experts to assist the staff in the preparation of the complex Wolf Creek rate case. There had not been a state siting bill when Wolf Creek was started, and so there had been no state hearing at the outset or state *imprimatur* saying that the plant was needed and the plan was sound.

Understandably, the financial analysts thought the Kansas commission and this legislative trend were "harsh," and designed to punish KG&E with hindsight information. Lennen spoke to the financial analysts several times, both before and during the rate case, and explained that there was no animosity toward KG&E and that "we think it is going to survive." He admitted that initially that statement did not allay a certain "uneasiness" among that group.[43]

Wilson Cadman saw among that financial group some outright fear. When asked by a reporter in February about KG&E's financial position, Cadman said, "What do you want to make me do, throw up or something?"[44] Before he spoke to them in February he asked the legislature to lock in a five-year rate phase-in. "We must be protected from capricious activity of future [Corporation] commissions and future legislatures," Cadman told legislators. "We must have some assurances that the ball game won't change next year."[45] He didn't get it.

There was some opposition to "rate shock" legislation. Ross Doyen, president of the Kansas Senate, for example, said he did not see how utilities could be blamed for overcapacity, and he did not think there was mismanagement. "Stockholders aren't going to do anything. If you own stock in KG&E, are you going to buy more stock to help them? No, so how are the stockholders going to pay for it?"[46] Doyen's legislative theory was virtual rather than actual representation. He thought one should vote based on the facts and common sense, and overall one's constituents would return you. His long career with its many stands in the minority, sometimes minorities of one, on issues from the severance tax to waste disposal to water usage in Kansas, seem to illustrate that point. Yet he was often charged with being in the pocket of "big oil" or the "big utilities," with the hope that perhaps his arguments would go away. Doyen's view was that there were few long-range thinkers in the legislature: "seems all we do is look to the next election." That boded ill for issues like the building of a nuclear power plant.[47]

Jim Haines of KG&E opposed it too, and asked the legislature to take no further action, arguing that once a plant was completed there should be no basis other than imprudence for denying charging its full cost to ratepayers. The legislative bills, he said, "condition the opportunity to earn a fair return on the ability to accurately predict the future. Nobody can simultaneously meet that burden and the duty to serve the public on demand."[48]

Wilson Cadman wrote one of his open letters to community leaders reminding them of Kansas in the early 1970s when some schools were closed down for lack of gas, and recalling the 1978 fuel use act. He went through the changes since Wolf Creek was projected in great detail, and pointed out that any temporary "excess" capacity was gas plants, which, before 1982, the company had not imagined it could legally use. KG&E was 75 years old in 1984, and while "we recognize that our motives and interests are being questioned by some people, particularly with Wolf Creek having become a major political issue," Cadman asked the leaders to think about KG&E's record in the past and ask themselves whether they believe the claims of the most suspicious. If not, they should write their legislators.[49] Some counties chimed in against the rate bills, worried about their property tax base. In Coffey County, Wolf Creek was providing 90 percent of the county's total assessed valuation. Said a county official in another county: "Divide electric generators this year, and you will be asked to divide oil refineries, sugar beet refineries, railroad yards and railroads in future years."[50]

A few opposed the rate shock bills on the grounds that they did not go far enough. The legislators, wrote one such critic, would talk in "distant and lofty phrases under the high chandeliers" and roll over the numbers, trying to obscure the blame for this "great chapter of chicanery." "Never in the history of this great state has duplicity been so pumped up in the name of equity." It was charged that the history of Wolf Creek was filled with "black secrets and white lies." "From the beginning we never had an answer. With the help of an indifferent and ignorant Legislature, we failed to demand one. We became a state of the sedated. . . . The bill before the Kansas legislature is an ulcer about to hemorrhage. It reeks of a putrid odor, of pandering in the name of pacification at the expense of our economy as we now know it."[51]

Governor John Carlin and House Speaker Mike Hayden, however, both supported such legislation, and Lennen predicted there would be a bipartisan bill.[52] "The KCC," wrote a Wichita editor, "merely is asking for a tool to help it better do its job: establishing that hard-to-define line between utilities' legitimate need to make a fair profit and the customers' legitimate need of affordable electricity." The newspaper objected to some versions of bills in the legislature that would deny KG&E due process by setting the amount of the overcapacity by statute, but sympathized with the idea of giving the KCC more flexibility in setting the rate and perhaps phasing in rates that were established.[53] Karen Adelson and Sam Rod of Westinghouse Corporation appeared in Topeka in January to brief legislators on nuclear power from fuel rods to decommissioning.[54] Early in February a supplemental appropriations bill passed, allowing $700,000 for the KCC to hire more consultants to study Wolf Creek's construction costs in preparation for the first rate hearings ever in Kansas on a nuclear plant. In fact, the KCC used Touche Ross, Project Management Associates, and Energy Systems Research Group of Boston for studies and expert testimony at the rate hearings in addition to several members of its staff.[55] "These are very, very complex issues we have never faced before," Brian Moline of the KCC staff told a legislative committee.[56] "This has a whole lot of gray areas."[57]

The utility lobbyists pushed for a phased-in rate increase over five years, while several versions of bills giving the KCC more discretion circulated. Polls taken of the legislators determined that most did not think customers should pay the full cost of the plant. Many were undecided, and only nine house members and seven senators were willing to say publicly that KG&E should have the full amount of its request.[58] Both the KCC and many newspaper editors opposed any legislative guarantee to KG&E on the phase in. Representative Robert Miller said such proposals, offered as a way to ease the shock to ratepayers, were a disguised bailout "designed to rip off ratepayers and at the same time would guarantee continued profits for stockholders. . . . This one really puts the Corporation Commission in handcuffs and keeps them there."[59] Miller noted that the legislators were concerned about the ratepayers. "We're not concerned about stockholders or the people on Wall Street. They weren't the ones who elected us to the Legislature."[60] "As utilities in Kansas always have," said one editor, "KG&E will have to take its chances with the K.C.C."[61]

There was quite a bit of evolution in the rate shock bills. James Haines of KG&E testified several times at the statehouse to present KG&E's view in detail. He noted two fundamental principles of regulation: first, that a public utility was obligated to meet every request for service within its service territory, and second, that, while the price of public utility service was subject to regulation, the owners must be given an opportunity to earn a fair return on their investment. As Haines was quick to point out, this latter is not the same as a "guarantee." He summarized once again for the legislators the history of Wolf Creek and the fundamental reasons for the decision to build it, and then pointed out what he considered basic flaws in the wording of the proposed legislation. For example, the penalty for excess capacity was not contingent upon a finding that such excess resulted from imprudent planning. A modern generating facility took 10 to 15 years from idea to use, and "future shock" was ever more a factor in times of rapid change. The legislation did not recognize that it is not always possible exactly to match generating capacity with demand. Electric load grew gradually, while generating capacity was added in large chunks, leaving some temporary larger reserve margins. The cost benefits of economies of scale involved in building a larger plant balanced the temporary cost of some capacity in excess of immediate need. Since electric service was indispensable to public welfare and business growth, Haines said that Kansas should have a system that erred in having too much generating capacity rather than too little. Long-term availability of power was a major factor in attracting industry. It was an advantage to have Wolf

Creek locked in at present rather than future costs, and in the versions of the bills denying eventual rate recognition of the carrying charges associated with excess capacity, the legislature was refusing to recognize this advantage. The bills refused to recognize cost advantages of the capacity to consumers, for example in fuel, while punishing its costs. "I sense," Haines said, "in House Bills 2927 and 2964 a legislative intent that shareholders should bear the entire risk associated with the planning, construction, and operation of generating facilities. I respectfully submit to you that the risk which shareholders bear under present law is quite substantial." Without CWIP, for example, during construction the stockholders bore all the risk.[62]

On March 10 Attorney General Stephan ruled that the state legislature did have the power to pass such a bill. The rate shock bill passed the House by a vote of 117 to 7 and the Senate on March 28 by a vote of 38 to 2.[63] It was signed by Governor Carlin in mid April.[64]

Meanwhile, the desperation to show the sort of imprudence that could lead the KCC under these rules to deny a rate increase was shown by the appearance of the Tompkins story, with its forged document, in the *Wichita Eagle* as the legislation was being formed in Topeka.[65] With its new color graphics capability the *Eagle* created a logo for stories on the plant with a green dollar sign and the phrase "Wolf Creek: The Bill Comes Due."[66] There was a certain pride in the press that "government of the people, by the Kansas Corporation Commission, and for the public utilities," was changing. "It's time our governor and Congress," wrote one newspaper reader, "tell Wilson Cadman and his partners that the people of Kansas will not pay for their white elephant."[67] Another wrote, "Let's face it; nuclear reactors have gone the way of the dinosaur. They have outlived their usefulness, which was zero to begin with. . . . What next? . . . If KG&E gets by with this, there will be no drawing the line."[68] The editor of the *Eagle* wrote that in contrast to editorials and letters to the editor, his news coverage had been "comprehensive and factual," and that no one had proved otherwise.[69] Cadman, however, in an open letter to the *Eagle*, complained that its news stories "read like editorials designed to promote a point of view."[70] "From this day forward," wrote a reader of that paper, "I am tossing reality (and the [*Eagle*]) out the window."[71]

The Kansas rate bill was an unprecedented move and created a furor of initial reaction, and considerable later study and analysis. Senator Ross Doyen felt that inviting the KCC to consider excess capacity as well as management mistakes would add immeasurably to the cost and difficulty of building plants. "I think we have seen the last of the power plants in Kansas."[72] Representative Jim Patterson commented: "Wolf Creek is very emotional (as an issue) and very difficult to deal with on a practical basis. . . . I think we've had people (in the Legislature) who were vindictive. Instead of just trying to solve the problem, they tried to punish. . . . It looks like we're putting the KCC in the board room of these corporations; in my opinion it's going to cost you." "It's bad to have high utility rates," said another senator, "but it's even worse not to have energy."[73]

Obviously, however, the bill had many defenders. Some of them participated in an extensive symposium on Wolf Creek legal issues held in February 1985. Involved in the discussion were state legislators, a KCC attorney, law professors, economists, and public interest advocates (utility executives were invited but declined)—all of whom addressed a large audience at Green Hall at the University of Kansas. HB 2927, the so-called "Rate Shock Bill," was the focus of much of the exchange, especially since the then-pending rate hearings would result in the first decision interpreting that legislation.

Robert Glicksman, in a paper called "Allocating the Cost of Constructing Excess Capacity: 'Who Will Have to Pay for It All?'," went through the history of the rate shock bill, calling it "the most comprehensive and detailed state statute in the nation concerning the regulatory consequences of constructing excess capacity." It gave the KCC wide discretion in determining prudence, and left that regulatory body with a wide range of possible actions if it determined there was imprudence. Specifically, the bill required the KCC to include in the rate base only property that is "used and required to be used," and the bill was narrowly amended to stop a provision that would have required disallowing the entire nuclear plant in the rate base until a waste site was found. If imprudence were found, the bill required that the cost of carrying or financing the excess capacity investment would be forever excluded from the rate base, and the utility could not be allowed to recover these costs in any other manner. The bill listed eleven factors bearing on prudence: 1) comparison of existing rates with rates if the new facility were in the rate base; 2) comparison of rates of any other utility in the state; 3) comparison of final costs with the cost of other plants constructed near the same time; 4) comparison of the original cost estimates by the owners with the final cost; 5) ability of owners to sell electric power at these new rates to others; 6) comparison of overruns in construction costs with overruns on other plants at the same time; 7) whether there was a waste disposal and decommissioning plan; 8) the extent of inappropriate or poor management decisions in construction or operation; 9) whether including the cost of the new plant or part of it would have an adverse economic impact on the people of Kansas; 10) whether the utility acted in the general public interest; and 11) whether the utility accepted risks in construction of the facility that were "inappropriate to the general public interest in Kansas." In addition to this specific list the rate shock bill presumed that any portion of the cost over 200 percent of the original cost estimate was, by legislative definition, incurred through lack of prudence. The utility would be required to rebut that assumption with a preponderance of evidence. Glicksman admitted there was some hindsight here, as well as a considerable number of "elastic clauses" for the KCC to determine the public interest. However, that was not all bad. "A review of the prudence of the utility's decision," he wrote, "is meant to provide an incentive for utility management officials to 'continuously rethink past decisions as new events unfold.'"[74]

A representative of ALERT at the symposium was happy that the hearings on the rate shock bill had allowed for citizen participation that was largely denied at the NRC operating license hearings; 1,400 "irate citizens" had appeared on a rate hike request by KG&E in February 1983, three times the previous record, and participation continued to increase. The Electric Shock Coalition and ALERT had organized legislative forums during the entire debate on the bill, and executives of these organizations thought it was a model for a "comprehensive utility reform bill." They saw it as a strong consumer bill rather than a complex evasion that passed the responsibility wholly to the KCC.[75] John Simpson, long an activist against the plant, noted that citizens had few rights in administrative agency proceedings, and that the bill was a first step to give them more standing.[76] Brian Moline of the KCC agreed, and thought the Commission was the ideal forum. "Regardless of the environmental, philosophical, and other controversies that swirl around the Wolf Creek Generating Station, the role of the State Corporation Commission is defined by statute." Moline thought that redefining it or restating the definition through the legislative process before this rate hearing was the right thing to do. There could be no avoiding the clash, but it should be a clash with rules, and he believed that "scientific regulation" as developed since the turn of the century was a democratic and rational answer. "Nettlesome or not, public participation is too important to be rejected for the sake of administrative efficiency.... In sustaining a civic culture, we must provide incentives for public administrators to listen to those who will be affected by their decisions; we must also provide administrators with sufficient authority to secure acceptance for their decisions." In Moline's opinion the rate shock bill helped in both goals.[77]

The major crafter of the bill, Robert Vancrum, held a positive opinion also. "The controversy of the Wolf Creek Power Plant," he recalled, "was destined to dominate the 1984 Kansas Legislative Session," and he thought the body had acquitted itself well in passing a rate relief bill that was virtually a "political imperative." Though Vancrum had had only one course in utility regulation at the University of Chicago law school and had never practiced in that area, he drafted the bill himself to get something on the floor. The bill, he thought, gave the intervenors some standing for their questions, and he personally hoped that they "will challenge the use of a 'cost-plus' contract to build a plant of largely experimental design."[78]

More detailed analysis came also from those who felt the bill was bad legislation. In October 1984, KG&E presented a Cresap, McCormick and Paget report on the bill and its consequences. Cresap simultaneously submitted a document entitled "A Prudence Review of KG&E's Involvement in the Wolf Creek Generating Station." Both reports were commissioned by KG&E, not by the KCC. They addressed specifically the question of management prudence, which the commission, thanks to the amendments to statute 66-128 (the rate shock bill), had such scope to evaluate. These reports also called attention to a study prepared by KG&E consultant Charles Huston entitled "Management Performance Evaluation, Wolf Creek Generating Station," which was issued by the owners in May 1984.[79] While KG&E's chief attorney, James Haines, thought that the 1984 legislation really only specified powers the KCC already had, he commented that "anyone who would say that KCC did not get a strong message from the legislature is wearing a blindfold."[80]

Cresap, McCormick and Paget defined *prudence* as, "Decisions and other actions judged to be reasonable at the time taken, based on considerations of what could reasonably be known by a person or persons qualified to make the decision or take the action."[81] It was not something judged against an abstract standard of perfection. Rather, a demonstration of prudence was process oriented—did the company use the right intellectual and physical processes to ensure that what could be known was considered? "Prudence," the consultants wrote, "cannot be assessed with hindsight, simply because the perfection of hindsight is not available to humans when they make decisions or take other actions. Therefore, the actual results of a decision or action are irrelevant to assessing the prudence of the decision or action." KG&E did not create Wolf Creek in a vacuum, and therefore all the historical dynamics must be considered.[82] "An assessment of prudence and an evaluation to secure improvement are totally different analytical processes, in purpose and in the approach used." A prudent driver, after all, could stop at a stop sign and be rammed by a vehicle following. An imprudent gambler could risk the mortgage money and win a fortune. That was good luck or bad luck, and had nothing to do with matters like "KG&E's concern for providing a reliable and economic supply of electricity, a concern required by law and manifest in a generation plant spanning 50 or more years of construction and operation and involving billions of dollars of expenditure." The obligation to serve was the "cornerstone" of electric utility planning and operation and placed on the industry "a standard and public expectation of reliability well beyond what is required of any other industry."[83]

Saying it was easier than showing it. The "Prudence Review" document was more lengthy than the 1980 Cresap report commissioned by the KCC, and detailed the history of the Wolf Creek plant under numerous headings: trends in the electric and nuclear industry, the coal alternative, regulation (federal and Kansas), power supply planning, and financial management. The report contained a year-by-year analysis of KG&E's performance in these areas and an extensive fold-out timeline, showing not only company events, but events in the surrounding regulatory and financial environment. Three trends stood out in the period since the plant was announced in 1973: unprecedented inflation in the U.S. domestic economy; severe social, and hence regulatory, concern for nuclear safety; and sharply lower growth in demand for electric power (at least before 1984). Cresap concluded that KG&E "noted the three fundamental factors as they emerged, weighed them, and prudently continued."[84] All the while the basis for planning judgment changed "sometimes radically and rapidly," playing havoc with projections around the country. Changes in technology and regulation, and a series of nuclear accidents, created "a permanently unsettled condition for nuclear technology and increase[d] the exposure of projects under design and construction to costly and delaying revision, retrofit, and so on." Regulatory bodies that had been "geared to a much less active and controversial setting" got clogged, and terms such as *attrition, regulatory lag,* and *pancaking* came into common parlance among utility people. As planning cycles for utilities got longer, given the larger capital investment and more delicate technology, the planning horizon of the political sector remained pretty much at the next election. The period of Wolf Creek planning and construction faced several public policy and regulatory priority cycles. That KG&E was able to complete its program at all, the consultants thought, demonstrated, "foresight, perception and prudence," as well as "unusual steadfastness of purpose."[85] KG&E's rates had been and remained low relative to the rest of the country (a 16% advantage *vis a vis* the national average in 1984) and many of the increases would have taken place whether Wolf Creek had been built or not.[86]

Cresap argued that KG&E was prudent with Wolf Creek in essentially five ways: 1) in the original perception of the need to diversify fuel sources and to meet capacity requirements; 2) continuing concern for minimizing the KG&E investment in Wolf Creek through SNUPPS and through attempts to reduce KG&E's ownership share; 3) early emphasis on the need for Wolf Creek energy to ensure a reliable and relatively economical supply of electricity; 4) repetitive analysis and evaluations by KG&E and consultants of needs for capacity and energy and of comparative generation economics; and 5) sound and well-executed financing strategies in increasingly difficult economic and financial market conditions.[87]

A similar perspective, stated in less restrained language, was offered by Gerald Charnoff, partner in Shaw, Pittman, Potts & Trowbridge of Washington, DC, who was invited to the 1985 University of Kansas symposium to represent the utility point of view on Wolf Creek. Charnoff's paper was entitled "Why Managers Did It All

Right: Overregulation and Other Acts of God." Nuclear plants had demonstrated splendid lifetime capacity factors when actually in operation, Charnoff said, and had proved, with the exception of hydro power, the lowest cost provider of electricity on the grids to which they were connected. Yet while operating plants were doing well, plants under construction were caught in what was probably a temporary down cycle in demand, and therefore applying hindsight to them was tempting. That, Charnoff thought, would be wrong. The definition of prudence by the legal standard in the common law of public utility regulation "precludes a judgment about past decisions based on present knowledge of whether the decisions proved in time to have been right or wrong. The proper inquiry is not 'why management did it all right,' which seems to rely on the application of hindsight. The proper inquiry, rather, . . . is 'whether the company's conduct was reasonable at the time, under all of the circumstances, considering that the company had to solve its problems prospectively." The exercise of prudence did not guarantee that the project would be on time or on budget. It did require that the decisionmaking be within the framework of "reasonable available alternatives." The state regulators, Charnoff said, should begin any prudence review of Wolf Creek "with a reconstruction of the context in which the decision at issue was made and should end with an evaluation of whether or not management acted reasonably (reasonably, not perfectly) under these circumstances." No second-guessing was allowed, "nor is it proper to saddle the evaluation with the baggage of events that could not have been reasonably foreseen." The more detailed definition of *prudence* in the new Kansas law raised legal and constitutional issues, but, Charnoff thought, did not change the fundamental definition. Regulatory change had "proceeded in an uncontrolled manner and has had a devastating impact on the costs and schedules of the plants under construction." U.S. intelligence did not predict the Iranian revolution, so why should the utilities have done so? "Did regulators any more wisely read the tea leaves in past years than did management?" and did hindsight disallowance of rate increases really serve the long-term interests of consumers?[88]

Charles Huston, more than the Cresap firm, was a KG&E advocate. Huston had been the project controls manager for Bechtel on the SNUPPS project in 1973, and so was acquainted with Wolf Creek from its inception. He was at the site regularly through the preparation of his 1984 report and in 1985 was, by all accounts, the most effective expert witness in the rate hearings for KG&E, and probably for either side. His spring 1984 report evaluated the KG&E management program prior to commercial operation of the plant, with special emphasis on comparing it to other nuclear projects similar in scope and timing and operating in a parallel regulatory environment. Though some in the hearings quarreled with his choices, none could deny that Wolf Creek's statistics compared very favorably with many of its contemporaries and indicated at least parity if not superiority in management efficiency. Huston focused, too, on explaining in detail the reasons for the cost and schedule changes at Wolf Creek from the time of the "definitive estimate" of 1977 to illustrate that the decisions were prudent under the circumstances. He gave KG&E high marks for the design, for joining SNUPPS, and for going with nonunion labor, and less high, but satisfactory ratings for its evolving relations with Daniel International in the field. KG&E, Huston wrote, had recognized the need for a centralized project management approach to Wolf Creek early in 1973 and had moved progressively toward implementing it. It had instituted any number of self-studies, particularly in the early 1980s, and had dealt openly and satisfactorily with the regulatory changes, delays, and public outcry.[89]

Some complained that the Huston report was just too favorable. Wrote the student newspaper at the University of Kansas, after looking at the report: "It is unlikely that KG&E has done much of anything in the saga of Wolf Creek that is worth congratulating itself about, and the company would do better, considering the runaway costs it wants to pass along to ratepayers, to show a little more modesty."[90] However, it could not be said that the report presented its facts in anything but the most straightforward manner. There was nothing in it that was very quotable in the press—nothing comparable even, for example, to the sweeping statements, favorable and unfavorable, that had and would appear in consultants' reports from Arthur D. Little in 1977, through Cresap and Touche Ross, right up through Richard Rosen's and Gui Ponce de Leon's conclusions in the rate hearings themselves. Huston was especially effective in the hearings also because he did not put himself wholly in the position of an inflexible advocate, though he certainly was retained by KG&E. He admitted there had been flaws in the companies' decisions, but argued they were well-intentioned ones. His willingness to see some of the other side's point of view made him more believable on those points where he refused to concede anything. And, of course, ultimately, in a long and at least quasi-judicial process, the authority and credibility of consultants and witnesses depend more on their facts and on the consultant's ability to present them clearly in the present context than on past glories or academic qualifications. Huston was in fact relatively new at the business of independent consulting, though since the Wolf Creek case, he has been in considerable demand by other companies with nuclear plants.[91]

Some of the public agreed with Huston's assessment, but stated their views in less matter-of-fact language. "It is wrong," wrote a man in Wilson County, "to call building for the future mismanagement."[92] Many others did not agree. They wanted simple answers to complex problems, said KG&E's new spokesman Lyle Koerper. "We live in a one-issue world where issues must be narrowly and simply stated."[93] Certainly they were and certainly some of the bumper sticker responses were memorable. The consultants' studies, said a man in Garnett, should be called "grunt" studies, since officials just grunted and paid the bill. As for Wolf Creek itself, it was, he wrote, "the biggest folly since aerosol toothpaste."[94]

The company expected opposition to its proposed rate increase, some of it colorful. After all, as Jim Haines once put it, "if I ask whether you want this head of lettuce for 10 cents or 20 cents, what will you say?" No one in the public was likely to support a rate increase, Haines noted, and they knew how to get quoted in the media, but "if ratemaking were to be the product of a popular vote the statutes would say that and, furthermore, no investment would be forthcoming to build utility systems."[95] Why, thought Haines, should the future value of any "excess capacity" determined now be ignored by banning it from the rate base forever? After all, the difference between a 100- and a 105-degree day was 120 megawatts of power. If the KCC declared capacity to be excess, would it give up all future jurisdiction over it?[96] HB 2927, Haines wrote, could be used to hold utilities to an impossible standard of perfection in their planning and operation. The KCC already had the power to punish imprudence and mismanagement, and the bill was just another roadblock.[97] You can't predict the future, he said, and still provide power on demand.[98] Given his views on how a rational process should work, Haines was understandably disturbed at what happened next.

The Kansas public as reflected in the press was not impressed by the rate phase-in. "It doesn't matter if you cut off the dog's tail a bit at a time, you're still cutting off its tail."[99] It became popular to call the phase-in plan a "stockholder bailout," though Wilson Cadman objected vociferously to the use of that term.[100] People were outraged too that KG&E continued to pay dividends, and they claimed that it borrowed money to do it (the company denied this). "When other companies get into financial trouble," one woman wrote, "they quit paying dividends, tighten controls, cut capital spending and take pay cuts. KG&E did none of these. This company is a monopoly selling a product with a built-in market. It takes real genius to louse up such a setup."[101]

People had been building resentment and, by the time of the legislative and KCC hearings on Wolf Creek rates, wanted to have their say one by one. "All the fever and clamor building up over electric rates," wrote an observer, "and the fires fanned by full-page articles in the *Eagle-Beacon,* are creating a lynch mob gathering together to hang an innocent party—namely KG&E."[102] A letter to the editor in Wichita suggested praying for a tornado to blow away Wolf Creek. "If Wilson Cadman thinks he has God in his pocket, he is in for a surprise."[103] The main problem with that plan of course was, as another writer put it, that "the structure is so ridiculously overdesigned that you theoretically could pick up the reactor building, roll it around, bounce it off a concrete walk, turn it upside down and hardly scratch the surface. To imply that any major part of a nuclear power plant is subject to tornado damage is about as intelligent as suggesting that a Brink's armored truck could be damaged by a BB gun."[104]

But the protests continued. The Electric Shock Coalition brought out nearly 1,500 people in seven meetings in Wichita in February to complain about their current and possible future electric bills.[105] Late in April a contingent from Wichita delivered petitions to Governor Carlin in Topeka against letting Wolf Creek operate. Seven wore yellow hardhats saying "Citizens for Affordable Power." They arrived on the steps of the Capitol in a white hearse and a white limousine, carrying their petitions in a black coffin that said on it, "Rest in Peace Wolf Creek." They were escorted to the governor's office by a trumpeter. One of their leaders was later elected to the Sedgwick County Commission.[106] Cadman personally remained a target. He had not bet KG&E on nuclear power, said one critic, "instead he bet the ratepayer upon which his false leadership preys." Officers at KG&E, it was said, were sitting in their offices saying to the customers, "Stand still, little lamb, to be shorn!"[107] In May a 90-minute meeting of 300 KG&E stockholders at the Century II convention center in Wichita was picketed by 50 protestors, representing such groups as the Gray Panthers, Home Owners Trust, and the International Association of Machinists. Signs said "Up Yours, Wolf Creek," and "Up Wolf Creek without a Paddle." Inside, stockholders learned that while profits were up slightly, KG&E stock had declined to $15.25 a share, down 11 percent from the first of the year.[108] Kansas cities were proposing to build their own power plants rather than pay the costs of the nuclear plant.[109] A poll taken in February 1985 of 990 Wichitans found only 2 percent who believed that KG&E should get the whole of its 95 percent rate increase; 53 percent thought the company should get no increase at all.[110] "This month's Henny Youngman award for guts," wrote an editor in Olathe, "goes to Kansas City Power and Light for asking us to accept a blind date with a dog and pay all the expenses."[111]

Prudence had been defined as a major issue, as had "excess capacity," though exactly what those would mean in the context of 1984 was still to be determined. The Wichita newspaper felt that the rate shock bill had gone far toward defining the all-important word in the lexicon of ratemaking, namely *prudence.*[112] But there was no question that the emotion would continue, no matter how much defining was done by how many bodies, no matter how many time-honored rules of civilized discourse were invoked, and no matter how often KG&E officials urged calm. "The real issue is people," wrote a Newton city commissioner, "—we, the people. And emotional? You're damn right!"[113] KG&E, the KCC, and the rate case intervenors girded their loins as the year ended for the last great public hearings struggle, the rate case. That was to be played out with all the forces at their maximum of determination and experience even as the final touches were put on the plant at Wolf Creek, and it stood ready to produce power for anyone who could or would pay for it. "There's pain to come," observed one editor, "very likely for everyone affected by the Wolf Creek dilemma, whose roots were sunk more than a decade ago. . . . All the KCC will be able to do at this late date is distribute the pain more fairly."[114]

10
"We Are Not a Monster"

> Right is right, wrong is wrong. It is only right that as many government forces as possible join forces to protect the people from unfair hardships going to be imposed upon them by the utility companies involved with the Wolf Creek nuclear power plant going on line this year. . . . The people did not ask for Wolf Creek.
> —George Collins, in *Leawood Squire*, Feb. 21, 1985

> It seems to me after the TMI accident in 1979, to argue that one needed a nuclear plant just to accomplish fuel diversity was very shortsighted because it didn't sufficiently take into account the risk of a serious problem with a nuclear plant.
> —Richard Rosen, at Wolf Creek rate hearings, June 20, 1985

> Merely identifying a problem doesn't indicate mismanagement.
> —Thomas Flaherty, at Wolf Creek rate hearings, June 10, 1985

In the middle of March 1985, following the issuance of a partial power operating license, fuel was loaded at Wolf Creek.[1] One reporter said it was an experience like no other, as he was checked into an antiseptically clean, highly polished building, which some had compared to the Taj Mahal in its simple elegance and near-sacred isolation. The entry lock was sealed, an airtight chamber—you waited for equalization and entry into the fuel load area. "You think you might be in a submarine, a time capsule, or something you've never experienced before." The KG&E people were "calm, practiced, and give you the feeling they know what they are doing. . . . It's a new venture into the future."[2]

In May the KCC rate hearings began. They lasted through June. Twenty groups filed requests to intervene and witnesses were scheduled to testify in 12 cities. Each witness might be cross-examined as many as 20 times by the intervenors before the three-member commission. The KCC hoped to finish the hearings by July 5 because hearings on infill drilling at the Hugoton, Kansas, gas fields were scheduled to begin then.[3] But it was to last 11 weeks and be the largest rate case in the history of Kansas. The hearings cost the ratepayers about $5 million, and generated nearly 20,000 pages (58 volumes) of testimony.[4] They did not end until July 27, far from the July 5 target, despite holding regular night and Saturday sessions. Sixty attorneys worked on the case, and 150 witnesses were examined.[5]

The atmosphere for KG&E's case did not appear promising. Richard "Pete" Loux had been replaced on the commission by Margalee Wright, a former member of the Wichita City Commission, mayor of Wichita, and the woman who ran the successful 1980 reelection campaign of Kansas 4th District representative Dan Glickman. While Wright was a friend of the wife of KG&E finance chief Howard Hansen, few felt that she would for that reason or any other be any more inclined to KG&E's point of view than had been her predecessor on the commission. She was not a Republican, she was not known to be especially friendly to corporate interests, she was certainly sympathetic to the kind of consumer interest groups that Loux had represented, and was definitely not a "good 'ole boy."[6] Governor Carlin had told Wright that he wanted someone on the Commission who could communicate with the public and had a sensitivity to Wolf Creek as a public policy issue.

Wright's experience with the hearings was probably typical. She had some personal opinions—she was, for example, a moderate environmentalist with a basically liberal outlook. She believed that there was an "innate wisdom" in the protests of the intervenors, however short they might sometimes be on technical detail, which told them that the bottom line was that "they were going to get the shaft and the big guys will get the roses." However, the hearings themselves were a profound and stimulating experience for her, and were an "enriching and intensifying purging of everything you believed individually and how that fit into your decision making model to solve the problem." Carlin had told his KCC appointees that 1985 would be a year they would remember forever, and it was. The hearings were "grindingly long and difficult," and in all the hours Wright perceived an evolution of her thinking. Perhaps she was a kind of female Thomas à Becket, placed in her office partly for a purpose, but impressed when there with the awesome responsibility of trying to be fair. There developed, she remembers, "a kind of culture of a gigantic problem to solve," which "took on a life of its own." The commissioners were not able to talk to each other about it outside the formal hearings, so they worked extensively with their administrative assistants. The staff was helpful, but it, like the utility attorneys, had an advocacy role to play and so was not the best neutral mirror, or backboard, for the commissioners to try their views on. More than anything else there was a lot of listening to do.[7]

In addition to Wright, who as a woman was an especially unexpected quantity, two other commissioners of recent appointment, Michael Lennen, chair, and Keith Henley, were likewise open to conclusions painful to KG&E, and the three, while far from clones, worked well together within a common understanding of their mission.

Lennen pointed out there had been "almost panic" on emergency legislation, and that there was a definite change to "really volatile" public and press opinion on the plant when the day of reckoning of paying for it actually arrived. There had been no state siting bill when Wolf Creek was first started, so there was no state record of approval for KG&E to depend upon or hark back to. A regulatory proceeding was not a judicial proceeding, though it had the trappings of one, but rather something between a legislative hearing and a judicial proceeding. Rate setting itself was a legislative, not judicial, function. The expert, technical witnesses, to be sure, would be the core of the hearings, but the public input would be significant, too. Lennen thought it was possible to get conceptual ideas from hearing hundreds of people speaking, even though many of them might not be well informed on the details. There was value, he thought, in having the public see and participate in the process, no matter how technical its content. While arguments were thus heard repeatedly sometimes, there were new and useful insights as well. As to the technical witnesses, the lengthy cross-examination process was helpful to the commissioners. Many who seemed impressive in their initial report could be tripped on cross-examination because, in Lennen's words, "there are a million things that happened and all of them interrelate." Flashy personalities sometimes did not wear well, and witnesses that at first seemed pedestrian could grow stronger under fire.[8]

The "rate shock" bills had tagged the attitude of the legislature, and much of the rhetoric coming from the public through the press was impatient about the technical rules of the hearings, and eager to get to the jugular on rate "relief." "Pardon us," wrote an editor, "if we don't take out the hanky and snivel in sympathy. . . . The state, through its citizens, should not be required to provide the company a profit on a poorly managed boondoggle like Wolf Creek."[9] The comment on the hearings often emphasized impatience with the technical testimony and the elaborate legal procedure. No wonder attendance was low, said a newspaper, as the hearings were mostly "esoterica on esoterica": "For week upon week, we've heard a parade of so-called expert witnesses and consultants hired for the expressed purpose of giving definitive answers about questions so arcane as to be meaningless to anyone except an actuary or an accountant." That reporter called it "mumbo-jumbo."[10] Still, for the first time in several years, KG&E had no pickets at its annual meeting in May. The focus was at the hearings.[11]

The immediate prelude to the hearings proper was a statement by the KCC staff very unfriendly to KG&E's rate request. The statement, issued early in April, said that Wolf Creek should have been "stopped and abandoned," and that cost overruns of 55 percent during construction were due to imprudent management decisions, and should not have to be paid by ratepayers ever. The utility requests for $505.5 million in rate relief should be drastically trimmed. KG&E should get just 40 percent of its $371 million request. It had used over 4 million hours of unnecessary labor during the construction and there were 14.5 months of avoidable delays. There were never enough studies. Headlines reporting these findings by the staff came out in tall letters in phrases like "KCC Staff Lambasts KG&E Management."[12]

The atmosphere was not confidence building for KG&E's attorneys and witnesses going in. If the KCC staff recommendations were followed, James Haines told the press, it could prevent paying a dividend on KG&E's preferred or common stock, the stock price might drop into the $4 to $6 range, the company might not be able to meet its day-to-day obligations, and it could go into bankruptcy, wiping out the savings of people who had invested in the stocks and bonds. "I think it would be a shame for KG&E to come this far and be cut so thin it can't survive."[13] But it was more than possible it would be.

Opening arguments by the attorneys took place May 13, 1985, in the old Supreme Court chambers at the Kansas state house.[14] James Haines of KG&E opened with the company's position. The issue involved, he said, was much larger than Wolf Creek: it involved the meaning of a public utility's obligation to serve and how to judge that. Hindsight was not the way, and historical empathy, if not sympathy, was. He asked the commission to recall the gas lines and coal strikes of the 1970s, the brownouts and the energy crises of those years. It should recall KG&E's 100 percent dependence on natural gas and the situation nationally with that fuel at the time that Wolf Creek was planned. It should take into account the immense financial, technical, and political changes that took place during the period of Wolf Creek's construction—a "severe and unexpected challenge." When in 1978, Kansas law was amended to remove the KCC discretion to recognize the value of CWIP in rates it increased the rate shock of the billion dollars in accumulated carrying charges included in Wolf Creek's cost. Federal regulatory changes were imposed after the fact and were costly. And on excess capacity, Haines contended that in the long run "the social cost of a shortage of capacity far exceeds the cost of an equal excess." The KCC staff had recommended that the commission completely deny rate recognition of nearly $450 million of the cost of Wolf Creek and deny a return to KG&E on more than 60 percent of its remaining investment in Wolf Creek. That, Haines said, would take the company to the brink of bankruptcy. There was no upside if the utility proved right and therefore no incentive for infrastructure investment in the future. Under the proposed rubric, Haines said, the company was being asked to give a tithe or gift to Kansas and take risks for nothing. He quoted William Hieronymous as saying: "If you fail this test, you lose everything not needed for the bare survival of the company. Now here is your big prize for entering this dangerous game: if you win, you get your money back." Unfortunately the utility had no alternative but to invest—that was its statutory mandate. And the company was not displeased. "KG&E is deeply satisfied, confident, and proud of the results of its fuel transition program."[15] Warren Wood for KCPL agreed, calling Wolf Creek "one of the finest nuclear plants in the world."[16]

The position of the KCC staff was summarized by Robert Fillmore. "The staff comes to hearing with a sense for the frustration felt by many thousands of ratepayers across the State of Kansas who have been told by utility managers for years that the nuclear option would provide needed energy reliability and at a very low cost." The staff, he said, had the sense that KG&E, relatively small and new to the nuclear business, had forged ahead without adequate tools or information and that Kansas ratepayers were footing the bill for mismanagement. In the past new utility technology and economies of scale had made even mediocre utility management look good. That was no longer true. Fillmore quoted a recent *Forbes* article entitled "Nuclear Follies," which claimed that "only the blind or the biased can think that most of the money [expended on nuclear plants] has been well spent. It is a defeat for the U.S. consumer and for the competitiveness of U.S. industry, for the utilities that undertook the program, and for the private enterprise system that made it possible." Costs for the plant had increased from an early estimate of $525 million to the latest estimate of $2.904 billion. The estimated commercial operation date had moved from April 1981 to April 1985, and the plant was still not on line. With the help of several consultants the staff had done quantitative analyses of management and contractor performance and found these lacking. He admitted that regulators should act with restraint in substituting their views for those of utility management on matters of policy, but stated that "regulation is reduced to an exercise in futility if it is barred or if it bars itself from reviewing management results for the recovery of costs running into billions of dollars in light of compelling evidence that management's inattention and imprudence resulted in costs sought to be passed on to ratepayers. Management immaterial prudence is not a charge which this Commission Staff has often made in the course of rate proceedings, and it does not lightly do so now." The staff, however, recommended that about $862 million of KG&E's $1.4 billion investment in Wolf Creek be excluded from the rate base.[17]

Attorneys for the intervenors were no gentler. Robert Eye, speaking for the Alliance for Liveable Electric Rates, said he was not arguing for perfection but that his 600 small and medium-sized business clients in the KG&E service area wanted "to have a modicum of business sense injected into the proceeding." The negative trends should have been foreseen; the SNUPPS commitment to a larger plant than needed should not have been made; labor and contractor costs were too high—all signals that could have been heeded. The intervenors intended to signal "that a wasteful commitment of resources will neither be tolerated nor rewarded, that management oversight of the projects must be commensurate with the magnitude of that project, that planning for projects, generating capacity, must be comprehensive and include all—a comparison of all meaningful alternatives."[18] Patrick Donahue, of Kansas Legal Services, who represented a 72-year-old woman with income limited to social security, asked how KPL could sell electricity at 7.5¢ per kwh, while KG&E was asking for 9 to 11¢ for the same thing. KG&E should be able to do as well as KPL. "If they can't, it's not the ratepayer who is to blame."[19]

There were several major expert witnesses documenting the staff's position in favor of extreme disallowance on the grounds of management imprudence and excess capacity. First in order was Gui Ponce de Leon, whose presentation and examination lasted for four days between June 12 and June 15. De Leon was a Ph.D., an adjunct professor in construction engineering and management at the University of Michigan, and president of the consulting firm Project Management Associates, Inc. (PMA). PMA was retained by the KCC as a subcontractor of Touche Ross to quantitatively study the management policies at Wolf Creek.[20] Another major witness, perhaps the most important one, questioning KG&E's rate requests for Wolf Creek, was Richard Rosen, whose testimony between June 18 and June 20 filled three thick volumes. His prefiled testimony alone was 268 pages long. Rosen worked for Energy Systems Research Group, Inc., in Boston, a nonprofit organization specializing in energy research, demand forecasting, conservation program analysis, electric utility dispatch and reliability modeling, generation planning, cost analysis, financial analysis, rate design, and a long list of other specialities. Rosen had an M.A. and a Ph.D. from Columbia University and had testified widely at nuclear plant hearings, including prominently on the economics of the Seabrook plant. Rosen's range of testimony included examining whether and to what degree the investment of the utilities involved in Wolf Creek "has made their electricity generating systems nonoptimal in the sense of leading to a situation of overcapacity and/or excessively costly electric supply costs." That is, Rosen addressed both physical and economic excess though an analysis of the processes of planning and execution in the construction of Wolf Creek. His testimony and quantitative analysis were particularly important, probably more so than any other witness's, to the case for severe rate disallowances on Wolf Creek.[21] Less extensive, but critical of KG&E, was testimony of Charles Komanoff, retained by ALERT. Komanoff was a consulting economist, an author on the societal costs of nuclear power, and the director of Komanoff Energy Associates of New York City. Komanoff addressed the effect of Wolf Creek on the ratepayer and how its construction performance and planning compared with the rest of the U.S. nuclear industry. Komanoff said that KG&E should have abandoned the plant, and that its decisions to continue "were based on significant misperceptions of relevant regulatory burdens and of the costs of coal-fired facilities and may have been imprudent."[22] There were staff witnesses on details—fuel costs, decommissioning, and so on—but these were the big three.

KG&E and KCPL brought forward a number of company people—Arthur Doyle and Donald McPhee of KCPL, Wilson Cadman, Gary Fouts, Robert Hagan, James Lucas, and Kent Brown of KG&E. Francis Andrews, George Roen, and Leonard Wass of Cresap, McCormick and Paget were there to clarify its consulting reports, as was Thomas Flaherty of Touche Ross, a staff witness. The consulting firm people, in trying to maintain an objective scholarly reputation, often backed off under cross-examination from some of the more extreme conclusions opponents were wont to draw from their reports and to that extent aided KG&E's cause. Roen went further and defended at length his firm's conclusion that KG&E's action at Wolf Creek had been not only prudent, but in some ways outstanding.

But unquestionably the strongest witness for KG&E, and probably the major key to the outcome of the entire rate case, was Charles Huston. Huston's May 1984 report, *Management Performance Evaluation*, had been a model of clarity, but doubtless the intervening attorneys, like the press, thought it self-serving, "bought and paid for," and probably vulnerable under intense and specific attack at the hearings. Huston was the first witness called and therefore in a particularly difficult position because emotion was high, the attorneys were fresh and confident of their ground, and literally no question had been disposed of.[23] Huston was relatively new at the consulting business, nearly unknown, and the president and owner of Challenge Consultants in Steamboat Springs, Colorado—not exactly the center of the corporate consulting business. He testified four full days, and the record of it filled four substantial volumes and over 1,000 pages.[24]

Michael Lennen remembered that the longer Huston talked the more impressive he was.[25] He told KG&E attorney James Haines later that Huston's testimony at the hearings had made a significant difference in Lennen's opinion, which in the beginning was as unfavorable to KG&E's rate request as that of the KCC staff.[26] While Huston did not have long experience as a consultant, he had a B.S. in civil engineering from Yale and an M.S. in construction management from Stanford, and a great deal of experience with nuclear plants. He had worked with Bechtel since the early 1960s, on generating plant projects since 1964, and on nuclear projects since 1966. He had been responsible for critical path scheduling on nuclear projects and for field engineering and quality control. He had been the civil superintendent of all work on two reactor buildings at the Calvert Cliffs project and early in 1973 had become a member of the Bechtel team involved with the organization of SNUPPS. Later he worked on the Davis Besse nuclear plant for Toledo Edison as the Bechtel construction manager and in the same capacity at the Sterling plant of Rochester Gas and Electric—like Wolf Creek, part of the SNUPPS group. One of his first jobs when he started his consulting firm in 1980 was an evaluation of the construction scheduling program and welding program at Wolf Creek. Shortly after that he was put in charge of a task force to improve electrical performance and then piping performance. Therefore his acquaintance with the Wolf Creek plant in particular was intimate and of five years duration by the time of the hearings. Any criticism that he was an "insider" was overcome by his knowledge and his credibility as an analyst rather than an advocate. Huston regularly conceded some of the points of the critics of Wolf Creek, never insisting that all decisions had been proper or that all actions had been efficient—only that as a large human work Wolf Creek stood up pretty well. His standard, he said, was "not a standard of perfection, but a standard of what real world people have been able to achieve as opposed to a hypothetical standard that is put together by some other individual which is based on really nothing other than that individual's definition of perfection which none of us ever achieve." He had not prepared or researched all of his reports, but he had approved and took responsibility for every page. By not going out on too-thin limbs, and through his deep knowledge and clear, open, and informal manner, he impressed with the points on which he did insist. James Haines commented that he had never seen a witness stand cross-examination nearly as long as Huston and that there were few instances where he did not answer a question.[27]

Huston started by summarizing his various reports to KG&E. He concluded that "owners and contractors exerted exceptionally strong and effective management and achieved commensurately outstanding results in the areas of implementation of standardized plant management concepts, schedule performance, the use of merit shop labor, and safety program performance. Areas of less than outstanding, but nonetheless acceptable, performance were labor productivity and overtime expenditures." Overall the performance was clearly better than the average for comparable projects. The cost was 18 percent less than average and the schedule duration was among the shortest for contemporary nuclear projects. Of the cost changes, 58 percent of the increases were caused by regulatory and codes changes, 24 percent by work scope changes by vendors and architectural engineers, 1 percent by estimate omission, 12 percent by underestimates, 1 percent by contingency, and "other" was 6 percent. Not a bad record for a utility supervising nuclear plant construction for the first time.[28]

Both in his initial statement and under cross-examination Huston admitted there had been problems. "I don't subscribe to a perfection in management theory," he reemphasized, "and I do believe that on any major project, you're going to have problems with your contractors. . . . It is the job of the owners who are managing all of those contractors to respond to those problems when they occur in a positive manner. . . . What really counts in my definition is how you finish." Immense time went into that responding: "I don't think for people that have not worked in the nuclear industry," said Huston, "they can appreciate just how much money and time and manpower goes into the development of procedures on a nuclear project." The scope of work and the regulatory atmosphere changed radically from the time Wolf Creek was begun to the time it was finished. The nuclear industry, Huston said, was not highly regulated in the 1960s—it was somewhat like building a fossil plant. All that changed in the 1970s, and particularly after the Three Mile Island accident in 1979. Large contingencies could have been put into the budget, but these would have been better for financial planning than they would have been for project management. "We did not want to allow contractors like Daniel and Bechtel to work up, and we approved specifically what we thought they should spend, and then say, well, let's put 100 percent out there for something else we might have to spend somewhere in the future." Therefore the contingency was only on the known scope, not speculation about how it might change. The regulatory changes, beginning with the Calvert Cliffs decision in 1971 and especially as interpreted by the new agency, the NRC, after 1974 did not have much regard for cost. "The NRC tells us today and then that the cost and schedule mean absolutely nothing to them. . . . Their only concern is safety and quality."[29]

Huston was followed by a series of witnesses generally supportive of KG&E's position. George Roen of Cresap, McCormick and Paget characterized KG&E's decisions on Wolf Creek as being prudent and sometimes showing "an unusually high degree of prudence." In this latter category he placed particularly the original company perception of the need for Wolf Creek to diversify fuel sources, the continued concern for minimizing KG&E's investment through SNUPPS and attempts to reduce its ownership share, good financial strategy through thick and thin, and the early and appropriate emphasis on the need for Wolf Creek energy for reliability. Forecasting was problematical in a time of change, but KG&E did it as well as any other. The "colored pencil and ruler" method was a "media fantasy," but admittedly all utilities were changing their methods and attempting "to develop a data base for this new world." The 1978 and 1979 forecasts, for instance, "were in effect both prepared on the edge of a cliff of unknowns."[30] Satisfying the various political constituencies was a challenge as difficult or more so than constructing and financing a nuclear plant.

There was a particularly germane exchange, given the broad issues of the case, between Roen and attorney Steve Dickson of the Electric Shock Coalition regarding both the concept of prudence and the use of hindsight in regulation. Dickson tried to get Roen to agree that "with regard to market regulated utilities . . . the prudence of management decisions is judged by the outcome of the market." Roen would not agree. How about in an unregulated industry? Dickson pursued. Roen replied that he did not know of an unregulated industry. Dickson said that he once worked for Ford Motor Company. Was it not true that when the product did not sell one looked back at the original decision and criticized the manager? Might the plant that made the unsuccessful cars be closed? Yes, said Roen. "However, your question speaks to an industry that is not economically regulated, regulated in a lot of other ways, and except for those who are completely wedded to [certain types of] automobiles, there is no particular penalty on the consumers except those whose pay is dependent on the plant or their relatives . . . there is no particular penalty on the consumers of that plant's ceasing to exist." But there, Dickson pursued, the manager was judged for a decision in hindsight, but the utility was saying the prudence of KG&E managers should be judged at the time the decision to build Wolf Creek was made. Why should that decision too not be judged by the results? "The most fundamental reason, sir," Roen replied, "is that it's beyond human ability to foretell the future accurately over as long a period of time as we are discussing here and a period of time that involves as much substantial change in matters affecting costs, fuel choices and so forth, usage of the product as occurred in this nearly two decades of time. Of course, that doesn't even consider the 30 to 40 years extending through commercial service and then on into the decommissioning phase." Given a utility's obligation to serve, errors on the high side on supply are better than errors of being too low. How high should they be before they are unacceptable, asked Dickson? Roen, like most others, could not answer that one exactly. Developing *an* answer was a key issue of the whole hearing.[31]

The utility case on a policy level was presented by officers. Wilson Cadman, who began his testimony on May 23, was the first of these. He filed only 14 pages of prepared testimony, but was extensively questioned by the attorneys. As someone who had joined KG&E immediately after getting his A.B. in personnel management from the University of Wichita in 1951, Cadman knew both the company and the region it served well. He had been in sales, he had been a division manager, and he had been vice president for customer and community services. His substantial involvement with Wolf Creek began late in 1979 when he became executive vice president, and it had taken an increasing amount of his time, energy, and emotion since that date. "To explain the significance of Wolf Creek," Cadman said during the hearings, "is to explain the significance of electric energy. Electric energy is fundamental to our way and quality of life. A flip of the switch brings us energy for light, warm or cool air, cooking and a multitude of appliances which provide information, entertainment, and freedom from many labor intensive tasks." It increases productivity and leisure time and removes danger and drudgery. Yet Cadman had a growing concern for the "sorry state" of the country's basic facilities. The world's richest nation was letting its infrastructure go to ruins. It would be worse in the future if some of the treatment of Wolf Creek was repeated. That Wolf Creek was finished amid such difficult times was remarkable, but even that, it appeared, was not enough—the company, it was proposed, would now be penalized for "isolated errors" and for "decisions which in hindsight were not perfect." The rate increase was needed for KG&E to survive—its "financial viability [was] on the line."[32]

Cadman stayed quite in character under cross-examination—determined and feisty. There were many questions about how possible abandonment was debated. "My response would be," Cadman said on one of these occasions, "that we were coming down to the wire with a plant that was well under way, minimum trouble. We looked at our ability to continue the financing of the plant and we set ourselves to the task of determining the way that we could bring the plant in with whatever restructuring of management was necessary, whatever steps had to be taken, and keeping in mind the foremost direction of the company and our policy, our stated policy, on the construction of Wolf Creek to bring that plant in safely and as nearly as reasonable as a contemporaneous plant could be built. . . . It was not wallowing in despair as were other plants in the United States that had now truly been canceled, not as paper entities, but as steel and concrete entities that stand there representing billions of dollars of investment that will never make a kilowatt of power. That is not the case in Wolf Creek. Our energies were turned to the management of the plant, continuing to adjust to the ever increasing requirements of completion and to bring on to the site whatever levels of management with new forms of expertise that could be found anywhere in the world to do that job. There were other—there were other issues at that point in time that were considerably more important to us than running a bunch of feasibility studies that were for all practical purposes moot." All had suffered, Cadman said—the stockholders, the officers, the customers. But it was not gratuitous suffering and it would not be in vain. "We have made some very, very long range decisions with the best kind of information available, and, believe me, with the very best intentions and we have dealt with a constant moving target with respect to regulations, changing in requirements, changing in, if you will, the public's attitude toward nuclear power."[33]

It was a good project, Cadman thought, not a magic one. He denied that "bureaucratic inertia" had worked against the abandonment of the plant, and denied also that stubborn, unreasonable pride had had anything to do with it. But, no question, he was proud, even at this dark hour. "I guess where we're headed," he said to one attorney, "is that we're a little dinky company that successfully built a nuclear plant with the lowest escalation rate and shortest construction duration and the least cost of any contemporaneous plant." It showed small companies with limited experience could do it. "Cincinnati Gas and Electric is a big company. Public Service Company is a big company, Consumers Power is a huge company. Their plants are dead. Wolf Creek is alive!" Still, Cadman could maintain a certain humility about his own role that had gotten him through a lot of abuse. Milo Unruh, the attorney for Vulcan Chemical in Wichita, asked, "Mr. Cadman, was it manifest destiny—I happened to notice that your initials are the same initials as this generation station. Did you ever think about that?" The answer was, "Yes, I've had that called to my attention. It is also Water Closet, Wichita Club . . ."[34]

Of the KCPL witnesses, Arthur Doyle and Don McPhee addressed the policy questions most broadly, while by no means omitting documentary detail. Doyle had been through Boston College and Boston College law school and had practiced law in Kansas City from 1949 to 1973, when he first joined KCPL to initiate its corporate law department. He was therefore particularly familiar with the legal process and effective at responding in that framework. He gave a capsule history of both KCPL and the Wolf Creek project, focusing on the need for such a move. The historical trend in rates had been downward, Doyle pointed out. In fact, KCPL's current residential rates were only 23 percent of its pre-Depression rates. However, a reversal in that trend had been caused by a) reaching the limits of economies of scale in generating units; b) the environmental movement, causing substantial non–revenue producing investments to clean up coal-fired generating plants and so forth; and c) the beginning of primary fuel shortages. All three of these trends became evident in the late 1960s, just when the decision was made to build Wolf Creek. It was unfortunate, Doyle thought, that many of these were blamed on Wolf Creek, which was a result of them as much as a cause. Uranium stabilized at a lower price than anyone predicted, the "acid rain" issue arose over coal, there were heat storms in Kansas, and in general Kansas City growth kept KCPL demand projections on the increase. Doyle admitted that people working on the project did not always feel upbeat about its prospects—"you go through a period of momentum and burn-out, momentum and burn-out, momentum and burn-out"—yet on the whole he evaluated Wolf Creek as an "absolute great project, clean as a whistle, just great." Would he do it again? No.[35]

Donald McPhee, formerly senior vice president of system power operations at KCPL, had been involved more intimately and longer than Doyle in the day-to-day development of Wolf Creek. He had high praise for his company both in its decision to join KG&E in the plant and in working with the SNUPPS consortium. He liked the people KG&E had hired in its nuclear department and found there "a resourcefulness and attention to underlying detail that gives us considerable confidence that the overall program will be successful."[36]

Hearings in May 1985 were devoted primarily to company witnesses and to consultants mostly favorable to the company position. In June came the KCC staff and intervenors' witnesses, who interpreted both the history and the future of the Wolf Creek plant quite differently.

First came a consultant, with the unlikely name for a twentieth-century nuclear power expert of Gui Ponce de Leon. His firm, Project Management Associates of Ann Arbor, Michigan, spent a good deal of time gathering data at Wolf Creek, especially on the efficiency of the use of labor. Like many of the witnesses unfriendly to the utility claims since 1976, de Leon used highly mathematical and quantitative methods for his analysis. This seemed more acceptable to the 1985 commission than when Michael Viren had tried it before the irascible Samuel Jensch and company nearly ten years earlier. Chairman Lennen was no Jensch, and controlled the hearings in a far less folksy manner. Quantitative analysis was definitely to be taken seriously this time and "seat of the pants" intuition as a counter would not be sufficient.

De Leon's most shocking number was that 4,036,685 worker hours employed on Wolf Creek construction could be classified as disallowable direct construction hours attributable to imprudent management actions or causes that were controllable by owner management. Controllable costs amounted to $446,575,500, over $3.5 million of this attributable to schedule extension and the rest the labor disallowances in eight direct labor cost categories.[37]

The cross-examination of de Leon was lengthy and intense, walking the line between losing the public and the commission in mathematics to counter mathematics and leaving de Leon's argument intact on its own ground. Attorney Ed Roach took the lead for the owners, driving early to try to discredit the witness on general competence. He did not know what AFUDC meant or understand the substance of it, even though much of his testimony hinged on that knowledge; he had changed his name, and so on. The core of the exchange, however, was lengthy discussions of exactly how long each kind of operation at Wolf Creek took and should take, and what the effects of regulation and other noncontrollable factors were on actual performance. Roach tended to characterize the regulatory requirements as incredibly arcane and sometimes nonsensical procedures which the average, though honest, workman could not be expected to understand. De Leon's response was that this is a nuclear plant, and people have to treat it as such. He was giving the utility the benefit of the doubt on most labor cost calculations, he said. "You've got a fella handling the additional pipe that's required," said Roach once. "Would you expect him to know why he's handling the pipe?" A. "Sure." Q. "You expect the guy sitting there lifting the pipe to know whether he's doing it because of 7914 or some other regulatory guide?" A. "Sure." Q. "He can figure out which regulatory guide he's handling the pipe for?" A. "He has to figure that out himself." De Leon's testimony used partly very technical critical path analysis, illustrating three critical paths (the BB reactor coolant system, the BG chemical and volume system, and the EG component coolant system), selected from fourteen possibilities, through the project and the maximum uncontrollable delays on each one. Analogies were used, like the one of driving a car through Kansas, taking a wrong turn and needing to drive faster to cover the extra miles. It is not certain that these homely analogies, however, were very helpful, and the commissioners and all attorneys doubtless had to spend some hours with the transcript and a headache being sure that de Leon's conclusions were justified by his data. De Leon and his team had been at the Wolf Creek site gathering data from March to September 1984. He was on the stand for three days explaining it.[38]

Richard Rosen, who was also on the stand for three days, made broader calculations by far than de Leon about cost overruns, management inadequacy, and overcapacity. Rosen saw no excuse for rate increases over the next five years of 101 percent for KG&E and 64 percent for KCPL, as proposed. His direct argument was that the Kansas utilities did not analyze the trends in nuclear power often and well enough and that their basic generation planning process was badly flawed and technically out of date. KG&E ended up with a reserve margin, with Wolf Creek, of 56.7 percent, according to Rosen's calculations, whereas the MOKAN reserve requirements for utilities in the area were only 15 percent. He estimated that 122 percent of KG&E's share of Wolf Creek was therefore excess in 1985, and that it would still be 67 percent in 1991, and not disappear until the mid 1990s. Fifty-eight percent of KCPL's share was excess. The operation of Wolf Creek over the next 30 years, Rosen said, would result in revenue requirements from ratepayers far in excess of an optimal plan. He estimated cumulative net ratepayer loss due to excess capacity for KG&E ratepayers at $400 million by the end of 1986, $1.4 billion by 1995, and over $1.6 billion by the time the plant was closed. These losses were about equal to revenues required for capital related costs: "Thus, if there were no capital costs at all, the facility would just break even over its lifetime." He did not, however, ignore capital costs, which he found excessive—in excess of 200 percent over the original estimates, a number defined in the rate shock bill as, by legislative definition, imprudent. From a "definitive" number of just over $1 billion, it was likely the final cost of Wolf Creek would rise to about $3 billion. To be fair, however, Rosen confessed that cost overruns in nuclear plants had been endemic owing in part to regulatory and technical changes. He proposed therefore to evaluate Wolf Creek's capital costs with relation to industry experience. He calculated that of all plants completed through 1984 Wolf Creek was 17 percent over the industry norm in cost and was therefore $430 million too high. The rate shock bill number would lop $922 million off the actual cost in allowable rate recovery, or about 31 percent of the bill. A Touche Ross study had come up with the number $447 million, or 14.9 percent of Wolf Creek's capital costs that had been unnecessarily or inefficiently incurred.[39]

Planning exercises had been too infrequent and were deficient in both design and execution, Rosen said. Had the planning been adequate, the proper decision would have been to abandon the plant at an early date, certainly as the effects of Three Mile Island became evident. It would have been a good decision to have abandoned it even as late as 1981 and even if the ratepayers or taxpayers were required to compensate the utility for costs to date. Cancellation in 1981 with "sunk" cost compensation would have benefitted ratepayers by $770 million, and without such compensation, by $1.1 billion. True, perhaps such a plant would be needed someday, but the question was the prudence of doing it now. It was a principle of regulation, Rosen said, that imprudent and unreasonable costs should not be borne by the ratepayers and that costs that are reasonable investment decisions, but which still lead to economic losses, should be shared equitably between ratepayers and utility stockholders.[40]

Linear and log-linear statistics aside, AFUDC (which this witness very well understood) forgotten, Rosen, like Huston, had a talent for getting to the summary bottom line in eloquent and clear English. Dr. Malcolm Burns at the 1976 NRC license hearings used quantitative methods to estimate the plant might cost $1.98 billion at a time when the utility estimate was $1 billion. That should have been a signal—"a quantitative warning . . . about potential escalation"—Rosen thought. KG&E did not pick up the signal and continued on. "By continuing . . . the Companies in effect assumed responsibility for the risk, and, indeed the economic outcome that has emerged." After 1981 no planning documents were produced at all. This was as it had always been, Cadman's claims about daily planning and Doyle's statements about not needing a bound report to see if the sun is coming up in the East notwithstanding. KG&E's forecasting method, Rosen averred, "was substandard during the 1970s when Wolf Creek was being planned, and remains substandard today. It still falls short of what one should expect from a modern electric utility." The same was true of the companies' study of alternatives. "I would characterize the co-owners' responses to escalating costs as essentially passive and fundamentally inadequate." Rosen called most of KG&E's financial planning "cursory economic analysis." They did not undertake detailed analysis of the forces underlying the increase in Wolf Creek's costs and "typically sought to explain recent capital cost overruns as they occurred and ignored their implications for future cost overruns," leading to an underestimate of the risk of continuing. "Utility commissions are increasingly having to confront the issue of how to apportion the growing financial burden of new power plants which contribute to sharp increases in electric rates."[41]

Just as the opponents' prime nemesis was Huston, to the proponents the strongest block was Rosen. The Rosen scenario was compelling enough that, even when used as a foil, it was taken seriously. Essentially, in the minds of the commission, the hearings narrowed to the world of Wolf Creek as Huston saw it and that world as Rosen saw it. Much of the rest of the detail could be attached and interpreted within that frame.

Again like Huston, Rosen hardly collapsed during cross-examination: he seemed to get stronger, and was quick and definite on the uptake. Naturally, the utility attorneys attacked his models, his assumptions, and the computer programs he used to calculate consequences. If the base data or axioms were incorrect, of course, it did not matter how sophisticated was the manner in which they were processed to arrive at conclusions—those conclusions would be erroneous. The attorneys chipped away at him on his assumptions about capacity factor, about the life and economics of the coal plants, and on many other technical questions that might influence the need for and efficiency of Wolf Creek. Rosen was no dummy, clearly, but the KG&E attorneys did establish that his specialization in physics was in quantum optics, particularly experiments with laser beams, that he had never taken even undergraduate economics courses, that he had never worked for a utility company, and that he had never so much as visited Wolf Creek or any other KG&E power plant. He had recommended abandonment or retirement before other commissions, and those commissions had ignored him wholly or in part. The question was whether his method had been invalidated or political compromises had had to be made. Particularly suspect were Rosen's long-term projections out to 30 years. He admitted they were "speculative," but argued that most of the losses to the ratepayers would take place in the first ten years anyway. He also had a fairly modest estimate of Wolf Creek's capacity factor—56.2 percent for the first ten years of operation. KG&E attorneys argued that it was likely to average more like 75 percent. The actual percentages when the plant began operating were 1986—70.4 percent, 1987—65.5 percent, 1988—67.1 percent, 1989—97.7 percent—going upward as the planned fuel replacement cycles purposefully got longer.[42]

Rosen remained devastatingly analytical and articulate. When quoted logic, he countered with the contention that commonsense, "seat of the pants" type thinking was simply not adequate here. "Logic can't help when you're doing a statistical analysis. I mean, people design multivariate regression analysis to try to be more precise than just saying what logically looks like it follows from this set of a few numbers." When dealing with hundreds of numbers and over the long term, Rosen argued, it would come out very close. Yes, there might be another TMI, and yes, the plant might work better for a time than he had projected—but in the long run his figures would be close. He had 95 percent certainty about them, he said. Typical of his poise was once when he was quoted a report he himself had written some years earlier giving different and more favorable figures for nuclear plants. His response was that he had not been busy planning a nuclear plant for ten years before that and did not have the resources to do a big study. Anyway, that was not the point: "The issue was what utility planners that were responsible should have been doing in 1981, not what Rich Rosen was doing or should have been doing in 1981; okay?" He stuck to his guns that "there is no performance level that Wolf Creek could possibly attain to pay for itself."[43]

Charles Komonoff took a still more extreme stance. KG&E's decisions to continue with Wolf Creek, he said, "were based on significant misperceptions of relevant regulatory burdens and of the costs of coal-fired facilities and may have been imprudent." To leave the Kansas ratepayers no worse off than if the companies had built a coal-fired plant, 93 percent of Wolf Creek's capital cost must be kept permanently out of the rate base. That is, $1.3 billion of KG&E's $1.4 billion investment there should be disallowed. This and other U.S. nuclear plants, Komanoff said, had "generally exhibited lackluster management at best." Wolf Creek should have been cancelled in the summer of 1979.[44]

Komanoff was hardly fond of KG&E. He said the company had

not cooperated well with him in gathering data, and that he felt little sympathy for its stockholders. "KG&E's shareholders participated voluntarily in the planning and execution of Wolf Creek—which cannot be said of KG&E's ratepayers." Cross-examination did establish that Komanoff had never been responsible for the construction of a power plant, had no training in nuclear power plant design, and had based his definition of prudence on hindsight. KG&E's Haines asked Komanoff repeatedly if he had ever asked to see the ten file cabinets of material brought together by KG&E for Komanoff's client, ALERT. Now that he was in Kansas, Haines said, the KG&E attorneys would try to make his testimony efficient so that he could see more of the state than the Supreme Courtroom. Komanoff answered that "it beats the New York Public Service Commission rooms." "It beats New York City, period," Haines responded. "No argument." That bit of friendly levity was about the only concession the company got out of him.[45]

Hindsight versus foresight—prudence versus perfection—the role of the regulatory commission as a surrogate market—permanent or temporary "punishment"—phase in or cold turkey—the significance of the utility obligation to serve—theory versus field intuition—mountains of testimony informed decisions that were in the end philosophical as well as legal and technical. But in the end, whatever the explanation and analysis, the question was how much of Wolf Creek should be paid for by ratepayers and when. The hearings closed early in the afternoon of July 27, and all parties awaited a decision.

The KCC members—Michael Lennen, Keith Henley, Margalee Wright—had more than the attorneys and the consultants and the expert witnesses to listen to as they examined the transcripts. There were the ratepayers themselves, and the thunder of ten years of active protest in the state. However "boring" the hearings were to the average person, they got more popular. At the small town of Pittsburg in June, a session drew 1,300 people.[46] One editor spoke of KG&E's "antics" during the last days of the rate hearings, when it "pulled out nearly all the stops, short of holding its breath until it turned blue in the face," and was contemptuous of the disagreements of experts, even when they worked for the same side.[47] There was little more sympathy for the NRC or the federal government generally. "My experience with them [NRC]," wrote one Kansan, "is like watching an Abbott and Costello movie. Nobody knows who's on first or second in that place. Nor do they have the kind of intention or desire to clean up their act."[48]

Events at Wolf Creek Station itself were not interrupted by the rate hearings. On June 18 at 2:05 A.M. the Wolf Creek plant was synchronized with the power transmission grids of KG&E, KCPL, and the Kansas Electric Power Cooperative and began supplying 80 mw of power during its initial production run.[49] Early in August, as Kansas awaited the rate decision of the KCC, Wolf Creek reached a milestone in its "power ascension test phase" when it produced full power for the first time.[50] On August 24, the KCC denied a temporary rate increase request by KG&E.[51] On September 3, 1985, at 1:16 P.M., the owners of Wolf Creek declared it to be officially "on line" like any other generating plant.[52]

Almost ignored in the flurry over who was to pay for it, the great white dome on the prairie, unlike so many of its siblings, finally made power. The history of every other nuclear plant suggested that from that point there was truly no going back. The "hot tests" of Wolf Creek had come just as the Shippingport Plant, the first commercial reactor in the United States, was being dismantled, and therefore the first full cycle in the history of American nuclear power was completed.[53]

On record for all time in myriad hearings and newspaper articles were the estimates and speculation of every second-guesser, poised to come back and haunt the corporation whenever future detail might vary from plan. The Kansas legislature was "sensitized" to an extreme; opposition groups were organized and networked as never before; the press propaganda machine had plenty of momentum left; and the regulatory commission unquestionably would have to toss a least a sop to the snarling critics.

There was no slack for celebration. On September 14, days after the plant came onto the electric grid, and amid rumors that KG&E would get only half its rate increase, large blocks of company stock were put up for sale. In two days, the per share price of KG&E common stock fell from 15 to 11¾.[54] It would touch 9 briefly. Yet the "little utility that could" had done it in the face of a fury of protest in the midlands that stereotypers of rural backwaters could never have imagined. The new public relations director for KG&E, Lyle Koerper, was low key in assessing the significance of the completion of Wolf Creek Station, Kansas, but understandably hesitant about making inflated claims for the future efficiency and cost of the plant. But he, like his compatriots at the KG&E headquarters in downtown Wichita, were as certain as they were of anything in the world that in time the critics of Kansas nuclear power were in for a surprise. With Koerper, the quiet confidence came down to one steady phrase. He said: "We are not a monster."[55]

Conclusion

All Are Punished

> Electric utility regulation should be designed to reward and reinforce good decisions and not protect, subsidize, and even reward bad ones.... If one goes bankrupt that is of no concern to the 'market' and should be of no concern to a regulatory commission.
> —James Sturgeon, at Wolf Creek rate hearings, June 21, 1985

> Its [KG&E's] executives probably never suspected that 1990 might appear on its corporate tombstone as its last year as an independent utility.
> —*Kansas City Star*, July 29, 1990

> All are punished.... A glooming peace this morning with it brings.
> —The Prince, in William Shakespeare,
> *Romeo & Juliet*, Act V, scene iii

The KCC decision came in a public meeting on September 27, 1985. James Haines in retrospect was cynical about the process and environment within which this decision had to be made. The brevity and content of the meeting confirmed Haines's concerns. While each commissioner read at least part of the transcript and was present for most of the hearings, any deliberation and debate they did together about the decision had to be done in public. The entire public session devoted to communicating the decision lasted one hour. Wright read a prepared statement on KG&E heat pump advertising and Wilson Cadman's salary. Keith Henley said that he agreed generally with the staff, but that KG&E made some good points. Then Lennen got into his physical and economic capacity argument, the others nodded and ordered the staff to draft an order. That part took just twenty minutes. It was inconceivable to Haines that a hearing so long and complex "would provoke no disagreement and discussion among three intelligent, diligent and fair minded people." Lennen, however, later assured Haines that the KG&E testimony, especially Huston's, had changed his mind about numerous things.[1]

In any case the rate decision, while not nearly as unfavorable as anticipated at the outset of the hearings, did not leave KG&E in a comfortable position *vis à vis* Wolf Creek. The KCC decided that a total of $183 million, or about 10 percent of the cost of construction, was imprudently or inefficiently incurred and denied the utilities recovery and return on that portion permanently. The other 90 percent could be recovered through annual depreciation expenses over the expected life of the plant. However, of that 90 percent no current return or profit was permitted on about $944 million on the basis that a portion of the costs constituted excess physical capacity not used or required to be used for current services. A further $266 million was disallowed on the basis of excess economic capacity. The argument here was that other types of generating plants would have been less expensive and should have been chosen. Amounts excluded would be eligible in the future for rate of return as the excess capacity was utilized. For the present, rate increases would be phased in over four years and would amount to 36.7 percent for KG&E, as contrasted with the 95 percent over five years originally requested.[2] KG&E under the order would get a full current return on only 22 percent of its declared prudent investment in Wolf Creek.[3]

The KCC report summarized reasons for this result. *Prudence* was defined as risks inappropriate for the general public interest, not general prudence as usually defined. SNUPPS, it was agreed, was a good idea. However, the KG&E managers should have taken more of a role earlier in negotiating contracts and supervising contractors. "The Commission finds that inherent problems arose from the management philosophy adopted by the owners in the early years. The evidence is persuasive that the owners neither defined nor understood the scope of the project. We find that the monitoring role was inefficient, ineffective and inappropriate under the circumstances." Improvement during later stages did not forgive earlier faults. The Wolf Creek schedule was shorter than other contemporary plants, but it was longer than it should have been "because the owners failed to avoid or mitigate controllable delay." The commission determined that 14.5 months of schedule slippage were in the control of the owners and the cost of this should be excluded as imprudent.[4]

The "Findings and Conclusions" section of the decision was

couched in stern language. The part of the Wolf Creek plant that was used and required, the commission said, "is an extraordinarily expensive means of providing base load capacity which could have been provided at more reasonable cost. The rates resulting from full rate base treatment of Wolf Creek would be unreasonably high for ratepayers to pay and unreasonably high compared to other electric rates in Kansas." The decision to continue constructing Wolf Creek, especially after 1981, the commission said, "was not based on adequate or realistic analysis and review and appears to have stemmed from institutional inertia." The valuation should include the estimated cost for a coal plant prevalent during the construction period, as well as the actual experience of recent facilities. The commission said it did not know how its decision would affect KG&E's financial health, but thought the company could take proper measures to allow it to continue to provide service. This might include reduction of executive salaries and elimination of a television advertising campaign "which appears to be primarily aimed at generating good will but seems to have the opposite effect."[5]

The Kansas Commission, in so deciding, placed itself at the national forefront on new ground in utility regulation. "The Commission cannot embrace totally the views that regulation should produce the same results as the competitive market place," the decision read. "As applicants observe, there are significant distinctions between the obligations of regulated and non-regulated firms. However, we agree with Dr. Rosen and other parties' witnesses that regulation must provide a mechanism which encourages good management planning. A comparison with the free market model in this light is of some value and is consistent with legislative directions to compare rates resulting from capacity additions with other utilities' rates."[6]

That language engendered considerable reaction from the Wolf Creek utilities and utilities around the country. "Utilities commissions," wrote the *Wall Street Journal*, "are sweeping aside a once-undoubted principle that utilities should earn a profit on all the money invested in generating facilities." Now there was examination of how the money was spent and the need for the capacity. "Regulators call the inspections 'prudency reviews.' Utilities call them something close to outrageous."[7] Commented the *Pittsburg Sun*: "Opponents of nuclear power did not stop the building of Wolf Creek. But they have succeeded in halting a major part of the effort to pay for the plant."[8]

While Kansas consumers cheered, corporate investors cringed. A Salomon Brothers survey rated the Kansas Corporation Commission as one of the two worst state regulatory bodies at protecting the interests of investors. KCPL securities got a D+ regulatory rating, and KG&E's were rated E.[9] KG&E got an irate call from a widow who held its stock, asking what had happened to her safe investment. "I was shocked by the KCC ruling," she said. "It's not fair to stockholders."[10] KG&E cut its quarterly dividend in half immediately, halted hiring, withdrew from the Chambers of Commerce and most other organizations, stopped paying dues of employees in civic organizations, no longer allowed employees to use work time for civic projects, curtailed most construction projects, eliminated all but emergency overtime, undertook extensive refinancings to lower both its cost of debt and retire much of its preferred stock, and implemented a list of other draconian measures designed to save $10 million in costs in 1986.[11] This allowed its stock to recover slightly to 11½, after having reached a 16-year low of 9¾ during the week of October 4, 1985. As news of the KCC decision became known the stock had plummeted from a price of over 18 at the end of August.[12] KG&E's senior debt was rated BB+ in the fall of 1985, and its preferred stock BB. Neither rating was investment grade, and both were among the lowest of all electric utilities in the nation. Yet Moody's seriously considered lowering it further.[13] "It's [KG&E stock] appealing strictly to speculators now," an analyst opined. "Aggressive buyers are the ones who are willing to look past the immediate dividend problems." The stock, he added unnecessarily, was "not for everyone."[14]

From the utility perspective the KCC evaluation was hindsight, and a "heads you win, tails I lose" proposition, where the utility took the risks and shouldered the public obligation without the prospect of the real upside return that rewarded more flexible risks taken in the less regulated part of the private sector. About the only positive elements company officials could see was that the 1985 KCC orders were designated "interim," with the possibility of adjustment as matters changed, and that the company was invited to be creative in making the best of living with the ruling.[15]

There was definitely a perceptual distance between the once

rather harmonious views of regulator and regulated. To the commissioners the ruling was moderate, and perhaps did not go far enough. Margalee Wright in the years following was upset that, from her perspective, nearly all the changes to the original ruling were in favor of the utility. Jim Haines, on the other hand, was upset at what he called reneging on promises made to the utility in that order.[16] In short, the atmosphere was hardly one of trust.

James Haines, who had the role of advocate through the rate hearings, took some of that with him to his new posthearing role as group vice president with responsibility for finance, accounting, rates, and revenue requirements. Haines thought the state legislature in passing the "rate shock bill" in 1984 had concluded that Wolf Creek would be finished, would operate, and that there would be nuclear power in Kansas. But the legislators were subject to great pressure on the rate increase, and so decided to make sure the KG&E shareholders picked up most of the tab—that is, as Haines put it, changing to "an exercise in property confiscation, as opposed to an antinuclear attempt." Haines said that when he had time to get in a reflective mood sometime in the far future he intended to write a law review article on the idea of "risk sharing" that was so prominent in the hearings and the rate decision on Wolf Creek. There was, he said, no legal basis for that, though no question there was a political one. It was made of whole cloth, Haines said, "the pipe dream of a consultant trying to figure out a rationale that would sound appealing for confiscating property." Richard Rosen, however, sold the argument (which was a trend in regulation nationally) well in Kansas, it stuck, and KG&E through the whole of the 1980s, Haines thought, was "trying to cope with what Rosen did to us."[17]

The problem, according to Haines, was in the odd position of a regulated monopoly and in the double standard that was applied to KG&E. Rosen, for example, said that KG&E's old gas and coal plants had to be evaluated on the basis of what the company paid for them, not their market value. In the wake of the rate hearings, as one of its strategies for restructuring its balance sheet and improving earnings per share, KG&E sold its interest in LaCygne 2 for $392 million; it was on the company books at $50 million. Had Rosen been "intellectually honest," Haines claimed, he would have allowed KG&E to value up its other assets, which would have had the same effect as charging what it asked on Wolf Creek. Instead, constantly two economic theories were used alternately, with the result that KG&E could not win for losing. Ford lost a ton on the Edsel, but was at least allowed to make it up on the Mustang. Haines was often told by entrepreneurs that "you guys don't know what it's like in the real world." His response to that was would they put their money into an investment that had the prospect of a 12 percent return and no more? That was the situation for KG&E investors. They had the hope of earning 12 percent and the risk of losing everything. And while hindsight regulation might be legally suspect, the man in the street understood it perfectly. When KG&E argued it could not be held responsible for decisions made under other conditions, the average Joe might say, "The hell you can't. My car broke down, and in hindsight I should never have bought it, but I am still responsible—I still have to pay—no one will bail me out. So why are you different?" With 1,000 people in the hearing audience, and streams of public witnesses whose testimony was not subject to cross-examination, those perceptions were hard to counter. "If I ask whether you want this head of lettuce for 10 cents or 20 cents, what will you say?"[18]

This new pattern applied to KG&E also was being applied nationally. Richard Pierce, writing in the *Georgetown Law Journal* in 1989, highlighted this. When Pierce first studied regulatory disallowances based on imprudence in 1983, he found that the Federal Energy Regulatory Commission (FERC) and its predecessor, the Federal Power Commission, had never disallowed an investment on the basis of imprudence in the 50-year history of the agencies. He found only a few cases where state agencies disallowed investments based on findings of managerial imprudence, and these, which happened about once a decade, were relatively trivial in amount. However, the same study for the period 1984 to 1988 gave much different results. In that period state agencies disallowed as imprudent portions of investment in 19 completed generating plants and the amount disallowed averaged $610 million per plant. It may be no accident that many of these plants were nuclear plants. "Apparently, for decades," wrote Pierce, "electric utility managers were almost uniformly individuals with outstanding business acumen. At some point in the 1980s, this entire generation of exceptional managers was replaced *en masse* by a generation of bumbling idiots."[19]

The trend was without doubt politicization of the regulatory process. Pierce noted that as a result of experiences with this trend some utility managers were not so sure regulated monopoly was any advantage, and were thinking cautiously of free competition among utilities.[20]

As it had been one of the first to feel the impact of the "extreme Hobbesian behavior" of state utility regulation in the 1980s, KG&E was also to be the first among modern U.S. utilities to experience a free market technique developed to a high pitch in the "real" business world of the 1980s—namely the corporate raid, the unfriendly takeover attempt. Not before, however, it had continued to its final *denouement* the struggle to survive as a Kansas nuclear producer within the framework of things as they now were.

As context, it must be emphasized that Wolf Creek itself in the late 1980s turned out to be unquestionably "the prettiest pig at the fair" among the controversial group of its sister nuclear plants. It outperformed all the others in volume of electricity, in cost of production, in availability, in capacity factor, in reliability, and in a host of other statistics. In nearly every operational way it outperformed not only what its critics allowed it, but what its best friends had hoped for. In its first year it produced 8,922,510 megawatt-hours, an alltime record for first-year nuclear plants.[21] The NRC commented during Wolf Creek's second year that "it is near the top of the stack in overall plant operations."[22] Again in the first six months of 1989 Wolf Creek produced more kilowatt-hours than any other commercial reactor of the 110 in the United States and was ninth among the 352 nuclear plants in the world. It operated during that period at an average capacity of 96.1 percent and electricity was available from it 97.2 percent of the time. Said spokesman Ronn Smith: "It was expected that we would do this well. Wolf Creek is a large power plant and should do well. It is well built, well designed, and run by well-trained, knowledgeable people. It is our aim to make Wolf Creek the top producer in the the world."[23] That pattern held through the year, with a production of more than 10 billion kwhs, which exceeded the production of every other U.S. plant of any kind. It ended the year available 99 percent of the time with a capacity factor of 95 percent.[24] In the 1985 hearings claims of capacity factors in the 70 percent range were thought considerably overdrawn by critics. As the fuel replacement cycle lengthened, the statistics became even stronger. In May 1991, Wolf Creek had run nonstop for 365 days. "It's like starting your car on May 21, 1990," said a manager, "and running it nonstop for 365 days."[25] That continuous run record was to extend well into September when a brief fuel load outage occurred. But in doing so, it set a world record by running 487 successive days, six more than any other plant. The plant's operating cost for 1990, despite a refueling outage that year, was the second lowest in the nation, and its radiation dose per worker was the lowest in the United States.[26]

Other factors mildly favorable to KG&E paralleled the major one of the plant's performance. Protest slowed some from its long peak, perhaps at last, with the decline of media coverage, reaching the "post-political" stage of moderate public acceptance. Instead of dozens of active groups, and a hydra-headed coalition, much of the rate protest was centered after 1988 in the single Consumer Utility Rate Board formed in January of that year by KCC chair Keith Henley after a failed attempt by a governor's task force to recommend legislation that would create an independent state agency. CURB was an active advocate indeed, and attached to the commission for funding with the strong voice of Linda Weir-Enegren of Wichita as its presence in the media.[27] But arguments over the technicalities of rate implementation did not have quite the drama of lying down in front of the reactor train in 1979 and CURB, though its members would not like to hear this, took on some of the characteristics of a centralized bureaucracy in trying to make the grassroots protest permanent.

A second factor giving KG&E a bit of breathing room was a change in the national economy resulting at long last in a decline in interest rates. Also, hot Kansas winds, and maybe a letup in conservation, resulted in increases in electric demand in KG&E's service area more in line with those predicted when Wolf Creek was planned. Instead of the 1 or 2 percent annual demand increases that embarrassed company witnesses at the 1985 hearings, the hot summer of 1988 increased demand about 14 percent. KCPL's demand in Kansas City was 332 mw more than the KCC said that company would need not in 1988, but in 1990.[28] KG&E's community reputation improved more to the level of old times. In 1986 a new corporation, Wolf Creek Nuclear Operating Corporation (WCNOC), was created solely to operate Wolf Creek, and had as one of its effects a distancing of KG&E itself from such direct connection with the project just as the Russian Chernobyl nuclear plant disaster hit the front pages.[29]

The company's "Project Living Green" for beautification was as popular as "Project Deserve" for paying poor people's utility bills. In 1991 the Utility Communicators named KG&E the nation's best overall utility communicator in its size class.[30]

These trends in their embryonic stages were combined with aggressive (some would say desperate) innovation by KG&E to try to avoid corporate financial disaster, given the Wolf Creek rate decision. While a detailed account of these innovations is beyond the scope of this study, several of the most striking were incorporated in something that became known as the "rate stabilization plan," which was presented by the company to the KCC in 1987 as a constructive alternative to the interim rate solution set in 1985.

KG&E had never accepted the 1985 decision. It requested a rehearing, giving 73 reasons in 52 pages why the KCC had made the wrong decision, and claiming that commission findings were "not based on any articulated standard of prudence" and were "arbitrary and therefore unreasonable."[31] The rehearing request was denied.[32]

KG&E then sued the commission. The Kansas Supreme Court in June 1986 sided with the KCC 6 to 1, which, despite a stinging dissent by Chief Justice Alfred Schroeder, put the KCC and the Wichita consumer groups in a "triumphant mood."[33] The case was, however, appealed late in the year to the U.S. Supreme Court which, to the surprise of the KCC counsel, accepted it.[34]

Both sides claimed that the pending Supreme Court case had nothing to do with what happened next. KG&E approached the KCC with a rate stabilization plan, an imaginative multifaceted proposal for delaying some of the rate increases authorized under the 1985 orders as well as returning the corporation to financial health in return for the commission's eliminating some of the long-term punitive features of the 1985 decision. The package was eventually approved by the commission.

The major architect of the plan was James Haines of KG&E. It involved accounting procedure changes to increase tax benefits, changing from a 30- to a 40-year depreciation schedule on the power plant, restructuring debt, and, most interestingly, providing for future cash flow by taking out life insurance policies on 82 of its executives and members of the board. That insurance would create a stream of income of $800 million over the next 40 years which would come to KG&E as beneficiary of these policies. KG&E agreed to delay two rate increases, which would save consumers $100 million, and in return asked the commission to provide a specific framework for the full rate recognition of KG&E's prudent investment in Wolf Creek and amortization of KG&E's commission-determined imprudent investment in Wolf Creek. The company was also to be allowed to retain the benefits of its cost cutting measures, refinancings, and benefits from the new federal tax law of 1986. The fourth increase in the commission's phase-in plan, which KG&E proposed to delay from September 1988 to January 1992, would be made a permanent increase. Certain accounting changes would be confirmed.[35]

Haines found it "incredible" that within three months of the 1985 rate order inflation and interest rates began to drop, helping reduce KG&E's interest cost on its large amount of variable interest debt and, more importantly, making it possible to refinance a good deal of debt that had been issued in the high interest rate environment of the early 1980s. The expectation of the company's stockholders for return on their equity also dropped, since utility common stock was sensitive to interest rate change. The Tax Reform Act of 1986 reduced the company's federal tax liability. Wolf Creek was operating flawlessly, giving the company an unexpected chance to sell power into the market. All these factors made it clear that the rate order might work, and Haines began struggling to make sure it did work.

A key conceptual breakthrough came in spring 1986 when an insurance salesman, one Bud Smith, called on KG&E to explain a plan to cover future health care costs. In explaining the plan it became evident that insurance was a way of building tax-free cash value, which could be borrowed against, with the interest used as a tax deduction. When the insured died, the proceeds came tax free and were used to pay off the loan. Haines asked the insurance man, why worry about $20 million of health care costs? Why not help to cover the capital costs of Wolf Creek by matching the insurance with the annual depreciation charges for the plant? Smith agreed. KG&E committed on a contingency basis for policies involving a $23 million annual premium, and went to the KCC with the entire proposal.[36]

The complex package, initially described in the press as "a mosaic of rate restructuring, insurance policies and accounting changes," was impressive to Topeka from the start.[37] Brian Moline of the Commission staff commented that "the plan is a very bold, innovative and unprecedented approach. It's creative and sincere and the way it's designed both customers and shareholders would benefit."[38] Haines, of course, joined in. "The KCC recognized," he said, "that its rate order would create financial difficulty for us and invited us to present innovative proposals to resolve that difficulty. . . . I emphasize that we do not view regulation as a scapegoat. It is management's responsibility to obtain good regulation. We accept that and will succeed in that responsibility."[39]

As might be expected, some doubts were also expressed. The *Kansas City Times* wrote that on the surface the plan was attractive, but there were risks. One was the murky area of depreciation. Writing off the investment more slowly would work if electrical demand and other key factors unfolded as the utility expected, but, as all had painfully learned, no one knew the future.[40] Moline said the commission must be aware "the plan makes major surgery on the existing Wolf Creek rate order," and drastically increased the company's future revenue requirements in return for short-term savings. The question was whether the stream of income created from the proceeds of the insurance plan combined with savings from debt restructuring would be sufficient to prevent the need for future rate increases.[41]

These issues were thrashed out in a KCC hearing in January 1987, with the musical name: "In the Matter of the Application of Kansas Gas and Electric Company for Approval of a Plan to Delay or Reduce $100 Million of Approved Rate Increases, Sustain KG&E's Progress in Restoring Its Health, Establish a Framework for Rate Recognition of KG&E's Prudent Investment in Wolf Creek, and Amortize KG&E's Commission Determined Imprudent Investment in Wolf Creek."

The opponents were there, some of them of long standing. Margaret Bangs wrote to her local paper that the KCC should not cave in and upset its 1985 order. "It is to be wondered who sets the KCC calendar—the regulators or the regulated." Bangs warned that KG&E's request to have its entire 540 mw share of Wolf Creek declared "used and useful" by 1992 could result in a sudden 50 percent rate increase at that time.[42] The KCC staff had the same kind of questions, and said that it would support the rate stabilization deal only if KG&E would legally bind itself never to ask for another Wolf Creek–related rate hike.[43]

There were some who were obviously annoyed that, whatever fiscal advantage might result for consumers, the plan involved in effect retracting the hand-slapping that KG&E had gotten in 1985 for poor management practices in the construction phase of Wolf Creek. Even the compliments on the brilliance of the plan often had an edge to them. Haines said at one point, as KG&E's stock price recovered into the low 20s and the stabilization plan was praised, that "I take great exception to the suggestion that innovation and creativity and good management are something that's new at KG&E."[44]

While the KCC itself had doubts, it did approve the rate stabilization plan in February 1987, just eight days before KG&E had to sign contracts for its insurance policies.[45] "As though exhausted by the intractable problem of justifying the unneeded, unaffordable $3 billion Wolf Creek plant," Bangs protested, "the KCC seems to have thrown in the towel and accepted as a solution KG&E's recent complex package of proposals. . . . The KCC has succumbed to the deceptive fiction that all the power from Wolf Creek will be needed in five years and that the cost of the plant was prudent." In fact, thought Bangs, the rate stabilization package was "a fragile house of cards, a Rube Goldberg contraption."[46]

Not to worry. True to the frustrating form of the nuclear power debate in Kansas since the first moves toward building Wolf Creek were made in 1968, the pendulum swung quickly again, and the seeming final wizardry of the rate stabilization compromise became simply the last in a series of patchworks that came unravelled.

First, the U.S. Supreme Court case was dismissed at the request of the KCC, which said that, given the rate stabilization agreement, there were no further issues between the commission and KG&E to be adjudicated.[47] KG&E did not like that, as it said the pattern with the KCC could be repeated, and it wanted a ruling. KG&E had claimed that the KCC action in 1985 was confiscatory, taking property without due compensation and thus violating the 5th and 14th amendments to the U.S. Constitution, and that the valuation for ratemaking of Wolf Creek differently than any other power plant in Kansas was a dangerous precedent that violated KG&E's right to due process and equal protection. Without a definite ruling on those principles, the company feared that those claimed constitutional violations could arise again between it and the KCC in a different context. However, the company had no choice but to accept the Supreme Court decision to drop the case.[48]

The next series of events was even less pleasing to the company. It did get permission late in 1987 to sell and lease back its share of LaCygne 2, which enabled the company to take better advantage of certain tax benefits, buy back 25 percent of its common stock, and refinance higher cost debt.[49] However, in the summer of 1988, prodded by the new CURB organization under its own wing, the KCC wiped out the fourth rate increase of the rate stabilization plan, to take effect in 1992, on the grounds that the sale and leaseback of LaCygne 2 had done enough for KG&E's stockholders. In that order, however, it reiterated its basic commitment to the rate stabilization plan and to the validity of the third rate increase, to take place in 1989. Then in December 1988, just before that rate increase was to take effect, the commission decided to make one-half of the January 1989 rate increase interim and subject to refund. In February 1990 it decided that in fact $8.7 million of that interim should be refunded. The economic overcapacity argument was reintroduced in those hearings, and other issues that had been matters of agreement between KG&E and the KCC since 1987 were treated in a punitive fashion.[50] At part of that hearing held in Wichita, Linda Weir-Enegren of CURB made an emotional appeal, and the commission, with Margalee Wright returning to her hometown in the chair, listened to several hours of pleas for rate relief from the elderly and handicapped organized for the occasion. In the audience that evening sat Wilson Cadman and many KG&E officers and employees, though it was late in the evening before the first witness with anything good to say about the company spoke.[51]

That evening in November 1989, when the emotional hearings in Wichita were reminiscent of the dozens of such confrontations with some of the same people for so many years before, Cadman and Haines believed the polarization was complete. People were locked into their positions and the opposition no longer depended entirely on the spontaneity of events.[52]

Some movement in the social and political climate was recognizable—it was just not of the magnitude that would have allowed the rate stabilization package to stick. There was a long pattern of KG&E and Wolf Creek bashing, a strong constituency for it, and it was not going to creep away quietly. Cadman and others in the company had absorbed great abuse for many years. "There was a cadre of maybe 20 people in this company who we decided would have the abuse heaped on us," said Haines. "We did that because we had to try and shelter the rest of our people and keep the damn electric company going." Cadman had even had part of his house blown up with a plastic bomb. And in the late 1980s the company had taken drastic cost-cutting measures: "We were looking for pennies. We were skating on the brink as our security ratings dropped down, down, down." And, Cadman said in a 1989 interview, perhaps a few of the critics came to have some grudging respect for the result. "Our great company and fine people are vindicated," he argued. "I detect in people I know a certain melancholy, a bit of guilt about the way we've been treated. They're really going out of their way now to reanalyze this thing and say, 'Hey, maybe this thing wasn't all bad.' If it were anything other than a nuclear power plant, people would say: 'Holy Christ! In Kansas, you've done this?' "[53]

There were signs at the turn of the decade of the 1990s that there not only might be a return to nuclear power, but that companies like Kansas Gas and Electric that had gone through the public gauntlet and owned completed and operating nuclear plants might find themselves in time in the catbird seat. Wilson Cadman commented in 1990 that he felt KG&E's temporary excess capacity was a "golden commodity." One industry observer agreed: "The companies that overbuilt in the 1980s are going to be in fat city in the 1990s."[54] While on the one hand voters in Sacramento, California, in 1989 became the first ever to close down a functioning nuclear plant (Rancho Seco) and protests continued full speed at Seabrook, on the other hand there was touting of new, smaller, and safer designs for nuclear plants alongside proposals to build power plants that ran on (this must have been painful for KG&E to listen to), of all things, now plentiful and relatively inexpensive natural gas.[55] The "cold fusion in a bottle" hype of April 1989 turned out to be a scientific April Fools' joke, and, ironically, as power demand increased across the country, brownouts and blackouts threatened with approximately the same range of technical solutions that had existed in the 1960s when Wolf Creek was first envisioned. A survey in 1991 showed "a sudden upsurge in support for nuclear power following a decade of rejection."[56] Low-key ads from an industry group appeared widely on television that year suggesting that the best choice for the environment was a nuclear plant.

Change in energy was again in the air in the 1990s. The Gulf War against Saddam Hussein and Iraq indicated to nuclear power's bitterest opponents some of the consequences of dependence upon alternative available energy sources. Subsidizing intervenors by allowing them full recovery of cost in nuclear cases and holding hearings where witnesses held forth with no cross-examination was different from simple public access, and the history of the 1970s and 1980s generating plant projects, when written, would illustrate the tradeoffs and the costs involved. While there were risks in advancing into a nuclear future, there were risks in not taking that action also. Dr. Jerome Suran of General Electric had spoken at Wichita State University in 1980 on the theme "Attack on Technology—Technology, Society and Conflict." We have, he said, "overglamorized Mother Nature. We've forgotten what the pre-technological world was like. We forget that while it was simpler, it was also more risky." Life required change and change involved calculated risks. "Life has always required man to change his conditions. It's future shock only to those people who refuse to accept the thesis that change is necessary."[57]

Both sides in the Wolf Creek controversy had mixed feelings about the public process in which they participated. James Haines thought the informal local hearing process with a press "pitched into a frenzy" in attendance was a "travesty" and "demeaning to the process."[58] Diane Tegtmeier of MACEA regretted that the adversarial hearing process led to the intervenors' error of "not putting our creative thinking into a more cooperative rather than adversarial" solution before egos became involved in such a way as to make people unable to compromise without losing face. All parties, she observed, had the mindset of emerging as the victor because the process demanded a victor.[59]

In evaluating the meaning of Wolf Creek history, there were also matters of accountability to consider. A newspaper, commenting in 1984 on some of the more extreme proposals of Wolf Creek's critics, noted that "such fantasies are three a penny with those who are not accountable to the public, but they are not available to those who are actually accountable for their actions and must always ask themselves 'compared to what?'"[60] Kent Frizzell, once attorney general of Kansas, noted in a speech in 1984 that the idea of a no-risk future was a "child-like fantasy." There was a finite supply of fossil fuels and Americans had an infinite appetite for energy. "There is no absolute safety. NO risk equates to no future. I submit that no risk is taking the greatest risk of all."[61] One analyst of the late 1980s national scene called the phenomenon "Fear of Living" and suggested that had the Vikings been so timorous, "their ships with the bold prows but frail hulls would have been declared unseaworthy. The Norsemen would have stayed home and jogged," and the world would have been greatly different.[62]

Certainly the 1970s and 1980s marked a large step in an attitude change of Americans toward business and industrialization, which had been going on in some form since the early part of the twentieth century. One might characterize it as a branch of the "Robber Baron" school of interpretation where profit is regarded as necessarily conspiratorial and exploitative, and mistakes become plots hatched by the evil rich in the secrecy of paneled offices insulated from the honest concerns of the "people." Related was the widely held idea that the economy was a "zero-sum" game, where wealth directed one way was denied to another.

There is also perhaps a feeling that, given such wonders, we have surely reached the point of diminishing returns, if not the end of the road in such economic endeavors. Marxist economists claim that citizens in capitalist countries are regularly brainwashed by advertising into perceiving "needs" that they do not really have, which sets off further unnecessary buying frenzies. Probably it is true, at least, that the public may temporarily lack the imagination to see what some new development could mean to them, and cannot therefore envision why they should not be more or less permanently satisfied with the latest wonder. It's like the person who has just eaten a fine meal, or purchased a very satisfactory new car, intended to be "the last car I ever need to own." Who with a brand-new IBM Selectric self-correcting typewriter in the 1960s could have imagined "needing" an electronic word processor? Yet most of us in the 1980s feel we could not possibly get along without one. Self-satisfied people will be clamoring soon for goods and services they are not going to take the lead in producing. "It is time we stopped making heroes of people who talk about things we can't do," said David Lilienthal, commenting on the age of nuclear power, "and honor those who believe there is no limit to human creative ability—political, economic, and technical. Nothing that has happened justifies this negativism we have been passing through. I think you can trace the beginnings of what is still called the recession [spoken in 1975] in the implanting of fear that we have reached the end of the road."

The opponents of nuclear power in Kansas and elsewhere spoke totally different languages. Instead of the next step in a growth psychology, to them the nuclear plant was "inappropriate technology," and the hubris involved in invoking the powers of the universe to run someone's hair dryer was a dangerous phenomenon. To opponents, the nuclear scientists and engineers were "reducing human lives to statistics in a probability equation," while the business people at the utilities were "ready to hop on whoever's bandwagon bolsters their profits." As it had been since it first appeared in print during World War II, the word *nuclear* was the ultimate mysterious and sinister lead media hook. People feared things nuclear as they feared snakes or spiders.

Scholarly literature, while emphasizing the emotional aspects, also often agrees with Margalee Wright that there is a certain innate wisdom or rationality there, which suspects that the scientists and planners have run amuck, that the marginal additions to an already affluent society must be carefully evaluated on the basis of total and real costs, to the environment and society as well as directly, and that the error should be on the side of safety.[63] Understandably it did not look that way to company people at KG&E. Wilson Cadman compared the volatile atmosphere he experienced to the situation that occurred in a yard full of turkeys, where if one turkey got a spot of blood on him, he would be attacked and eaten by the others.[64]

This attitude clearly had an impact on the local and national regulatory environment, and it caught KG&E in the midst of a fundamental change in the nature, scope, and organization of its generating plants of the future. The company in the Wolf Creek era took a big step into an unfamiliar technological environment (nuclear), and an unfamiliar corporate environment (jointly owned power plants), just at the time of maximum external resistance, from which utilities were less protected politically than ever, when there was technological uncertainty in the nuclear industry, and in the midst of a highly unfavorable financial environment. Wolf Creek's history is an ideal case study of adjustment to rapid change, of the kind that may become ever more typical of the future. Ironically, that rate of change escalated just as the planning lead time for the building of a generating facility increased and regulation increased, leaving the utility less flexible than ever in dealing with the changes. It is little wonder there is thought of deregulation, and of the increased use of competition as a regulator in the future.

Arthur Doyle, president of KCPL, told the KCC at the 1985 hearings that he was satisfied, but tired. "If you make Wolf Creek disappear tonight and give me my opportunity election, I would say: give me back Wolf Creek with its present cost and condition. But if I'm looking at it also, which I must, from the standpoint of the stockholder who has for years been subject to a huge risk, emotion, all uncompensated and seeing his investment degrade tremendously so even with dividends in many instances have a negative total yield, I would have to consider and say, no, you know, maybe we ought to do something else because of the political situation and the regulatory situation that has gone on in this country. That's why, of course, we're not going to have any more nuclear plants until there is a major change in the national thinking which I believe is going to come."[65] Bob Hagen put it more simply by saying that no company person who had been through the Wolf Creek experience ever wanted to go through anything like it again.[66]

However, there were others besides Doyle who thought that change would come, or at least *might* come soon, just as the unexpected had happened to change the "givens" quickly and largely in the 1970s. A writer in western Kansas commented in 1984 that "what are now belabored and controversial points [will] be viewed in the future as pinnacles of foresight and wisdom. Given the bizarre and unexpected turns of the past ten years, to anticipate such a scenario is not at all beyond reason."[67] More than one internal expert in the 1980s gave the figure "ten years" from the date Wolf Creek came on line (or about 1995) as a date by which the despised plant would be seen by most of its detractors as a stroke of genius.[68] In time, said Dean Eckhoff at Kansas State, just when the TMI accident had left morale at Wolf Creek at a low point—in time "you'll be eternally glad it's built."[69]

As the 1990s began, there was some evidence that these optimistic prophets might be right, and that the seeming permanent nationwide change occasioned by the virtual shutdown of the U.S. nuclear industry by 1970s and 1980s protest might be at least partially a cycle, or an aberration. The financial situation improved dramatically in the late 1980s, the regulatory environment in Kansas showed some flexibility, the protest was less homogeneous, and nuclear technology began to be less of a pariah in the United States when people spoke of a future which, again, appeared to be largely an electric one.

One result of this shift was that KG&E was again caught between changes, burdened with characteristics fixed partly in what suddenly looked like a passing era. Wolf Creek in the 1990s, complete, operating perfectly, and beyond the agony of its construction, was an attractive asset, while KG&E itself, weakened by protest, by costs, and by supremely punitive regulation, was vulnerable, not so much to the bankruptcy it had feared, but to a takeover, the possibility of which it had been forced largely to accept as an unavoidable risk associated with gradual restoration of financial health. The corporate "raid" had been perfected in the business world generally in the 1980s, but was unheard of in the utility industry. There had not been a hostile takeover attempt there in over 50 years, and there had never been a straight cash offer directly to stockholders.[70] There had also not been a change in the Soviet government in well over 50 years, and no one expected the centralized bureaucracy there to come apart in a matter of days in 1991.

KG&E was in 1990 in the midst of its yearlong 80th birthday celebration. It was putting out old pictures from 1910 forward of its service to the southeast Kansas community, and Wilson Cadman looked forward to a quiet retirement with Wolf Creek pumping out power as a symbol of the company's latest innovation. Then late in July came a piece of surprising, even shocking, news: Kansas City Power & Light, KG&E's partner in the ownership of Wolf Creek, had arranged a credit line of $1 billion and made a tender offer directly to KG&E stockholders of $27 a share, or about $875 million, to purchase Kansas Gas and Electric lock, stock, and barrel.[71] A cartoon in the *Wichita Eagle* showed the familiar KG&E symbol Reddy Kilowatt in a state of shock at receiving a disconnect notice.[72]

KCPL's public reasons were simple. Cadman was approaching retirement age, and the time for a corporate change was before a new generation of leadership took over in Wichita. KCPL's electrical demand was growing and it was faced with building new generating capacity. The price for a single new coal plant would exceed the probable cost to buy KG&E and thus obtain proven and geographically well-located nuclear generating capacity at Wolf Creek.[73]

Analysts enjoyed speculating about more subtle motives, and

about the reasons for the opportunity. Fundamentally, KG&E was vulnerable, not only because of the burden of Wolf Creek, but because of the regulatory treatment of that plant. The KCC had "swallowed hard," said the Monday morning quarterbacks, in approving the rate stabilization bill in March 1987. Then in September 1987 the commission approved the sale and leaseback of KG&E's 50 percent share of LaCygne 2. In a sort of footnote to that decision lay the "Trojan Horse" that had opened the way to the regulatory reverses and the takeover. The KCC in the LaCygne case had ordered the KCC staff to conduct a cost of service audit of the company. "The KCC was now in a position to review all of the post–Wolf Creek regulatory adjustments and make whatever changes it wished." On completion of that audit in July 1988, the commission predictably modified the rate stabilization plan. Not only did subsequent KCC actions negate the regulatory benefits achieved in 1986 and 1987 "but a substantial portion of the gains derived from the austerity program had also been turned over to the ratepayers." The company's per share earnings went from $2.10 in 1988 to $1.36 in 1989. Its return on equity in 1989 was only 6.9 percent. The stock price dropped from 25 3/8 in March 1987 to 19 3/4 in July 1990. In addition, the number of shares held by the public declined because of the sale and leaseback, and therefore market capitalization declined from $1.02 billion in March 1987 to $610 million at the time of the takeover offer. That reduced financial requirement for a cash takeover made such a takeover almost irresistible.[74] Whatever the subtleties, however, the whole train was hooked to one engine—the long history of the building of Wolf Creek. "Kansas Gas and Electric would not be in this position," wrote an analyst for Salomon Brothers, "if they hadn't built the Wolf Creek plant. This is, in a way, the final revenge of a nuclear power plant—to cause the company to be put out of existence."[75]

All recognized that KG&E certainly had a chance to play the takeover, and to use every technique besieged companies had developed in the 1980s to resist it. While Drue Jennings of KCPL downplayed the "unfriendly" part of the "raid," Wilson Cadman thought it was bad manners at best and said so. Cadman, now described as "a direct, intense man who shines in a crisis," had himself a final battle.[76] His opening shot was to advise KG&E shareholders against accepting the KCPL tender offer. As for Jennings's kindly comments,

Cadman compared them to those of the Japanese admiral who told Roosevelt that he had not meant to hurt anyone at Pearl Harbor, but just needed to get the attention of the United States.[77] Reid Ashe of the *Wichita Eagle* wrote that the KG&E–KCPL merger might be a marriage made in heaven—"too bad they're trying to begin it with a rape."[78] A cartoon was pasted in the company notebook showing a bemused couple viewing a sign reading, "Notice: Due to a hostile takeover, today's sensitivity training workshop will be replaced by an assertiveness training workshop."[79]

At first the KCPL offer showed strength. Some KG&E stockholders sued the executive officers of that company, accusing them of rejecting lucrative merger offers in the past at the expense of stockholders and asking that they accept this one.[80] About 43 percent of KG&E's stockholders had by the end of August agreed to sell their shares to KCPL, a record one Wall Street source called a "home run" for KCPL, especially considering that KG&E would not give it access to its stockholder list. The Kansas City company extended its offer and hinted it might raise it.[81] KG&E went looking for a "white knight" to divert the drive by making a competing offer.[82] Meanwhile a date in January 1991 was set for hearings on the merger before the KCC.[83]

The white knight that emerged was The Kansas Power and Light Company (KPL), headquartered in Topeka. It was announced late in October 1990 that KG&E and KPL had agreed to a $1 billion merger that would offer shareholders a cash and stock transaction worth $32 a share.[84] There were questions right away. Wall Street analysts questioned KPL's ability to outbid KCPL and noted that KPL did not have the immediate need for Wolf Creek power.[85] John Hayes, chairman, chief executive, and president of KPL, did not show particular public enthusiasm for the deal. KPL would never have made the offer, he said, except as a defensive move against KCPL. Hostile takeovers, he thought, had no place in the utility industry.[86] Still, on the news of a second bidder, KG&E's stock increased 20 percent in what otherwise was a bad quarter for the regional market.[87]

The Wichita newspaper gave a slight edge to KPL in desirability for Wichita, although, the editor said, "we'll have heartburn either way." Whatever happened, it would be interesting to watch the personalities, particularly with "KG&E's Wilson Cadman, the crusty, strong-willed veteran, facing off against KCPL's Drue Jennings, the polished, calculating financier." As in the whole history of Wolf Creek, there was a marvelous supporting cast—this time including shareholders, employees, regulators, and incumbent managers— each with a different stake and a different point of view.[88] The struggle was billed locally and nationally as "The Great Utility War."

The "war" part, however, soon disappeared. KCPL in December 1990 announced that it was not going to get involved in a bidding war. It was losing support from KG&E stockholders and withdrew its takeover bid officially at the middle of the month.[89] As U.S. aircraft bombed Baghdad, KG&E prepared to return to Topeka for another round with the corporation commission.

The next steps could almost have been predicted by a student of Wolf Creek's history. In February the KCC staff recommended against the merger, largely on the grounds that too much of a premium was being paid by KPL, and KG&E's stock dropped.[90] The CURB organization was against it based on the specifics, though it said the concept was OK, particularly the promise of consumer rate freezes.[91] In March came the KCC hearings.[92] Cadman noted in those hearings that his company had spent $6 million fending off the KCPL bid, and that the end might not be in sight. If KG&E and KPL merged and that new company remained a partner with KCPL in Wolf Creek, another hostile takeover bid by KCPL to swallow the whole thing was "certainly a possibility."[93] It was the second biggest case ever handled by the KCC, next only to the Wolf Creek rate case itself.[94] While all waited for the decision, KG&E gained public relations kudos by distributing service flags to Gulf war troops' families, by issuing a booklet on the "Amazing People of Kansas," and by responding with dispatch to a killer tornado that swept through its trade area. In September came approval of the merger by the KCC, announced in headlines so negative one would almost think it had disapproved. (In May 1992 the merged company was formally renamed Western Resources.) The "strict conditions" imposed would save customers an estimated $223.5 million through 1995.[95] The same month KG&E made a final settlement with CURB over the last of the outstanding Wolf Creek rate issues, which resulted in a refund to customers of more than $7.5 million.[96] As this history is being written, at the end of 1992, KG&E employees are checking maps of Topeka, and expecting that very soon another corporate headquarters in Wichita will become a subsidiary office.

One last "So what?"; maybe not the cosmic "So what?" but the broadest one a book like this one can responsibly address. A medium-sized utility in the middle of Kansas gets in a fuel mix crunch in the midst of an energy crisis, decides to build a nuclear plant, finds that its long lead time catches the center of a sea change in the nuclear issue and the political position of utilities in the United States generally as well as unprecedented inflation, perseveres at the loss of much of its local reputation and financial strength, and is absorbed with its new plant by a neighbor utility only slightly larger. Is that as much as anyone but a stockholder or ratepayer of those concerns, maybe academics interested in business history or regulation, perhaps Kansans in general, needs to know?

Hardly. As stated at the outset, Kansas has been and is a kind of bellwether for the nation—events there often a harbinger of change that is basic rather than merely faddish. Wolf Creek Station was not the first nuclear plant in the United States, but there were indications, not yet entirely disproved, that it might be one of the last. KG&E, the smallest utility in the country attempting to build a nuclear plant, was dealing with a population and a regulatory commission whose populist propensities went back to the very origin of the modern term. The setting for the Wolf Creek story was one of the most rapid change in the rules and in the stakes of nuclear power, and energy generally, of any time in American history, and certainly one where there was no such thing as a purely local phenomenon. Waves from national, even international, events impacted Wolf Creek and vice versa every month of its existence. It was watched. In the bibliography of scholarly accounts of nuclear plants, this study stands as one of the few yet in existence, and there is every reason to believe that understanding the history of these plants in detail is going to be a requirement for improving the performance—public and private, technological and managerial—when (it does not at the moment appear that the question is *if*) another round of nuclear power plants is built in this country.

Wolf Creek was finished because, despite problems, KG&E did certain things right. The siting was generally right. It was relatively isolated, had enough cooling water, and contained space for two plants. The SNUPPS decision was right. Standardization of design is being much touted as a *sine qua non* for the return of nuclear power in the future. SNUPPS allowed much learning and vastly more attention to a conservative design than would otherwise have been possible. It doubtless was a major factor in the technical success of the Wolf Creek reactor. Public relations was right, if not in prescience at least in persistence. Bob Rives was hard to hate, and the managers, however much teeth grinding went on, hung in there and developed responses to each challenge. The fuel deal, brought out of the Westinghouse controversy of 1976, was right and gave Wolf Creek a fuel cost advantage in the long run over every other nuclear plant in the country. The legal team was right, and was able in the rigorous cross-examinations at the extensive hearings to have an impact on the regulatory commissions that created a plausible, if difficult, resolution. The financial innovation was right, allowing KG&E to survive financially in times of extreme challenge and to take advantage of favorable trends and unique opportunities in the era of the rate stabilization agreement. And finally the merger, unprecedented as it was in style, was probably right in creating a broader corporate constituency for Wolf Creek power. In 1992 Wichita is grunching that it still pays higher rates than Kansas City. No doubt in time that historical legacy will smooth out also as inflation of demand and costs for alternative energy, combined with the nuclear advantage in operating costs, catches up with rates. Nuclear plants are supposed to have advantages in the long term, particularly if one ignores the continued bugaboos of decommissioning and waste storage. Wolf Creek at least survived to test that contention, and the determined managers at KG&E were the reason it did.

Clearly, management also did a number of things wrong, and was subject to outside events (like Three Mile Island) with devastating impact. Cost projections were shockingly off; the supervision of construction, especially early, was weak and probably the idea that the utility could subcontract so much of it was flawed; relations with the state legislature and the KCC were poor, partly because Wichita was Wichita and Topeka was Topeka, but partly because of arrogance and mishandling; and there was overconfidence—born partly of fascination and a desire to be high-tech, for all the mundane arguments about the requirement for mixed-fuel use—in the benefits of nuclear power.

But perhaps the most fundamental weakness was in broad aspects of public relations, which in their tactics and style have been listed as a strength. Despite Rives, KG&E shared the fundamental "engineering mentality" of other utilities of this era, and made flawed assumptions about the "growth mentality" of the public over these decades. In making that mistake, KG&E was far from alone. "In a historical sense," one history of the electric industry comments, "the success of nuclear energy seemed almost predestined" as the next step in a succession of fuel changes that had resulted in great takeoffs of economic growth.[97] Yet past technological changes, from the railroad to the airplane to electricity itself, were more effectively "sold" to the public than was nuclear energy. When in the 1950s the "chrome-plated" dreams so widely shared were expressed by the phrase "Better Living Through Chemistry," it was widely assumed that whatever was made could be unmade through science, and that generally science was something that saved us from danger, as in the famous experiment of mixing hydrochloric acid and lye together in a drinkable substance. By the 1980s that attiude toward science had changed, almost without a fight.[98] There was perhaps more recognition, conscious or unconscious, than in earlier, less specialized times, that the introduction of a new device was not purely a technical problem to be debated only among experts, but was a social phenomenon—a humanistic challenge of broad import.[99]

Railroads, wrote Nathaniel Hawthorne, "spiritualized" travel. He called electricity "the demon, the angel, the mighty physical power, the all-pervading intelligence. . . . By means of electricity, the world of matter has become a great nerve vibrating thousands of miles in a breathless point of time. Rather, the round globe is a vast head, a brain, instinct with intelligence! Or, shall we say, it is itself a thought, nothing but thought, and no longer the substance which we deemed it. . . . An almost spiritual medium, like the electric telegraph, should be consecrated to high, deep, joyful and holy missions."[100] I do not suggest that Hawthorne's rhetoric would be appropriate for nuclear plant public relations people today, but something like it is clearly necessary. It is not enough to convince people a new technology is safe, or even that it is desirable in a kind of pedestrian, functional way, but rather that it is somehow humanizing, that it improves human life in some fundamental manner that justifies its various physical and social costs. Otherwise the backers will have the problem of Prometheus.[101]

At the highest level of generalization Wolf Creek teaches three large lessons. First, that public opinion can be brought effectively to bear upon even the most technical issues and in the most seemingly "conservative" places; second, that while the formation of that opinion depends heavily upon emotion, its results are economic; and third, that the public regulation of "natural monopolies" is a device flawed in advancing the interests of either corporations or consumers, assuming that these interests are in fact necessarily separate.

A conclusion that might be drawn from the events discussed here is that building nuclear plants that were reasonably satisfactory to all elements of society was beyond the capability of the United States in the 1980s. Wolf Creek, at least in hindsight, is seen to be one of the best operating nuclear plants ever built, and it was built at no more than average expense with no more than average protest. Yet witness its unquestionably traumatic story. Perhaps the times were a little "out of joint," focused, as one author contends, overmuch on fear and "fretting" while dreaming of a risk-free society, and one need not make assumptions of an exactly parallel environment in preparing for the future.[102]

It appears that the nuclear industry will survive, but that as a result of the saga of Wolf Creek and its sisters in the 1970s, the part of American companies and American workers in it will be severely diminished. The parts boxes at Wolf Creek in 1991 often read "Hitachi." The National Power Development Company, located in Overland Park, Kansas, is a subsidiary of the Marubeni Corporation of Tokyo, a giant Japanese trading company. Marubeni established this subsidiary in Kansas in 1986, just after the Wolf Creek rate decision, to investigate the possibility of building new nuclear plants in the United States, maybe even in Kansas.[103]

What of the flaws in the process? How might the history have been different with a different system, and therefore, by implication, how might it be different in the future should the basic adventure of entrepreneurial growth still remain attractive to many Americans? Clearly, a question arising from the history of Wolf Creek is, "Who did government protect and from what, to justify the cost added by regulation to the project?" Perhaps at least there should be some kind of "value detracted" calculation to evaluate the role of regulation in such projects. The WPSS story in Washington state clearly indicates that one alternative to regulated monopoly, public power, would not necessarily have helped. The bumper sticker summary of the irate ratepayers there about direct public supervision of nuclear plants was that "they promised us power without cost, and they have delivered cost without power."[104]

The details are in the narrative, but at base, the Wolf Creek story calls into question the model of the regulated "natural monopoly," and calls it into question from the point of view of both the protestors and the utility companies. According to the theory, centralized power production creates overwhelming cost and efficiency advantages, and regional monopoly adds to that by preventing duplication. Of course, such monopoly also prevents competition, and to protect the public against the abuse that situation might bring, a political body, presumably representative of the "people," stands in place of the market and tries to substitute for its actions. Some problems with this are that centralized planning utilizes the inadequate wisdom of only a few, fixes the model in time without flexibility for change or innovation, and subjects decisionmaking to the dictates of the politically effective—with all the implications of emotionalism, electioneering, and lack of accountability that implies—rather than the thousands of quiet, but personally meaningful decisions of individual consumers in a market. It is possible that both consumers and utilities would have been better off in the Wolf Creek situation had both made decisions that were confirmed or rejected by a competitive marketplace.

There is every reason to believe that future utility technology will be in the direction of smaller-sized plants, as well as vastly more efficient and miniaturized transmission systems. That, combined with bitter experience with the Insull quasi-public monopoly model in Kansas and elsewhere, may suggest to all the punished in the nuclear battles that a fundamental change in the system is in order. Wolf Creek's story suggests that the proper incentive may not have been present with either the business, the politicians, or the consumers to make the best decisions for all. Good intentions, after all, do not necessarily lead to good results. And, however heretical it may seem to some involved in the Wolf Creek debate, under the right conditions, capitalism can indeed be a generous system. When businesses are forced to serve consumers' needs or are threatened by competitors who do, and when consumers are forced to vote with their money rather than their mouths, decisions become more realistic.

A characteristic of the late twentieth century, as it has been to a lesser degree of the entire century, is escalating rapidity of change and of complexity. This makes decisionmaking more difficult, but does not obviate the necessity. As long as humankind is stuck on earth and responsible for decisionmaking and commitment at a certain time, and in the face of some uncertainty about the present and much uncertainty about the future, such decisionmaking is going to be a feature of meaningful, dare we say "progressive," civilization. One is reminded of the Zen poem about overthoughtfulness: "The centipede was happy quite / Until a frog in fun / Said, 'pray which leg comes before which?' / Since, the poor fellow has lain in a ditch / Considering how to run." Yes, the decisionmakers must decide, and the second-guessers will second-guess, and there will be risk. Doubtless such a thing as nuclear power is not something subject to "pure" free-enterprise with no social and environmental agenda set by a political process. But those elements that are, that must be, set politically could perhaps be better done if others were relieved from the stress of deciding them that way, and they were left to the market. The tragedy of Wolf Creek was that the rules of engagement with nature and with the choices of customers were so many, and were therefore often unclear and inadequate, and that the lead time on rule changes shortened as the lead time on generating plant construction lengthened. Politics and the accompanying legal maneuvering is a polarizing process, and it will polarize to the point of helplessness if it is too broadly applied. That, among other things, was the wisdom of the founding fathers' philosophy of limited government. It is also one of the lessons of the history of Wolf Creek Station.

There were fundamental questions in the Wolf Creek situation of nature versus culture. As Spencer Weart puts it in *Nuclear Fear: A History of Images*, people are constantly trying to balance wilderness and civilization, wild and controlled things, Dionysian and Apollonian, "natural" impulses and self-control and planning, hierarchy and authority versus liberty, even the contrast of male and female seen in the makeup of the conflicting sides in nuclear confrontations. The planning and control associated with the building of an industrial artifact like Wolf Creek Station can be frightening and appear cold, unintimate, even inhuman. It, therefore, is instinctively perceived as being as dangerous as radiation itself.[105] "Who so hath his minde on taking, hath it no more on what he hath taken," wrote Montaigne, quoted in a new context in the 1970s by Wendell Berry.

Marge Setter, a KG&E director, observed that the protestors seemed to think "some divine providence had promised them that everything was trouble free, and they had a right to expect that." It was as though, she said, "they were defying even the street lights that made the traffic move more smoothly," and seemed to want an insurance policy against being trampled by an elephant in downtown Wichita. They debated things on the level of Aquinas's first cause uncaused, which a woman like Setter thought was fine in philosophy class, but not in the real world where real-time decisions with real, and relatively short-term consequences, must be made. "You have to sit on your own blisters," she said, make your decision and live with it until you can change it.[106]

Weart admits that the abstract, and maybe highly philosophical contrasts, and therefore seeming choices, that he mentions are more rooted in psychology and in images than in reality. Still, clearly, the appeal to "nature" was a strong way to build a constituency—for who could be against it? It was not enough to call the mindset of your opponent "ludicrous," and then to attack it with your own unshared assumptions. Passion and self-consciousness were as prominent among the players at Wolf Creek as common sense. Without changing the rhetoric within which nuclear debates take place, without calling into fundamental question some of the assumptions that are probably axiomatic to both sides, as well as endemic to each, changes in the political terms of engagements, or improvements in technology will not alone have adequate effect.

In some ways Wolf Creek was a symbol as much as a functional artifact, and the controversy swirling around it involved as much art as craft. In 1893 at the Columbian Exposition, Henry Adams was taken into the great hall of dynamos. There he mused famously on the new electric technology as a cultural, even religious, symbol equivalent in motivating and awe-inspiring power to the Virgin in the Middle Ages: in fact, he called that machine "a symbol of infinity."[107]

Doubtless Adams's famous comments, like so many of their type, were considerably overdrawn. Talk in the 1970s about the "Electric God" was just that—talk. There is no evidence that the power plant was ever a religious icon to Americans, but plenty of evidence that it was a symbol of a powerful secular ideal. Secular ideals and religious icons in America have not always stayed conveniently in their separate spheres, but mix awkwardly in the roots of human action. Separating them legally, as though spirit and intellect were separable, may be one of the fundamental problems of our constitutional processes.

However, such symbols are vital to any culture. If we destroy the dynamo as symbol if not in fact because we no longer believe in what it represents, then the question arises, What do we believe in, and what are its appropriate symbols and earthly manifestations? Do we go back to the Virgin, or forward to what? Is it possible to be an age without ideals—self-satisfied, free of ambition, wanting only peaceably to be left alone? Nothing suggests a lack of passion and vaunting ambition in our own age, but our force appears disjointed and therefore, to some degree, self-destructive. There are unhealthy extremes of individualism as well as of centralization. More than one scholar has suggested that "paradigms," however much they may involve some simplification and a compromise of the best individual perception, are absolutely vital to progress toward any end. Certainly there are cultures fixed on some ideal ready to take the ground that Americans may abandon. Therefore it is vital that we abandon it at least on purpose.

It is easy to say that the real answer suggested by the nuclear power conflict in Kansas is that to avoid mutual punishment we must bring our discourse, procedures, and attitudes closer into line with the complicated and often ambiguous nature of things. That, of course, requires vocabulary, background, information, sophistication in a large number of people, and a media that plays to the best in us rather than the most easily aroused. It requires engineers who are at least a little humanist, and philosophers who are a little businesslike. It requires rational tradeoffs, and an understanding that good always produces evil, but that it is a question of a positive change in the mix. Otherwise, we will not only kill the goose that lays the golden eggs, but also the one that lays the ordinary eggs. There is no unhappiness greater than the vain and single search for perfection, unless it is to have no ambition at all. The moderate mean has fallen out of favor, but with it, perhaps, so has wisdom.

CONCLUSION

"Fain wou'd I have persuaded you to think with more Equality of NATURE," wrote Anthony, Earl of Shaftesbury, in a 1709 essay called "The Moralists: A Rhapsody": "and to proportion her Defects a little better. My Notion was, that the Grievance lay not altogether in *one* part, as you placed it; but that *everything* had its share of inconvenience. Pleasure and Pain, Beauty and Deformity, Good and Ill, seem'd to me every-where interwoven, and one with another made, I thought, a pretty Mixture, agreeable enough, in the main. Twas' the same, I fancy'd, as in some of those rich Stuffs, where the Flowers and Ground were oddly put together, with such irregular Work, and contrary Colours, as look'd ill in *the Pattern*, but mighty natural and well *in the Piece*. But you were still upon extremes."[108]

Notes

PREFACE

1. T. B. Macaulay, "History," from *Edinburgh Review*, May 1828, in Macaulay, *Critical Historical and Miscellaneous Essays by Lord Macaulay*, 6 vols. in 3 (Boston: Houghton Osgood, 1878), 2:377, 387–88.

2. Anthony, Earl of Shaftesbury, "Advice to an Author," in *Charakteristiks of Men Morals Opinions and Times*, 3 vols., 5th ed. (Birmingham: John Baskerville, 1773), 1:135, 193.

3. Charles Schulz, "Peanuts," in *Wichita Eagle*, January 13, 1991.

4. Ralph Waldo Emerson, *An Oration Delivered Before the Phi Beta Kappa Society at Cambridge, August 31, 1837* (Boston: James Munroe, 1837), p. 7.

INTRODUCTION

1. For example, see Leo Marx, *The Machine in the Garden: Technology and the Pastoral Ideal in America* (New York: Oxford University Press, 1964) and John Stilgoe, *Metropolitan Corridor: Railroads and the American Scene* (New Haven: Yale University Press, 1983).

2. Wilson Cadman, *Kansas Gas and Electric Company: Eighty Years of Innovation* (New York: Newcomen Society of the United States, 1989), p. 9; Andre Millard, *Edison and the Business of Innovation* (Baltimore: Johns Hopkins University Press, 1990), pp. 105–6.

3. Mark Hertsgaard, *Nuclear Inc: The Men and Money Behind Nuclear Energy* (New York: Pantheon, 1983), p. 10.

4. See Herbert Muller, *The Children of Frankenstein: A Primer on Modern Technology and Human Values* (Bloomington: Indiana University Press, 1970); Michael Adas, *Machines as the Measure of Men: Science, Technology, and Ideologies of Western Dominance* (Ithaca, NY: Cornell University Press, 1989); Arnold Pacey, *The Maze of Ingenuity: Ideas and Idealism in the Development of Technology* (New York: Holmer & Meier, 1975).

5. Connell's novel *Mr. Bridge* was published in 1969, just as KCPL's involvement in the Wolf Creek project was beginning.

6. Robert Bader, *Hayseeds, Moralizers, and Methodists: The Twentieth Century Image of Kansas* (Lawrence: University Press of Kansas, 1988).

7. Ibid, pp. 112–13, 128–29.

8. Paola, Kansas newspaper 1905, quoted in Craig Miner, *Discovery: Cycles of Change in the Kansas Oil & Gas Industry 1860–1987* (Wichita: KIOGA, 1987), p. 111.

9. For the context, see Sally Foreman Griffith, *Home Town News: William Allen White & the Emporia Gazette* (New York: Oxford University Press, 1989).

10. For example, see Richard Hirsh, *Technology and Transformation in the American Electric Utility Industry* (Cambridge: Cambridge University Press, 1989).

11. The quote is from Henry Bedford, *Seabrook Station: Citizen Politics and Nuclear Power* (Amherst: University of Massachusetts Press, 1990), p. xi.

12. Bedford, in *Seabrook*, p. 19, calls it "cynical theater." Richard Rudolph and Scott Ridley, in *Power Struggle: The Hundred Year War Over Electricity* (New York: Harper & Row, 1986), p. xii, comment that "regulation of the industry was steadily undermined by a coordinated system of political influence and lobbying."

13. *Servicegraph* [KG&E company magazine] (May 1974), p. 2.

14. For background, see Harold Passer, *The Electrical Manufacturers, 1875–1900: A Study in Competition, Entrepreneurship, Technical Change and Economic Growth* (Cambridge: Harvard University Press, 1953). A summary of Insull's thinking is in Sheldon Novick, *The Electric War: The Fight Over Nuclear Power* (San Francisco: Sierra Club, 1976), pp. 113–36, 219ff. See also Forrest McDonald, *Insull* (Chicago: University of Chicago Press, 1962).

15. This point is made in Hirsh, *Technology and Transformation*, p. 33.

16. *Servicegraph* (Dec. 1959), p. 8.

17. Kansas Gas and Electric Company, "A Response to the 1984 Amendments of K.S.A. 66–128, Oct. 1984," typescript, p. 150, KG&E archives; Federal Power Commission, *Reclassification of Electric Plant in Accordance with Uniform System of Accounts and Order of May 11, 1937 Issued by the Federal Power Commission. Statements 'A' to 'T' Inclusive of Kansas Gas and Electric Company*, KG&E archives. This document with its forbidding title is a sound historical compendium, especially section 'A' on the origin and development of KG&E. The company, in preparing its input to the report, hired a researcher who copied every energy-related item he could find in the Wichita newspapers from 1872 to 1940. Seldom has a summary for a regulatory body been based on more thorough primary historical investigation. For further background history see *Servicegraph*, Oct. 1974; Dec. 1959, pp. 1–3, 8; Aug. 1949, p. 3; C. V. Waddington, "The Development of the Kansas Gas and

Electric Company System from an Engineering Point of View," (BS thesis, University of Kansas, April 28, 1939); and Kansas Gas and Electric Company, *Information Pertaining to the Company's Business and Operations* (Wichita: 201 N. Market, Feb. 1949).

18. *Servicegraph* (April 1964), p. 7.

19. A good overview of the history and nature of electric utilities is found in Leonard Hyman, *America's Electric Utilities: Past, Present and Future* (Arlington, VA: Public Utilities Project, 1983).

20. Ralph W. Emerson, "Beauty," in *Conduct of Life* (New York: Ticknor and Fields, 1860), p. 249.

21. William Dean Howells, "A Sennight of the Centennial," *Atlantic Monthly* 38 (1876): 96.

22. Thomas P. Hughes, *American Genesis: A Century of Invention and Technological Enthusiasm, 1870–1970* (New York: Viking, 1989), p. 24.

23. For an analysis, see Alan Trachtenberg, *Brooklyn Bridge: Fact and Symbol* (New York: Oxford University Press, 1965).

24. Henry James, *The American Scene* (New York: Harper & Brothers, 1907), p. 72.

25. *The Collected Poems of Hart Crane*, ed. Waldo Frank (New York: Liveright, 1946), p. 4.

26. Ronald Inglehart, "The Fear of Living Dangerously: Public Attitudes Toward Nuclear Power," *Public Opinion* 7 (1984), 1:41–44.

27. Hughes, *American Genesis*, pp. 1, 8, 13.

28. Hirsh, *Technology and Transformation*, p. 3.

29. Henry D. Lloyd, *Wealth Against Commonwealth* (New York: Harper & Brothers, 1894), p. 2.

30. David Shi, *The Simple Life: Plain Living and High Thinking in American Culture* (New York: Oxford University Press, 1985).

31. This summary comes from a speech the author heard by Jackson, entitled "Learning from the Land" in the spring of 1992. Two recent books are helpful in understanding this outlook: Wes Jackson, *Altars of Unhewn Stone: Science and the Earth* (San Francisco: North Point Press, 1987) and Wendell Berry, *Home Economics* (San Francisco: North Point Press, 1987).

32. Paul Pilzer, *Unlimited Wealth* (New York: Crown, 1991). Pilzer is a former officer of Citibank and economic advisor to the Reagan and Bush administrations. His book is only one example of a genre.

33. Quoted in Hyman, *America's Electric Utilities*, p. 29.

34. Hirsch, in *Technology and Transformation*, p. 73, argues that the mindset of the engineer/managers was that "simple profitability" was subordinate to technological leadership.

35. The phrase was used by KG&E Vice President James Haines in an interview with the author, June 27, 1990.

36. Margaret Bangs, interview with the author, April 2, 1990.

37. Charles Cobb, Jr., "Living with Radiation," *National Geographic* 175 (April 1989), 4:410.

38. The author was told this during a tour of Wolf Creek while fuel rods were being changed, April 1990. The reactor was not operating, but the reason for the alltime low radiation levels in the plant was not that, the operators explained, but rather the fact that the containment building could be opened and the radon could escape.

39. Spencer Weart, *Nuclear Fear: A History of Images* (Cambridge, MA: Harvard University Press, 1988), preface, pp. 15, 59, 183 ff.

40. Margaret Bangs, interview with the author, April 2, 1990.

41. Samuel McCracken, *The War Against the Atom* (New York: Basic Books, 1982), pp. 95–96.

42. James Haines, interview with the author, July 10, 1990.

43. Euripedes, *The Bakkhai*, translated by Robert Bagg (Amherst: University of Massachusetts Press, 1978), pp. 4–5.

44. McCracken, *The War Against the Atom*, p. 104.

45. Diane Tegtmeier, interview with the author, June 19, 1990.

46. A good summary of the impact of these works upon alternative thinking is in Hughes, *American Genesis*, p. 443ff.

47. E. F. Schumacher, *Small is Beautiful: Economics as If People Mattered* (New York: Harper & Row, 1975), pp. 265–67. A summary of the reading and thinking of the counterculture toward technology especially as it manifested itself in the 1960s is in Theodore Rosak, *The Making of A Counter Culture* (New York: Doubleday, 1969).

48. Robert Hirsh, in *Technology and Transformation*, suggests that most utility managers had an engineering background, and therefore were fixed on using the engineering method to solve problems, even in contradistinction to the profit motive.

49. McCracken, *The War Against the Atom*, p. 99.

50. James Haines, "Opening Statement, Wolf Creek Rate Case, May 13, 1985," typescript, KG&E legal department, p. 1.

CHAPTER 1

1. Robert Branyan and Lawrence Larson, eds., *The Eisenhower Administration 1953–1961: A Documentary History* (New York: Random House, 1971), pp. 194–200.

2. Peter Stoler, *Decline and Fall: The Ailing Nuclear Power Industry* (New York: Dodd, Mead & Co., 1985), pp. 16–39, provides a good summary of these events. For the earlier background Richard Rhodes's book, *The Mak-*

ing of the Atomic Bomb (New York: Simon & Schuster, 1988), can hardly be improved upon. For the corporate involvement see Mark Hertsgaard, *Nuclear Inc: The Men and Money Behind Nuclear Energy* (New York: Pantheon, 1983).

3. Richard Rudolph and Scott Ridley, *Power Struggle: The Hundred Year War Over Electricity* (New York: Harper & Row, 1986), p. xi. On the early history of electric utilities, see also Thomas Hughes, *Networks of Power: Electrification in Western Society, 1880–1930* (Baltimore: Johns Hopkins University Press, 1983).

4. Hirsh, *Technology and Transformation*, pp. 7, 73–75.

5. *Servicegraph* (Nov. 1933).

6. *Wichita Eagle*, Feb. 24, 1938, quoted in *Servicegraph* (March 1938).

7. *Servicegraph* (June 1951), p. 11.

8. Ibid. (May 1952), p. 10.

9. Ibid. (April 1953). KG&E, *Annual Report 1954*, p. 8.

10. Speech by Gordon Evans, in *Servicegraph* (Jan. 1957).

11. KG&E, *Annual Report 1952*, p. 6 and passim.

12. Ibid., *1953*.

13. *Servicegraph* (Oct. 1958).

14. Hirsh, *Technology and Transformation*, pp. 111–17.

15. James M. Jasper, "The Political Life Cycle of Technological Controversies," *Social Forces* 67, no. 2 (1988): 360–61.

16. Elmer Hall, interview with the author, Feb. 16, 1989. Mr. Hall died during the second year of research on this history.

17. KG&E, *Annual Report 1954*, pp. 14–15.

18. Ibid., *1955*, p. 12.

19. *Servicegraph* (Dec. 1954), p. 14.

20. *Wichita Eagle*, Aug. 11, 1957; *Servicegraph* (April 1957), p. 9. Although the *Eagle* undergoes several name changes during this period, finally returning to the original, it will be cited throughout as *Wichita Eagle*.

21. *Servicegraph* (Aug. 1957), pp. 6–8.

22. Jean Worth, in *Wichita Eagle*, Dec. 14, 1958.

23. Samuel McCracken, *The War Against the Atom* (New York: Basic Books, 1982), pp. 3–10; Rhodes, *The Making of the Atomic Bomb*; Michael Golay and Neil Todreas, "Advanced Light-Water Reactors," *Scientific American* (April 1990), p. 82; William Lawrence, *Men and Atoms: The Discovery, the Uses and the Future of Atomic Energy* (New York: Simon and Schuster, 1959).

24. Jean Worth, in *Wichita Eagle*, Dec. 14, 1958.

25. *Servicegraph* (Dec. 1959), p. 12.

26. Ibid. (Jan. 1961), pp. 2-3; (Jan. 1962), p. 3.

27. KG&E, *Annual Report 1963*, pp. 10–11; *Annual Report 1962*, p. 8.

28. *Lawrence Journal World*, July 18, 1982. See also *Kansas City Times*, Oct. 6, 1982. The decommissioning of this reactor in the 1980s was a much bigger public issue than its commissioning in the 1960s.

29. J. D. Hixson, *SEFOR Plant Operating Experience* (Sunnyvale, CA: General Electric Corp., 1972), pp. 3-2, 1-1; *Servicegraph* (Aug. 1967), pp. 6–7.

30. Mel Johnson, interview with the author, Nov. 29, 1989; *Servicegraph* (March 1966), p. 7. Johnson was at SEFOR representing GE from 1967 on and was manager in the early 1970s.

31. *Servicegraph* (Jan. 1967), p. 8.

32. Ibid. (Nov. 1965), p. 3.

33. McCracken, *War Against the Atom*, pp. 33–35. McCracken calls the furor about plutonium "melodramatic piffle." *Kansas City Times*, April 15, 1982.

34. Mel Johnson, interview with the author, Nov. 29, 1991. However, as shall be seen, it continued to be a potent attention-getter to a public unconvinced by these denials. The Arterburn story is from Harley Macklin, interview with the author, July 17, 1989.

35. *Servicegraph* (Aug. 1967), p. 6.

36. U.S. Nuclear Regulatory Commission, "In the Matter of Kansas Gas and Electric Company and Kansas City Power and Light Company (Wolf Creek Generating Station, Unit No. 1)." Docket no. 50-482 (20 vols., 1975–1976), vol. 17, Feb. 25, 1976, pp. 2785–86, transcript, KG&E archives. Hereafter cited as Construction Permit Hearings.

37. *Servicegraph* (Feb. 1965), pp. 6–7.

38. Elmer Hall, interview with the author, Feb. 16, 1989. *Servicegraph* interview with Hall on blackout, Jan. 1966, pp. 2–3. There is an extensive foldout "Chronology of Events Affecting KG&E and the WCGS" contained in Cresap, McCormick and Paget, "A Prudence Review of KG&E's Involvement in the Wolf Creek Generating Station," (Oct. 1984), KG&E archives. Hereafter cited as Cresap, "Prudence Review"; "timeline" added where applicable.

39. Testimony of Arthur Doyle, May 29, 1985, in Kansas Corporation Commission, "In the Matter of a General Investigation of the Commission of the Projected Costs and Related Matters of the Wolf Creek Nuclear Generation Facility at Burlington, Kansas." Docket no. 120, 925-U et al. Transcript of Proceedings, May 1985, 39 vols., 13:3452. Hereafter cited as 1985 Rate Case.

40. Cresap, McCormick and Paget, "Report on the Financial and Operational Study of the Wolf Creek Nuclear Generating Facility," (Nov. 1980), typescript, KG&E archives, p. I-15. "Chronology of Major Events," memo from Bob Rives to the author, Feb. 8, 1985.

41. Testimony of George Roen, May 20, 1985, 1985 Rate Case, 6:1948.

42. *Kansas City Times*, Nov. 18, 1971.

43. Harley Macklin, interview with the author, July 17, 1989.
44. "Symposium on the Wolf Creek Nuclear Power Plant," *University of Kansas Law Review* 33 (Spring 1985), p. 421.
45. Harley Macklin, interview with the author, July 17, 1989; Cresap, "Prudence Review," timeline.
46. Cresap, "Prudence Review," timeline.
47. Testimony of Arthur Doyle, May 29, 1985, 1985 Rate Case, 9:3543.
48. Testimony of Wilson Cadman, May 23, 1985, 1985 Rate Case, 9:2537–38, 2587, 2590.
49. Cresap, "Prudence Review," timeline.
50. Testimony of Arthur Doyle, May 29, 1985, 1985 Rate Case, 13:3446, 3462.
51. Testimony of Donald McPhee, May 30, 1985, 1985 Rate Case, 14:3892.
52. Cresap, "Prudence Review," IV-58ff, timeline; Harley Macklin, interview with the author, July 17, 1989; *Servicegraph* (April 1968), back of front cover.
53. Harley Macklin, interview with the author, July 17, 1989; Donna Dilsaver, interview with the author, July 17, 1989; testimony of James Lucas, May 28, 1985, 1985 Rate Case, 11:3208.
54. *Topeka Capital Journal*, Feb. 20, 1977.
55. Harley Macklin, interview with the author, July 17, 1989.
56. *Wall Street Journal*, June 14, 1977.
57. Harley Macklin, interview with the author, July 17, 1989.
58. *Wichita Eagle*, Aug. 8, 1976.
59. Cresap, "Prudence Review," III-62, IV-75.
60. Harley Macklin, interview with the author, July 17, 1989.
61. *Kansas City Times*, Dec. 4, 1980.
62. Testimony of Arthur Doyle, May 29, 1985, 1985 Rate Case, 13:3447, 3452, 3455, 3465; Cresap; "Prudence Review," timeline.
63. "Chronology of Major Events," Feb. 8, 1985.
64. Cresap, "Prudence Review," III-28.
65. Testimony of Arthur Doyle, May 29, 1985, 1985 Rate Case, 13:3652–53, 3679–80.
66. Cresap, "Prudence Review," III-27–29, IV-60–62, 79.
67. Testimony of Donald McPhee, May 30, 1985, 1985 Rate Case, 14:3842. Studies indicated that the incremental cost of increasing the plant from 950 to 1150 mw was only $2.5 million, or $12.50 per kw.
68. Gerald Charnoff, "Why Managers Did It All Right: Overregulation and Other Acts of God," "Symposium on Wolf Creek," *University of Kansas Law Review*, p. 485.
69. Cresap, "Prudence Review," IV-60–62, 79, timeline.

70. Harley Macklin, interview with the author, July 17, 1989.
71. Testimony of Arthur Doyle, May 29, 1985, 1985 Rate Case, 13:3469.
72. Cresap, "Prudence Review," IV-61.
73. Harley Macklin, interview with the author, July 17, 1989. Kansas Gas and Electric Company, Kansas City Power & Light Company, Kansas Electric Power Cooperative, Inc., *Management Performance Evaluation. Wolf Creek Generating Station* (May 1984), p. 11. This is known as the "Huston report" because consultant Charles Huston was its main author. It will be so cited hereafter.
74. Huston report, pp. 11–12.
75. Testimony of Arthur Doyle, May 29, 1985, 1985 Rate Case, 13:3670; testimony of Donald McPhee, May 30, 1985, 1985 Rate Case, 14:3838, 3853; testimony of George Roen, May 20, 1985, 1985 Rate Case 7:1965–66. An exact breakdown of estimate of cost savings from SNUPPS is in Huston report, p. 10.
76. *Emporia Gazette*, Sept. 29, 1975.
77. Testimony of Warren Wood, May 13, 1985, 1985 Rate Case, 1:55; Cresap, "Prudence Review," timeline.
78. *Servicegraph* (March 1973), inside cover.
79. Testimony of Donald McPhee, May 29, 1985, 1985 Rate Case, 13:3469.
80. *Kansas City Times*, March 7, 1973.
81. KG&E, *Annual Report 1973*.
82. KG&E, *Annual Report 1968*, p. 11.
83. KG&E, *The Core of the Great Plains* (Wichita, KS: Author, 1955), p. 19.
84. *Wichita Eagle*, March 4, 1984.

CHAPTER 2

1. Wilson Cadman, interview with the author, March 10, 1989. *Wichita Journal*, June 18, 1977, discusses the early opinion surveys; *Neodesha Daily Sun*, June 10, 1977.
2. *Servicegraph* (Nov. 1956), p. 4.
3. Ibid. (June 1969), p. 6.
4. Ibid. (Jan. 1962), p. 2.
5. The book, by John Fuller, was published by the Reader's Digest Press in 1975. Samuel McCracken, in *The War Against the Atom*, p. 36, characterizes Fuller's book as "extremely ignorant and sensational." Of course, McCracken's book is an *apologia* for nuclear power. See also Richard Lewis, *The Nuclear Power Rebellion: Citizens vs. the Atomic Industrial Establishment* (New York: Viking, 1972), p. 244, and Stoler, *Decline*, p. 99. There was coolant blockage at Fermi that caused a partial meltdown. The plant was reopened in 1972 and then closed, some say for safety, others for economic reasons.

6. Kenneth Keniston, *Youth and Dissent: The Rise of a New Opposition* (New York: Harcourt Brace Jovanovich, 1971), pp. viii, 27, 292.

7. Cresap, "Prudence Review," III-30, 34; *University of Kansas Law Review* (Spring 1985), p. 486.

8. James Haines, interview with the author, July 10, 1990.

9. For a careful discussion of this phenomenon in Kansas, see Sid Shapiro, "Utility Regulation and Public Input," in *University of Kansas Law Review* (Spring 1985), pp. 491–500.

10. Cresap, "Prudence Review," III-68–69.

11. The Quantrill's raiders quotation is from Lewis, *Rebellion*, where a summary of these events is found on pp. 148–70.

12. Ibid., p. 158.

13. *Yates Center* (Kansas) *News*, Aug. 28, 1980. See also McDowell's history of the controversy in *Emporia Gazette*, Nov. 29, 1980.

14. *Wichita Journal*, June 18, 1977.

15. For pollution and aesthetic issues see *Servicegraph* (March 1970), p. 13 and (Aug. 1970), p. 1. Catfish are documented in (Jan. 1971), p. 6.

16. Ibid. (May 1970), pp. 1–6.

17. Ibid. (July 1971), pp. 2–3; (Dec. 1973), p. 5.

18. Ibid. (July 1973), p. 2.

19. *Iola Register*, Feb. 6, 1974.

20. Ibid., May 14, 1974.

21. Quoted in *LeRoy* (Kansas) *Reporter*, Jan. 4, 1974. The 30,000-page collection of newspaper clippings in the KG&E archives provides extensive documentation of the counternuclear movement in Kansas and the evolution of regional public opinion on the issue.

22. *Topeka Daily Capital*, Nov. 25, 1974. The Union of Concerned Scientists and the Sierra Club said at that time that they "didn't dispute the contention that major reactor accidents are less probable than other typical human activities," but were concerned about the severity when and if they did happen.

23. *Kansas City Star Magazine*, May 1, 1977; *Kansas City Star*, April 6, 1980; *Wichita Eagle*, May 6, 1974.

24. Jane Edwards, in *Burlington* (Kansas) *Daily Republican*, Feb. 21, 1974, quoting 1973 letters.

25. *Kansas City Star Magazine*, May 1, 1977; *Iola Register*, May 14, 1974; Dec. 11, 1974; *Kansas City Star*, June 25, 1978; *Emporia Gazette*, June 6, 1977.

26. Diane Tegtmeier, interview with the author, June 12, 1990. For a sample of Salava's sources see her letter to *Iola Register*, March 20, 1974, where she quotes Daniel Ford and Hannes Alfven.

27. *LeRoy* (Kansas) *Reporter*, Jan. 4, 1974.

28. *LeRoy* (Kansas) *Reporter*, Feb. 22, 1974; *Wichita Eagle*, May 6, 1974; *Salina Journal*, Feb. 8, 1976.

29. *Topeka Capital Journal*, Oct. 19, 1975.
30. *Burlington Daily Republican*, Sept. 4, 1974.
31. Francis Blaufuss to Bob Rives, Nov. 13, 1974, KG&E nuclear clippings.
32. Paid advertisement in *Burlington Daily Republican*, Oct. 3, 1974.
33. Francis Blaufuss to Bob Rives, Nov. 13, 1974, KG&E nuclear clippings.
34. There is a picture of him and this getup in *Topeka State Journal*, March 3, 1975.
35. *Burlington Daily Republican*, Feb. 24, 1975; Oct. 24, 1974.
36. Wanda Christy, in *Chanute Tribune*, April 15, 1974.
37. *Iola Register*, May 8, 1974.
38. *Chanute Tribune*, Nov. 23, 1974; *Kansas City Star*, Dec. 6, 1974.
39. *Kansas City Times*, March 4, 1974.
40. The phrase comes from *Burlington Daily Republican*, March 24, 1975, and was coined by Dr. Peter Beckmann, a professor of electrical engineering at the University of Colorado.
41. *Chanute Tribune*, April 22, 1975.
42. *Burlington Daily Republican*, April 24, 1975, quoting *St. Louis Globe Democrat*, April 12, 1975.
43. Loretta Young to Bob Rives, May 5, 1974, KG&E nuclear clippings.
44. *Iola Register*, May 9, 1974.
45. *Ottawa Herald*, May 17, 1974.
46. *Wichita Eagle*, Nov. 5, 1974.
47. *LeRoy* (Kansas) *Reporter*, Jan. 31, 1975.
48. The account of the founding of MACEA is drawn from Diane Tegtmeier, interview with the author, June 12, 1990; *Wichita Eagle*, May 19, 1977; *Topeka Capital Journal Magazine*, Nov. 13, 1977.
49. Jack King, interview with the author, Feb. 17, 1989; *Servicegraph* (May 1972), p. 4.
50. *Burlington Daily Republican*, Jan. 4, 1974.
51. *Chanute Tribune*, March 29, 1974; *Garnett Anderson Countian*, April 4, 1974.
52. *Chanute Tribune*, April 11, 1974.
53. *Coffeyville Journal*, April 22, 1974.
54. *Burlington Daily Republican*, Nov. 8, 1974.
55. *Kansas City Star*, Dec. 6, 1974.
56. *Kansas State Collegian*, Nov. 6, 1974.
57. *Servicegraph* (Oct. 1973), pp. 1–3, outlines the content of these.
58. *Burlington Daily Republican*, April 24, 1974.
59. *Servicegraph* (May 1975), pp. 3–5.
60. *Lyons Daily News*, Jan. 10, 1975.

61. *LeRoy Reporter,* June 7, 1974.
62. *Lebo Enterprise,* June 13, 1974; *Wichita Eagle,* June 15, 1974.
63. *Ottawa Herald,* July 18, 1974.
64. *Topeka Daily Capital,* Jan. 2, 1975.
65. *Chanute Tribune,* April 18, 1974.
66. *Wellsville Globe,* July 25, 1974; *Pittsburg Morning Sun,* Dec. 7, 1974.
67. *Burlington Daily Republican,* Jan. 22, 1975.
68. *Iola Register,* May 14, 1974.
69. Ibid., May 16, 1974.
70. Wm. Miller, in *Wichita Sun,* Feb. 19, 1975.
71. *Burlington Daily Republican,* March 24, 1975.
72. *El Dorado Times,* Jan. 1, 1975.
73. *Chanute Tribune,* July 3, 1975; *Burlington Daily Republican,* July 10, 1975; *Lebo Enterprise,* Oct. 16, 1975.
74. *Sunflower* (Wichita State University), July 17, 1975. *Interchange,* a publication of Wichita Free University, Sept. 11, 1975.
75. *Hutchinson News,* Sept. 21, 1975.
76. *Wichita Sun,* Oct. 8, 1975.
77. *Howard Courant-Citizen,* Oct. 16, 1975.
78. *Kansas City Star,* July 25, 1976.

CHAPTER 3

1. Joseph A. Camilleri, *The State and Nuclear Power: Conflict and Control in the Western World* (Seattle: University of Washington Press, 1984).
2. James Jasper, "The Political Life Cycle of Technological Controversies," abstract, pp. 358–59.
3. Allan Mazur, "Media Influences on Public Attitudes Toward Nuclear Power," in William Freudenberg and Eugene Ross, *Public Reactions to Nuclear Power: Are There Critical Masses?* (Boulder: Westview, 1984), p. 99. Mazur emphasizes that this effect happens even when the media is generally favorable to the technology covered, as in the case of water fluoridation.
4. William A. Gamson and Andre Madigliani, "Media Discourse and Public Opinion on Nuclear Power: A Constructionist Approach," *American Journal of Sociology* 95 (1989), 1:8.
5. Mazur, "Media Influences," pp. 98–99.
6. Gamson and Madigliani, "Media Discourse," p. 7.
7. Wayne H. Sugai, *Nuclear Power and Ratepayer Protest: The Washington Public Power Supply System Crisis* (Boulder: Westview, 1987), p. 392.
8. Ibid.
9. *Burlington Daily Republican,* April 1, 1974; *Osawatomie Graphic-News,* May 2, 1974; "Administrative History," in U.S. Nuclear Regulatory Commis-

sion, Office of Nuclear Reactor Regulation, *Final Environmental Statement related to the Operation of Wolf Creek Generating Station, Unit No. 1* (June 1982), p. 1-1.

10. *Wichita Eagle*, May 5, 1974.
11. Unidentified clipping, Sept. 4, 1974, KG&E nuclear clippings.
12. *Lebo Enterprise*, May 22, 1975.
13. *Wichita Eagle*, March 24, 1975. A detailed account of the accident appeared in *Emporia Gazette*, Oct. 21, 1976, just as the Kansas hearings were to get underway.
14. *Iola Register*, Feb. 7, 1975.
15. George Mazuzan and Samuel Walker, *Controlling the Atom: The Beginnings of Nuclear Regulation 1946–1962* (Berkeley: University of California Press, 1985), p. 281.
16. *Kansas City Star*, Nov. 13, 1974.
17. *Wichita Sun*, Jan. 15, 1975.
18. *Goodland Daily News*, Nov. 14, 1974.
19. *Topeka Daily Capital*, May 24, 1975.
20. *Servicegraph* (Oct.1974), pp. 1–2.
21. Ibid. (May 1975), pp. 1–2.
22. *Iola Register*, Dec. 2, 1974.
23. *Electric Light and Power* (Dec. 1974) in Jack King scrapbooks, vol. 1.
24. Quote in *Iola Register*, Dec. 11, 1974.
25. *Wichita Sun*, Jan. 15, 29, 1975.
26. *Wichita Sun*, Jan. 22, 1975.
27. Fred Kimball, interview with the author, April 5, 1989.
28. *Wichita Sun*, Feb. 5, 1975.
29. Ibid., Feb. 19, 1975.
30. In Jack King scrapbooks, n.v.
31. *Wichita Sun*, Jan. 29, 1975.
32. Ibid., March 19, 1975.
33. Ralph Fiebach to KG&E employees, July 10, 1974, Jack King scrapbooks, n.v.
34. Undated clipping and *Wichita Eagle*, March 8, 1975, in Jack King scrapbooks, n.v.
35. Ralph Fiebach, interview with the author, March 29, 1989.
36. *Kansas State Collegian*, Nov. 5, 1975.
37. *Wichita Eagle*, Nov. 13, 1975.
38. *Iola Register*, Feb. 5, 1976.
39. *Topeka State Journal*, Sept. 27, 1975.
40. *Wichita Eagle*, Aug. 14, 1976.
41. U.S. Nuclear Regulatory Commission, *Safety Evaluation Report Related to Construction of Wolf Creek Generating Station, Unit. No 1* (Sept. 1975) Docket no. STN 50-482, p. 3 and passim.

42. U.S. Nuclear Regulatory Commission, *Final Environmental Statement Related to Construction of Wolf Creek Generating Station Unit 1* . . . (Oct. 1975), Docket no. STN 50-482, pp. iv, xix.

43. Ibid., pp. iii–vi.

44. *Wichita Eagle*, Feb. 14, 1975.

45. Ibid., March 31, 1975.

46. *Wichita Sun*, March 26, 1976.

47. Construction Permit Hearings, May, 19 1975, 2:8, 13, 17–18, 23, 29.

48. *Wichita Eagle*, Jan. 7, Nov. 13, 1975.

49. Jay Silberg, Nov. 12, 1975, in Construction Permit Hearings, 3:105–28.

50. Bill Ward, ibid., pp. 137–44.

51. Diane Tegtmeier, interview with the author, June 12, 1990.

52. *Kansas City Star*, Jan. 25, 1976.

53. Various speakers, Construction Permit Hearings, 3:148–350; 4:362–72.

54. Margaret Bangs, interviews with the author, April 2 and 9, 1990. On the Wichita hearings see *Wichita Sun*, Jan. 2, 1976; *Wichita Eagle*, Jan. 22, 1976.

55. Margaret Bangs, Jan. 26, 1976, Construction Permit Hearings, 5:416–19.

56. Margaret Bangs, interview with the author, April 2, 1990.

57. Paul Schaefer, Jan. 26, 1976, Construction Permit Hearings, 5:466.

58. Construction Permit Hearings, Jan. 26, 1976, 5:471–81.

59. *Servicegraph* (Dec. 1975), pp. 6–7.

60. *Burlington Daily Republican*, Aug. 18, 1975.

61. *Manhattan Mercury*, Feb. 11, 1976.

62. Quoted in *Topeka State Journal*, May 29, 1975.

63. *Wichita Eagle*, Feb. 20, 1976.

64. Ibid., Nov. 13, 1975.

65. *Burlington Daily Republican*, Nov. 17, 1975.

66. Rev. Frederick Ashworth, in *Burlington Reporter*, Nov. 14, 1975.

67. *Wichita Sun*, Jan. 2, 1976.

68. *Wichita Eagle*, Jan. 22, 1976.

69. Ibid., Jan. 23, 1976.

70. Ibid., Jan. 23, 1976.

71. Ibid., Jan. 24, 1976.

CHAPTER 4

1. Hirsh, *Technology and Transformation*, p. 150.

2. Rudolph and Ridley, *Power Struggle*, p. 153.

3. Bert Useem and Mayer Zald, "From Pressure Group to Social Move-

ment: Organizational Dilemmas of the Effort to Promote Nuclear Power," *Social Problems* 30, no. 2 (1982): 144–56.

4. Robert C. Mitchell, "From Elite Quarrel to Mass Movement," *Society* 18, no. 5 (1981): 76–84; Stanley Rothman and Robert Lichter, "Elite Ideology and Risk Perception in Nuclear Energy Policy," *American Political Science Review* 81, no. 2 (1987): 383–404. Rothman and Lichter argue that elite groups' concern about the risks of nuclear technology were a surrogate for underlying ideological criticisms of U.S. society. See also Anthony Ladd et al., "Ideological Themes in the Antinuclear Movement: Consensus and Diversity," *Sociological Inquiry* 53, no. 2 (1983): 252–72.

5. Marx, *The Machine in the Garden.*

6. "Notes and Comments," in *New Yorker* 59 (July 25, 1983): 19–20.

7. U.S. Nuclear Regulatory Commission, "Partial Initial Decision Authorizing Limited Work Authorization," Docket no. STN 50-482, Jan. 18, 1977, typescript, KG&E archives, p. 8 and passim.

8. Construction Permit Hearings, Jan. 27, 1976, 8:731–802, 835.

9. For press coverage of the fuel question, see *Wichita Eagle*, April 21, 1975 and March 20, 1976.

10. *Kansas City Star*, March 24, 1977, Feb. 5, 1978; *Wichita Eagle*, June 20, 1977.

11. Dr. Robert Hagen, interview with the author, Nov. 19, 1992.

12. *Kansas City Times*, Feb. 5, 1976.

13. *Wichita Eagle*, Sept. 11, 1975; *Kansas City Star*, Jan. 28, 1976.

14. Dr. Robert Hagen, interview with the author, Nov. 19, 1992.

15. *Wichita Eagle.*, Oct. 2, 1975.

16. Ibid., Dec. 9, 1976.

17. *Burlington Daily Republican*, Jan. 16, 1976.

18. *Wichita Eagle*, April 21, 1977.

19. Ibid., May 7, 1977; KG&E, *Annual Report 1976*, p. 2.

20. *Kansas City Times*, Oct. 28, 1978; *Wichita Eagle*, Feb. 23, 1980.

21. KG&E, *Annual Report 1979*, p. 5.

22. Arthur D. Little, Inc., "Management and Operations Review, KG&E," (1977), typescript, KG&E archives, p. III-12.

23. Cresap, McCormick and Paget, "Report on the Financial and Operational Study of the Wolf Creek Nuclear Generating Facility," (Nov. 1980), typescript, KG&E archives, p. X-3.

24. Dr. Robert Hagen, interview with the author, Nov. 19, 1992.

25. *Kansas City Star*, Feb. 5, 1978.

26. *Wichita Eagle*, March 20, 1976.

27. KG&E, *Annual Report 1975*, p. 3.

28. Testimony of M. Jarvin Emerson, Feb. 2, 1976, Construction Permit Hearings, 10:1189 ff.

29. Ibid., pp. 1190–99.

30. Testimony of Malcolm Burns and Michael Viren, Feb. 2, 1976, Construction Permit Hearings, 11:1433ff. Viren's prepared testimony begins at 1438, and is separately numbered.

31. Viren cross-examination, Feb. 4, 1976, ibid., 12:1510, 1580–81, 1587, 1597, 1707, 1716. The intervenors' argument on demand growth is in ibid., 10:90 ff. of Emerson prepared testimony.

32. Testimony of W. K. Woolery, Feb. 5, 1976, Construction Permit Hearings, 13: Woolery statement following p. 1759, separately paged. W. K. Woolery, interview with the author, April 26, 1989.

33. Testimony of James Lucas, Feb. 5, 1976, Construction Permit Hearings, 13: Lucas statement following p. 1759, separately paged. James Lucas, interview with the author, March 6, 1989. Much of volumes 15 and 16 of the hearings is taken up with detailed discussions of forecasting.

34. Dr. Robert Hagen, interview with the author, Nov. 19, 1992.

35. Testimony of Donald McPhee, Feb. 5, 1976, Construction Permit Hearings, 13: prepared statement following p. 2125, separately paged.

36. Testimony of Donald McPhee, Feb. 25, 1976, Construction Permit Hearings, 17:2599ff.

37. Testimony of Jesse Arterburn, Feb. 24, 1976, Construction Permit Hearings, 16:2426, 2454.

38. Testimony of Frank Schwoerer, ibid., p. 2496ff. Decommissioning is extensively treated in vol. 17.

39. Testimony of Gary Boyer, Feb. 25, 1976, ibid., 17:2765ff.

40. Testimony of Jesse Arterburn, ibid., p. 2782 ff.

41. Testimony of George Leroy, Feb. 26, 1976, ibid., 18:2851–60.

42. Testimony of Leonard Sagan, ibid., pp. 2923 ff.

43. Testimony of Jacob Frenkel, March 3, 1976, ibid., 20: prepared testimony following p. 3341.

44. Samuel Jensch, ibid., p. 3480.

45. The major part of the exchange is contained in vols. 22, 24, and 25 of Construction Permit Hearings.

46. *Parsons Sun*, Jan. 24, 1976.

47. Daryl Glannmann, in *Hutchinson News*, March 25, 1976.

48. Ruth Luzzati, interview with the author, Nov. 17, 1992.

49. *Salina Journal*, March 30, 1976.

50. Ibid., Jan. 23, 1976.

51. *El Dorado Times*, Jan. 28, 1976.

52. *Winfield Courier*, Feb. 11, 1976; *Chanute Tribune*, Feb. 11, 1976; *Kansas City Times*, Feb. 12, 1976.

53. *Kansas City Times*, Feb. 12, 1976.

54. Ross Doyen, interview with the author, Nov. 17, 1992.

55. *Wichita Eagle*, Feb. 12, 1976.
56. *Syracuse Journal*, Jan. 28, 1976.
57. Harold Munger, in *Manhattan Mercury*, March 18, 1976.
58. *Columbus Advocate*, Jan. 26, 1976.
59. *Chanute Tribune*, Jan. 29, 1976.
60. *Burlington Republican*, Feb. 2, 1976.
61. *Chanute Tribune*, Feb. 5, 1976.
62. *Parsons Sun*, Jan. 29, 1976.
63. *Topeka State Journal*, Feb. 9, 1976.
64. *Iola Register*, Feb. 13, 1976.
65. *Independence Reporter*, Feb. 16, 1976.
66. *Parsons Sun*, Feb. 20, 1976.
67. *Topeka Daily Capital*, Feb. 28, 1976; *Emporia Gazette*, Feb. 28, 1976.
68. *Dodge City Daily Globe*, March 1, 1976.
69. *Emporia Gazette*, Feb. 17, 1976; *Newton Kansan*, Feb. 17, 1976.
70. *Emporia Gazette*, Feb. 5, 1976.
71. *Oswego Independent-Observer*, Feb. 5, 1976.
72. *Topeka Daily Capital*, Feb. 24, 1976.
73. *Chanute Tribune*, Feb. 24, 1976.
74. *Kansas City Times*, Feb. 26, 1976; *Parsons Sun*, Feb. 26, 1976; Ross Doyen, interview with the author, Nov. 17, 1992.
75. *Kansas City Times*, March 10, 1976.
76. Typescript, Jan. 26, 1976, Jack King scrapbooks, vol. 2.
77. *Burlington Daily Republican*, Jan. 26, 1976.
78. Ralph Fiebach to "all KG&E people," Feb. 11, 1976, Jack King scrapbooks, vol. 2.
79. Ruth Luzzati to Jack King, Feb. 19, 1976, Jack King scrapbooks, vol. 2.
80. Ruth Luzzati, interview with the author, Nov. 19, 1992.
81. Ruth Luzzati to editor, *Wichita Eagle*, Feb. 9, 1976, handwritten draft, Ruth Luzzati papers, Wichita, Kansas.
82. Ruth Luzzati to Doug King, Margaret Bangs, both Feb. 9, 1976, Luzzati papers.
83. Ruth Luzzati to Paul Burmeister, March 1, 1976, Luzzati papers.
84. For example, statement against water contract prepared by Carl Kruse, Olathe, for Kansas House and Senate Hearings, Feb. 18, 1976, Luzzati papers.
85. Jim Lawing to Morris Krouse, n.d., Luzzati papers.
86. *Burlington Daily Republican*, Feb. 6, 1976.
87. *Kansas City Times*, Oct. 31, 1975.
88. Nancy Jack of Kansas Sierra Club to members, Feb. 12, 1976, Jack King scrapbooks, vol. 2.
89. *El Dorado Times*, Feb. 17, 1976.

90. *Wichita Eagle*, March 6, 1976.
91. *Hutchinson News*, March 9, 1976.
92. Quoted in *Junction City Daily Union*, March 6, 1976.
93. *Hutchinson News*, March 10, 1976.
94. *Arkansas City Traveler*, June 30, 1976; *Wichita Eagle*, Dec. 8, 1976. The suit was dismissed by the court in December.
95. *Parsons Sun*, Jan. 29, 1976.
96. Ibid., March 12, 1976.
97. *Kansas City Times*, May 1, 1976.
98. *Wichita Eagle*, Jan. 26, 1976.
99. *Kansas City Star*, May 6, 1976.
100. *Burlington Daily Republican*, Jan. 25, 1977.

CHAPTER 5

1. Testimony of Donald McPhee, May 30, 1985, 1985 Rate Case, 14:3842–60.
2. Testimony of Thomas Flaherty, June 10, 1985, ibid., 17:4786–4800.
3. Testimony of Charles Huston, May 16, 1986, ibid., 4:905.
4. KG&E et al., *Management Performance Evaluation* (1984), pp. 212, 215ff., 263; *Burlington Daily Republican*, March 29, 1976.
5. *Servicegraph* (April 1976), n.p., Jack King scrapbooks, vol. 2.
6. *Parsons Sun*, May 17, 1976.
7. *Wichita Eagle*, June 26, 1976.
8. *Iola Register*, June 28, 29, 1976.
9. *Newton Kansan*, May 6, 1976.
10. *Kansas City Times*, May 6, 1976; *Parsons Sun*, May 7, 1976. The November ballot issues were defeated in six of seven states. One where some limits passed was Missouri, where the twin to Wolf Creek was under construction; it did not mention nuclear power by name, but only prevented utilities from charging for current cost of money invested in construction work in progress. *Wichita Eagle*, Nov. 4, 1976.
11. *Kansas City Star*, May 26, 1976.
12. Freudenberg and Rose, *Public Reactions to Nuclear Power*, pp. 23–24.
13. Jim Lawing, interview with the author, Nov. 20, 1992.
14. *Kansas City Kansan*, June 3, 1976; *Iola Register*, June 4, 1976.
15. *Humboldt Union*, June 10, 1976.
16. *Wall Street Journal*, June 10, 1976.
17. *Wichita Eagle*, June 9, 1976.
18. *Garnett Review*, June 28, 1976.
19. *Wichita Eagle*, June 18, 1976.
20. *Wichita Eagle*, Aug. 24, 25, 1976.

21. Ibid., Aug. 24, 25, 27, 1976.
22. Ibid., Sept. 4, 1976.
23. *Hutchinson News*, Oct. 13, 1976.
24. *Wichita Eagle*, June 22, 1976.
25. *Topeka Daily Capital*, June 23, 1976.
26. *Topeka State Journal*, July 21, 1976.
27. *Arkansas City Traveler*, June 22, 1976.
28. Robert Glicksman, "Allocating the Cost of Constructing Excess Capacity: 'Who Will Have to Pay for it All?'" *University of Kansas Law Review*, 33:433–35.
29. Cresap, "Prudence Review," timeline.
30. *Topeka State Journal*, Jan. 27, 1977.
31. Ibid., Jan. 27, 1977.
32. Ibid., Jan. 28, 1977.
33. Ibid., Feb. 17, 1977.
34. *Kansas City Times*, Sept. 8, 1976.
35. *Parsons Sun*, Aug. 16, 1976.
36. *Wichita Eagle*, Nov. 6, 1976; *Kansas City Times*, Nov. 6, 1976. The decision was announced Nov. 5.
37. *Chanute Tribune*, Nov. 9, 1976.
38. *Emporia Gazette*, Dec. 11, 1976.
39. U.S. Nuclear Regulatory Commission, "Partial Initial Decision Authorizing Limited Work Authorization," Jan. 18, 1977, pp. 9(a), 184.
40. Jensch, in *Kansas City Star*, Feb. 3, 1977.
41. U.S. Nuclear Regulatory Commission, "Partial Initial Decision," passim. The finance issue is treated on p. 118.
42. *Wichita Eagle*, Jan. 19, 1977.
43. *Servicegraph* (Feb. 1977), pp. 3–4.
44. *Emporia Gazette*, Jan. 21, 1977; *Burlington Daily Republican*, Jan. 25, 1977.
45. *Kansas City Star*, Feb. 20, 1977.
46. *Wichita Eagle*, Dec. 31, 1976. Books on nuclear power are sometimes not much more helpful. Henry Bedford, in *Seabrook Station*, says CWIP was "jargon of utility accountants," and a "device" that "allowed the company to receive a return on investment in new generating capacity before it became productive, thereby forcing consumers to provide part of the requisite capital." (p. 101).
47. *Wichita Sun*, Nov. 17, 1976. A careful discussion of CWIP, the history of its restriction in Kansas, and the effects on KG&E's costs is Kansas Gas and Electric Company, "A Response to the 1984 Amendments of K.S.A. 66-128, October, 1984," p. IV-31 ff. I have been aided here also by several talks with James Haines of KG&E.

48. Cresap, "Prudence Review," III-9–24; Cresap, McCormick and Paget, "Report on the Financial and Operational Study of the Wolf Creek Nuclear Generating Facility, November, 1980," typescript, KG&E archives, II-7.
49. McCracken, *War Against the Atom*, pp. 46–47.
50. *Kansas City Star*, Feb. 27, 1977.
51. *Wichita Eagle*, Dec. 31, 1976; Jan. 13, 1977.
52. *Topeka Daily Capital*, Feb. 23, 1977.
53. Ibid., March 2, 1977.
54. *Parsons Sun*, March 5, 1977.
55. *Topeka State Journal*, Sept. 22, 1977.
56. "Statement of James Haines, House Bills No. 2927, 2964, 2810 [1985]," typescript, KG&E legal department.
57. Ruth Luzzati, 84th District Representative, to members of the energy committee, Sept. 15, 1977, Luzzati papers.
58. Ruth Luzzati, interview with the author, Nov. 19, 1992.
59. Ross Doyen, interview with the author, Nov. 19, 1992.
60. *Wichita Eagle*, July 27, 1978.
61. Testimony of Arthur Doyle, May 29, 1985, 1985 Rate Case, 13:3789–3806.
62. Testimony of Wilson Cadman, May 23, 1985, ibid., 9:2808–11, 2890.
63. Glicksman, "Allocating the Cost of Excess Capacity," *University of Kansas Law Review*, 33:439.
64. *Wichita Eagle*, Feb. 1, 1977.
65. *Iola Register*, March 8, 1977.
66. *Kansas City Star*, March 21, 1977.
67. Cresap, McCormick and Paget, "Report (1980)," III-2–3, 7, 11.
68. Ibid., IV-1–4.
69. Testimony of Leonard Wass, July 1, 1985, 1985 Rate Hearings, 34:10278.
70. Testimony of Charles Huston, May 14, 15, 16, 1985, 1985 Rate Hearings, 2:159–62; 3:598, 604, 677; 4:803–5.
71. Testimony of Richard Rosen, June 18, 1985, 1985 Rate Hearings, 23:6692–99.
72. Jim Lawing, interview with the author, Nov. 20, 1992.
73. *Wichita Eagle*, April 20, 1977; *Servicegraph* (April 1977), p. 5.
74. *Kansas City Star*, May 8, 1977.
75. *Kansas City Star*, May 12, 1977.
76. *Wichita Eagle*, May 13, 1977.
77. Steven Barkan, "Strategic, Tactical, Organization Dilemmas of the Protest Movement Against Nuclear Power," *Social Problems* 27 (1979): 19–35.
78. Diane Tegtmeier, interview with the author, June 12, 1990.
79. Dr. Robert Hagen, interview with the author, Nov. 19, 1992.

80. *Wichita Eagle*, May 2, 1977; Bedford, *Seabrook Station*, pp. 76–77.

81. Margaret Olwine, "Showdown Time in Mid-America," *Kansas City Star Magazine*, May 1, 1977.

82. *Wichita Eagle*, May 19, 1977.

83. Ibid., May 13, 1977.

84. Arthur D. Little, Inc., "Management and Operations Review, KG&E," Feb. 1977 contract, KG&E archives, I-1–5; II-8; V-12–13; VII-1–3; Cresap, "Prudence Review," timeline.

85. *Wichita Eagle*, Dec. 22, 1977.

86. KG&E, *Annual Report 1974*, p. 5; News Update, KG&E, May 16, 1977, Jack King scrapbooks, vol. 2.

87. *Wichita Eagle*, Aug. 11, 1976.

88. KG&E, *Annual Report 1975*, p. 11; *1978*, p. 9.

89. *Wichita Eagle*, July 15, 1978.

90. Ibid., Aug. 11, 1976.

91. Ibid., June 18, 1978.

92. KG&E, *Annual Reports, 1974, 1976,* and *1978*.

93. Elmer Hall, interview with the author, Feb. 16, 1989.

94. National Electric Reliability Council, *1977 Annual Report* (Princeton, NJ, 1978), pp. 5–7.

95. *Kansas City Times*, Sept. 17, 1977.

96. *Wichita Eagle*, Sept. 17, 1977.

97. Ibid., Sept. 14, 1977.

98. Ibid., Sept. 15, 1977.

99. *Wichita Journal*, May 21, 1977.

100. Wilson Cadman, interview with the author, March 10, 1989; *Wichita Eagle*, Feb. 18, July 21, 1978; *Kansas City Times*, Feb. 11, 15, 1978; *Wichita Eagle*, Feb. 9, 1978.

101. *Kansas City Times*, Jan. 5, 1978; *Kansas City Star*, Sept. 3, 1977.

102. *Wichita Eagle*, April 13, 1978.

103. Cresap, McCormick and Paget "Report (1980)," IV-66; *Kansas City Star*, Jan. 19, 1978.

104. *Wichita Eagle*, Sept. 5, 1977, June 10, 1978.

105. Ibid., Feb. 15, 1977.

106. Ibid., Oct. 6, 1977.

107. *Osawatomie Graphic News*, Jan. 26, 1978.

108. *Emporia Gazette*, May 20, 1977; *Iola Register*, May 20, 1977; *Lebo Enterprise*, May 26, 1977.

109. *Ft. Scott Tribune*, May 21, 1977.

110. *Neodesha Daily Sun*, June 10, 1977.

111. *Kansas City Star*, June 25, 1977; *Ft. Scott Tribune*, May 21, June 1, 1977; *Iola Register*, May 20, 1977. The *Emporia Gazette* reported on April 1 that the housing market there was more active than at any time in the last 20 years.

112. Betty Brown, in *Coffey County Reporter,* Jan. 12, 1978.
113. Edith Lange, in *Kansas City Star,* June 25, 1977.
114. Ibid., May 20, 1977.
115. *Parsons Sun,* May 15, 1977.

CHAPTER 6

1. Wiebe Bijker, Thomas Hughes, and Trevor Pinch, eds., *The Social Construction of Technological Systems* (Cambridge, MA: MIT Press, 1987), pp. 1, 9, 30, 68, 76, 80, 83, 90.

2. William Least Heat Moon, *PrairyErth* (Boston: Houghton Mifflin, 1991), p. 14.

3. Margalee Wright, interview with the author, Nov. 20, 1992.

4. *Ft. Scott Tribune,* June 1, 1977; *Leon News,* July 7, 1977; *Independence Reporter,* July 26, 1977.

5. For a detailed account of the Washington protest, see Wayne Sugai, *Nuclear Power and Ratepayer Protest: The Washington Public Power Supply System Crisis* (Boulder: Westview, 1987).

6. *Chanute Tribune,* Nov. 10, 1977.

7. *Newton Kansan,* June 15, 1977.

8. *Wichita Eagle,* May 25, 1977.

9. Jeffrey Hart, in *Independence Reporter,* May 24, 1977.

10. *Emporia Gazette,* July 27, 1977.

11. Ibid., Aug. 2, 1977.

12. *Wichita Eagle,* Aug. 5, 1977.

13. Ibid., Aug. 7, 1977; *Burlington Daily Republican,* Aug. 8, 1977; *Emporia Gazette,* Aug. 8, 1977.

14. *Wichita Eagle,* Aug. 1, 1977.

15. *Servicegraph* (Oct. 1977), p. 1; Wilson Cadman to KG&E employees, Sept. 20, 1977; undated pamphlet, Jack King scrapbooks, vol. 2.

16. *Servicegraph* (Nov. 1977), p. 2.

17. John Delahanty, interview with the author, May 4, 1990.

18. *Servicegraph* (Nov. 1977), n.p.; Jack King scrapbooks, vol. 2.

19. *Kansas City Star,* Nov. 13, 1977; *St. Louis Post Dispatch,* Dec. 11, 1977.

20. *Kansas City Star,* Nov. 23, 1977.

21. *Servicegraph* (Nov. 1977), p. 5.

22. Ibid. (Jan. 1978), pp. 2–3; *Burlington Daily Republican,* Dec. 14, 1977 contains photos.

23. KG&E, *Annual Report 1978,* p. 2.

24. *Kansas Grass and Grain,* Dec. 20, 1977.

25. *Wichita Eagle,* Dec. 9, 1977.

26. Ibid., Dec. 31, 1977.

27. *Burlington Republican,* Jan. 27, 1978.

28. *Wichita Eagle,* Jan. 31, March 12, 1978.

29. Craig Miner, *Wichita: The Magic City* (Wichita, KS: Wichita-Sedgwick County Historical Museum, 1988), pp. 39, 74.
30. *Wichita Eagle,* June 30, 1976.
31. Ibid., Feb. 25, 1977.
32. Ibid., Feb. 15, 1977.
33. Ibid., Feb. 10, 24, 1977.
34. Ibid., March 10, 14, 1977.
35. Ibid., May 2, 1977.
36. *Wichita Journal,* Oct. 29, 1977.
37. *Wichita Eagle,* Nov. 10, 1977.
38. *Wichita Journal,* Nov. 5, 1977.
39. Ibid., Nov. 12, 1977.
40. *Wichita Eagle,* Nov. 16, 1977.
41. *Wichita Journal,* Dec. 10, 1977.
42. Ibid., Dec. 3, 1977.
43. Ibid., Jan. 18, 1978.
44. *Wichita Eagle,* Jan. 9, 1978.
45. Ibid., Jan. 10, 1978.
46. Ibid., Jan. 25, 1978.
47. Ibid., Feb. 3, 1978.
48. *Wichita Journal,* Feb. 25, 1978.
49. *Wichita Eagle,* March 12, 1978.
50. Ibid., March 30, 1978.
51. Ibid., Sept. 1, 1978.
52. Testimony of George Roen, May 10, 1985, 1985 Rate Hearings, 6:1784–92.
53. Testimony of Wilson Cadman, May 23, 24, 1985, 1985 Rate Hearings, 9:2615, 10:2755.
54. Wilson Cadman, interview with the author, March 10, 1989.
55. *Kansas City Times,* March 1, 1978; *Topeka Daily Capital,* March 2, 1978.
56. Testimony of Arthur Doyle, May 29, 1985, 1985 Rate Hearings, 13:3473.
57. *Wichita Eagle,* March 2, 1978.
58. Ibid., March 4, 1978.
59. Ibid., March 24, 1978.
60. Ibid., March 7, April 13, 1978.
61. Ibid., April 14, 1978.
62. Testimony of Arthur Doyle, May 29, 1985, 1985 Rate Hearings, 13:3471.
63. *Wichita Eagle,* April 22, 1978.
64. Ibid., May 2, 1978.
65. Ibid., May 4, 1978.

NOTES TO CHAPTER 6   355

66. Ibid., April 13, 1978.
67. *Kansas City Times*, April 13, 1978.
68. *Burlington Daily Republican*, Oct. 19, 1978.
69. *Topeka Daily Capital*, April 20, 1978.
70. Cresap, "Prudence Review," p. IV-81. The KEPCo deal for 17%, as shall be seen, was anything but a given.
71. *Topeka State Journal*, April 20, 1978.
72. *Servicegraph* (May 1978), p. 3.
73. *Humboldt Union*, Jan. 11, 1978.
74. *Parsons Sun*, March 9, 1978.
75. *Wichita Eagle*, Oct. 7, 1978; *Humboldt Union*, April 26, 1978.
76. *Wichita Eagle*, June 26, 1978; *Kansas City Times*, June 26, 1978.
77. *Burlington Daily Republican*, June 19, 1978.
78. *Wichita Eagle*, June 26, 1978.
79. *Topeka State Journal*, July 26, 1978.
80. *Chanute Tribune*, July 26, 1978.
81. *Kansas City Star*, Nov. 12, 1978.
82. *Wichita Eagle*, Oct. 10, 1978.
83. *Kansas City Times*, Oct. 14, 1978.
84. *Wichita Eagle*, Oct. 15, 1978.
85. *Topeka State Journal*, Oct. 9, 1978.
86. *Wichita Eagle*, Nov. 7, 1978.
87. *Topeka Daily Capital*, Oct. 19, 1978.
88. Wilson Cadman to KG&E families, Sept. 12, 1978, Jack King scrapbooks, vol. 2.
89. *Servicegraph* (Nov. 1978), n.p.
90. Wilson Cadman to Dr. Barry Commoner, March 6, 1978, ibid.
91. *McPherson Sentinel*, June 29, 1978.
92. *Kansas City Times*, Oct. 13, 1978.
93. *Emporia Gazette*, Feb. 13, 1978.
94. Series in *Emporia Gazette*, Sept. 27, 28, 1978.
95. *Servicegraph* (Nov. 1978), p. 6.
96. *Ft. Scott Tribune*, April 11, 1978.
97. *Chanute Tribune*, Nov. 6, 1978.
98. *Kansas City Star*, Aug. 16, 1978.
99. Testimony of Arthur Doyle, May 29, 1985, 1985 Rate Hearings, 13:3476–78.
100. *Wichita Eagle*, Dec. 5, 1978.
101. Ibid., Jan. 23, 1978.
102. Ibid., Oct. 28, 1978.
103. Ibid., Dec. 15, 16, 30, 1978; *Burlington Daily Republican*, Dec. 15, 1978.

104. *Kansas City Star*, Dec. 24, 1978.
105. *Wichita Eagle*, Oct. 8, 1978.
106. *Burlington Daily Republican*, Dec. 22, 1978.
107. *Independence Reporter*, Sept. 10, 1978.
108. *Kansas City Times*, Oct. 13, 1978.
109. *Lawrence Journal World*, Nov. 25, 1978.
110. *Emporia Gazette*, Dec. 4, 1978.
111. *Lawrence Journal World*, Nov. 25, 1978.

CHAPTER 7

1. *Wichita Eagle*, Dec. 22, 1978.
2. *Wichita Eagle*, Dec. 30, 1978.
3. *Kansas City Star*, Dec. 24, 1978.
4. *Wichita Eagle*, Dec. 24, 1978.
5. *Burlington Daily Republican*, Dec. 29, 1978.
6. *Kansas City Star*, Dec. 31, 1978.
7. Ibid., Dec. 21, 26, 1978. In January, columnist Sidney Harris suggested sending nuclear waste to the moon in missiles. *Wichita Beacon*, Jan. 10, 1979.
8. *El Dorado Times*, Jan. 3, 1979.
9. *Wichita Eagle*, Jan. 5, 1979.
10. Ibid., Jan. 11, 1979.
11. Ibid., Jan. 10, 1979.
12. *Parsons Sun*, Jan. 12, 1979.
13. *Wichita Eagle*, Jan. 12, 1979.
14. *Topeka State Journal*, Jan. 12, 1979.
15. *Lawrence Journal World*, Nov. 25, 1978. The author was in St. Louis at the time of this event working on a history of the Missouri Pacific Railroad, and was aware of the elaborate arrangements with the railroad and police to be sure no one was injured.
16. *Topeka State Journal*, Jan. 12, 1979.
17. *Emporia Gazette*, Dec. 4, 1978.
18. Tony Blaufuss, in *Journal Free Press*, Jan. 3, 1979, Jack King scrapbooks, vol. 3.
19. *Wichita Eagle*, Jan. 13, 1979. This and the *Kansas City Times* article of the same day contain photos.
20. *Kansas City Star*, Jan. 14, 1979; *Kansas City Times*, Jan. 13, 1979.
21. *Servicegraph* (Jan. 1979), n.p.
22. *Kansas City Times*, Jan. 13, 1979.
23. *Iola Register*, Jan. 30, 1979.
24. *Burlington Daily Republican*, Jan. 18, 1979.

25. Kenneth Keniston, *Young Radicals: Notes on Committed Youth* (New York: Harcourt, Brace & World, 1968), p. 28.

26. Clipping, Jan. 26, 1979 from Clay Center, Kansas, Wolf Creek clip book no. 10, KG&E archives.

27. *Ft. Scott Tribune*, Jan. 25, 1979.

28. Quoted in *Topeka Daily Capital*, Jan. 23, 1979.

29. *Wichita Eagle*, Jan. 20, 1979.

30. Ibid., March 10, 1979; *Kansas City Star*, March 12, 1979.

31. Memo, March 21, 1979, clip book no. 12, KG&E archives; *Wichita Eagle*, March 8, 1979; *Wichita Eagle*, March 24, 1979; Edison Electric Institute, "Some Important Considerations Regarding *The China Syndrome*," n.d., Jack King scrapbooks, vol. 3.

32. There was a day-by-day report on the crisis in *Wichita Eagle* from the Associated Press on April 8, 1979. See also *Evening News* (Harrisburg, PA), March 29, 1979 and *Reports of President's Commission on the Accident at Three Mile Island* (Washington, DC, 1979). The author was helped here also by KG&E engineers.

33. Bedford, *Seabrook Station*, p. 147.

34. Some examples of the analysis are Connie DeBoer et al., "The Impact of Nuclear Accidents on Attitudes Toward Nuclear Energy," *The Public Opinion Quarterly*, 52, no. 2 (1988): 254–61; Joseph Hugey and Eric Sandstrom, "Perceptions of TMI and Acceptance of a Nuclear Power Plant in a Distant Community," *Journal of Applied Social Psychology*, 18, no. 10 (1988): 880–90; Edward Walsh and Rex Warland, "Social Movement Involvement in the Wake of Nuclear Accident: Activists and Freeriders in the TMI Area," *American Sociololgical Review*, 48, no. 6 (1983): 764–80.

35. For an account of TMI's impact on the specific protest movements surrounding it see Edward Walsh, *Democracy in the Shadows: Citizen Mobilization in the Wake of the Accident at Three Mile Island* (New York: Greenwood, 1988).

36. *Kansas City Star*, letter from Ben Nicks, April 8, 1979.

37. *Wichita Eagle*, April 7, 1979.

38. *Burlington Daily Republican*, May 7, 1979.

39. *Chicago Sun-Times*, quoted in *Parsons Sun*, April 2, 1979.

40. *Wichita Eagle*, May 1, 1979.

41. *Parsons Sun*, April 3, 1979.

42. The cartoon appeared in *Wichita Eagle*, April 7, 1979.

43. *Kansas City Times*, May 2, 1979.

44. *Emporia Gazette*, May 24, 1979.

45. *Wichita Eagle*, May 7, 1979.

46. Ibid., April 6, 1979.

47. Ibid., May 24, 1979.

48. *Burlington Daily Republican,* June 5, 1979.
49. *Wichita Eagle,* June 11, 1979.
50. *Wichita Eagle,* April 7, 1979.
51. *Wichita Eagle,* April 9, 1979.
52. Ibid., May 13, 1979.
53. Ibid., March 30, 1979.
54. *Topeka Capital Journal,* March 31, 1979.
55. *Wichita Eagle,* April 3, 1979.
56. *Emporia Gazette,* April 3, 1979.
57. Ibid., July 5, 1979.
58. Jim Lawing, interview with the author, Nov. 21, 1992.
59. Dr. Robert Hagen, interview with the author, Nov. 19, 1992.
60. *Wichita Eagle,* June 24, 1979. The Schorr article, "Second Thoughts on Wolf Creek," appeared in the *Wichita Eagle,* May 5, 1979. McDowell was dismissed by the *Gazette* also in November 1979. The editor there said that "It now appears the *Gazette* is being used mainly as a sounding board for your antinuclear views." *Wichita Eagle,* Nov. 8, 1979.
61. *Wichita Eagle,* May 5, 1979; for the union case see *Wichita Eagle,* May 19, June 6, 1979. The Kansas Building and Construction Trades Council asked for a stop to Wolf Creek on the grounds that the work was "substandard and inadequate."
62. *Wichita Eagle,* May 8, 1979.
63. *Kansas City Star,* May 16, 1979.
64. Glenn Koester, interview with the author, Feb. 10, 1989.
65. *Kansas City Star,* May 16, 1979.
66. *Wichita Eagle,* May 15, 1979.
67. Ibid., Jan. 5, 1979.
68. Ibid., Jan. 10, 1979; Glenn Koester, interview with the author, Feb. 28, 1990.
69. *Wichita Eagle,* March 2, 1979.
70. Ibid., May 16, 1979; *Emporia Gazette,* May 24, 1979. The best information forthcoming was that Bechtel had sort of a "one-year warranty" on the design. McDowell's history of the base mat controversy appears in *Emporia Gazette,* April 11, 1979.
71. *Kansas City Star,* June 29, 1979.
72. A complete summary is in KG&E, "Supervisor's Digest," Jan. 4, 1979, Jack King scrapbooks, vol. 3.
73. *Wichita Eagle,* July 7, 1979.
74. Glenn Koester, interview with the author, Feb. 28, 1990. A complete chronology of basemat events is in an insert in *Servicegraph* (July 1979).
75. Ibid., Aug. 15, 1979.
76. *Wichita Eagle,* July 24, 1979.

NOTES TO CHAPTER 7

77. Ibid., July 24, 1979.
78. Cresap, McCormick and Paget, "Financial and Operational Study," (1980), p. 1.
79. Margie Miller Caney, *Coffeyville Journal*, Oct. 17, 1979.
80. James Kirkpatrick, in *Kansas City Times*, Oct. 2, 1979. *The Wichita Eagle*, May 7, 1979, reported attendance of 65,000 at a Fonda antinuclear rally in Washington, DC.
81. John Chamberlain, column in *Emporia Gazette*, Oct. 2, 1979.
82. *Hutchinson News*, Nov. 14, 1979.
83. *Wichita Eagle*, Nov. 10, 1979.
84. Ibid., Nov. 24, 1979.
85. *Wichita Eagle*, Nov. 27, 1979.
86. Bob Rives, interview with the author, June 21, 1990; directors' reactions and experience are in Dwight Button, interview with the author, Feb. 22, 1989, and Marge Setter, interview with the author, June 27, 1989.
87. Marge Setter, interview with the author, June 27, 1989.
88. *Wichita Eagle*, April 4, 1979.
89. *Kansas City Star*, Oct. 12, 1979.
90. Cresap, "Prudence Review," p. IV-73.
91. *Emporia Gazette*, Aug. 6, 1979.
92. *Wichita Eagle*, Oct. 28, 1979.
93. *Ottawa Herald*, Oct. 16, 1979.
94. *Kansas City Star*, Dec. 2, 1979.
95. *Wichita Eagle*, Nov. 30, 1979.
96. Ibid., Sept. 19, Oct. 9, 1979.
97. Ibid., Dec. 16, 1979.
98. Ibid., July 21, 1979.
99. Ibid., Dec. 16, 1979.
100. Glenn Koester, interview with the author, Feb. 28, 1990.
101. Deposition of Jesse Arterburn, June 11, 12, 1985, "In the Matter of Kansas City Power & Light Company . . . for authority to file tariffs increasing the rate for electric service. . . . , No. ER-85-128, EO-85-185," pp. 12, 17, 23–25, 28, 33, 35–36, 40–41, 48, 51, 53, 55, 82, 92, 210, KG&E archives. There are 254 pages of testimony and a similar volume of exhibits in this document.
102. Kent Brown, interview with the author, June 11, 1990.
103. *Wichita Eagle*, Dec. 24, 1979.
104. Wilson Cadman, interview with the author, March 10, 1989.
105. Kent Brown, interview with the author, June 11, 1990. Brown was hired by KG&E as a full-time employee in 1982. Duddy was brought in for the completion work in 1983. Bob Rives, interview with the author, June 21, 1990, touches on the same point.

106. *Wichita Eagle*, Oct. 23, 26, 1979; Wilson Cadman, interview with the author, March 10, 1992.

CHAPTER 8

1. *Kansas City Star*, Dec. 30, 1979.
2. *Burlington Daily Republican*, Jan. 16, 1980.
3. *Kansas City Star*, Feb. 27, 1980.
4. Cresap, McCormick and Paget, "Financial and Operational Study," (1980), II-1–3; III-1–3
5. *Wichita Eagle*, June 26, 1980; *Yates Center News*, June 26, 1980; *Iola Register*, July 15, 1981.
6. *Wichita Eagle*, Dec. 5, 1981.
7. *Yates Center News*, Dec. 24, 1981.
8. *Wichita Eagle*, April 22, 1982.
9. One of these cards was given to the author by Glenn Koester.
10. *Chanute Tribune*, May 15, 1982.
11. *Kansas City Times*, June 7, 1982.
12. *Emporia Gazette*, April 22, 1982.
13. *Kansas City Star*, April 6, 1980.
14. R. Jacqueline Marsh, in *Burlington Daily Republican*, July 2, 1980.
15. *Kansas City Star*, April 6, 1980.
16. Ibid.
17. *Burlington Daily Republican*, Aug. 31, 1982.
18. George Swank, in *Emporia Gazette*, Sept. 9, 1982.
19. Bill Burns, Personnel Manager, Daniel International, in *Wichita Eagle*, April 23, 1983.
20. *Wichita Eagle*, April 27, 1980.
21. Ibid., June 6, 1979.
22. Ibid., April 27, 1980. Several investigations of drug use at the plant were instigated by the company and outside agencies, ibid., May 5, 1980.
23. *Parsons Sun*, Dec. 9, 1983.
24. *Emporia Gazette*, Nov. 13, 1981.
25. *Lawrence Journal-World*, May 21, 1980.
26. *Kansas City Star*, March 23, 1980.
27. *Burlington Daily Republican*, June 20, 1980.
28. *Wichita Eagle*, June 25, 1980.
29. *Winfield Courier*, July 2, 1980.
30. *Wichita Eagle*, July 17, 1980; *Independence Reporter*, Dec. 29, 1980.
31. KG&E bonds in March 1980 were downgraded to BBB by Moody's and BBB- by Standard and Poor. *Wichita Eagle*, March 13, 1980.

NOTES TO CHAPTER 8

32. Dale Lyon, in *Burlington Daily Republican,* May 22, 1979. Actually, the money for the REC came from REA, part of USDA, or a federally backed "bank" for co-ops, and thus more from the general tax fund than from farmers specifically.

33. *Fredonia Herald,* May 24, 1979.

34. *Humbolt Union,* May 1, 1980.

35. *Kansas Country Living,* (June 1979).

36. *Kansas City Star,* March 23, 1980.

37. *Wichita Eagle,* May 16, 1980.

38. Ibid., June 11, 1980; *Kansas City Star,* July 27, 1980.

39. Dr. Robert Hagen, interview with the author, Nov. 19, 1992.

40. *Wichita Eagle,* June 15, 1980.

41. *Topeka Daily Capital,* July 9, 1980.

42. *Burlington Daily Republican,* June 13, 1980.

43. *Wichita Eagle,* June 15, 1980; Cresap, "Prudence Review," IV-79.

44. James Haines, interview with the author, June 27, 1990; Wilson Cadman, interview with the author, March 10, 1989.

45. James Haines, interview with the author, June 27, 1990. Brian Moline of the KCC staff heard a similar rumor, indicating that state senator Frank Gaines had met with company officials with this offer. Moline said had he been the company he would not have relied on that offer, either. Brian Moline, interview with the author, June 8, 1990.

46. Brian Moline, interview with the author, June 8, 1990.

47. *Wichita Eagle,* Aug. 17, 1980.

48. Brian Moline, interview with the author, June 8, 1990.

49. *Wichita Eagle,* Oct. 31, 1980.

50. Ibid., Jan. 13, 1981.

51. Ibid., Feb. 1, 1981.

52. *Wellington Daily News,* Dec. 15, 1980.

53. *Wichita Eagle,* Dec. 19, 1980.

54. Ibid., Oct. 31, 1981.

55. Ibid., Oct. 8, Oct. 31, 1980.

56. Ibid., Jan. 13, 1981.

57. *Emporia Herald,* Nov. 11, 1980.

58. Robert Rives, in *Parsons Sun,* Nov. 17, 1980.

59. Wilson Cadman to "Kansas Leaders," Feb. 6, 1981, Jack King scrapbooks, vol. 4.

60. *Kansas City Star,* July 27, 1980.

61. *Topeka Capital Journal,* March 18, 1981.

62. *Wichita Eagle,* Nov. 29, 1980.

63. *Parsons Sun,* Feb. 10, 1981.

64. Les and Scott Davis, in *Wichita Eagle,* Feb. 14, 1981.

65. *Hutchinson News,* Jan. 27, 1981.
66. *Burlington Daily Republican,* Jan. 28, 1981.
67. *Topeka Capital Journal,* Jan. 29, 1981.
68. *Wichita Eagle,* Feb. 1, 1981.
69. *Pittsburg Sun,* Feb. 18, 1981.
70. *Parsons Sun,* Feb. 18, 1981.
71. *Topeka Capital Journal,* March 27, 1981; *Wichita Eagle,* April 3, 1981.
72. Undated clipping [April 1981], KG&E Wolf Creek clippings.
73. *Emporia Gazette,* March 14, 1981.
74. *Wichita Eagle,* July 23, 1981.
75. *Kansas City Star,* Aug. 2, 1981; Brian Moline, interview with the author, June 8, 1990.
76. *Topeka Capital Journal,* Aug. 1, 1981.
77. *Parsons Sun,* Oct. 5, 1981.
78. *Wichita Eagle,* Oct. 27, 1981.
79. Ibid., Jan. 1, 1982.
80. *Burlington Daily Republican,* Oct. 12, 1981.
81. *Wichita Eagle,* Oct. 27, 1981; *Ottawa Herald,* April 30, 1982; *Larned Tiller and Toiler,* May 17, 1982.
82. *Wichita Eagle,* May 6, Nov. 17, 1981; *Topeka Capital Journal,* Nov. 26, 1981; *Kansas City Times,* Oct. 10, 1981.
83. *Wichita Eagle,* Sept. 1, 1981.
84. *Topeka Capital Journal,* Nov. 26, 1981; *Servicegraph* (Sept. 1981).
85. *Wichita Eagle,* Dec. 29, 1979.
86. Cresap, McCormick and Paget, "Financial and Operational Study," (1980), IV-1-32; VII-32.
87. Ibid, VI-512.
88. Ibid., VII-12-13, 27; Section IX contains the recommendations.
89. Ibid., I-1.
90. KG&E flyer, "The Outlet," (Jan. 1981).
91. *Topeka Capital Journal,* Jan. 3, 1981; *Wichita Eagle,* Nov. 28, 1980.
92. *Parsons Sun,* Feb. 11, 1982.
93. *Wichita Eagle,* Nov. 20, 1981.
94. Wilson Cadman, interview with the author, March 10, 1989.
95. *Wichita Eagle,* Aug. 21, 1982.
96. Flyer "Warning to the people of the Wichita area," Oct. 26, 1982, in Jack King scrapbooks, vol. 4. The flyer was a campaign piece for Kansas attorney general candidate Lance Burr.
97. *Wichita Eagle,* Nov. 30, 1983.
98. *Ottawa Herald,* Nov. 20, 1981.
99. *Kansas City Times,* Aug. 19, 1981.
100. *Wichita Eagle,* March 29, 1982.

101. Ibid., July 17, 1983.
102. C. and M. Abbot-Mills, in *Wichita Eagle*, Jan. 19, 1982.
103. *Louisburg Herald*, Sept. 30, 1982.
104. *Chanute Tribune*, Oct. 4, 1982.
105. Ibid, Jan. 7, 1983.
106. *Olathe Daily News*, Feb. 4, 1983.
107. *Olathe Daily News*, Oct. 1, 1983.
108. Bob Rives, in *Parsons Sun*, Feb. 24, 1982.
109. *Emporia Gazette*, Oct. 13, 1981.
110. *Independence Reporter*, June 15, 1982.
111. *Salina Journal*, June 28, 1982.
112. John Flick, in *Wichita Eagle*, Sept. 14, 1982.
113. *Independence Reporter*, Feb. 17, 1982.
114. *Kansas City Star*, March 13, 1983; *Olathe Daily News*, Nov. 24, 1983.
115. Joseph Hosley, in *Wichita Eagle*, Sept. 2, 1982.
116. *Olathe Daily News*, April 26, 1983.
117. *Ottawa Herald*, March 26, 1983.
118. Lee Gorman, Carla Cornett, in *Wichita Eagle*, Dec. 21, 1983.
119. Bernard Cohen, professor of nuclear physics, University of Pittsburgh, in *Kansas City Star*, Oct. 16, 1983.
120. *Wichita Eagle*, Nov. 23, 1983.
121. *Servicegraph* (Sept. 1980), p. 3.
122. *Marion County Record*, Oct. 19, 1983.
123. Al Noland, in *Wichita Eagle*, Aug. 31, 1982.
124. *Wichita Eagle*, May 1, 1982.
125. *Kansas City Star*, Sept. 2, 1982.
126. *Wichita Eagle*, July 13, 1982.
127. *Kansas City Star*, Sept. 12, 1982.
128. *Parsons Sun*, Sept. 12, 1982.
129. *Wichita Eagle*, July 26, 1983.
130. *Topeka Capital Journal*, Jan. 11, 1983.
131. *Kansas City Star*, Sept. 2, 1982.
132. *Wichita Eagle*, May 23, 1982. In an internal memo, Rives noted that the Wichita papers had left out a comment by Pete Loux of the KCC: "Before we started, they had no handle on cost. While a cost of $2 billion or $2.5 billion seems large, it could have been twice that without our investigation. They didn't have any management. The contractors were running amok. No one at KG&E or KCP&L had the ability to supervise the contractors." Memo dated July 17, 1982, in KG&E, Wolf Creek clippings.
133. *Pittsburg Sun*, Dec. 24, 1982.
134. Cresap, "Prudence Review," IV-64.
135. *Wichita Journal*, March 26, 1983.

136. *Wichita Eagle*, April 20, 1983.
137. Ibid., Nov. 20, 1983. KG&E stock declined that year to a low of under 17. It was to go far lower.
138. Ibid., Feb. 16, 1984.
139. Ibid., Feb. 23, 1984. Because the KG&E trade territory did not grow as fast as did that of KCPL, the customers there paid relatively more for Wolf Creek power than did residents of Kansas City.
140. *Kansas City Times*, March 27, 1984.
141. Wilson Cadman, interview with the author, March 10, 1989.
142. *Kansas City Star*, May 13, 1984.
143. Joe Kramer, in *Kansas City Times*, April 24, 1984.
144. William Woolery, interview with the author, April 26, 1989.
145. *Kansas City Star*, May 13, 1984.
146. Cresap, "Prudence Review," V-47. This section of the report contains a complete summary of KG&E's financial innovations in funding Wolf Creek.
147. *Kansas City Star*, May 13, 1984.
148. William Woolery, interview with the author, April 26, 1989.
149. *Kansas City Star*, May 13, 1984.
150. *Wichita Eagle*, Dec. 8, 1983.
151. *Ottawa Herald*, May 17, 1983.
152. *Wichita Eagle*, March 4, 1983.
153. *Coffeyville Journal*, Sept. 20, 1983.
154. *Wichita Eagle*, Nov. 20, 1983.
155. William Woolery, interview with the author, April 26, 1989.

CHAPTER 9

1. Camilleri, *The State and Nuclear Power*, pp. 280–83.
2. *Wichita Eagle*, Jan. 14, 16, 1984.
3. Edwin Yoder, in *Washington Post*, quoted in *Wichita Eagle*, Jan. 5, 1984.
4. *Independence Reporter*, Jan. 22, 1984.
5. *Wichita Eagle*, Jan. 12, 1984.
6. *Olathe Daily News*, Jan. 18, 1984.
7. *Wichita Eagle*, Feb. 29, 1984.
8. *Coffeyville Journal*, Feb. 22, 1984.
9. John Brown, in *Wichita Eagle*, March 2, 1984.
10. Grover McKee, in ibid., March 4, 1984.
11. Patric Rowley, in ibid., March 8, 1984.
12. *Pittsburg Sun*, Feb. 8, 1984.
13. *Parsons Sun*, Jan. 31, 1984.

14. *Kansas City Times*, Dec. 28, 1982.
15. *El Dorado Times*, March 3, 1984.
16. *Kansas City Star*, Feb. 28, 1984.
17. *Wichita Eagle*, March 1, 1984.
18. Ibid., Feb. 12, 1984.
19. Ibid., Feb. 18, 1984.
20. Willard Garvey, in *Wichita Eagle*, March 2, 1984.
21. Bill Earnest, in ibid., March 9, 1984.
22. Joyce Dutton, in ibid., March 10, 1984.
23. Ibid., March 11, 1984.
24. Ibid., Feb. 12, 1984.
25. Elmer Hall, interview with the author, Feb. 16, 1989.
26. Wilson Cadman, interview with the author, March 10, 1989. See *Wichita Eagle*, March 28, 1984 for Tompkins's resignation.
27. *Wichita Eagle*, March 11, 1984.
28. U.S. Nuclear Regulatory Commission, Atomic Safety and Licensing Board, "In the Matter of Kansas Gas and Electric Co. et al . . . NRC Docket no. 50-482 OL, ASLBP Docket no. 81-453-03 OL, July 2, 1984, Initial Decision," typescript, KG&E archives, passim; *Wichita Eagle*, Dec. 8, 1983, Feb. 8, 1984.
29. U.S. Nuclear Regulatory Commission, "Initial Decision, July 2, 1984," p. 1.
30. *Lebo Enterprise*, Jan. 23, 1985; *Miami Republican*, Jan. 30, 1985; *Iola Register*, March 12, 13, 16, 1985; *Howard Courant-Citizen*, March 13, 1985; *Liberal Southwest Daily Times*, June 4, 1985; U.S. Nuclear Regulatory Commission, *Final Environmental Statement relating to the Operation of Wolf Creek Generating Station, Unit No 1* (Washington, DC: NRC, June 1982); U.S. Nuclear Regulatory Commission, *Safety Evaluation Report Related to the Operation of Wolf Creek Generating Station, Unit No 1* (Washington, DC: NRC, April 1982).
31. *Dodge City Daily Globe*, Dec. 28, 1984.
32. *Wichita Eagle*, Nov. 9, 1983.
33. Ibid., June 9, 1983.
34. *Pratt Tribune*, Feb. 15, 1983.
35. *Olathe Daily News*, April 26, 1983.
36. *Salina Journal*, Feb. 19, 1984.
37. Paul Wilde, in *Kansas City Star*, Feb. 29, 1984.
38. *Emporia Gazette*, Feb. 17, 1984.
39. *Chanute Tribune*, Jan. 5, 1984. Three Mile Island, however, had its effect. Three states—California, Connecticut, and Maine—passed legislation in 1980 similar to that proposed in Kansas in 1984. Five other states proposed new initiatives to limit nuclear power. See Rosa and Freudenberg, "Nuclear Power at the Crossroads," pp. 24–25.

NOTES TO CHAPTER 9

40. *Wichita Eagle,* Jan. 25, Feb. 19, 1984.
41. Ruth Luzzati, interview with the author, Nov. 19, 1992.
42. Margalee Wright, interview with the author, Nov. 20, 1992.
43. Michael Lennen, interview with the author, July 26, 1990.
44. *Wichita Eagle,* Feb. 12, 1984.
45. Ibid., Feb. 8, 1984.
46. Ibid., March 1, 1984.
47. Ross Doyen, interview with the author, Nov. 17, 1992.
48. *Wichita Eagle,* Feb. 23, 1984.
49. Wilson Cadman to community leaders, Feb. 24, 1984, in Jack King scrapbooks, vol. 4.
50. *Wichita Eagle,* Feb. 23, 1984.
51. *Olathe Daily News,* Feb. 29, 1984.
52. *Wichita Eagle,* March 1, 1984.
53. Ibid., Jan. 28, 1984.
54. *Servicegraph* (Feb. 1984), n.p.
55. *Kansas City Kansan,* May 8, 1984; *Wichita Journal,* July 6, 1985.
56. *Wichita Eagle,* Feb. 2, 1984.
57. Ibid., Feb. 19, 1984.
58. Ibid.
59. Ibid., Feb. 11, 1984.
60. *Kansas City Star,* March 4, 1984.
61. *Wichita Eagle,* Feb. 10, 1984.
62. James Haines, Legislative Testimony, House Bills 2927, 2964, 2810, and 2927 as amended, undated typescript, James Haines files, KG&E.
63. *Wichita Eagle,* March 2, 28, 1984.
64. *Parsons Sun,* April 14, 1984.
65. The Tompkins story was on Feb. 12 and retractions were not printed until March, by which time the rate shock bill was well under way.
66. *Wichita Eagle,* Feb. 19, 1984.
67. Frank Myers, in *El Dorado Times,* March 6, 1984.
68. Joyce Dutton, in *Wichita Eagle,* March 10, 1984.
69. *Wichita Eagle,* Feb. 22, 1984.
70. Ibid., Feb. 15, 1984.
71. Marc Francoeur, in ibid., March 6, 1984.
72. *Wichita Eagle,* March 28, 1984.
73. *Coffeyville Journal,* March 31, 1984.
74. "Symposium on the Wolf Creek Nuclear Power Plant," *University of Kansas Law Review* 33:3 (Spring 1985), 429–57.
75. Keith Weins, "Citizen Perspective in the Wolf Creek Rate Case," ibid., pp. 469–70.

76. John Simpson, "Equal Rights for Citizens Before Administrative Agencies," ibid., p. 503.
77. Brian Moline, "Wolf Creek and the Rate-Making Process," ibid., pp. 509–18.
78. Robert Vancrum, "The Wolf Creek Excess-Cost Capacity Bill," ibid., pp. 475–77.
79. KG&E, "A Response to the 1984 Amendments of K.S.A. 66-128, October, 1984," typescript, KG&E archives, p. I-2.
80. James Haines, interview with the author, June 27, 1990.
81. KG&E, "Response," p. II-1.
82. Cresap, "Prudence Review," pp. I-1–4.
83. KG&E, "Response," pp. II-4–7.
84. Ibid., p. II-22.
85. Cresap, "Prudence Review," pp. II-2, 5; III-36, 52, 59, 66.
86. KG&E, "Response," pp. III-2, 4.
87. Ibid, pp. VI-1–2.
88. Charnoff, "Why Managers Did It All Right."
89. [Charles Huston], *Management Performance Evaluation* (May 1984), pp. 16, 18, 122, 257.
90. *University Daily Kansan*, Aug. 30, 1984.
91. James Haines, interview with the author, July 10, 1990.
92. *Wilson County Citizen*, Feb. 27, 1984.
93. *Independence Reporter*, March 20, 1984.
94. RMT, in *Garnett Review*, March 12, 1984.
95. James Haines, interview with the author, June 27, 1990.
96. James Haines, in *Topeka Capital Journal*, March 15, 1984.
97. James Haines, in *Coffey County Today*, March 16, 1984.
98. James Haines, in *Kansas City Times*, March 15, 1984.
99. *Hutchinson News*, Feb. 27, 1984.
100. *Wichita Eagle*, Feb. 28, 1984.
101. Mrs. R. M. Bond, in *Wichita Eagle*, Feb. 28, 1984.
102. John Brown, in Ibid., March 2, 1984.
103. Don Eastman, in Ibid., March 27, 1984.
104. *Wichita Eagle*, April 7, 1984.
105. Ibid., Feb. 26, 1984.
106. *Chanute Tribune*, April 27, 1984.
107. Ronald Force, in *Wichita Eagle*, March 4, 1984.
108. *Wichita Eagle*, May 24, 1984; *Arkansas City Traveler*, May 23, 1984.
109. *Kansas City Star*, May 27, 1984.
110. *Ottawa Herald*, Feb. 18, 1985.
111. *Olathe Daily News*, June 13, 1984.

112. *Wichita Eagle,* March 30, 1984.
113. Lewie Kreuger, in ibid., March 3, 1984.
114. Ibid., Feb. 29, 1984.

CHAPTER 10

1. *Miami Republican,* Jan. 30, 1985; *Junction City Daily Union,* March 13, 1985. The full power license was granted early in June; *Liberal Southwest Daily Times,* June 4, 1985.
2. *Coffey County Today,* March 15, 1985; another full description is in *Iola Register,* March 16, 1985.
3. *Wellington Daily News,* Feb. 12, 1985; *Dodge City Daily Globe,* March 5, 1985.
4. *Lawrence Journal-World,* July 23, 1985.
5. *Olathe Daily News,* July 27, 1985; *McPherson Sentinel,* July 27, 1985.
6. *Pittsburg Morning Sun,* Jan. 12, 1985.
7. Margalee Wright, interview with the author, Nov. 20, 1992.
8. Michael Lennen, interview with the author, July 26, 1990.
9. *Chanute Tribune,* May 15, 1985.
10. *Arkansas City Traveler,* June 19, 1985.
11. *Colby Free Press,* May 23, 1985.
12. *Newton Kansan,* April 8, 1985; *Ottawa Herald,* April 8, 1985.
13. *Humbolt Union,* May 15, 1985.
14. *Salina Journal,* May 13, 1985.
15. Statement of James Haines, May 13, 1985, 1985 Rate Hearings, 1:26–54.
16. Statement of Warren Wood, ibid., p. 56.
17. Statement of Robert Fillmore, ibid., pp. 69–105. Within a few months of the conclusion of the Wolf Creek case, Robert Fillmore went to work for a law firm in Dallas that represented Texas Utilities. His assignment was to guide TU's rate application and prudence review at the Texas Commission for the $10 billion plus Commanche Peak Station. Fillmore argued from 1986 to 1991 that $10 billion plus was a good deal for TU consumers. Haines had changed situations, too, when he went from attorney for the Missouri Public Service Commission to a job at KG&E. Interview with James Haines, September, 1991.
18. Statement of Robert Eye, 1985 Rate Hearings, 1:113–18.
19. Statement of Patrick Donahue, ibid., pp. 133, 135.
20. Testimony of Gui Ponce de Leon, June 12, 1985, ibid., 18:5266–70.
21. Testimony of Richard Rosen, June 18, 1985, ibid. , 23:6501, 6520–21, 6530–31, 6534.

22. Testimony of Charles Komanoff, July 1, 1985, ibid. 34:9951–53.
23. Michael Lennen, interview with the author, July 26, 1990.
24. Testimony of Charles Huston, May 13, 1985, 1985 Rate Hearings, 1:147.
25. Michael Lennen, interview with the author, July 26, 1990.
26. James Haines, interview with the author, July 10, 1990.
27. Testimony of Charles Huston, May 13, 14, 16, 1985, 1985 Rate Hearings, 1:147–51, 154; 2:236, 284; 4:990.
28. Ibid., May 13, 1985, 1:154–56. Totals 102 percent due to rounding.
29. Ibid., May 14, 15, 16, 1985, 2:310; 3:499–500; 4:677, 679–80, 689.
30. Testimony of George Roen, May 20, 1985, ibid., 6:501–3, 1581, 1621.
31. Ibid., May 21, 1985, 7:1867–80.
32. Testimony of Wilson Cadman, May 23, 1985, ibid., 9:253–40.
33. Ibid., May 24, 1985, 10:2797–98, 2802, 2898.
34. Ibid., May 25, 1985, 11:2950, 2952–54, 3006.
35. Testimony of Arthur Doyle, May 29, 1985, ibid., 13:3443–44; 3453, 3473–75, 3584, 3702–3.
36. Testimony of Donald McPhee, May 30, 1985, ibid., 14:3860.
37. Testimony of Gui Ponce de Leon, June 12, 1985, ibid, 18:5270.
38. Ibid., June 12, June 15, 1985, 18:5277, 5309, 5440; 20:5814, 21:5882.
39. Testimony of Richard Rosen, ibid., June 18, 1985, 23:6510, 6531, 6534, 6542–46, 6549.
40. Ibid., 6550–51, 6554.
41. Ibid., 6733–36, 6739, 6784–85, 6787.
42. Ibid., June 18, 19, 1985, 23:6922; 24:6943, 6977, 7002–3. George Roen, whose recommendations were generally favorable to KG&E, had majored in Near Eastern Studies, which was quite a bit more beside the point. *Great Bend Tribune*, May 23, 1985.
43. Testimony of Richard Rosen, June 19, 20, 1985, 1985 Rate Hearings, 24:7039, 7046, 7069, 7107–9; 35:7329.
44. Testimony of Charles Komanoff, July 1, 1985, ibid., 34:9953, 9962–63.
45. Ibid., 34:9965, 9970, 10021–24, 10077, 10081.
46. *Concordia Blade Empire*, June 13, 1985.
47. GNF, in *Wamego Smoke Signal*, July 31, 1985.
48. *Concordia Blade Empire*, Aug. 19, 1985.
49. *Coffeyville Journal*, June 18, 1985.
50. *Beloit Daily Call*, Aug. 9, 1985.
51. *Winfield Daily Courier*, Aug. 24, 1985.
52. *Humbolt Union*, Sept. 11, 1985.
53. *Wichita Eagle*, Sept. 9, 1984.
54. *Wichita Journal*, Sept. 14, 1985.
55. *Chanute Tribune*, March 14, 1985.

CONCLUSION

1. James Haines, interview with the author, July 10, 1990.
2. U.S. Supreme Court, *In Re Kansas Gas and Electric Co v. State Corporation Commission* (Oct. term, 1985), Appellant's Appendix to Jurisdictional Statements, pp. 24–25a, KG&E archives; *Coffeyville Journal*, Sept. 30, 1985.
3. Kansas Corporation Commission, "In the Matter of the Application of Kansas Gas and Electric Company for a Determination of the Efficiency or Prudence of the Retirement from Service of the Ripley Steam Electric Station . . ." Docket no. 142, 098-U, Rebuttal Testimony of James Haines, n.d., p. 4, KG&E archives.
4. U.S. Supreme Court, *In Re Kansas Gas and Electric Co.*, "Order of the Kansas Corporation Commission," Sept. 27, 1985, pp. 19c, 20c, 24c, 47c, 60c, 67c, 72c, 89c, 91c.
5. Ibid., pp. 99c–155c. Actually, the total executive salaries and TV advertising in 1985 would have been less than $1 million. Had salaries been cut by half and TV ads eliminated there would have been an after-tax saving of about $300,000, hardly significant in the circumstances. James Haines, note to the author, Oct. 20, 1991.
6. U.S. Supreme Court, *In Re Kansas Gas and Electric Co.*, "Order of the Kansas Corporation Commission," p. 92ff.
7. *Wall Street Journal*, Oct. 2, 1986.
8. *Pittsburg Sun*, Oct. 3, 1985.
9. *Kansas City Times*, Oct. 1, 1986.
10. Ibid., Oct. 1, 1985.
11. *Kansas City Star*, Oct. 4, 1985; *Wichita Eagle*, Oct. 10, 1985. A complete summary of the cost-cutting measures is in Kansas Corporation Commission, "In the Matter of the Application of Kansas Gas and Electric Company for Approval of a Plan to Delay or Reduce $100 Million of Approved Rate Increases . . ." (cited hereafter as Delay of Rate Increases). Testimony of James Haines, Jan. 5, 1986 [1987], p. 6.
12. *Wichita Eagle*, Oct. 5, 1985.
13. *Kansas City Times*, Oct. 17, 1985.
14. Ibid., Oct. 1, 1985.
15. Testimony of James Haines, Delay of Rate Increases, Jan. 5, 1986 [1987], p. 6. Haines surmised it was as though the KCC had said, "Here is a level of revenue which we believe is reasonable for your customers to pay and which, if you just muddle through, will barely keep you out of bankruptcy. But, if you work at it, we think that level of revenue will permit you to make minimally acceptable progress in restoring financial health." Ibid., Ripley Retirement, rebuttal testimony, n.d., p. 6.

16. Margalee Wright, interview with the author, Nov. 21, 1992; James Haines, interview with the author, June 27, 1990.
17. James Haines, interview with the author, June 27, 1990.
18. Ibid.
19. Richard J. Pierce, Jr., "Public Utility Regulatory Takings: Should the Judiciary Attempt to Police the Political Institutions?" *Georgetown Law Journal*, 77:2050–51.
20. Ibid., p. 2074. James Haines to William Steinmeier, Feb. 6, 1990, KG&E archives, expresses Haines's views on this subject.
21. *Emporia Gazette*, Sept. 17, 1986.
22. *Kansas City Times*, May 30, 1987.
23. *University Daily Kansan*, Aug. 30, 1989.
24. *Coffey County Today*, Dec. 29, 1989.
25. *Wichita Eagle*, May 22, 1991; "Record Runs Signal New Hope for the Future of Nuclear Power," *Electrical World* 205 (December 1991): 73–74.
26. *Coffey County Today*, June 21, 1991; *Kansas This Week*, Aug. 29, 1990. Interestingly, one of the three best performing plants in the nation was Three Mile Island Unit 1, doubtless under special scrutiny.
27. *Wichita Eagle*, Aug. 14, 1991.
28. *Kansas City Star*, Aug. 15, 1988; *Pittsburg Morning Sun*, Aug. 24, 1988.
29. *Wichita Eagle*, Dec. 3, 1985; *Coffey County Today*, Sept. 28, 1986; *Topeka Capital Journal*, Dec. 13, 1986.
30. *Wichita Business Journal*, June 21, 1991.
31. *Wichita Eagle*, Oct. 8, 1985; *Kansas City Star*, Oct. 8, 1985.
32. *Wichita Eagle*, Nov. 14, 1985.
33. Ibid., June 16, 1986.
34. *Independence Reporter*, Jan. 14, 1987; *Wichita Eagle*, Feb. 24, 1987; *Kansas City Times*, Feb. 24, 1987.
35. Testimony of James Haines, Delay of Rate Increases, Jan, 5, 1986 [1987], pp. 11–13.
36. James Haines, interview with the author, July 10, 1990.
37. *Wichita Eagle*, Dec. 5, 1986.
38. *Topeka Capital Journal*, Jan. 6, 1987.
39. *Kansas City Times*, Dec. 10, 1986.
40. Ibid., Dec. 9, 1986.
41. *Topeka Capital Journal*, Jan. 6, 1987.
42. *Wichita Eagle*, Jan. 17, 1987.
43. Ibid., Feb. 2, 1987.
44. Ibid., Jan. 11, 1987.
45. Ibid., Feb. 2, 6, 1987.
46. Ibid., April 5, 1987.

47. *Topeka Capital Journal,* April 11, 1987; *Kansas City Times,* May 19, 1987.

48. James Haines, interview with the author, July 10, 1990; U.S. Supreme Court, *Kansas Gas and Electric Company and Kansas City Power & Light Company v. State Corporation Commission of Kansas* (Oct. term, 1986), Brief for Appellant Kansas Gas and Electric Company, May 9, 1987, KG&E archives.

49. James Haines, interview with the author, July 10, 1990; Kansas Corporation Commission, *In the Matter of the Application of Kansas Gas and Electric Company for Approval of the Sale of its 50% Interest in Unit 2 of the LaCygne Generating Station . . . ,* Sept. 1, 1987, transcript of proceedings, KG&E archives.

50. James Haines, interview with the author, July 10, 1990.

51. The author was personally present that evening.

52. James Haines, interview with the author, July 10, 1990.

53. *Wichita Eagle,* Nov. 26, 1989.

54. Ibid., Nov. 13, 1990.

55. *Time,* June 19, 1989; *Wichita Eagle,* May 21, 1989.

56. *Business Week,* April 10, 1989; *Wall Street Journal,* May 18, 1989; Golay and Todreas, "Advanced Light-Water Reactors;" "Nuclear Power: Do We Have a Choice," *Time,* April 29, 1991, pp. 54–61.

57. *Wichita Eagle,* Feb. 20, 1980.

58. James Haines, interview with the author, June 27, 1990.

59. Diane Tegtmeier, interview with the author, June 12, 1990.

60. *Kansas City Star,* April 22, 1984.

61. *Arkansas City Traveler,* March 1, 1984.

62. Henry Farlie, "Fear of Living," *New Republic,* Jan. 23, 1989, p. 16.

63. This analysis, beginning with the "Robber Baron" quotation, is derived from Jack D. Kartez, "Rational Arguments and Irrational Audiences": "Psychology, Planning, and Public Judgement," *Journal of the American Planning Association* 55 (Autum 1989), 445–56.

64. Wilson Cadman, interview with the author, March 10, 1989.

65. Testimony of Arthur Doyle, May 29, 1985, 1985 Rate Hearings, 13:3533.

66. Dr. Robert Hagen, interview with the author, Nov. 19, 1992.

67. JLS, in *Lyons Daily News,* Feb. 29, 1984.

68. *Wichita Eagle,* Feb. 19, 1984.

69. *Wichita Eagle,* Jan. 18, 1979.

70. *Ingrams* (Sept. 1990); *Wichita Eagle,* Oct. 28, Nov. 13, 1990.

71. *Wichita Eagle,* July 24, 1990.

72. *Wichita Eagle,* July 25, 1990.

73. *Kansas City Star,* July 24, 1990.

74. Charles Studness, "Utility Financial Policy and Vulnerability to Hostile Takeovers," *Public Utilities Fortnightly* (Sept. 27, 1990), n.p. James Haines

replied to this article in detail, arguing that Studness emphasized the reverses KG&E's regulatory strategy experienced rather than its successes. He denied that KG&E "allowed" the KCC to conduct a cost of service audit, but only that the KCC exercized its authority to order such an audit as any regulatory body could. KCPL's strength, on the other hand, was not, noted Haines, due to its superior regulatory strategy, but to phenomenal sales growth in the Kansas City area. KG&E was never unaware of takeover possibilities, but had to work within severe restraints. James Haines to Charles Studness, Oct. 9, 1990, KG&E archives.

75. *New York Times,* July 24, 1990.
76. *Wichita Eagle,* Nov. 13, 1990.
77. *Energy Daily,* Oct. 31, 1990.
78. *Wichita Eagle,* Aug. 5, 1990.
79. Nuclear clippings, KG&E archives, 1990.
80. *Independence Reporter,* July 27, 1990.
81. *Wichita Eagle,* Aug. 30, 1990; *Energy Daily,* Aug. 22, 1990.
82. *Wichita Eagle,* Sept. 1, 1990.
83. Ibid., Sept. 6, 1990.
84. *Kansas City Star,* Oct. 29, 1990.
85. *Wichita Eagle,* Sept. 13, 1990.
86. *Kansas City Star,* Oct. 29, 1990.
87. Ibid., Oct. 31, 1990.
88. *Wichita Eagle,* Nov. 4, 1990.
89. Ibid., Dec. 4, 14, 1990.
90. *Topeka Capital Journal,* Feb. 8, 1991.
91. *Wichita Business Journal,* Feb. 1, 1991.
92. *Wichita Eagle,* March 26, 1991.
93. *Newton Kansan,* April 12, 1991.
94. *Kansas City Star,* April 22, 1991.
95. *Wichita Eagle,* Sept. 11, 1991.
96. *Parsons Sun,* Sept. 6, 1991.
97. Freudenberg and Rosa, *Public Reactions to Nuclear Power,* p. 22.
98. This analogy was made by Jim Lawing, interview with the author, Nov. 20, 1992.
99. Literature turning on this and analyzing it from an "American Studies" perspective includes Marx, *Machine in the Garden,* Joseph Corn, *The Winged Gospel: America's Romance with Aviation, 1900–1950* (New York: Oxford University Press, 1983), and David Nye, *Electrifying America* (Cambridge, MA: MIT Press, 1991).
100. Nathaniel Hawthorne, *The House of the Seven Gables* (Boston: Ticknor, Reed & Fields, 1851), pp. 279–83.

101. The Japanese are much more aware of this element than are Americans. See, for example, Shiro Sasaki, "Building Public Acceptance of Nuclear Power," *Business Japan* 36 (Feb. 1991): 38–39, which is typical of a large body of such recent literature.

102. Farlie, "Fear of Living," pp. 14, 16, 17.

103. *Kansas City Star*, Nov. 13, 1990.

104. Sugai, *Nuclear Power and Ratepayer Protest*, p. 245.

105. Weart, *Nuclear Fear*, p. 354. These dichotomies are analyzed in numerous more or less contemporary books. An especially eloquent statement is in Wendell Berry, *The Unsettling of America: Culture & Agriculture* (New York: Avon, 1978).

106. Marge Setter, interview with the author, June 27, 1989.

107. Henry Adams, *The Education of Henry Adams: An Autobiography* (Boston: Houghton Mifflin, 1918), p. 380.

108. Shaftesbury, *Chacteristiks of Men*, 2:200.

Bibliography

Most of the primary material was researched in the corporate archives of Kansas Gas and Electric Company, Wichita, Kansas. However, much of this material, and most of that substantial part generated by regulatory bodies, is available to the public in a special collection at the library of Emporia State University, Emporia, Kansas, where it has been deposited as it was generated. The extensive statewide and national newspaper coverage is cited by newspaper and date, but was researched, for the most part, in the voluminous, definitive, and nonselective clippings files maintained by KG&E.

PRIMARY

Documents

Arthur D. Little, Inc. "Management and Operations Review, KG&E," prepared for Kansas Corporation Commission under Feb. 1977 contract, typescript.
Cresap, McCormick and Paget. "Report on the Financial and Operational Study of the Wolf Creek Nuclear Generating Facility," Nov. 1980, typescript, KG&E Archives.
———. "A Prudence Review of KG&E'S Involvement in the Wolf Creek Generating Station," Oct. 1984, typescript.
Haines, James. "Opening Statement, Wolf Creek Rate Case, May 13, 1985," typescript, KG&E legal department.
Hixson, J. D. *SEFOR Plant Operating Experience*. Sunnyvale, CA: General Electric Corp., 1972.
Kansas Corporation Commission. "In the Matter of the Application of Kansas Gas and Electric Company for a Determination of the Efficiency or

Prudence of the Retirement from Service of the Ripley Steam Electric Station . . ." Docket no.142,098-U, Transcript of Proceedings, n.d.

———. "In the Matter of the Application of Kansas Gas and Electric Company for Approval of the Sale of its 50% Interest in Unit 2 of the LaCygne Generating Station . . ." Sept. 1, 1987, Transcript of Proceedings.

———. "In the Matter of a General Investigation of the Commission of the Projected Costs and Related Matters of the Wolf Creek Nuclear Generation Facility at Burlington, Kansas." Docket no. 120, 925-U et. al. Transcript of Proceedings, Spring 1985, 39 vols., over 17,000 pages.

Kansas Gas and Electric Company. "A Response to the 1984 Amendments of K.S.A. 66-128," Oct. 1984, typescript.

———. *Annual Reports*, 1945 to present.

———. *Information Pertaining to the Company's Business and Operations.* Wichita: 201 N. Market, Feb. 1949.

———. ,Kansas City Power & Light, Kansas Electric Power Cooperative, Inc., *Management Peformance Evaluation*, May, 1984.

———. James Haines, "Legislative Testimony, House Bills 2927, 2964, 2810 and 2927 as Amended," undated typescript.

———. Nuclear Clippings, 1974–1991 (35 loose leaf volumes, 2 boxes loose clips, c. 20,000 pages).

———. Statement of James Haines, House Bills No. 2927, 2964, 2810 [1985], typescript.

———. *Servicegraph* (company magazine), 1933–1982.

———. *The Core of the Great Plains.* Wichita: KG&E, 1955.

———. Transmittal Clippings, July 1976 to July 1983 (4 large boxes [3 smaller boxes in each], c. 20,000 pages).

King, Jack. Personal scrapbooks on Wolf Creek, 4 volumes.

Luzzati, Ruth. Personal Papers, Wichita, Kansas.

National Electric Reliability Council. *Annual Report 1977.* Princeton NJ: NERC, 1978.

"Record Runs Signal New Hope for the Future of Nuclear Power," *Electrical World* 205 (Dec. 1991): 73–74.

Superior Court of the State of California, for Missouri Public Service Commission, "In re Deposition of Jesse O. Arterburn, In the matter of Kansas City Power and Light Company of Kansas City, Missouri, for authority to file tariffs increasing rate for electric service . . ." no. ER-85-128, no. EO-85-185, KG&E archives.

"Symposium on the Wolf Creek Nuclear Power Plant," *University of Kansas Law Review* (Spring 1985).

U.S. Federal Power Commission. *Reclassification of Electric Plant in Accordance with Uniform System of Accounts and Order of May 11, 1937 Issued by Federal Power Commission—Statements "A" to "I," Inclusive of Kansas Gas and Electric Company Wichita, Kansas.* (n.p., n.d.), file E-4 Federal.

U.S. Nuclear Regulatory Commission. "In the Matter of: Kansas Gas and Electric Company and Kansas City Power and Light Company (Wolf Creek Nuclear Generating Station, Unit No. 1)," Docket no. 50-482. Bethesda Maryland, various locations in Kansas, Feb. 1975–1977 (30 vols).

———. "Initial Decision," Docket no. 50-482, July 2, 1984, typescript.

———. *Final Environmental Statement Related to Construction of Wolf Creek Generating Station Unit 1.* . . , Oct. 1975 NUREG-75/096 Docket no. STN 50-482. (Washington, DC: Office of Nuclear Reactor Regulation).

———. "Partial Initial Decision Authorizing Limited Work Authorization," Docket no. 50-482, Jan. 18, 1977, typescript.

———. *Safety Evaluation Report Related to Construction of Wolf Creek Generating Station, Unit No 1.* Docket no. STN 50-482, Sept. 1975. NUREG-75/080.

———. *Supplement No. 1 to the Safety Evaluation Report by the Office of Nuclear Reactor Regulation, U.S. Nuclear Regulatory Commission in the Matter of Kansas Gas and Electric Company and Kansas City Power & Light Company Wolf Creek Generating Station No 1,* Jan. 14, 1976.

———. *Safety Evaluation Report Related to Construction of Wolf Creek Generating Station, Unit. No 1 . . . Supplement No. 2.* Feb 1976. NUREG-0033.

United States Supreme Court. *Kansas Gas and Electric Company, Appellant* v. *State Corporation Commission of the State of Kansas, Appellee,"* Oct. term, 1986 (Washington, DC: Wilson-Epes, 1986).

Wichita (Kansas) *Eagle (*and predecessor names), 1955 to present.

Interviews

John Bailey (Feb. 6, 1989, April 6, 1990); Margaret Bangs (April 2, 9, 1990); Kent Brown (June 11, 1990); Dwight Button (Feb 22, 1989); Wilson Cadman (March 10, 1989); John Delehanty (May 4, 1990); Donna Dilsaver (numerous interviews); Ross Doyen (Nov. 17, 1992); Ralph Fiebach (March 29, 1989); Ralph Foster (July,1991); Dr. Robert Hagen (Nov. 19, 1992); James Haines (Feb 17, 1989, Feb. 22, 1990); Elmer Hall (Feb. 16, 1989); Norman Jacobshagen (April 7, 1989); Mel Johnson (Nov. 29, 1989); Fred Kimball (April 5, 1989); Jack King (Feb. 17, 1989); Lyle Koerper (Nov. 16, 1992); Glenn N. Koester (Feb. 10, 1989, Feb. 28, 1990); Jim Lawing (Nov. 20, 1992); Michael Lennen (July 26, 1990); James Lucas (March 6, 1989); Ruth Luzzati (Nov. 17, 18, 1992); Harley Maklin (July 17, 1989); Robert A. McFarren (March 22, 1989); Brian Moline (June 8, 1990); Bob Rives (June 21, 1990); Marge Setter (June 27, 1989); Ronn Smith (Feb. 6, 1989); Nora Steg (July 31, 1989); Diane Tegtmeier (June 12, 1990); Bill Woolery (April 26, 1989); Margalee Wright (Nov. 20, 1992).

SECONDARY

Adams, Henry. *The Education of Henry Adams: An Autobiography.* Boston: Houghton Mifflin, 1918.

Bader, Robert. *Hayseeds, Moralizers and Methodists: The Twentieth Century Image of Kansas.* Lawrence: University Press of Kansas, 1988.

Barkan, Steven. "Strategic, Tactical, Organization Dilemmas of the Protest Movement Against Nuclear Power," *Social Problems* 27 (1979): 19–35.

Bedford, Henry. *Seabrook Station: Citizen Politics and Nuclear Power.* Amherst: University of Massachusetts Press, 1990.

Berry, Wendell. *Home Economics.* San Francisco: North Point, 1987.

Branyan, Robert, and Larson, Lawrence, eds. *The Eisenhower Administration 1953–1961: A Documentary History.* New York: Random House, 1971.

Cadman, Wilson. *Kansas Gas and Electric Company: Eighty Years of Innovation.* New York: Newcomen Society of the United States, 1989.

Camilleri, Joseph A. *The State and Nuclear Power: Conflict and Control in the Western World.* Seattle: University of Washington Press, 1984.

Cobb, Charles E. "Living With Radiation," *National Geographic* 175, no. 4 (April 1989): 403–37.

Colmer, Donald. *The Gammarae: A Story of Grand Gulf Nuclear Station.* Jackson, MS: Northtown, 1989.

Crane, Hart. *The Collected Poems of Hart Crane.* Edited by Frank Waldo. New York: Liveright, 1946.

DeBoer, Connie, and Catsburg, Irene. "The Impact of Nuclear Accidents on Attitudes Toward Nuclear Energy," *Public Opinion Quarterly* 52, no. 2 (1988): 254–61.

Emerson, Ralph W. *An Oration Delivered Before the Phi Beta Kappa Society at Cambridge, Aug. 31, 1837,* Boston: James Munroe, 1837.

———. *Conduct of Life.* New York: Ticknor and Fields, 1860.

Farlie, Henry. "Fear of Living," *New Republic,* Jan. 23, 1989, pp. 14–19.

Freudenbert, William, and Ross, Eugene. *Public Reactions to Nuclear Power: Are There Critical Masses?* Boulder: Westview, 1984.

Gamson, William A., and Madigliani, Andre. "Media Discourse and Public Opinion on Nuclear Power: A Constructionist Approach," *American Journal of Sociology* 95, no. 1 (1989): 1–37.

Golay, Michael, and Todreas, Neil. "Advanced Light-Water Reactors," *Scientific American* (April 1990).

Hawthorne, Nathaniel. *The House of the Seven Gables.* Boston: Ticknor, Reed & Fields, 1851.

Hertsgaard, Mark, *Nuclear, Inc.: The Men and Money Behind Nuclear Energy.* New York: Pantheon, 1983.

Hirsh, Richard. *Technology and Transformation in the American Electric Utility Industry.* Cambridge: Cambridge University Press, 1989.

Howells, William D. "A Sennight of the Centenntial," *Atlantic Monthly* 38.
Hugey, Joseph, and Sandstrom, Eric. "Perceptions of TMI and Acceptance of a Nuclear Power Plant in a Distant Community," *Journal of Applied Social Psychology* 18, no. 10 (1988): 880–90.
Hughes, Thomas P. *American Genesis: A Century of Invention and Technical Enthusiasm, 1870–1970.* New York: Viking, 1989.
———. *Networks of Power: Electrification in Western Society, 1880–1930.* Baltimore: Johns Hopkins University Press, 1983.
Hyman, Leonard. *America's Electric Utilities: Past, Present and Future.* Arlington, VA: Public Utilities Project, 1983.
Inglehart, Ronald. "Fear of Living Dangerously: Public Attitudes Toward Nuclear Power," *Public Opinion* 7, no. 1 (1984): 41–44.
Jackson, Wes. *New Roots for Agriculture.* Lincoln: University of Nebraska Press, 1980.
———. *Altars of Unhewn Stone: Science and the Earth.* San Francisco: North Point, 1987.
James, Henry. *The American Scene.* New York: Harper & Brothers, 1907.
Jasper, James M. "The Political Life Cycle of Technological Controversies," *Social Forces* 67, no. 2 (1988): 357–77.
Kartez, Jack D. "Rational Arguments and Irrational Audiences: Psychology, Planning, and Public Judgment," *Journal of the American Planning Association* 55 (Autumn 1989): 445–56.
Keniston, Kenneth. *Young Radicals: Notes on Committed Youth.* New York: Harcourt, Brace & World, 1968.
———. *Youth and Dissent: The Rise of a New Opposition.* New York: Harcourt Brace Jovanovich, 1971.
Kolflat, Alf, and Patterson, Robert. *The Sargent & Lundy Story: Consultants to the Power Industry Since 1891* [Chicago?] Sargent & Lundy, [1987].
Ladd, Anthony; Hood, Thomas; and Vanliere, Kent. "Ideological Themes in the Antinuclear Movement: Consensus and Diversity," *Sociological Inquiry* 53, no. 2 (1983): 252–72.
Lawrence, William. *Men and Atoms: The Discovery, the Uses and the Future of Atomic Energy.* New York: Simon and Schuster, 1959.
Lewis, Richard. *The Nuclear Power Rebellion: Citizens vs. the Atomic Industrial Establishment.* New York: Viking, 1972.
Lloyd, Henry D. *Wealth Against Commonwealth.* New York: Harper & Brothers, 1894.
Marx, Leo. *The Machine in the Garden: Technology and the Pastoral Ideal in America.* New York: Oxford University Press, 1964.
Mazuzan, George T., and Walker, J. Samuel. *Controlling the Atom: The Beginnings of Nuclear Regulation 1946–1962.* Berkeley: University of California Press, 1985.
McCauley, T. B. "History," from *Edinburgh Review,* May 1828, in *Critical His-*

torical and Miscellaneous Essays by Lord Macauley. 6 vols. in 3. Boston: Houghton, Osgood, 1878.

McCracken, Samuel. *The War Against the Atom.* NY: Basic Books, 1982.

Millard, Andre. *Edison and the Business of Innovation.* Baltimore: Johns Hopkins University Press, 1990.

Miner, Craig. *Discovery: Cycles of Change in the Kansas Oil & Gas Industry 1860-1987.* Wichita: KIOGA, 1987.

———. *Wichita: The Magic City.* Wichita: Wichita-Sedgwick County Historical Museum Association, 1988.

Mitchell, Robert C. "From Elite Quarrel to Mass Movement," *Society* 18, no. 5 (1981): 76-84.

Moon, William Least Heat. *PrairyErth.* Boston: Houghton Mifflin, 1991.

"Notes and Comments." *New Yorker* 59 (July 25, 1983): 19-20.

Novick, Sheldon. *The Electric War: The Fight Over Nuclear Power.* San Francisco: Sierra Club, 1976.

"Nuclear Power: Do We Have A Choice?" *Time* (April 29, 1991) pp. 54-61.

Nye, David. *Electrifying America.* Cambridge, MA: MIT Press, 1991.

Passer, Harold. *The Electrical Manufacturers, 1875-1900: A Study in Competition, Entrepreneurship, Technical Change and Economic Growth.* Cambridge, MA: Harvard University Press, 1953.

Pierce, Richard J. "Public Utility Regulatory Takings: Should the Judiciary Attempt to Police the Political Institutions?" *Georgetown Law Journal,* 77: 2031-77.

Pilzer, Paul. *Unlimited Wealth.* New York: Crown, 1991.

Rhodes, Richard. *The Making of the Atomic Bomb.* New York: Simon & Shuster (Touchstone paperback), 1988.

Rothman, Stanley, and Lichter, Robert. "Elite Ideology and Risk Perception in Nuclear Energy Policy," *American Political Science Review* 81, no. 2 (1987): 383-404.

Rudolph, Richard, and Ridley, Scott. *Power Struggle: The Hundred Year War Over Electricity.* New York: Harper & Row, 1986.

Shaftesbury, Anthony, Earl of. *Charakteristics of Men Morals Opinions and Times.* 3 vols, 5th edition. Birmingham, England: John Baskerville, 1773.

Shi, David. *The Simple Life: Plain Living and High Thinking in American Culture.* New York: Oxford University Press, 1985.

Schumacher, E. F. *Small is Beautiful: Economics as If People Mattered.* New York: Harper & Row, 1975.

Stoler, Peter. *Decline and Fall: The Ailing Nuclear Power Industry.* New York: Dodd Mead, 1985.

Studness, Charles. "Utility Financial Policy and Vulnerability to Hostile Takeovers," *Public Utilities Fortnightly* (Sept. 27, 1990), pp. 43-46.

Sugai, Wayne H. *Nuclear Power and Ratepayer Protest: The Washington Public Power Supply System Crisis.* Boulder: Westview, 1987.

Trachtenberg, Alan. *Brooklyn Bridge: Fact and Symbol.* New York: Oxford University Press, 1965.

Useem, Bert, and Zald, Mayer. "From Pressure Group to Social Movement: Organizational Dilemmas of the Effort to Promote Nuclear Power," *Social Problems* 30, no. 2 (1982): 144–56.

Waddington, C. V. "The Development of the Kansas Gas and Electric Company System From An Engineering Point of View." B.S. thesis, University of Kansas, April 28, 1939.

Walsh, Edward. *Democracy in the Shadows: Citizen Mobilization in the Wake of the Accident at Three Mile Island.* New York: Greenwood Press, 1988.

Walsh, Edward, and Warland, Rex. "Social Movement Involvement in the Wake of Nuclear Accident: Activists and Freeriders in the TMI Area," *American Sociological Review* 48, no. 6 (1982): 764–80.

Weart, Spencer. *Nuclear Fear: A History of Images.* Cambridge, MA: Harvard University Press, 1988.

Whitehouse, Sheldon. "Perestroika for Public Utilities? (Second Thoughts on a Conservation Incentive)," *Public Utilities Fortnightly* (Feb. 1, 1990), pp. 37–38.

Index

Abzug, Bella, 215
Adams, Henry, 329–30
Adelson, Karen, 265
Advanced Epithermal Thorium Reactor (AETR), 37
Advisory Committee on Reactor Safeguards, 103
Advisory Council on Historic Preservation, 99
Advocates for Clean Energy (ACE), 216
Aker, John, 80
Allen, Andrew, 202
Allendale, NJ, 77
Alliance for Liveable Electric Rates (ALERT), 258, 269, 283, 285, 298
Allowance for Funds Used During Construction (AFUDC), 154–57, 293, 295
American Civil Liberties Union, 72, 82, 90, 102
American Power & Light Company (AP&L), 10
Anderson, George, 89
Andrews, Francis, 285
Ann Arbor, MI, 292
Arkansas City, KS, 130, 140
Arlington, TX, 213–14
Army Corps of Engineers, 213
Arterburn, Jesse, 39–40, 53, 66, 103, 110, 115, 124–26, 145, 180, 205, 210, 221–24
Arthur Little Company, 118, 144, 166–67, 239, 274

Ashe, Reid, 321
Atomic bomb, 2, 13, 18, 73, 105, 110, 126, 140, 179, 193, 197
Atomic Energy Act, 27, 85
Atomic Energy Commission (AEC), 27, 37, 49, 51, 58, 60, 62–63, 66, 70–71, 77, 79, 81, 89–92, 114
Atomic power. *See* Nuclear power
Atomic Safety and Licensing Board, 89, 117, 147, 151–52, 159, 162, 260–61
Atomics International, 34
"Atoms for Peace," 25
Australia, 114

Babcock & Wilcox Company, 47, 51–52, 115–16
Bacon, Francis, 15
Bader, Robert, 4
Bailey, David, 208
Bailey, John, 205
Bangs, Margaret, 18–19, 105, 107, 311–12
Base mat. *See* Wolf Creek Station
Bechtel Company, 6, 44, 120, 143–44, 160–61, 213, 229, 260, 274, 286, 288
Beckmann, Peter, 81
Beems, William, 200
Bennett, Robert, 133, 140, 146–47, 186
Berman, Arnold, 149, 156, 189
Berry, Wendell, 329
Bethesda, MD, 89, 113, 203
Beto Junction, KS, 142–43, 231

384 INDEX

Bijker, Wiebe, 175
Biological Effects of Ionizing Radiation (BEIR) report, 127
Bishop, James, 206
Black & Veatch Company, 123
Black Fox power plant, 247
Blackout (1965), 41, 169
Blaufuss, Francis, 69–71, 106, 176–77, 179, 193, 205, 209
Blaufuss, Tony, 69, 77, 105, 204–5
Bodine, Louis, 193
Bogart, Larry, 77–78
Bosin, Blackbear, 7, 232
Boston College, 291
Boyer, Gary, 125
Breeder reactor, 26, 32, 35–36, 40, 94
Brennan, Peter, 198
Brinkley, John, 4
Brooklyn Bridge, 13
Brooks, Ted, 170, 185–87
Brown, Betty, 142
Brown, Jerry, 141, 227
Brown, Kent, 225, 259, 285
Browns Ferry power plant, 124, 179
"Buddhist Economics," 22
Bunker, Archie, 227
Burgner, Donald, 230
Burlington, KS, 45, 53, 57, 64, 67, 71, 76–77, 103, 113, 138, 142, 151, 172–73, 179–80, 212, 229
Burlington Republican, 67, 72
Burns, Malcolm, 119, 152, 295
Burr, Lance, 246
Byron power plant, 256

Cadman, Wilson, 43–44, 57–58, 60–61, 76–78, 155, 158, 162, 165, 167, 180, 188, 195–96, 214, 220–21, 225, 238–39, 241, 248, 250–51, 257, 259–60, 263–64, 267, 276–77, 285, 289–91, 295, 301, 313–14, 317, 319–22
California: Proposition 15, 146–48
Callaway power plant, 2, 52, 151, 165, 170, 242
Calvert Cliffs decision, 60, 104, 288
Calvert Cliffs power plant, 286

Camilleri, Joseph, 85, 255
Campaign Against Nuclear Energy (CANE), 216
Capacity factor, 101, 124, 217, 297
Carlin, John, 146, 164, 194, 198, 210–11, 236–37, 240, 242, 262, 265, 267, 279
Carson, Rachel, 13, 21
Carter, Jimmy, 146, 169
Cartwright, Robert, 254
Catfish, 65, 67
Challenge Consultants, 285
Chamberlain, John, 215
Charnoff, Gerald, 272–73
Chattanooga, TN, 202
Cherenkov effect, viii
Chernobyl power plant, 23, 87, 308
China Syndrome, The, 20, 207, 210, 217, 256
Christy, Wanda, 71, 76, 106, 260
Cimarron River power plant, 103
Cincinnati Gas and Electric, 291
Cities Service Company, 41–42
Citizens Concerned for the Future, 70
Citizens Environmental Council, 73
Citizens Utility Rights Board (CURB), 79, 82, 258, 308, 313, 322
Clack, Robert, 77, 96, 105–6
Clamshell Alliance, 165, 192, 207
Clapp, Mildred, 142
Clean Air Act (1965), 41, 49, 60
Coal, 41, 43–44, 46–50, 105, 123–24, 126, 183–84, 198–99. *See also* Jeffrey Energy Center; LaCygne power plant; Wichita, KS: coal gas plant
Coalition for Renewable Energy Sources (CREST), 216
Coffey County, KS, 57, 99, 203–4, 256, 264
Cohen, Karl, 38
Cold fusion, 314
Cole, Maverik, 138,
Collins, George, 278
Colorado, 147
Columbia University, 284
Combustion Engineering Company, 52
Commerce Bank (Kansas City), 251–52

Common Cause, 79, 82, 195
Commoner, Barry, 21, 61, 195
Commonwealth Edison Company (Chicago), 256
Computer, 45
Conger, Joan, 192
Connell, Evan, 3
Conservation, 94
Construction Permit (CP), 89, 163
Construction Work in Progress (CWIP), 48, 153–59, 217, 248, 282
Cooling lake, 99
Corbin Reservoir, 45
Cox, Danny, 192
Crane, Hart, 13
Credit Suisse, 251
Cresap, McCormick and Paget Company, 118, 161, 215, 226–27, 239, 242–44, 270–72, 274, 285, 288
Critical Mass, 203, 252

Daniel International Company, 144–45, 151, 161, 171–72, 180–81, 212, 221–23, 225, 288
Day After, The, 252
DeBoer, Jack, 7
Decker, John, 105
Definitive estimate. *See* Wolf Creek Station: cost
Delehanty, John, 181
Denton, Gene, 186
Department of Energy, 184, 186
Descartes, Rene, 15
Dickson, Steve, 288–89
Dilsaver, Donna, xii, 46, 196
Docking, Robert, 62
Dodge City, KS, 5
Dole, Robert, 250
Donahue, Patrick, 284
Donnell, James, 108, 185
Doppler effect test, 38
Douville, Arthur, 110, 140
Doyen, Ross, 130, 134, 254, 263–64, 268
Doyle, Arthur, 43–44, 52, 157–58, 241–42, 252, 284, 291–92, 295, 317
Dresden power plant, 27

Drexel-Burnham-Lambert Company, 250
Duddy, Frank, 221–22, 252
Dylan, Bob, 56

Earnest, William, 259
Easton, William, 258
Ebasco Company, 42–44, 50
Eckhoff, Dean, 96, 101, 318
Econometrics. *See* Economics
Economics, 15–17, 107, 108, 119, 121–22, 195–96, 225–26, 255, 305–6
Edison, Thomas, 2, 8, 13, 32, 198
Edison Institute, 207
Eisenhower, Dwight, 2, 25–26
El Dorado, KS, 81, 129–30, 139
Electric Bond & Share Company, 10
Electric Shock Coalition, 245, 258, 269, 276
Electrical Reliability Council, 22
Electricity, 1, 8–10, 23, 27–28, 32, 40–41, 249, 290, 325
Elliott, Donald, 83, 184, 212
Ellis, Charles, 240
Ellsberg, Daniel, 194
Elmdale, KS, 211
Emerson, Ralph Waldo, xi, 12
Emerson, M. Jarvin, 119
Eminent domain, 75–76
Emporia, KS, 142, 151, 180–81, 256
Emporia Citizens for Energy Conservation, 178
Emporia Gazette, 131, 177, 210–11, 246
Energy crisis, 42, 54, 169–70
Energy Reorganization Act (1974), 60
Energy Research and Development Administration (ERDA), 60, 114
Energy Systems Research Group, 265, 284
Enrico Fermi power plant, 59
Environmental Protection Agency, 47, 99
Environmental Report (ER), 77, 89, 98–100, 102, 113, 123
Estes, Sue, 258
Euratom, 40

Euripedes, 20
Eurodollars, 250
Evans, Gordon, 12, 29–30, 33, 41, 54, 93–94, 166, 249
Excess capacity, 262, 268–69, 275, 294–95, 301, 314. *See also* Kansas: rate shock bill; Kansas Gas and Electric Company: Wolf Creek rate hearings
Eye, Robert, 283–84

Faust, 19
Fayetteville, AK, 37
Federal Communications Commission (FCC), 193–94
Federal Energy Regulatory Commission (FERC), 196, 306
Federal Power Commission, 25, 40, 50, 94, 99, 118, 306
Fiebach, Ralph, 54, 66, 96–97, 135, 148, 181, 220–21
Fillmore, Robert, 282–83
First Boston Company, 198, 250
Fish, 134. *See also* Neosho madtom
Flaherty, Thomas, 144–45, 278, 285
Fluor-Pioneer Company, 143
Fonda, Jane, 19, 209, 215
Ford, Daniel, 27
Ford, Henry, 215
Forecasting, 121–22
Ft. Scott, KS, 206
Foster, Ralph, 131, 133, 215, 220
Fouts, Gary, 221, 242, 285
Freeman, Earl, 204–5
Frenkel, Jacob, 71–72, 74, 77, 100, 127–28
Friends of the Earth, 72, 75
Frizzel, Kent, 315
Fuel Use Act (1978), 188, 225
Fund for Peace, 82

Gaar, Norman, 210
Gaddis, John, 79
Gale, Susan, 227
Gamson, William, 87
Garnett, KS, 77, 79, 105, 275
Garten, Scott, 177–78, 210
Garvey, Willard, xi–xii, 258–59

Gas, vii, 10, 12, 28, 37, 41–42, 44, 105, 114, 130–31, 184, 188, 264, 279. *See also* Gordon Evans power plant; Murray Gill power plant; Wichita, KS: coal gas plant
General Electric Company (GE), 6, 10, 27, 29, 37–38, 51, 54, 65, 133
Georgetown Law Journal, 306
German, Glenn, 67
Gerstenhaber, Jan, 195
Gill, Murray, 12, 55
Glaves, Jack, 214–15
Glickman, Dan, 184, 209–10, 279
Glicksman, Robert, 158, 268–69
Gordon Evans power plant, 183–84
Governor's Nuclear Energy Council (Kansas), 45
Gray Panthers, 277
Groves, Frank, 130–31, 140
Gulf General Atomics Company, 52
Gulf Oil Company, 115

Hagen, Robert, 78, 115, 122–23, 164, 210, 223, 234, 285, 317
Haines, James, 20, 23, 235–36, 238, 241, 264, 266–67, 270, 275–76, 282, 286, 298, 301–2, 305–6, 309–11, 313–15
Hall, Elmer, 7, 31, 41, 45, 51, 169, 259–60
Hansen, Howard, 249–50, 279
Hawks, William, 95
Hawthorne, Nathaniel, 111, 325
Hawthorne power plant, 4
Hayden, Mike, 265
Hayden, Thomas, 209, 215
Health. *See* Wolf Creek Station: safety
Hearings, 84–5, 104, 110–11. *See also* Wolf Creek Station
Hegwald, James, 208
Hendricks, Ron, 74
Henley, Keith, 280, 301, 308
Hersey, John, 21
Hertsgaard, Mark, 1
Hieronymous, William, 282
Hirsh, Richard, 14
History, x, 1
Hofstadter, Richard, 256

Home Owners Trust, 277
Howells, William, 12
Hughes, Thomas, 14, 175
Hugoton, KS, 279
Hunt, Bian, 203
Hussein, Saddam, 315
Huston, Charles, 52, 161, 223, 270, 273–75, 285–88
Hutchinson, KS, 62

Indian Point power plant, 27
Ingram, Steve, 219
Insull, Samuel, 8, 13, 17
Insurance, 95–96, 309–10. *See also* Price-Anderson amendments
International Association of Machinists, 277
Iola Register, 66–67, 81, 192
Iraq, 315
Iraq war (1991), 23
"Irrational Fight Against Nuclear Power, The," 197

Jack, Nancy, 107
Jackson, Wes, 15, 72, 179
James, Alfred, 114, 209
James, Henry, 13
Jameson, Stan, 180
Japan, 326
Jasper, James, 31, 85
J. E. Gegenheimer, 203
Jefferson, John, 131–32
Jefferson, Thomas, 14
Jeffrey, Balfour, 168
Jeffrey Energy Center, 49, 168, 191, 214, 240, 248–49
Jennings, Drue, 320–22
Jensch, Samuel, 40, 89, 102, 107, 119, 124–26, 128, 147, 151, 292
John Redmond Reservoir, 45, 51, 55, 71, 77, 82, 100, 107, 131, 134–35, 138–40, 192, 209, 228, 247
Johnson, Mel, 39
Johnson, W. E., 58
Julius, Haldeman, 4

Kansans for Sensible Energy (KASE), 216, 260
Kansas, 43; CWIP debate, 153–59, 248; history, 3–5, 9–10, 14, 28, 98, 108, 130–31, 220, 223; Lyons protest, 62–64, 90; nuclear politics, 44–45, 82, 90–93, 99, 102, 113, 117, 146–48, 164, 167, 177, 188–91, 194, 198–99, 236–37, 239–40, 323; rate shock bill, 262–71, 305; Siting Act (1976), 149–50; water debate, 128–40; weather, 170, 213, 232. *See also* Kansas Corporation Commission
Kansas Building and Construction Trades Council, 219
Kansas City, 3, 57–58, 73, 100, 107, 113, 291, 324
Kansas City People's Energy Project, 179
Kansas City Power & Light (KCPL), 3, 154–55, 162–63, 247, 277; generation needs, 53, 123; relation with KG&E, 41–44, 51–54, 117, 180, 222–23, 235, 251, 319–22; sale of power to Nebraska, 189–91. *See also* Doyle, Arthur; McPhee, Donald
Kansas City Star, 165
Kansas City Times, 197, 200, 311
Kansas Corporation Commission, x, 9, 60, 91, 149, 156, 166–67, 171, 185, 190, 214–15, 219–20, 230, 259, 261–63, 265–68, 277, 322; KEPCo hearings, 235, 237–42, 245, 249, 270–71; rate stabilization (1987), 309–13, 320; Wolf Creek rate hearings, 278–305
Kansas Electric Power Cooperative, Inc. (KEPCo), 3, 189; hearings on share of Wolf Creek, 232–41
Kansas Electrical Generation Siting Act (1976), 149
Kansas Energy Advisory Council, 148
Kansas Farmers' Union (KFU), 72, 77, 82, 233, 239. *See also* Lyon, Dale
Kansas Gas and Electric Company (KG&E): analysis of nuclear role, 3, 7, 254–55, 289–91, 305–9, 314–19, 323–31; demand, 121–22, 152, 170, 189, 191, 288, 308; early history, 10–12;

Kansas Gas and Electric (*continued*)
  early nuclear plans, 29–41; finance, 6, 24, 30, 45–46, 48, 94, 152, 157, 198–99, 219–20, 241–43, 248–52, 260–61, 263, 299, 304, 309–11; fuel, vii, 28, 37, 41, 43–44, 120, 183, 188; legal, 114–18, 131–32, 139, 146–49, 153, 220, 309, 312; management, 166–67, 218–26, 243–44, 251, 253, 270, 295, 302–3; mergers, 251, 319–23; public relations, 7, 23, 29, 55–56, 64–65, 76–79, 96–97, 167, 176, 180–81, 217, 246, 309, 322, 325; rates, 11, 29, 92, 149, 167, 170–71, 194–96, 214, 243–45, 252, 261–71, 275–77; rate stabilization plan (1987) 309–13; sponsor of history, vii–x, xii, 6; Wolf Creek rate hearings, 258, 278–300. *See also* Jeffrey Energy Center; LaCygne power plant; Wolf Creek Station
Kansas Gas and Electric International Finance NV, 250
Kansas Geological Society, 62
Kansas Legal Services, 284
Kansas Libertarian Party, 259
Kansas Municipal Energy Agency, 191, 239, 241, 248–49
Kansas Municipal Utilities, Inc., 105
Kansas Natural Guard, 192, 194, 200, 204–7
Kansas Natural Resource Council, 258
Kansas Newman College, 73
Kansas Organic Producers, 209, 233
Kansas Power and Light (KPL), 43, 46, 168, 321–22. *See also* Jeffrey Energy Center
Kansas State University, 71, 77–79, 96–97, 105, 107, 195–96, 318
Kansas Supreme Court, 149, 309
Kansas Water Resources Board, 100, 129–30, 133
Kant, Immanuel, 15
Kassebaum, Nancy, 209
Kassebaum, Philip, 234, 239
"Keeper of the Plains," 7, 65
Kennedy, Edward, 169
Kenniston, Kenneth, 59, 206

Kerr-McGee Company, 97, 103, 256
Kilowatt, Reddy, 7, 29, 32, 178, 319
Kilpatrick, James, 208
Kimball, Fred, 30, 94–95
Kindall, James, 229–30
King, Jack, 75–76, 135–36
Kinney, Charles, 180
Klemmer, Jo, 105
Knighten, Phillip, 118
Koerper, Lyle, xii, 252, 275, 300
Koester, Glenn, 74, 76, 116, 173, 180, 212, 214, 221, 223, 225, 229, 242
Komonoff, Charles, 285, 297–98
Kornblith, Lester, 89
Krause, Keith, 131
Ku Klux Klan, 194

Labor *See* Wolf Creek Station: construction
LaCygne power plant, 46–49, 92, 123, 153, 167–68, 171, 191, 248, 313, 320
Lake Cayuga power plant, 85
Lance, Purl, 73
Land Institute, 15
Lange, Edith, 105, 108, 173, 179, 205–6
Larkin, Wade, 51
Lawing, James, 89, 102, 138, 147, 162, 210, 223
Lawrence, KS, 245, 252. *See also* University of Kansas
League Against Nuclear Dangers (LAND), 73, 82
League of Women Voters, 247
Least Heat Moon, William, 176
Lebo, KS, 84
Lehman Brothers Kuhn Loeb, Inc., 187
Lennen, Michael, 262–63, 280, 286, 293, 301–2
Leroy, George, 126
Lilienthal, David, 73, 108
Limited Work Authorization (LWA), 89, 152, 158, 162
Lippmann, Walter, 14
Lloyd, Henry, 14
Long Term Credit Bank of Japan, 251
Loux, Richard, 153, 167, 220, 230, 235, 237, 249, 279

INDEX 389

Lovins, Amory, 164, 194, 251, 257–58
Lucas, James, 121–22, 285
Luzzati, Ruth, 135–37, 147, 155–57
Lyon, Dale, 72, 77, 129, 232–33
Lyons, KS, 5, 62–64, 79, 90, 164, 211

Macauley, Thomas, x
Machine in the Garden, 111
Macklin, Harley, 45–46, 51
Madigliani, Andre, 87
Mainey, Donald, 189
Management Analysis Company (MAC), 225
Mann, Michael, 81
Marble Hill power plant, 250
Marcuse, Herbert, 22
Martin, Keith, 130–31, 140
Marubeni Corporation, 326
Marx, Leo, 111
Marxism, 17, 68
Matthews, Jack, 1
Maxey, Margaret, 191
McCracken, Samuel, 20, 23, 25
McDaniel, Clifford, 46
McDowell, Max, 63–64, 211–13
McGinnis, Donald, 261
McKee, Grover, 56, 184–86, 257
McPhee, Donald, 123–24, 180, 223, 285, 291–92
McPherson Anti-Nuclear Alliances (MANA), 216
McPherson Sentinel, 197
Media, 85–89, 101, 206, 211–12, 216–17, 247–48, 257, 259–61
Mennonite church, 193
Messler, Russell, 77
Mid-American Coalition for Energy Alternatives (MACEA), 21, 73–75, 77, 82, 89, 100–101, 104, 113, 119–20, 134–35, 140, 150, 153, 159, 162, 164, 183, 210, 233, 258
Miller, David, 131
Miller, Robert, 150, 164, 189, 266
Miller, Verne, 90–92
Mills, Chuck, 216
Mills, Mary, 216
Missouri, 155

Missouri Kansas Power Pool (MOKAN), 43, 45, 50–51, 54, 294
Missouri Public Service Company, 54–55, 191, 249
Missourians for Safe Energy, 179
Moline, Brian, 237–38, 241, 265, 269–70, 310–11
Mondale, Walter, 168
Montaigne, Michael de, 329
Moore, Anne, 231
Moore, Thomas, 231
Moore, Vincent, 84, 105, 130, 148
Mulberry, KS, 31
Mumford, Lewis, 22
Murdock, Marcellus, 28
Murray Gill power plant, 33, 185
Myth, 88–89

Nader, Ralph, 61, 66, 70, 81, 93, 126, 155, 177, 203, 209, 213, 215, 252
National Academy of Sciences, 127
National Advisory Committee on Reactor Safeguards, 97
National Association for the Advancement of Colored People (NAACP), 191
National Council of Teachers of English, 217
National Electric Reliability Council, 122, 169
National Environmental Policy Act (1969), 49, 60, 98–99
National Organization for Women (NOW), 193
Natural Gas Policy Act (1978), 188
Nebraska Public Power, 75, 189–91, 232
Nelson, Kay, 73
Neosho madtom, 100
Neosho River, 45, 100, 113, 129, 131, 134, 138
Netherlands Antilles, 250
New Strawn, KS, 76, 143, 171
New York State Electric & Gas Company, 85
Nichols, Mike, 256
Nixon, Richard, 63
Nolan, Kay, 73

North American Aviation, Inc., 34
North Dakota, 187
Northern States Power Company, 51–52, 125, 170, 218
Northwest Kansas Municipal Energy Agency, 233
Novik, Sheldon, 73
Nuclear power, viii, 1–2, 13–14, 17–19, 25, 30–31; early plans, 25–28, 37; in Europe, 85, 177, 180; national scope, 50, 146–47, 154–55, 159–60, 169, 177, 215, 219, 249–50, 252, 255–56, 283, 306–7, 315–16; theory of, 34–36, 175–76, 314–15; waste, 36–37, 62–64, 150–51, 203
Nuclear Projects, Inc. (NPI), 143–45, 170, 221
Nuclear Regulatory Commission (NRC), x, 60, 82, 89, 93, 98, 101, 103, 147, 150–52, 159, 182, 189, 199, 202, 211, 213–14, 219, 221, 243–44, 260–61, 288, 298–99
Nuclear submarines, 27

Operating permit, 77
Oregon, 147
Organization of Petroleum Exporting Countries (OPEC), 42, 54
Orwell, George, 254
Ottawa, KS, 142

Panhandle Eastern Pipeline Company, 184, 187
Paris, Barry, 94–95
Parsons, KS, 11, 129, 146, 209, 246
Parsons Sun, 139, 150, 156, 173, 246
Patterson, Jim, 268
Patterson, John, 114
"Peanuts" (cartoon), xi
Peck, Robert, 95
People's Energy Project (PEP), 82, 191
People's Party, 4, 14
Peters, Connie, 108
Petrick, Nicholas, 143
Petroleum, 19, 42
Pierce, Richard, 306–7

Pioneer Service and Engineering Company, 32
Pittsburg, KS, 31, 254, 304
Pilzer, Paul, 16
Pinch, Trevor, 175
Platt, Lois, 106
Plutonium, 35–36, 38–39, 105
Poe, Robert, 127
Pointer, Wade, 180
Pollard, Robert, 203
Ponce de Leon, Gui, 274, 284, 292–94
Portland Cement Association, 213
Pratt, KS, 262
Preliminary Safety Analysis Report (PSAR), 77
Price-Anderson amendments, 27, 146
Price, Peggy, 178
Privatization, 27
Project Deserve, 252
Project Living Green, 309
Project Management Associates, 265, 284
Protest, 153, 165, 194; analysis of, 19–23, 80–81, 85–86, 104, 106, 110–12, 163–64, 177–79, 191, 196–98, 206, 214–16, 238, 245, 257, 313–14, 316–17. *See also* Economics; Silkwood, Karen; Technology; Wolf Creek Station: activism against
Prudence: as a utility cost measure, 23, 271–74, 277, 288, 293, 302, 306
Public opinion, 207–8; polls, 103, 107, 149, 191, 247, 265–66, 277
Public Service Company of Indiana, 250
Public Utility Holding Company Act, 10

Quality Assurance Program, 202
Quantrill, William, 63

Radiation, 17–19, 34–35, 38–39, 49, 98, 100–101, 124, 126–27, 248
Radioactive Free Kansas (RFK), 216
Radon, 18
Railroads, 27–28, 43, 48, 131, 150, 172, 203–5, 325
Rancho Seco power plant, 314

INDEX

Reagan, Ronald, 227
Reed, Clyde, 129, 146, 173, 246
Regulation, 8–10, 27–28, 47, 54, 60–62, 159, 169, 171, 227, 240, 243, 266–67, 272, 287–88, 303–4, 306, 315. *See also* Atomic Energy Commission; Nuclear Regulatory Commission
Reich, Charles, 22
Rickover, Hyman, 26
Ripley, L. O., 12
Risk sharing, 305
Ritchey, Clark, 65
Rives, Robert, vii–ix, 55, 64, 70, 74, 76, 78, 116, 131, 141, 147, 180, 196, 203, 209, 212, 216–17, 246, 249, 252, 259, 324–25
Roach, Edward, 293
Robel, Robert, 148
Rochester Gas & Electric Company, 52, 218
Rockford, IL, 256
Rod, Sam, 265
Roen, George, 41, 285, 288–89
Roosevelt, Theodore, 221
Rosen, Richard, 162, 274, 278, 284–85, 294–97, 303, 305–6
Ross, Charles, 234, 241
Royko, Mike, 208
Rural Electrification Corporation (REC), 232–33, 241
R. W. Beck and Company, 239

St. Louis, MO, 75, 92–93
Safety report (SR), 97–98
Sagan, Leonard, 127
Salava, Donna, 107
Salava, Mary, 67–68, 84, 89, 93, 107, 260
Salina, KS, 15
Salinans for Alternatives to Nuclear Energy (SANE), 216
Salomon Brothers Company, 320
Salt City Alliance for Responsible Energy (SCARE), 216
San Onofre power plant, 120, 181
Sargent & Lundy Company, 76, 143, 160, 229

Schaefer, Paul, 107, 191–92, 200, 204
Schama, Simon, 1
Schlesinger, James, 169, 195, 215
Schneider, Kurt, 90, 92, 117, 131, 133, 147–48
Schorr, Daniel, 211–12
Schroeder, Alfred, 309
Schumacher, E. F., 21
SCRAM system, 38, 207
Seabrook power plant, 3, 153, 165, 192–94, 206–7
Servicegraph, 32, 65
Setter, Marge, 217–18, 329
Shaftesbury, Anthony, Earl of, xi, 331
Shakespeare, William, 301
Shaw, Pittman, Potts & Trowbridge, 272
Shepard, Karl, 193,
Shippingport power plant, 26, 33, 299
Shriver, Garner, 148
Sickel, S. J., 33–34, 36–37
Sierra Club, 71–72, 107, 138–39
Silberg, Jay, 103
Silkwood, Karen, 97, 103, 193, 207, 256
Simpson, John, 136, 150, 179, 189, 193, 269
Skubitz, Joseph, 63, 159
Smith, Adam, 22
Smith, Bud, 310
Smith, Ronn, 307
Socialist Workers Party of Kansas, 209
Solar power, 165, 180, 196
"Some Risks of Modern Life," 127
Southwest Atomic Energy Associates (SAEA), 33, 36–37, 40, 44
Southwest Experimental Fast Oxide Reactor (SEFOR), 37–40, 58, 65–66, 125, 145
Southwest Power Pool (SWPP), 54, 234
Sowby, F. T., 127
Standard & Poor Company, 219, 248
Standardized Nuclear Unit Power Plan Systems (SNUPPS), 51–54, 89, 92, 98, 103, 124, 143–45, 161, 165, 170, 212, 218–19, 274, 284, 286, 288, 302, 323–24
Stanford University, 286

State and Nuclear Power, The, 85
Steamboat Springs, CO, 285
Steam systems, 36, 47, 52, 143, 228
Stephen, Robert, 202, 256, 267
Stevens, John, 82
Stoler, Peter, 197
Stone & Webster Company, 43, 45
Streep, Meryl, 256
Stroup, Louis, 105
Sturgeon, James, 301
Sunbelt Alliance, 203, 228
Sunflower Alliance, 192–93, 209, 245, 258
Suran, Jerome, 315
Syfrit, Karl, 213

Taylor, Lester, 120
Taylor, Thomas, 230, 240
Tax Reform Act of 1986, 310
Technology: attitudes toward, 13–17, 31, 85–86, 174–76, 315
Tegtmeier, Diane, 21, 68–69, 73–75, 88–89, 100–102, 104, 163–66, 189, 210, 315
Teller, Edward, 215
Thompson, Art, 82
Thorium-232, 35
Three Mile Island power plant, 2, 23, 151; 1979 accident at, 86–87, 124–25, 147, 162, 207–10, 214–15, 217, 220, 223, 227, 244–45, 278, 295, 324
Thiasos, 20
Times Beach, MO, 249
Tompkins, Steve, 259–60, 267
Topeka, KS, 3, 46, 80, 100, 142, 149, 191, 193, 211, 220, 234, 323–24
Touche Ross Company, 144, 265, 274, 284–85, 295
Tulsa, OK, 200, 202–3
Twain, Mark, 185

U-235, 34–35
Uniform Commercial Code, 115
Union Electric Company, 47, 52–53, 165, 170
Union of Concerned Scientists, 27, 203

United Mine Workers, 198, 209
University of Arizona, 121
University of Colorado, 81
University of Kansas, 38, 71, 77, 193–94, 200, 268, 272, 274
University of Michigan, 284
University of Southern California, 31
University of Washington, 89
U.S. Fish and Wildlife Service, 134
U.S. Supreme Court, 309, 312
Unruh, Milo, 291
Utilities. *See* Electricity
Utility Fuels Company, 117

Vancrum, Robert, 270
Veblen, Thorstein, 14
Vietnam war, 13, 58, 85, 197, 206
Viren, Michael, 120, 152, 163–64, 190, 292
Vulcan Chemical Company, 199, 291

Wallis, L. R., 65–66
Wall Street Journal, 67, 303
"War of the Worlds," 193
Ward, William, 74, 77, 89–91, 102, 104, 107, 110, 119, 124, 126–27, 136, 152, 159, 179, 189, 203
WASH studies, 49–50
Washington, 177, 249
Washington Public Power Supply System (WPSS), 249–50, 326–27
Wass, Leonard, 161, 285
Waste. *See* Wolf Creek Station: waste
Water. *See* Wolf Creek Station: water supply
Water Appropriations Act (1945), 131, 134
Water Pollution Control Act, 152
Watts, Alan, 81
We Almost Lost Detroit, 59
Weart, Spencer, 19, 328–29
Weaver, Fred, 129, 136, 140
Weidenbaum, Murray, 92
Weik, Mary, 79
Weir-Enegren, Linda, 258, 308, 313
Western Resources, Inc., xiii, 322

INDEX

Westinghouse Company, ix, 6, 27, 51–52, 103, 112, 114–18, 143, 219, 223, 265
Westphalia, KS, 72
White, Mometh, 106
White, William, 5
Whitman, Walt, 57
WIBI TV (Topeka), 211–12
Wichita Chamber of Commerce, 258
Wichita Eagle, 136–37, 183, 212, 256–57, 259, 267, 321
Wichita Gas Utility, 186
Wichita Journal, 185
Wichita, KS, 7, 9, 30, 45–46, 57–58, 64–65, 73, 90, 100, 105, 107, 117, 130, 145, 167, 194, 220, 232, 279, 323, 324; coal gas plant, 176, 183–88, 257; hearing before city commission, 108–9
Wichita Labor Federation, 105
Wichita State University, xii, 33, 79, 82, 259, 289, 315
Wichita Sun, 91, 93–96
Wigglesworth, John, 150
Williams Brothers Engineering Company, 184, 186
Wilson, Harold, 105
Winn, Alfred, 69
Wolf Creek Express. *See* Wolf Creek Station: reactor vessel arrival
Wolf Creek Nuclear Operating Corporation, 208
Wolf Creek Nuclear Plant Opposition, Inc., 67, 73, 79, 82, 113, 179
Wolf Creek Station: activism against: 57–83, 153, 176–80, 188–89, 191–206, 209, 216–18, 276–77; base mat issue, 182–83, 199, 202–3, 212–14, 225, 243; construction, 54, 143–45, 153, 159–60, 171–73, 199–200, 202, 211–12, 225–26, 228–31; construction permit hearings, 84, 89, 102–8, 113, 119–29, 133, 140–41, 151–52; cost, 53, 101, 112, 119–20, 124–25, 150, 153–63, 227, 235–36, 239–40, 242–43, 245, 248–49, 251, 257, 259–60, 281, 283, 287, 293–95; description, viii, 13, 180, 218, 229–30, 278; design, 33, 45–46, 50–53, 98, 153, 212–13, 219; fuel, 112–18; KEPCo hearings, 232–41; logo, 7, 231–32; operating permit hearings, 252, 256, 260–61; operation of, 299, 307–8; reactor vessel arrival, 202–6; safety, 125–28; site, 44–45, 53, 57–58, 99–100, 57–83; studies of, 77, 89, 97–100, 118, 144–45, 166–67, 175, 215, 239, 242–44, 250, 268–73; waste, 62–64, 128, 262; water supply, 45, 77, 100–101, 112–13, 128–40, 146–47, 153. *See also* Kansas; Kansas Gas and Electric Company; Media; Nuclear power; Protest
Women Insisting on Sensible Energy (WISE), 216
Women's International League for Peace and Freedom, 82, 105
Wood, Warren, 282
Woodcock, Helen, 193
Woolery, William, 121–22, 252–53
Workingman's Advocate, The, 4
Wright, Margalee, 176, 279–80, 301, 305, 313, 317
Wyoming, 43, 48, 167–68, 185

Yale University, 286
Youth and Dissent, 59
Young, Annette, 105
Young, Loretta, 72
Yucca Flats, NV, 203